D0970570

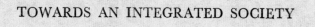

TOWARDS AN INTEGRATED SOCIETY

TOWARDS
AN INTEGRATED SOCIETY

*REFLECTIONS ON PLANNING, SOCIAL
POLICY AND RURAL INSTITUTIONS*

TARLOK SINGH

GREENWOOD PUBLISHING CORPORATION
WESTPORT, CONNECTICUT

Copyright © 1969 by Orient Longmans Ltd.

Library of Congress catalog Card Number : 76-95507
SBN : 8371-2338-0

ALL RIGHTS RESERVED. NO PORTION OF THIS BOOK MAY BE
REPRODUCED BY ANY PROCESS OR TECHNIQUE, WITHOUT
THE EXPRESS WRITTEN CONSENT OF THE COPYRIGHT HOLDER

PRINTED IN INDIA

BY S. N. GUHA RAY AT SREE SARASWATY PRESS LTD.
32, ACHARYA PRAFULLA CHANDRA ROAD, CALCUTTA-9
AND PUBLISHED BY GREENWOOD PUBLISHING CORPORATION
51 RIVERSIDE AVENUE, WESTPORT, CONN. 06880 (U. S. A.)

13⁵⁰

HC
435.2
S547
1969

abel

H

10/16/70

TO

GUNNAR MYRDAL

FOR WHOM THERE IS NOT A LAND
WHICH IS NOT HIS OWN

286579

PREFACE

Certain aspects of our problems of poverty and economic and social development have long been of concern to me. Both before and since Independence, specially during the years of intimate participation in India's national planning, they have been constantly in my mind. Therefore, as occasions arose outside work on the Five Year Plans in which I was immersed, I found myself turning to these topics. This is how several of the papers brought together in this book came to be written.

The thirty-four papers which are here presented fall into three groups: Rural Institutions and Problems, Planning and Plan Implementation, and Social Policy. Though these are broad descriptions, the scope of the papers is more limited. In the main, those aspects have been discussed which seemed to me to need special emphasis. In a collection of this nature, certain thoughts will recur from time to time, both because they bear on the argument and because they have become part of one's view of life and society.

Separate pieces on the range of themes covered in this volume have a certain limitation to which attention should be drawn. They are extensive rather than intensive in treatment, and they differ in their purpose from systematic and detailed study in depth devoted to specific topics. However, they are closely related and form part of a larger design of change and of a concept of social democracy deriving from the background and conditions of India. They point to significant questions which merit closer investigation and call for social action. They also reflect changes in mood and circumstance, which are as much a part of the processes of economic and social development, as they are of the way in which each of us reacts towards events in which, in howsoever small a measure, we are privileged to participate.

The title of this book sums up the central theme which runs through many of the papers and was stated in these words in the last of the Five Year Plans which bore the name of Jawaharlal Nehru:

> "In the last analysis, economic development is but a means to an end—the building up, through effort and sacrifice widely shared, of a society without caste, class or privilege, which offers to every section of the community and to all parts of the country the fullest opportunity to grow and to contribute to the national well-being."

Through circumstances which are apparent enough, in retreats which follow one upon another, the concept of India as an Integrated Society is now being weakened. This should not be. India's unity, her future, and the role of the masses of her people, are bound up with this vision and this faith. As a nation, our assets are fully equal to the challenges we face, and the many unfinished tasks before us are well within our capacity to accomplish.

Work on this volume was completed at the Institute for International Economic Studies of the University of Stockholm and was made possible by a grant to the Institute from the Wenner-Gren Foundation in Stockholm. The sojourn there in the summer of 1967 and the day-to-day stimulus of exchange and reflection with Professor Gunnar Myrdal and colleagues and friends at the Institute meant much to me. From a distance many of our emerging problems could be seen more sharply and with greater detachment. The opportunity to see at work a free society which, through its continuing pursuit of equal welfare and opportunity for all, had gone far towards achieving economic and social integration, helped me both to view the past and to prepare for tasks in the future. In attempting to understand the development of Swedish employment and economic policies since the thirties and in the post-war period, I received special help and guidance from Professor Ingvar Svennilson. My sense of obligation to the Institute, therefore, goes well beyond the present work.

I wish also to express my gratitude to various organisations, academic authorities and journals for generous response to the request for permission to reproduce, adapt or draw upon papers originally prepared and published under their auspices. Wherever necessary, I have taken the liberty of making small changes.

January, 1968   Tarlok Singh since the above, and to the post-war period, I received special help and guidance from Professor Stewart S. Hamilton. Versions of material to the Institute, therefore, goes well beyond the present work.

I wish also to express my gratitude to various organizations, academic authorities, and journals for generous response to the request for permission to reproduce, adapt or draw upon papers originally prepared and published under their auspices. Wherever necessary, I have taken the liberty of making small changes.

January, 1968   Daniel Singh

CONTENTS

PART THREE

SOCIAL POLICY

PART ONE

INTRODUCTION AND RURAL INSTITUTIONS

INTRODUCTION

TODAY INDIA finds herself overwhelmed by her current problems. Internal economic, social and political conditions have combined with external developments to produce a situation marked by growing uncertainty in the present and lack of direction for the future. Many a serious purpose, which evoked response not so long ago, is becoming empty of content. With barely twenty years of freedom behind us, we have entered a period, not of transition to a new order, but of small aims, of weakening of values, of loss of social ideals, perhaps even of disintegration.

I

The main elements of a classic revolutionary situation are already taking shape, but without either the preparation or the organisation for guiding fundamental changes in system and structure. The roots of the processes at work can be traced back over many years. They are still in their early and manageable phase. If the mind and heart of India could be exposed to eventualities which lie around the corner and there is greater understanding of what is at stake, it is possible to bring these processes to a halt and to turn symptoms of failure and frustration into acts of faith and creative energy. Though immediate problems may oppress us, it has never been more important for the people of India to feel and think beyond them, to discover and build upon their own sources of strength, and together to mark out steps for the future.

There are portents to be observed. Within the country, in terms of practical action, every single idea, which gave constructive expression to the belief in freedom and democracy, is becoming weaker: equality, employment and education for all; land reform and redistribution of income and wealth; diffusion of industry, rural industrialisation and balanced regional development; local democracy, building up of a co-operative commonwealth and the development of a socialist society. Planning, democracy and economic and social reconstruction were inter-dependent movements and gave support to one another. The main strength of India's planning lay in its continuity, organic growth and view of the nation as a whole. These attributes have now been allowed to come under eclipse.

In the past, a national five year plan, which also embodied State plans and plans for the private sector, served, however imperfectly, as a continuing guide to governmental action and to the people at every level. Changes in the composition of governments in the States or in personnel at the Centre did not affect the main directions of public policy or the commitments which the Centre and each of the States had accepted. In the total concept which was built up with much labour over a long period of years, five year plans were not merely projections of investment or optional guides to policy or a selective approach to India's problems. They were a major part of the effort to build up the country's resources, to reorganise the structure of the economy, to lift the masses from the state of poverty, and to establish a just society.

They were a vital and indispensable framework for India's stability, continuity and integrity as a nation. In a country in India's situation, these conditions cannot be taken for granted and must remain an object of constant vigilance and ceaseless endeavour.

Weaknesses in economic management and in administrative and political leadership at many levels provide some part of the explanation of unsatisfactory economic performance of recent years. These weaknesses will be further accentuated on account of the interruption which has virtually occurred in systems and processes which were evolved for achieving and implementing a national consensus on economic and social development. Droughts and scarcities and the relative stagnation in agriculture reveal not only the unstable character of the agricultural economy and inadequacies in planning and organisation, but also the deeper crisis which runs through the structure of rural society in every part of the country.

At the same time as aid is sought from others, India's own internal resources—manpower, industrial and other capacities, knowledge, talent and ability to invent, adapt and improvise—are not pressed far enough and remain but partially employed. Too little of the nation's energy and effort are now being given to the achievement of basic social objectives. Growth in numbers bears with particular harshness on all the weaker sections of our people, as increase in prices and in costs of living and decline in standards of maintenance and efficiency do on the community as a whole. Movements in favour of the under-privileged— specially landless agricultural workers, tenants, Harijans, the tribal people and the urban poor—are still weak in resources and leadership. In the absence of speedy transformation, they will increasingly take on political expression. It is all too easy for local discontents to link up and turn into large-scale movements of revolt.

Without national goals which evoke widespread response and sacrifice, as administrations with uncertain political and moral authority meet new problems and crises from day to day, sections of the community, such as students, youth, the unemployed, the tribal communities and those who are still denied the minimum opportunities or who come under the severe impact of high prices and artificial scarcities, are being successively alienated. So much of what is being said lacks the true ring. The chasm between the values and premises of the Directive Principles and the Fundamental Rights in the Constitution and the working of our political, economic and social institutions in terms of the daily life and satisfactions of large numbers of people is becoming too wide to be sustained for long. Lenin's dictum that all governments are sleeping on a volcano is specially true of India at the present juncture.

Meanwhile, the distress aid in food sought from friendly countries, itself in part a substitute for the greater effort which the country can and must make to secure larger food stocks from within its own production, greatly increases the consequences of dependence on external economic aid. As within a nation, so in relations between nations, shifts in economic capacity bring their own political equations. All over Asia and Africa, many countries have been forced away from the economic and social objectives and the political ideals which inspired them before they became free and independent. Though there are difficulties enough, this need not happen in India, if we so will. But it can, if we do not make in time the necessary effort in thought and action. For a nation of India's size and diversity, with all her major tasks still half accomplished, what the sequel may be, no one can tell. The opportune moments in history pass before we are aware of them. In truth, every idea and every institution which, in the past, has given hope and led to action, is now on test. The challenge is pervasive, making demands, at the same time, on the intellect, on social purpose and the sense of sharing, on the institutional structure, on leadership in every walk of life and at every level. In its barest form this is the nature of the crisis upon us. No one can stand aside from it.

II

Both in her earlier history and since Independence, India has enjoyed advantages which few other nations possessed. Used with confidence and understanding of social forces and concern for the future, despite current evidence of political exhaustion, these advantages can enable her to meet the present problems and prepare the ground for completing the larger economic and social tasks which lie behind them. Periods of stress and change can also be periods of opportunity and renewed faith. To attack the roots of poverty through social change, to mobilise the inner strength and resources of the community as a whole, to appeal to self-reliance and the welfare of all, is in the tradition of the movement for freedom and the best part of our legacy as a nation.

In the earlier phases, it was scarcely possible to foresee all the specific problems which our experience with development has thrown up. There is a great deal new that we have learnt, from our own experience and that of other countries and systems. We see now, more sharply than before, that economic growth is a condition for social advance, as social and technological change is itself the crucial element in economic growth and that, by itself, neither one nor the other is a sufficient objective. With the development of industry which has already occurred, to a large extent further progress can be secured through more adequate economic policy, improved tools of economic management, strengthening of the apparatus of political decision and administrative action, and insistence upon the social and national interest as against individual and sectional claims. The problems still to be resolved in agriculture and the rural economy are, however, more deep-rooted. Here, progress achieved over the past fifteen years, significant in some parts of the country, less so in many others, has nowhere altered the pattern of land-holding and cultivation in any fundamental sense. There is no serious answer yet to the human and economic problem represented by the landless, by tenants, by small peasants or by tribal communities, all of whom live on the margins of subsistence and under conditions of increasing stress and privation. A few favoured regions, a few dynamic groups in the community, a few individuals with income and wealth which mark them out from the rest, cannot be a true measure of economic development, nor do they make for a society sufficiently at peace within itself to be able to advance as a whole.

Nations which have achieved economic development fall into two broad groups. The first group includes countries in which, with some differences in emphasis and institutions, welfare capitalism has brought about a high degree of integration and equality of opportunity among nearly all sections of the population. In these countries, educational and technological and industrial changes go back over many decades and were well advanced even before the first world war. It needed the expanding world economy of the period since the end of the second world war and improved tools for economic management and planning in market economies to turn these advantages to full account and to achieve continuing growth. The second group of countries fall within the fold of socialism and communism. They had a much narrower educational and industrial base and carried many handicaps from the past. It was essential for them to undertake large structural changes and changes in property and land relationships before they could hope for industrial and economic progress and could build up internally cohesive societies.

At different stages, both groups of countries have become acutely aware of weaknesses in their economic and social systems and in the scheme of incentives and opportunities embodied in them. Both are still engaged in economic reform and in improving the instruments and techniques at their disposal. However, it is important to note that in their different ways, both welfare capitalism and socialism now give their main attention to the provision of educational opportunities for all, full employment, essential welfare measures, the care of the young and training and retraining of youth, increase in productivity and spread of new industry and technology, development of natural and human resources, efficient use of existing capacities, reduction in costs and improved management, development of backward regions, and maintenance of economic independence within a framework of expanding economic and trade relationships. Without these, whatever the tenets of their systems, they could not succeed in mobilising their inherent skills and resources and expanding their economies fast enough, nor in greatly reducing social and economic disparities and differences in opportunity between various sections of the population and between different regions.

These, indeed, are among the leading characteristics of any society which seeks to be economically and socially integrated from within. In India, as a consequence of planning over the past fifteen years, those regions and urban and industrial centres and those sections of the community which already possessed certain of the preconditions of growth have become, as it were, active agents of change and innovation. Thus, irrigated areas, metropolitan cities, industrial centres, established business houses, large and medium-sized farmers and certain professional and skilled groups would conform to this description. The gap between them and the others is steadily increasing. Having already gained a start, they also obtain a greater share in the facilities and opportunities whose steady expansion is a necessary element in planned development.

In making these observations, we must be careful not to under-estimate the contribution to overall growth in the economy which the dynamic or potentially dynamic elements are able to make. In the larger interest, this contribution needs to be drawn upon, and doubtless there is a problem in the short run of determining the minimum conditions for securing it. At the same time, it is necessary to assess certain implications for longer-term development. The new disparities, though frequently deriving from the old, are more far-reaching in significance and, in turn, have other consequences. They express themselves in many ways: in the widening of the gap between industrial and agricultural productivity and between urban and rural wages, in the greater imbalance in distribution within the rural community and in more rapid economic advance in some areas as against lags and stagnation in others. At the level of policy and programmes of development, evasion of laws enacted in pursuance of land reform, unwillingness to provide for urgent problems of mass unemployment and under-employment in many densely populated areas, neglect of the minimum needs of disadvantaged sections, and failure to evolve systematic long-term plans for under-developed regions, are also to an extent a reflection of the growing disparities and their influence on fiscal policy, economic and social priorities and political judgement and action.

And yet, in a real sense, while there are limitations, according to its resources and its needs, no society is so poor that it cannot provide an essential minimum of work and an essential minimum of education to every single individual. Nor can any society, which seeks to grow from its own strength and establish the conditions of equal

opportunity for all, fail to undertake structural changes
and make substantial adjustments in property and income
relationships. Contrasts and privileges have to be ended
at the same time as positive measures are adopted for
stimulating individual and group effort. Beyond the planning
of investments, the extension of public and co-operative
sectors and the regulation and guidance of private activity,
there is need also for a wide range of supporting policies
and strategies. These will concern, for instance, determination of industrial priorities, distribution of scarce resources,
linking up of large and small industries, choice of major
locations, techniques of urban and regional planning,
integration of rural and industrial development, intensive
area development, pursuit of minimum standards of consumption for the community as a whole, utilisation of local
manpower and other resources, and planning for the development of various regions as an integral part of the growth
of the national economy.

III

The achievement of an integrated society is the central
purpose of economic growth and the very essence of planned
development. It represents a vital, unifying goal and is a
means for harnessing the energies and initiative of the
people in all fields of activity. It is a comprehensive objective
on which, both in the general approach and more so on
points of specific action, even politically differing groups,
with the total interest of the nation in mind, will find it
possible to agree. Rapid economic and industrial growth
and the urgent solution of the agricultural problem are, of
course, essential conditions for advance towards economic
and social integration. In the design of development broadly
outlined in India's plans, aspects of which are discussed in

several of the papers in this volume, there is a close connection between current management of the economy and longer-
term planning and between measures for increasing agricultural and industrial productivity and strengthening the
social base and the social structure. The system of incentives
for greater production by enterprises and by groups and
individuals as well as the role assigned to the public and
the co-operative sectors and to private effort, which are
implicit in India's scheme of planned development, constitute
on the whole a considered response to the objective conditions
of the Indian economy.

Determination of practical objectives which will provide
for at least a minimum approach towards the achievement
of an integrated society can be of great importance during
a period in the evolution of India when the capacity of
the political system to solve the problems of the people is
being rapidly weakened and no single group is in a position
to propose or implement overall national goals. The focus
has, therefore, to shift to a few central tasks and commitments which go beyond party labels held out in the past
and can serve as the basis of a common plan of action for
which sufficient agreement can be secured at the national
and regional levels. From this aspect, in the present circumstances, the following would appear to be the essential
ingredients in working towards an integrated national
democratic community:

1. A systematic and planned approach to economic
and social development supported by medium-term national
and regional plans which cover *all* aspects of the economy
and of social policy.

2. A national food policy designed to meet the requirements on a fair and equal basis of all parts of the country
and to reduce import of food to the minimum.

3. The maximum physical effort for agriculture and the
development of rural resources, including strengthening of

co-operative institutions and enterprise and development of rural industry.

4. Honest implementation and early completion of the programme of land reform embodied in the Second and Third Five Year Plans on which, for the most part, legislation already exists.

5. A scale of investment effort and domestic resource mobilisation capable of ensuring the effective utilisation of the main industrial and other capacities which have been already built up and of providing for their expansion at least to the limits of the country's own resources and talent for innovation.

6. Measures to strengthen self-reliance in all its aspects and modification of existing priorities with the object of reducing external assistance to the minimum and limiting it to forms consistent with freedom in planning economic and social policies for the domestic economy.

7. Employment for all who are able and willing to work, including rural public works for the landless and others similarly placed, subsidiary work opportunities for women, and training and re-training of youth.

8. Education for the mass of the people, including expansion of primary education, reorientation of secondary education and a national movement for adult literacy both for men and for women.

9. Measures for preventing the growth of disparities in wealth and income and for reducing the existing disparities.

10. Combined national, regional and local plans for developing the resource potential and solving the urgent problems of mass unemployment and under-employment in the most densely populated areas and in areas of intense poverty.

11. Policies and measures directed *specifically* towards enlargement of opportunities for the weaker sections of the community such as the landless, Harijans, tribal communities and the urban poor.

12. Reconstructing the administrative system at all levels with the major emphasis on responsibility for action and results, on respect and consideration for the citizen equally with obligations, and on organised support and participation of local communities.

These are the main elements in a common programme for putting the nation to work, for increasing the capacity for self-reliance and community effort, and for countering the negative and divisive forces which are now gaining dominance. In the phase through which the country is passing, there is too little genuine debate on great issues of public policy, on how the problems of the people can be resolved through the approach of planning and freedom within the framework of a multi-party federal democracy, and on steps which may lead towards a new synthesis of national objectives and values. To wait on events will be a dangerous course.

IV

A political system based on the concept of freedom will survive and grow in the measure in which its values are genuinely expressed in the everyday life and opportunities of the common people and in human and social relationships at the level of the community. Such a system is under compulsion both to correct injustices and handicaps of the past and to create conditions of equality for the future. To this end, it must give effect faithfully to the laws and policies and the measures which make for structural change. Both in outlook and action, it must be ruthless in enforcing justice, integrity, efficiency and the interest of the community as a whole. In these respects, the failures and evasions which have occurred and have already weakened the hold of our principal institutions were and are avoidable. A democracy, whose main claim is the welfare

of the people, has its own ethics and philosophy, a fundamental core of principles and rights and obligations, which
are the attributes of citizenship in its full sense, and no
narrow loyalty to group or faction or to caste or creed may
detract from them. Within each community, these principles and rights and obligations have to be applied openly
and fearlessly to all facets of life until a truly integrated
society comes into being.

In looking at developments within India, it is also
important to recognise that many countries in Asia and
Africa have now less hope of sustained economic progress
than they could entertain a decade ago and that the distance
between the richer and the poorer countries of the world is
steadily increasing. Even if they had a stronger will and no
conflicting interests, the richer countries have only limited
capacity to assist. The tide no longer runs in favour of under-
developed countries. More decisively than before, they
have no course but to turn to themselves and to their own
intrinsic resources and to put these to the best advantage.
That this should be so is on the whole a gain. There can be
little doubt now that in the difficult years which lie ahead
the ability to withstand the strains of economic and social
development and to overcome internal tensions will determine the political and economic future of India and of many
other countries, their capacity to grow, their stability and
integrity, their relations with one another as well as with
the more advanced countries. In this sense, whatever the
nature and dimensions of her current problems, India has
much to count upon. If she is true to herself, with the
development already accomplished, in a large measure
she possesses the resources, the technical and organising
capacity and the moral reserves to meet the challenge of
her own mass poverty and to redeem the promise of
freedom.

1

THE RURAL ECONOMY
AND ITS INSTITUTIONAL FRAMEWORK*

I

IN THE present phase of India's economic development, there are several circumstances which suggest the need for fresh consideration of the structure and pattern of growth of the rural economy. Towards the end of the First Five Year Plan, influenced by favourable harvests over a period of three years, some observers felt confident that irrigation and improved techniques were spreading fast enough to enable the agricultural economy to maintain a steady and continuous advance. Some others, engaged in the study of progress, thought that India was well set on the path of modernisation and industrialisation and there would be such uninterrupted progress in industry as could pull the agricultural economy out of its ruts. They saw in the secondary effects of industrialisation the main solution both to the problems of urban unemployment and to that of mass under-employment in rural areas. The long-term perspective against which the Second Five Year Plan was formulated, which visualised a doubling of national

* Adapted from a contribution to *Studies in Indian Agricultural Economics*, ed. J. P. Bhattacharya, pages 300-315, The Indian Society of Agricultural Economics, Bombay, 1958.

income by 1971 and of per capita income by 1976, also reflected this optimism.

It was not then appreciated sufficiently that, despite the recent upward trend, the growth of agricultural production might follow a course so uneven as to put the country's food economy into jeopardy and that, after a relatively short period, the pace of industrialisation could show signs of slowing down or might encounter difficulties which might severely test the whole scheme of national development. In a situation such as this, instead of rising steadily in real terms from year to year, levels of living might follow a seesaw course, with the growth of population exerting a depressing influence.

Periods of economic stress may be expected to lead to re-examination of past assumptions and to the formulation of new ones. There is already some measure of questioning in the air. It seems to take the form not so much of carrying forward the thinking on basic problems of change in the rural economy which the First and the Second Plans embodied as of doubting their relevance to the solution of current problems. Some policies which were conceived of as means for mobilising the community and freeing it from past rigidities are being placed on the defensive before they have been carried out to any great extent. There may be some value, therefore, in a short restatement of some of the more fundamental issues affecting the institutional framework of India's rural economy.

The institutional framework of any sector of the economy could be seen from several angles. In the first place, it might be seen in terms of the place the sector occupies in the national economy and in the scheme of national development. This would provide some of the major tests by which to judge the adequacy of the structure and of the directions of change. Other ways of looking at the institutional framework are in a sense particular facets of this

approach. Thus, the structure might be seen from the point
of view of the principal types of workers engaged in the
sector. The picture of the rural economy which emerges
when we study it from the standpoint of the tenant cultivator, the small peasant, the middle peasant, the landless
labourer and the rural artisan, or from that of the larger
landowner, the village merchant and the village money-
lender, the wholesale trader in agricultural produce and
the industrial entrepreneur in rural areas, points as much
to the hopes and frustrations of each representative type
as to the strength and weakness of the rural economy as
a whole. A third way of looking at the institutional framework of the rural economy might be to trace each of its
main economic and social links with the non-rural urban
economy. Finally, one might place oneself outside the rural
economy, as it were, and work back to each point of contact,
conflict or co-operation with it.

At a time when both the rural and the urban economy
are passing through several parallel processes of change
and the relationships between them are also undergoing
much change, it is by no means easy to see all aspects of the
picture together. The focus of analysis has, therefore, to
be somewhat limited. The guiding consideration in the
present review is whether the existing institutional framework
and the changes which are being sponsored are likely to
create, say, by the end of the Fourth or the Fifth Plan, the
essential conditions of an expanding economy which can
keep pace with the growth of population and an integrated
rural society which provides full equality of status and
opportunity to all its members. Two main tasks will be
attempted in this paper. The first is to review the present
institutional framework of India's rural economy in relation
to production, occupational patterns, marketing, processing, distribution, price relationships, rural incomes,
savings and capital formation and technological and social

change. The second task will be to look at some of the processes and programmes for change in the existing institutional framework which are in progress through community development, land reform, co-operation and industrialisation, especially through village and small industry programmes. Different aspects of the problem are necessarily related at many points and cannot be easily isolated, but it is hoped that analysis on these lines may suggest some broad conclusions. Within the compass of this paper both tasks can be attempted only briefly and even somewhat summarily.

II

The leading characteristics of an under-developed economy are its low rate of growth in relation to the available manpower resources and the lack of balance between different sectors of the economy. The main purpose of planned development is to mobilise the total resources of the economy from all sectors and to channel them into directions where, within each given period, they will make the maximum contribution to the growth of national income and the building up of a just and progressive social order. The relative contribution of different sectors to capital formation and the allocation of resources between them will, therefore, vary from one stage of development to another.

Every country is under obligation to develop to the maximum extent possible from its own resources. This has no other meaning than that in the early period of planned economic development agriculture must provide for a considerable part of the initial resources for investment. These take the form, firstly, of manpower released for non-agricultural work; secondly, of supply of foodgrains and raw materials for meeting the increased demands from industries and towns; thirdly, of savings to be employed in agriculture both by way of self-financing and for meeting

2

the costs of loans and credits; and finally, foreign exchange resources to be earned through exports of agricultural products. Rationalisation of agriculture, increase in its total production and in its productivity, the creation of a surplus and its mobilisation, and the ability to export a part of the production are all complementary aspects of rural economic growth. The main test of adequacy to apply to the institutional structure of a rural economy is the extent to which it enables the rural sector to maximise resources in the fourfold sense described above. The test has to be applied not merely to one section of the rural community or the other as, for instance, the larger landowners and traders and entrepreneurs in rural areas, but to the rural economy of each area taken as a whole.

By themselves institutional changes afford only part of the answer to any problem but, to the extent they are a condition precedent to massive development and mobilisation of latent resources and to the effective utilisation of resources made available from outside the rural economy, they deserve a degree of priority which has not yet gained sufficient recognition. If the rural economic structure is viewed in terms of production alone, it will be readily seen that on account of the prevailing patterns of land distribution, the vast majority of producing units are inefficient, unable to go much beyond subsistence agriculture, unable to use the available manpower resources and deficient in the means for achieving higher standards of production and technology. Since the existing units of production derive essentially from property relationships, rigidities are being only slowly broken, and economic and social disadvantages continually accentuate one another.

Institutional changes affecting the rural economy have four principal objectives:

    (i) To promote scientific agriculture based on steadily improving technology and diminishing costs per unit of output;

(ii) To bring about a balanced distribution of the rural population between farm and non-farm occupations and to assure work opportunities to all rural workers, both men and women, who offer for work. It is by expanding the scope of productive work in rural areas that unemployment can be eliminated and under-employment reduced substantially, with consequent improvement in levels of living. One of the central facts to grasp is that it is only through more continuous employment for an increasing proportion of the present and potential labour force of each village and area that the worst forms of rural poverty can be removed;

(iii) To replace a diminishing upper class, whose comparative prosperity has in the past rested on fixed and out-of-date patterns of land distribution, by a growing body of farmers with skill, productivity and education; and

(iv) To bring into existence rural communities functioning as units of a larger co-operative economy, in which the rights and obligations of the individual and the community are secured through freedom and democracy and, at the same time, each community is able to mobilise its surpluses and solve many of its problems through its own initiative.

How far the surplus obtained from agriculture can be utilised for the development of the economy as a whole depends on the economic relationships between the rural and the non-rural sectors of the economy. In the past, in some countries these relations have been based on the dominance of private capitalism, in others of State capitalism. The choice of the democratic method has the important implication that the pattern of industrialisation and urban growth, while strengthening the national economy as a whole, should specially justify itself in terms of the highest attainable levels of rural incomes and rural employment.

When social changes are brought about through democratic consent and the development of responsible citizenship, all sections of the community have to prepare for their new role in the economy, those who stand to gain no less than those who stand to lose in the first instance. Once the nature of the basic changes and the means for achieving them are clear and sufficiently accepted there is, on the one hand, a sense of direction and, on the other, time, opportunity and help from the community as a whole

available to all sections of the people for effecting the
transition from the old to the new. This involves, of course,
an immense educational process at all levels of national
life and a determination to achieve social and economic
integration along the chosen paths. The essence of the
democratic approach, therefore, is that social, economic
and political conditions are created for advance on broadly
agreed lines by the community as a whole, leaving local
or special problems to be resolved as they arise.

III

One of the central issues in the reorganisation of the
rural economy is the role of the village structure and the
village community. Until the Rural Credit Survey the
general consensus of opinion was that the village had to
be the primary unit of development.* The Rural Credit
Survey questioned this assumption mainly on the ground
that caste on the one hand and the rural landlord and the
trader on the other had gained too dominating an influence
in rural life. In this, as in other fields, the same facts may
admit of different emphasis. The theme, however, is of such
importance that it may be useful to explain the context
in which the village and the village community are to be
understood as primary units in rural development and the
limitations as well as the possibilities of this conception.

It is conceded that the 'village' does not represent an
identical social and economic entity in every part of the
country, that villages vary in size and that their configuration has been greatly influenced by various historical factors
and, more especially, by the nature of land settlements
undertaken during the eighteenth and the nineteenth
centuries. Nevertheless, with all these qualifications, it is

* All-India Rural Credit Survey, Report of the Committee of Direction,
Vol. II, General Report, Reserve Bank of India, Bombay, 1954

true to say that the village is one of the more outstanding
facts of the rural scene. Whether we seek a unit larger than
the village or smaller than it, in some way it must be related
to it. Whatever adjustments may be considered necessary,
the village provides a frame of reference as well as a point
of departure.

It should also be readily admitted that the social structure
of the village is rooted in a traditional scheme of stratifica-
tion based on caste and occupation, and in essentials this
scheme still persists, that within each village the benefits
of capitalist economic development and of the extension
of public services have gone in greater measure to the
privileged sections, and that village life is marked by
factions in which caste and vested interests are significant
factors. These have been the natural characteristics of
a comparatively static rural society in which both the effort
and the impulse for social and economic progress, whether
from within or without, were largely lacking, as indeed
was to be expected until the period of alien rule came to
an end. When the aim is to transform an existing structure
as part of a scheme of national development, in which a
fundamental role is assigned to the initiative and leadership
of the people and to changes in attitudes, it becomes
necessary to select and revitalise some of those elements in
the existing situation which are capable of making a
positive contribution. Four of these may be specially
mentioned:

(1) Invariably, the village community is a compact group whose members
    know one another intimately and, despite differences, owe a degree
    of loyalty to or consideration for the group and the village unit as a
    whole.
(2) Despite the unequal station accorded to and the unequal opportu-
    nities enjoyed by different sections, the village community or group
    is still conscious of a degree of responsibility or concern towards them
    all. This becomes apparent both in good times and in bad.
(3) Even though the state of poverty is not identical for all sections of the
    village community and there are special factors working in favour of

or against different sections, their problems are closely related, and their common source is the condition of the village economy with its low productivity, pressure on land and lack of employment opportunities; and

(4) Although caste and possession of land have been important factors in rural leadership, there are several dynamic elements at work. Some of these strengthen the role of caste, some weaken it, but the long-term trend, which can be further strengthened, is in favour of greater democracy in economic and social life and activity.

These elements can be turned to account if the village and the village community have a clearly assigned place in the scheme of development. With the base established, they can be of value also in a larger framework; without this, there may be a certain loss of direction, with no corresponding attributes of leadership, group loyalty, group responsibility and common need being readily available at levels above the village.

It is not to be expected that by itself the village community will be an activating, dynamic force. It can become so only in virtue of the catalytic forces released by planned economic development on a national scale. Once this precondition exists, the village community is seen as a readily available agency for development between the State and its organs on the one side and the individual on the other, and the village can serve frequently as the primary area within which the organised local community fulfils its role. On purely pragmatic considerations with reference to the character of each region, both the village and the local community can be suitably 'adjusted' to meet the needs of development. They are not to be viewed as altogether fixed or rigid. Two conditions should, however, be stressed. The first is that by definition a primary community must be concerned with all aspects of the life and work of those who form part of it. For different purposes, it will be linked with units or organisations embracing a larger area or several communities, but in respect of each purpose in view, the village community will have distinct, though necessarily a varying measure of responsibility in relation to its members. The second condition is that the primary community should not be so small that it cannot efficiently discharge its functions, nor so large that its members cannot form a reasonably compact group bound by ties of loyalty, responsibility, sense of obligation and common interest.

The appropriate size for the primary community will itself depend on a variety of circumstances, notably on the level of development, the state of technique and the prevailing economic conditions and structure. As these change, the appropriate size will tend to become larger. In other words, even though we may urge that *at this stage* the emphasis has to be on the village community and the village as primary units in the development of the rural economy, a steady and continuous process in which village communities and villages amalgamate into or become part of larger working units is to be anticipated as a necessary consequence of economic development. The process, however, is one of growth and adaptation to new needs, not one of creation of units superimposed from above by the administration and seeking to reduce the smaller units into a position of subordination or insignificance as operational units. In the second place, the process assumes the creation of a strong community base which gradually expands in size and range of functions as against a structure which is set up from above for specific and limited tasks to be carried out in relation to individuals *qua* individuals. In the latter scheme of organisation, there is no single level at which the members of the community and their various needs are effectively integrated.

The question may be asked why there need be a level at all in the organisation of rural life at which such integration should be attempted. Would it not speed the break-up of caste and feudal vestiges if, through the weakening of the village unit, their influence at the primary level is greatly reduced and there are organisations serving larger areas which are strong economic units in themselves and to which individual farmers and others can turn for aid irrespective of the size of their farms and the economic power they wield ? Social and economic change involves both the dissolution of the old and the creation of a new scheme of institutions and incentives. Unless the new structure and the processes by which it is to be brought into existence are clearly visualised, it is by no means sufficient to prescribe only the initial phase of the strategy for transforming rural life. It is necessary to form a clear conception of the ultimate goals as well as of the instruments through which they are to be reached and the incentives and motivations upon which reliance is to be placed. It is in this context that the picture drawn in the Rural Credit Survey remained incomplete. While this might have been inevitable because the Rural Credit Survey had certain limited objectives, it should be stressed that the structure and problems of the rural economy have to be seen as a whole and that, if they are approached in segments, numerous contradictions arise and the results achieved will be small.

In any comprehensive outlook on the rural economy, at least four basic questions have to be posed. Taken together, the answers to these questions will largely determine the paths of change.

The first of these is the part the people are expected to play. Economic development in the framework of democracy limits the role both of political parties and their cadres and of the machinery of administration. Both exert an indirect influence, the former by leading opinion, the latter by rendering assistance and providing technical guidance. In the second place, where responsibility and initiative rest with the people, the institutions through which they are enabled to exercise these in relation to their local affairs are of paramount importance in the reshaping of rural

life. These institutions can be built up on either of two
principles, namely, (a) fusion of diverse interests and classes
and the strengthening of organisations which stand for the
community as a whole, or (b) conflict between different
interests and classes and the organisations which serve them.
It is a major assumption in democratic growth that the
ending of inequalities and privileges based on the accidents
of birth and economic circumstance is a common value
which admits of no compromise. Without this premise
there would be little reason to believe that far-reaching
changes could be brought about peacefully through democratic processes. If this premise is granted, as it is under
the Constitution as well as in all responsible declarations
of policy, it provides the vital principle for the integrated
development of the community towards a classless society
through the building up of an expanding economy and
a just social structure founded upon the welfare of all
and more especially of the under-privileged. The second
question, therefore, bears on whether or not institutions
such as panchayats and co-operatives are to be based on the
principle of class fusion rather than class war.

There has been sometimes a temptation to look upon
the village as a self-contained and largely self-sufficient
unit and to build upon these features. The third question,
therefore, concerns the limits of planning at the village
level and the way village planning has to be related to
the planning of larger local areas such as development
blocks, *tahsils*, *taluks* or sub-divisions of which the district
is composed. Important elements of most problems, social,
economic and other, are to be found in the village. While
the reorganisation of village life has a most important
contribution to make towards their solution, the attack
upon them has to come simultaneously from several
positions and on several fronts. In particular, in the planning
of resource development and the expansion of employment

opportunities, village planning needs to be fitted into schemes of area planning.

Finally, it is necessary to consider the contribution towards the transformation of the rural economy of changes in structure and organisation, technical development programmes and economic and financial measures relating to credit, marketing, distribution and price and fiscal policies. In all under-developed economies, when measures in these three categories go together, their combined effects are much greater than when they are conceived of as separate planks. This is the situation more especially in rural areas. The lines along which these various policies and measures may be integrated are broadly understood, but so far the amount of integration achieved between them in terms of practical action at various levels has been small. This is in part due to the fact that frequently technical, social and economic aspects of development are not seen together as inter-acting and inter-dependent parts of the same process of growth. They are dealt with in isolation from one another and not as parts of a well-knit philosophy of social action. Without such an approach, it is difficult to form a clear view of the place of the village in the rural economy of the future and the scheme of institutions and incentives through which the objectives of rural community development are to be realised.

IV

The main inquiry in this paper was whether the present institutional framework and the changes now being sponsored are likely to create, say, by the end of the Fourth or the Fifth Plan, the essential conditions of an expanding economy and an integrated rural society. In the nature of things, it is too early to attempt a definite answer. In recent years, the Agricultural Labour Enquiry, the Rural

Credit Survey and the bench-mark surveys and evaluation reports of the Programme Evaluation Organisation and other studies have added appreciably to the precision of our knowledge regarding the pattern of land holdings, occupational structure, and rural incomes and capital formation. During these years, large programmes of development and new social policies have also been initiated. At this stage one can at best attempt a tentative statement of the precise points at which changes in the institutional framework are called for and the extent to which these are likely to be achieved through the impact of various programmes of development. The institutional framework of the rural economy can be analysed broadly in relation to land, manpower resources and marketing and distribution and the accompanying price relationships. Programmes of development, which are among the instruments of change, can be considered in three groups, namely technical, economic and social development programmes, extension and other services provided by the State and its organs, and the measures taken to build up peoples' organisations. There is a wide gulf between the problems to be solved and the changes which are called for and the impact achieved in the actual process of implementing various programmes. The issue to be considered is whether, on an objective assessment, the gulf is being diminished rapidly enough and the directions in which measures now being attempted need further strengthening.

Until a few years ago, the pattern of land distribution throughout the country was extremely rigid and the general trend was in the direction of concentration of ownership in the higher deciles and greater sub-division in the lower deciles. The former trend seems to have halted. Measures taken to eliminate intermediaries and protect tenant cultivators as well as the fear of ceilings on agricultural holdings have somewhat diminished the value of land as investment outside zones of urban influence and some favoured areas. Whatever the delays that might yet occur in giving effect to land reform policies, in the course of the next few years, the principal problem in relation to land may be, not concentration of ownership, but the widespread distribution of land into small and highly uneconomic holdings and the need to improve their management and to raise their productivity. Consolidation of holdings is a necessary step in many areas, but the indications are that its progress will be slow and that its total impact on agricultural production is not likely to be as great as its key role would in fact justify.

With land distributed into large numbers of small holdings, of which only a proportion can be regarded as adequate family holdings, the pooling of land into sizeable farm units is a far more urgent requirement than has been commonly accepted during the past decade. In the light of experience available within India as well as from other countries, given a clear view on policy and the necessary effort to experiment and to educate, it is perfectly feasible to implement a programme involving the progressive development of co-operative farming which will preserve the essential freedoms of the individual, be broadly acceptable to public opinion and, at the same time, be capable of increasing agricultural production and ensuring the more intensive use of manpower resources. Much of the discussion on co-operative farming has been lacking both in the sense of urgency and in the appreciation of consequences should India's agricultural economy continue for long to be wholly unequal to the requirements of economic development. The proposal in the Second Five Year Plan that such steps should be taken during this period as would provide sound foundations for the development of agrarian co-operatives so that, within a period of ten years or so, a substantial proportion of agricultural land is cultivated on co-operative lines has not yet begun to be implemented. It is not too much to suggest that in this respect, as in several others, time runs short. Both co-operative and individual farming are envisaged within the framework of village plans. Services and assistance available to co-operatives should be available equally to individuals, but conditions have to be created in which, through positive measures of assistance and guidance, it becomes worthwhile for peasants to join co-operative farming groups of their own choice.

Within each village one can visualise a growing sector composed of co-operative farming groups, a community sector in which land belongs to and is worked in the name of the community as a whole, and an individual sector composed of individual farms. The significance of the community sector is likely to be greater than the actual area comprised within it, for this sector will include not only land but also rural industry, and its existence should enable the village community organisation to set the pace in technological and social development. One can foresee co-operative groups beginning separately in a relatively small way and coming together gradually for reasons of economic advantage into larger units within the village. One can also foresee a steady, if limited, growth in the community sector and a steady diminution in the individual sector. In the Indian context, co-operation in cultivation is sought without affecting the rights of ownership which will be moderately rewarded. As the village economy develops, the return due to the ownership of land will become a less and less important element in the total income of each farm family, an increasing proportion of the income being derived from work. Problems of farm management, improved agricultural practices, production of improved varieties of seed and the full utilisation of local manurial resources, which now seem so formidable, will be much simpler to deal with if the co-operative development of agriculture is taken up with sincerity and earnestness and co-operative farming is organised as a movement essential to the success of the rural economy and, above all, in the interests of the peasants themselves.

The doubt is often expressed whether the pooling of small holdings into larger co-operative units may further accentuate the problems of rural employment. To put forward the plea that the larger units will merely involve the throwing out of surplus labour leading to conditions worse than those of disguised unemployment is to assume an altogether static picture. In theory, it was always clear that if manpower resources could be pooled, they could be put to a variety of tasks not previously undertaken, provided food supply and finance to meet the wage bill were available. Whatever its other limitations or lessons, the experience of China since the organisation of agrarian co-operatives has provided conclusive practical proof of this fact. It will be readily agreed that on the whole in Indian agriculture manpower resources are not employed intensively. In part, this is due to the dependence on rainfall, the small size of holdings, excessive numbers on land and the vagaries of the seasons. In part also this is due to the fact that where agriculture is undertaken through small peasant holdings, it is extraordinarily difficult to organise the use of manpower resources in the common interest of the community as a whole. This has been one of the main reasons for the small success achieved over the past several years in labour-intensive minor irrigation works. It is true that, even with individual farming, given village planning and an expanding community effort, there is scope for better use of local manpower resources, and all possible steps in this direction are to be supported. It should be stressed, however, that in a predominantly agricultural economy in which there is heavy pressure on land, the maximum use of manpower resources cannot be achieved within the existing system of agriculture. In relation to the development of the national economy, this is another way of saying that, next to land, by far the most important resource available to the country will remain under-utilised so long as the greater part of agriculture is not organised along co-operative lines. Thus, the rate at which village planning and co-operative farming develop will determine in substantial degree the rate at which the economy as a whole develops. It should also be added that, with village planning and co-operative farming, the community assumes an obligation to provide work to everyone willing to work. This creates both a pressure for bringing into existence new forms of work and services and the means, as part of area planning and national planning, for meeting the demand for new work opportunities. Full employment of rural manpower and reduction in the proportion of the population dependent on cultivation are difficult aims to achieve even under favourable circumstances. Without the organisation of co-operative farming and the development of some system of co-operative village management as part of a wider scheme of area planning, these goals are not merely distant but are beyond the capacity of the rural economy to achieve.

The third important aspect of the institutional framework of the rural economy concerns the organisation of rural trade, marketing and processing. Over the years a system comprising markets for foodgrains and other crops, traders and commission agents, and entrepreneurs owning processing plants has come into existence in all parts of the country. As with the prevailing system of agriculture, these institutions are also frequently accepted as lasting and inevitable. There is little doubt that in their time these institutions have served to expand the economy of rural areas. In large part, however, they have now outlived their period of service and need to pass through a process of radical change along with the agricultural economy itself. In a co-operative rural economy there would not only be a growing measure of joint cultivation but also an increasing degree of co-operative marketing of agricultural produce and distribution of consumer goods and production requisites, and processing of agricultural commodities would be undertaken through co-operative organisations. In point of sequence and significance, it is even more urgent to complete the transfer of the bulk of trade and processing activities from individual into co-operative hands in the course of the next decade than it is to complete the transformation of agriculture from the individual to the co-operative basis. This priority arises from several factors, of which the three most important are the management of the food problem in the interest of steady economic development, the problem of rural credit and the maintenance of stable agricultural prices. In recent years, one of the principal areas in which there has been a wide gap between what was intended in the plans and what occurred in practice is that of agricultural price policy. It is now clear that the development of co-operative marketing, distribution and processing are essential no less in the interest of the rural community than in the interest of the national economy as a whole. Another aspect deserving of mention is that a co-operative rural economy in which the profits of trade and industry belong to the rural population (as in Yugoslavia) is likely to provide to them the means for the expansion of welfare services and social opportunities which it is beyond the power of government budgets to establish to any adequate extent for many years to come.

Recent studies of migration from rural to urban areas have shown that, as at present organised, rural society fails to offer adequate work opportunities either to unskilled workers or to those who have education, skills and ambition. The latter, therefore, tend to move into towns. In some degree this must affect the rate of economic progress in rural areas. Although the statistical data available are meagre, it is now apparent that, as industrial development proceeds, the gap between urban and rural incomes is likely to widen further and more rapidly. In the existing rural economy there are no forces at work which will counteract this trend. An expanding rural economy should provide not only for larger employment opportunities but also for a fair proportion of jobs at income levels which, after allowing for rural living conditions, are at least comparable with those in urban areas. A planned rural economy organised on co-operative lines alone can meet this test.

The main programmes of development which are now under way bear directly or indirectly on the major problems which have been briefly discussed above. Thus, it is the aim of agricultural production, irrigation and rural industry and other technical programmes to raise productivity, promote intensive agriculture and expand work opportunities. To achieve these goals, on the one hand, the network of extension services is being strengthened and, on the other, an attempt is being made, specially in community project areas, to build up representative institutions. The various technical programmes will be further improved as it comes to be more widely recognised that their full potential by way of increased production and employment is not yet being realised. The main weaknesses at present lie in the fields of land reform and co-operation. In the case of land reform, these are related to the partial fulfilment of tasks set out in the plans. In the case of co-operation, however, the objectives set out in the plans need to be greatly enlarged and made more concrete, and more dynamic programmes have to be implemented. In particular, the transformation of the rural economy through agrarian co-operatives and the organisation of co-operative marketing, distribution and processing should now be placed boldly right at the centre of the national plan. Such transformation involves the setting up of new units as well as the progressive conversion of

3

existing units and existing businesses from an individual to a
co-operative basis in all sectors of activity which provide fair
scope for application of the principle of co-operation.
Programmes of co-operative development on these lines,
supported by effective land reform and technical programmes, are calculated to make a direct attack on the
fundamental problems of the rural economy. In this respect
the efforts now under way continue to fall short of the
minimum requirements in speed and intensity of action.

2

AGRICULTURAL POLICY AND RURAL ECONOMIC PROGRESS*

I

FOR MORE than a decade, continuous efforts have been made to transform India's economy through a series of Five Year Plans. The formulation of each Plan has brought up prominently issues concerning the place of the rural sector in the economic development of the country, its rate of growth and investment requirements and the relations between the rural and the non-rural sectors of the economy. Large changes have taken place in many directions, new institutions have been established and the rural environment today is different in many ways from that of ten or twelve years ago. Yet, a general impression remains that economic progress in rural areas has not been achieved in adequate measure, that partly in consequence of planned development, the gap between levels of income and opportunity in rural and non-rural areas is widening, and that the agricultural economy has not been

* Adapted from the Presidential address to the Twenty-second All India Agricultural Economics Conference, held at Ahmedabad, in December, 1962. See Indian Journal of Agricultural Economics, Volume XVIII, No. 1, January-March 1963, pages 10-23.

strengthened sufficiently to meet the demands of rapid industrial and economic development. At this juncture, when a crisis in our affairs has forced us to re-examine our assumptions and practices, it would be useful to explore how far the common beliefs concerning the progress of the rural economy are borne out by the available evidence, whether the framework of policies and institutions on which the Five Year Plans are based calls for fundamental changes in emphasis and direction and, finally, whether the instruments through which the various objectives are sought to be attained are adequate for the purpose. These questions, important as they are for an appraisal of the past, become even more significant in relation to the perspectives for the future.

In recent years, a vast amount of statistical, economic and other data regarding conditions in rural areas has become available. There is much new wealth of knowledge to be explored for gaining deeper understanding of the basic problems of our rural economy. Doubtless, there would still be many aspects on which answers might be difficult. Nevertheless, in the degree to which we formulate issues correctly, even if precise answers are not to be had immediately, means now exist for gaining greater insight and devising new policies on the basis of tested knowledge. However, to use these means to the best advantage, there is need for much closer interchange of experience and for a common frame of reference between those engaged in carrying out studies and surveys and the workers, both official and non-official, who are actively participating in specific tasks for the development of the rural economy.

In assessing the progress of a national economy, growth in national and per capita income, rates of growth in different sectors and rates of investment and domestic savings are among the principal indicators. Statistical measures have considerable validity in the organised sector of an economy.

In the unorganised sector and more specially in relation to the rural areas, such indicators are not always readily available. To the extent statistical data can be obtained, even apart from inherent limitations, they throw only partial light on the total process and degree of change that occurs over a period. Data which permit comparison with given benchmarks exist at present only to a small extent. Moreover, many aspects of rural change are not sufficiently susceptible of measurement. Without, therefore, under-estimating the importance of statistical measures of economic progress in rural areas, one may legitimately suggest that for any just appraisal, it is essential to take a wider view of the changes through which the rural economy is passing under the impact of planned development and the economic, technical, social and administrative policies and measures associated with it.

II

Before proceeding to this appraisal, certain broad magnitudes and trends may be briefly stated. These are not intended to be a summing up of the total picture, but may at least point to some of the problems. The rural sector accounts for about 70 per cent of the total net national output. Its pace of advance is, therefore, the most dominant factor in the overall growth of the economy. The growth of population is throwing an increasingly heavy burden on the rural areas. According to the final population totals for the 1961 census, during the decade 1951-61, as against an increase of 34 per cent in the total number of workers and of 35 per cent among non-agricultural workers, the addition in agriculture was of the order of 33 per cent. In terms of absolute figures, this has meant an increase in the number of agricultural workers from about 98 million to about 131 million, the proportion of agricultural workers to the total working force remaining at about 70 per cent.

This large increase in the pressure of population on land should have been balanced by corresponding increase in production in rural areas. Between 1950-51 and 1960-61, as against increase in national income of 42 per cent, the net output of agriculture, animal husbandry and ancillary activities rose by 33 per cent. It has been estimated that over the period 1950-51 to 1960-61 the average net output per worker increased by 21·5 per cent. Against this, the net output per worker in agriculture rose by about 15 per cent, while that outside agriculture increased by 25·5 per cent. Consequently, a small decline is observed in the proportion between the net output per agricultural worker and the net output per worker outside agriculture. At the same time, such statistical data as are available suggest that capital formation in rural areas has increased during the first two Plans at a much lower rate than outside the rural sector or in the economy as a whole.

Since agriculture accounts for most of the economic activity in the rural sector, the presumption is that in an economy which, as a whole, has been advancing only at a moderate pace, agriculture has tended to lag behind and, secondly, that with the growth of population the gap between incomes in rural and urban areas may have actually widened. Over the period 1961-76, the total increase in population may be of the order of 187 million, the increase in the labour force being about 70 million. With this prospect of population growth, it becomes all the more imperative that there should be the most concentrated attack on the development of agriculture and the rural economy. It is from this aspect that we have to give thought to changes in policy and, what is not less important, to changes in the machinery and methods of practical implementation which are called for in the light of experience. The trends which have been cited suggest that the task of lifting the rural economy from the stagnation which characterised it in the past and of enabling it to function in a truly dynamic manner is much bigger and more difficult and will make larger demands on our resources and our institutions than might have been allowed for.

III

As different policies and programmes embodied in the Five Year Plans are executed, it is important to keep in mind the character of the rural problem as a whole and of the strategy which has been evolved for dealing with it. Prior to the First Plan, much study was devoted to the problem of uneconomic holdings and of rural indebtedness, and the need for agrarian reform was widely felt. In the Five Year Plans, an attempt was made to approach the rural economy in an integrated manner. From a more or less static rural structure, which laboured under feudal tenures, the aim was to build up a progressive and rapidly growing economy founded on peasant proprietorship and organised increasingly on co-operative lines. The main features of this approach may be briefly stated.

To secure the development of the rural economy, the entire machinery of district administration had to be strengthened and identified with the welfare of the people. This involved steps in three directions: firstly, provision of technical skills through a network of extension services; secondly, a co-ordinated approach to the village community and the problems of the peasant; and thirdly, building up institutions by means of which the people could largely undertake development through their own initiative and participation. These steps led to the emergence of Community Development and the National Extension Service and, in due course, to the establishment of democratic Panchayati Raj institutions at the district and block levels in addition to panchayats in the villages.

The Plans have sought to raise the productivity of land,

above all, through irrigation, supplemented to an increasing extent by programmes for soil conservation, extended use of fertilizers, development of local manurial resources and adoption of improved agricultural practices.

The Five Year Plans visualise the rural economy being reorganised and developed basically along co-operative lines. The precise content of this co-operative approach has taken shape more slowly than had been hoped for. While large parts of what is broadly accepted in principle still remain to be carried out in practice, the objective clearly is that co-operation should become as speedily as possible the principal basis of organisation in many branches of economic life, notably in agriculture, small industry, processing, marketing, distribution, supplies, rural electrification, housing and construction, and in the provision of essential amenities for local communities.

The scheme of land reform has been regarded from the beginning as being fundamental to development. Its main features have now been embodied in the legislation which has been enacted in the States. The primary aims were to eliminate intermediary tenures, establish security and reasonable rents for tenants, limit the size of agricultural holdings, progressively provide the rights of ownership to tenant cultivators, and create conditions for the growth of a co-operative rural economy. In the earlier stages, it was also hoped that substantial areas of surplus lands would become available for distribution to the landless.

The fact that a sizeable proportion of the rural population consists of landless or virtually landless agricultural labourers has been a source of anxiety in each of the Plans. In practice, the scheme of land reform has provided mainly for tenant cultivators. Even in its conception, it did not seek to provide to every agricultural labourer a piece of land, however small it might be, as it seemed that such a step could have rendered peasant farming untenable and could have also led to the weakening of the agricultural economy. Measures for raising agricultural productivity could bring only gradual and limited benefits to agricultural labourers. The main hope of bringing agricultural workers on to a level of equality in status and opportunity with others in the village community, therefore, lay in the development of industry and in the diversification of the rural economy. This is one of the major compulsions for rural industrialisation, for closer integration of the rural with the industrial economy, and for accelerated development both in regions which have favourable conditions for growth and in those with considerable rural unemployment and under-employment. It should be added that in the *social* field, through community development and other programmes, there has been already some impact on the life and conditions of rural labour.

Thus, in terms of policy, the Five Year Plans provided the machinery for rural development and set out the economic and social goals to be achieved. They were weak in dealing with the problem of landless labour, but it was thought that with the growth of the economy as a whole, increase in the productivity of land, development of co-operation and changes in the agrarian structure, this problem might become more manageable. In reviewing economic progress in rural areas, particular attention should be given both to the strengthening of policy and objectives and to eliminating the gaps between policy and implementation which have tended to reduce the social and economic impact of planned development. Such a review should encompass changes in the rural environment which are under way, changes in the agrarian structure which need urgent thought, directions in which the process of building up a co-operative rural economy must be strengthened, measures required for speeding up technological change in agriculture and for raising the productivity of land, and policies designed to achieve intensive development in each area and closer integration between the rural and the industrial economy.

IV

In the building up of the rural economy, changes of an environmental and social character have a significance which is not fully described in statistical terms. There is an intimate and growing connection between economic, social and technical change. The emergence of an environment in many rural areas favourable to economic progress is a vital fact. In bringing about such an environment many factors are at work. The general development of the economy and expansion of industry and trade and of transport and power and increasing urbanisation would in any case exert a powerful and continuing influence on the rural environment. The main role of community development thus far has been to serve as an agent of change close to the rural population and as a link between national and local planning. The process of community organisation has not yet gone far enough to be able to tap sufficiently the local manpower and other resources of each area. Social research and improvements in organisation and planning could help in reducing this shortcoming. The existence of institutions through which the people of each area can largely determine their own course of development should be a factor of increasing importance in the coming years and one capable of imparting richness and vitality to the process of growth at the grassroots. Already, the development of an expanding network of communications has brought the town and the village nearer one another. The benchmark surveys undertaken by the Programme Evaluation Organisation have shown that in most areas there is increasing readiness to adopt improved agricultural practices. Thus, in the eighteen blocks which were studied, between the first survey in 1953-54 and the second survey five years later, the percentage of households using improved seeds increased by 70, of those using improved implements by about 50, and of those making use of fertilizers by about 150. In many areas the limits to the acceptance of improved practices are now set less by resistance on the part of farmers and far more by the ability of the extension services to make the necessary supplies and technical guidance promptly and readily available.

In the nature of things, changes in the rural environment are by no means evenly spread. They are more marked in areas in which new resources have come to be developed, whether by way of irrigation or rural electrification or the growth of processing and other industries or of new communications. However, these changes are being stimulated in all areas by developments in education, health and other social services. Although the replanning of village sites and improvement of rural housing are necessarily long-term undertakings, to which much greater attention should now be paid, it is interesting to observe that in several areas the proportion of brick-built houses is increasing fairly rapidly. Thus, in the Programme Evaluation Organisation's studies, in one area in the Punjab, the proportion rose from about 3 to 23 per cent, in another from 7 to 34 per cent. Increases, somewhat smaller in dimensions, are also reported from a number of other States and are borne out by several re-surveys of villages which have been undertaken in recent years. Changes in the rural environment, which are now proceeding under the influence of developments outside as well as within each local area, have to be harnessed purpose-fully as a positive factor for accelerated economic development through the mobilisation of local man-power resources, specially for creating new community assets, improving living conditions for the weaker sections of the village community and expanding agricultural production.

V

The scheme of land reform was evolved in detail over a period of several years after Independence. As its main features came to be accepted at the level of policy, legislation followed in the States, however, responding in this process to local pressures and permitting variations which were often better avoided. The piecemeal character of land reform legislation and its excessive reliance on the machinery of revenue administration, without adequate education of rural opinion and support by way of credit and supplies and programmes for resettlement on land, have unfortunately tended to diminish the impact of land reform on rural welfare and development. The main consideration at the present time is the need for early completion of the process which has been initiated and intensification of development in areas in which land reform entails substantial changes in the distribution of rights in land.

Land reform comprises four sets of measures—abolition of intermediary tenures, tenancy reform, ceilings on agricultural holdings and conferment of rights of ownership on tenant cultivators. Once accomplished, these measures are intended to pave the way for the growth of a co-operative rural economy. At Independence, intermediary tenures accounted for about 40 per cent of the total area of the country. Except for the payment of compensation—a process spread over 20 to 40 years—this phase of land reform has been completed. Similarly, despite difficult problems arising from attempts by owners to resume land for 'personal cultivation' and with certain variations between States, the programme for tenancy reform has been also substantially undertaken.* Together, abolition of intermediary rights and tenancy reform involve considerable *de facto* redistribution

---

* However, later investigations have revealed serious deficiencies in implementing measures for tenancy reform.

of land. On the other hand, proposals for imposing ceilings on agricultural holdings have only slowly found their way into legislation, and a high proportion of potentially 'surplus' lands has passed out of hand through 'transfers,' many of them being essentially evasive of land reform. In due course, large holdings will disappear in fact as in law but, for the time being, an important public purpose sought through land reform has not been served. Nevertheless, whatever the limitations of the legislation, it is essential that it should be implemented as early as possible.

Apart from ceilings, the next major step in land reform is the grant of rights of ownership to the bulk of tenant cultivators, specially to those occupying non-resumable lands. The direction of policy was that this task should be accomplished before the end of the Third Plan. Some States have undertaken the necessary legislation and are giving effect to it, elsewhere the objective has not been given so far the priority due to it.

In theory, land reform was urged and broadly accepted as part of the Plans. In its actual implementation, instead of being developed as a movement rooted in mass opinion, land reform has been generally treated as an isolated programme. In every area in which land reform is carried out, there is need, firstly, for an intensive agricultural drive and provision of supplies, credit and other services; secondly, for greater emphasis on the organisation of co-operative activity; and thirdly, for supporting rural employment programmes. Without such measures, the positive gains from land reform cannot be fully realised.

For the agricultural economy to be placed on a sound basis, the problem of small and uneconomic holdings still remains to be faced. To an extent, in most States, extreme fragmentation of holdings is now sought to be avoided, but the limits are necessarily very low. Consolidation of individual holdings has been undertaken on a notable scale only in three or four States. It is doubtful if at any time the total area benefited will be much in excess of 50 or 60 million acres, the largest scope for consolidation being in areas which are irrigated or are likely to come under irrigation. Co-operative farming, rural works programmes, land settlement schemes and intensive development of rural industry are essential not only in themselves but as means for securing efficient cultivating holdings and completing the reorganisation of the agrarian structure. These elements have to be brought into the Five Year Plans on a much larger scale than at present.

Over the past few years a distinctive co-operative sector has begun to take shape. The principal advances have been in the field of credit, specially short-term credit, in processing, in particular, of sugarcane, and in the handloom industry. At the end of the Second Plan, there were about 200,000 primary agricultural credit societies with a total membership of about 17 million. Of these, nearly 8000 with a membership of over 3 million were large-sized societies. The total short and medium-term credit advanced through co-operatives amounted to more than Rs. 200 crores, as against about Rs. 50 crores five years earlier and Rs. 20 crores at the beginning of the First Plan. The number of co-operative sugar factories increased steadily from 3 with a total production of 30,000 metric tons in 1955-56 to 30 with a total production of 440,000 metric tons. The number of industrial co-operatives increased from about 8000 in 1951 to about 15,000 in 1956 and, at the end of the Second Plan, to about 30,000, of which about 8000 were co-operatives of handloom weavers. For the rest, despite some advances, the role of co-operative institutions is still quite small, and the main task of building up a strong and diversified co-operative movement remains to be accomplished.

The magnitude of the task ahead will be seen from some of the goals which have been indicated even in the Third Five

Year Plan. These goals will not be attained at the present rate of progress. The volume of agricultural business conducted by co-operative marketing societies was estimated at the end of the Second Plan at about Rs. 200 crores—itself a mere fraction of the total trade in agricultural produce—which it was hoped at least to double during the Third Plan. In the field of co-operative processing, the Plan called for reorganisation as co-operatives of the existing units engaged in the processing of agricultural produce as well as for allocation to the co-operative sector of the greater part of the expansion in processing industries based on planned increases in the production of agricultural raw materials and in the consumption of final products. In co-operative farming, the broad aim is that over a period of ten years or so a substantial proportion of agricultural land should be cultivated on a co-operative basis. However, in two directions some advance is now expected, namely, consumer co-operatives and, under the impulse of the rural works programme, in the organisation of labour and construction co-operatives.* In the reconstruction of the rural economy and in the harnessing of the resources of rural areas, there are no larger or more far-reaching objectives than those connected with the building up of a strong and dynamic co-operative sector. These objectives have not yet been fully incorporated into the concepts and practice of community development at the level of the block and the village. Their attainment is a vital part of the country's agricultural effort and indeed of the entire scheme of planned development.

VI

To bring about a sharp increase in agricultural production and a rise in the productivity of land have been among the

---

* The organisation of labour and construction co-operatives and the rural works programme did not in fact receive the attention and the resources contemplated in the Third Five Year Plan.

central aims of planning for more than a decade. These tasks have been approached from several directions. In considering the impact of planned development on the rural economy, it is difficult to separate various policy elements. The scope of the agricultural effort under the Five Year Plans may be summed up in three broad propositions. Firstly, the scale of investment in agriculture has increased from about Rs. 800 crores in the First Plan to about Rs. 1200 crores in the Second Plan and to about Rs. 2000 crores in the Third Plan. Secondly, at the end of the Second Plan, some 14,000 agricultural graduates, 5000 veterinary graduates and about 40,000 village level workers trained in agricultural extension were engaged largely in the task of providing technical guidance and improving the level of agriculture in different parts of the country. Thirdly, steadily increasing resources by way of water, improved seed and fertilizers have been made available, so that the essential technical foundations for raising the productivity of land have been strengthened. Thus, over the first two Plans the net area irrigated increased from about 51 million acres to about 70 million acres, the consumption of nitrogenous fertilizers rose in terms of nitrogen from 55,000 to 230,000 tons, and about 4000 small government farms were set up for multiplying improved varieties of seeds produced in research stations.

These measures have led to perceptible results, but certain important deficiencies have also been revealed. Between 1950-51 and 1960-61, the total agricultural area increased by about 19 per cent, the area under foodgrains by about 15 per cent and that under crops other than foodgrains by about 39 per cent. Agricultural production as a whole rose by about 40 per cent, production of foodgrains by 36 per cent and of crops other than foodgrains by 49 per cent. Despite year to year fluctuations, the output of cotton increased nearly twofold and of sugarcane by about 74 per cent. The average agricultural productivity rose by about 18 per cent, the increase in respect of rice, wheat, jowar and cotton being distinctly higher than, for instance, for maize, pulses and sugarcane. In some States, progress in agricultural production has been fairly marked, although the crops whose output has increased vary widely in different areas.

Increase in irrigation and changes in demand have led in many areas to the substitution of more remunerative for less remunerative crops. This is borne out by special surveys which have been undertaken and is also reflected in changes which have taken place in the crop patterns of different States. Thus, while there are important variations between States, areas under crops such as jowar, bajra, small millets, barley and sesamum have tended to diminish, while those under crops like rice, wheat, gram, groundnut, sugarcane, cotton and jute have increased.

In a planned economy, in those areas in which crop prospects are reasonably secured through irrigation and assured rainfall, cropping patterns should be a matter for systematic and studied planning and should not be subject to any great extent to short-term shifts in prices and demand.

We may next attempt to identify certain weaknesses shown by the agricultural trends of the past decade or so. This will suggest the directions in which policy, planning and adminis-tration need to be strengthened. Under conditions of planned development in India, three important tests should be met in planning for agricultural development. The first is that the agricultural economy should be developed and stimulated to the extent of providing for increase in the requirements of food and raw materials in accordance with the estimates of the Plan. Variations on account of seasonal factors could be progressively provided against through buffer stocks and other regulatory measures. Apart from such varia-tions, in keeping with the crop plan, the relative prices and other economic incentives should be as nearly equal as

4

possible as between different crops. Secondly, there should be steady increase in production and yields in all parts of the country and, in particular, in areas with irrigation and assured rainfall. In the third place, through increase in yields, adoption of improved techniques and improvements in the size of the unit of cultivation, cost per unit of production should be kept down and even reduced. The high level of costs in Indian agriculture at present is both an index of backwardness and a drag on the development of the economy as a whole. On these three tests, both the techniques of agricultural planning which have been actually followed and the performance of agriculture have on the whole fallen short, the gap being much larger in some directions than in others. Thus, for oilseeds which are important for domestic consumption as well as for exports, over a period of ten years, the yield per acre scarcely increased. Though the output of cotton has increased considerably, both on account of improvement in yields and increase in area, the output is still significantly short of requirements. In the case of an export crop like tobacco, the yield per acre has not materially improved. In respect of foodgrains, the goal of self-sufficiency, which was set for the First Plan and again for the Second, has yet to be reached.

The benchmark surveys undertaken by the Programme Evaluation Organisation show that except in a few areas there has been relatively small increase in the double-cropped area. A number of re-surveys of villages which have been undertaken, for instance, in Maharashtra, Punjab, Uttar Pradesh, Mysore and elsewhere, indicate that even where irrigation has led to changes in cropping patterns, in the methods of cultivation and in the tools and implements employed by cultivators, there have been few radical improvements. This points to a persistent inadequacy both in the organisation and in the techniques and objectives of extension work.

Lags in the utilisation of irrigation present a more complex problem reflecting, on the one hand, deficiencies in irrigation and agricultural policy and administration and, on the other, existing weaknesses in the organisation of community effort and in extension methods. On the available data, it appears that at the end of the Second Plan, as against a total potential of about 12 million acres from major and medium irrigation projects, the actual utilisation was of the order of 9 million acres. The gap between potential and actual utilisation may be even larger. The same problem also exists in respect of minor irrigation works such as tanks and tubewells. It is obvious that a many-sided approach has to be adopted to achieve the speedy utilisation of irrigation facilities. This must include more precise knowledge of the water resources of an area through surveys and investigations, co-ordinated action by different agencies, evolution of suitable crop patterns, supported by measures to facilitate their adoption on the part of cultivators, acceptance of the obligation to construct and maintain field channels, not only by the beneficiaries individually but by the village community as a whole, and policies relating to irrigation cesses and the distribution of water which are better designed to promote speedy utilisation. Since a variety of factors are responsible for what is doubtless a critical weakness in the present agricultural situation, in addition to steps which are already being initiated, it would be desirable to take up some areas on a pilot basis with the deliberate object of evolving techniques under field conditions for eliminating the time lag between the creation of irrigation potential and its utilisation and for promoting a higher level of agricultural technology simultaneously with the introduction or expansion of irrigation facilities.

This brief review points to four main conclusions. Firstly, in the planning of agriculture a much more central role should be assigned to price policy and the organisation of

marketing than has been done so far. This involves both
closer analysis of costs and returns for different crops as well
as continuous study of the conditions of cultivation and
marketing actually prevailing in different parts of the
country. Secondly, there are definite indications that the
existing agricultural administrations in the States, the
numbers and quality of extension personnel and the techniques of extension do not answer adequately to the requirements of rapid development in agriculture. The community
development organisation in the blocks has to be greatly
strengthened in terms of technical, agricultural and extension
personnel. The earlier expectation that the village level
worker, as the common agent of the various development
agencies functioning in the block, would also meet adequately
the requirements of agricultural extension needs to be reviewed. For this there are two reasons. With the development
of Panchayati Raj institutions, even if agriculture is always
given the first place, the more general administrative and
organisational functions will frequently tend to take precedence over normal and technical work. Secondly, the
progress already achieved in agriculture and the new
environment and outlook which has emerged in the villages
in many parts of the country have created a demand for
skill and knowledge on the part of agricultural extension
services at standards higher than those which village level
workers can at best be expected to provide. There is also
need for a much more intimate connection between agricultural research and its application in the field. An expert
committee has recently listed outstanding agricultural practices in a number of areas and has attempted to identify the
practices to which the high yields of crops like rice, wheat,
sugarcane and cotton obtained in these areas may be attributed. Variations in yields and in the general level of
agriculture even between different parts of the same State
are extraordinarily wide. In the effort to bring up levels of

cultivation and agricultural practices to similar standards, it is important not to spare resources in men or in money. The requisite agricultural personnel can be provided only over a period. However, recent developments such as the accelerated programmes for cotton and oilseeds, for soil conservation, and in the intensive agricultural districts emphasise the urgency of a new outlook on agricultural administration and the development of extension services.

The third main conclusion which may be drawn from current experience concerns the place of community action in the scheme of agricultural development, specially at the level of the village. This is an indispensable condition for realising substantial increases in agricultural production, widespread adoption of superior techniques and practices and the organisation of co-operatives, specially for marketing and production. The most important aspect of such community action must be the full utilisation of the manpower resources of each village and each area. In a system of peasant farming, the labour of each household may be expected to be well utilised. However, in the Indian situation the existence of small and uneconomic holdings and of large bodies of agricultural labourers, accompanied by rapid growth of population, leave a considerable reserve of manpower which could be mobilised for productive work. With a large and better organised labour input, it is possible to extend irrigation, undertake soil conservation, dry farming, land reclamation and afforestation, and adopt labour intensive agricultural practices on a scale far exceeding that yet attempted in any part of the country. Hiring of labour by individual households cannot provide for continuity of work and is inadequate as a method of harnessing all the manpower available in the village. Such a task can only be undertaken by the village community as part of a wider area plan which ensures the requisite resources, technical guidance and other facilities. It is, therefore, necessary to redefine the relationship between the individual landholder or cultivator and the community in terms of the present imperatives of rapid economic development and the fullest utilisation of manpower.

In many areas it should be possible to create conditions in which the demand for labour could be greatly increased, not merely in busy seasons but throughout the year. As is well known, in present day Europe, a number of countries receive a regular influx of workers from other countries which have larger labour reserves and are absorbing a proportion of these workers permanently within their own economies. This is because their own economic development is rapid and renders them continually short of labour. In the same manner, agricultural activities could be intensified in areas with irrigation and assured rainfall on a scale which could, in time, not only assimilate the local labour force but also create conditions in which there would be additional demand for labour from other areas and, in some cases, even from other States. Thus, a policy aiming at the fullest utilisation of rural manpower resources will also bring out the possibilities of planning for the redistribution of the rural population within individual States and, progressively, between different States.

A marked intensification of agricultural operations, supported by extension activities, community action and the full use of manpower and by co-operative organisations, will call for a bolder and more forward-looking approach to investment in agriculture. The agricultural growth potential of many areas cannot be realised without a much higher level of investment than the present schemes of community development and agriculture provide for. The consequence is that planning becomes rigid, the local manpower resources are not fully harnessed to productive effort and the growth of the agricultural economy is in fact retarded to an extent that may not be always realised. There should be a special provi-

sion in the scheme of annual allocations under the national
and State plans for additional resources beyond the customary
norms for areas in which intensive agricultural operations
are likely to yield significant additions to output. In these
areas, to begin with, the scheme of land utilisation, cropping
patterns, the inputs of capital, labour, fertilizers, and others
as well as the marketing and processing of agricultural
produce should be planned for the village and the block as a
whole, and responsibility for the enforcement of standards
and for the fullest utilisation of manpower and other available
resources should be placed on the community.

VII

In the numbers it engages and in the contribution it makes
to the national product, agriculture will always be India's
leading industry. In the more advanced countries, on account
of improvements in the techniques of agriculture, production
has continually increased even as numbers on the land have
diminished. At the same time, with agriculture still the main
occupation in rural areas, the distance between the village
and the town has been broken down. In fact, the rural and
the urban areas, while retaining their distinct character,
yet form part of a single integrated national economy. In
these countries it is the urban areas which constantly pull
the rural areas in their own direction. The nature of the
problem of poverty in India, the size of the rural mass, the
limited number of centres of major industrial activity and
the very process of planning for development both in economic and human terms to which we are committed, lead to
the conclusion that the pattern of relationships between the
rural and the urban and the industrial economy which we
seek to build up over the next fifteen or twenty years should
be carefully thought out at this stage in our development.
In the nature of things, many decisions have to be taken

which involve choice of location, choice of technology, selection of industries and the building up of economic and social overheads. These decisions have profound long-term effects and set in train further chains of action and reaction which will later leave little room for manoeuvre to those concerned with planning or legislation or the making of policy. Sooner than may be perceived, the balance and momentum of a complex economic structure largely begin to dictate the course.

In what manner, then, should we plan for agriculture and the rural areas so that, in time, the rural and the urban economies will merge into one ? As mentioned earlier, the gap between the value of output per worker in the villages and in the towns is already appreciable and, in the absence of a larger strategy of development, the forces leading to a further widening of this gap will prove too powerful to resist. However intensive the process of industrialisation and urbanisation, by its very nature, its influence will be felt most fully in small and limited areas and the impact further afield will be much smaller. In other words, one of the essential aims of economic planning in India must be to find a way to avoid a marked and continuing dichotomy in the pace and direction of development in urban and rural areas. An impelling reason for this is the existence of a large labour surplus in the villages which no amount of agricultural development can by itself absorb to the extent of providing full-time gainful employment. Moreover, beyond a point, the growth of agricultural output will be held back unless there are strong incentives towards increase in agricultural production associated with new economic opportunities and improvements in levels of living.

Under the existing conditions of agricultural organisation, the rural economy is not well placed for mobilising its manpower and other resources and gaining adequately from the processes of industrial and economic development which have been initiated. There is a vicious circle in as much as an under-developed region cannot secure or sustain the economic and social overheads needed for rapid growth and, without these, the balance of economic advantage continues to turn against it. It may need all the skills and leadership it can muster and more. Yet, these it must lose to regions which are developing more rapidly. There is, thus, a close connection between securing rapid increase in agricultural production, creating in the rural areas expanding opportunities for non-agricultural employment, and building up a dynamic rural economy along co-operative lines. It is in the measure in which these three aims are pursued as parts of the same basic concept of agricultural policy that it will be possible to achieve the necessary integration between the rural and the industrial economy and to raise significantly the levels of income and living for the bulk of the people in the rural areas.

3

PLANNING AND PRODUCTIVITY IN AGRICULTURE*

I

THE CHALLENGE OF AGRICULTURE

Agriculture and Economic Growth

THERE IS no precise historical parallel to the conditions and assumptions under which India is seeking to rebuild her economic and social structure. For particular facets of this effort analogies can be found. In specific directions, the experience of other countries and other periods bears on our problems and can be drawn upon. But the combination of circumstances under which India's planned development is being undertaken can be considered unique. Therefore, while drawing upon the experience, for instance, of the early stages of the Industrial Revolution in Great Britain, of the

* Adapted from a contribution to the Dr. P. S. Lokanathan Seventy-second Birthday Commemoration Volume, *Economic Development: Issues and Policies* (1966), pages 117-152, Vora & Co., Bombay. The paper is based on three Extension Lectures at Osmania University, Hyderabad, delivered on January 27, 28 and 29, 1965.

building up of a system of national economy in Germany, of the development of agriculture and small industry in Japan, of rural extension in U. S. A., of planning and state enterprise in USSR, or of co-operative development in the Scandinavian countries and elsewhere, it is even more essential to analyse our own experience in depth. The materials available for such study are already plentiful; they need to be supplemented by field investigations, by systematic exchange of experience and a wider range of enquiry encompassing economic, social, scientific and technological problems as well as institutional possibilities. In particular, the problems of agriculture and the rural economy call for the combined application of several disciplines of knowledge and fields of experience accompanied by a vivid appreciation of the nature of rural life, the functioning of rural communities and human relations between different groups.

Planned development commences from a situation of lack of balance and proportion within the economy as a whole and in agriculture in relation to the rest of the economy. To establish a satisfactory balance and the conditions of self-sustained growth is among the main purposes of planning, of industrialisation and of social reconstruction. These are in the nature of processes of development to be carried forward from one stage to the next and realised over a period. In range and scope, the developmental effort changes and grows as it proceeds and as new problems arise. Nevertheless, in its limited sense, there has to be, within each given period, a certain quantitative balance between the demand for and supply of agricultural commodities, both in the aggregate and in relation to the non-agricultural sector of the economy. Therefore, given certain assumptions as to growth of population, growth of national, sectoral and per capita incomes, requirements of raw materials for industry, estimates of exports, nutritional and other standards to be met and the elasticities of demand for different products, it is possible to determine broadly the quantities in which different commodities should become available at each stage during the period of planning. The estimates will invariably be crude and will need revision from time to time. To a considerable extent, gaps in availability can be anticipated and provided for. In the measure in which this does not happen, they will express themselves before long through changes in price levels, in the terms of trade between agriculture and industry, and in the balance of payments.

The problem of the marketable surplus is a special case of this general relationship between agriculture and the national economy. To begin with, the specific issue may be how the towns and the industrial centres are to be fed. The conditions under which the producer takes his surplus to the market change. Depending on the institutional arrangements which may exist, in the short period, the marketable surplus may diminish sharply if the grower and the trader have the ability to hold back or are permitted to do so. However, as more and more transactions within the rural economy take the form of sales for cash, the problem of the marketable surplus moves from the towns into the countryside. Hence, sooner rather than later, in a developing economy, marketing of agricultural produce has to be organised within a framework of social control, state trading and co-operative marketing. Both co-operatives and individual traders and growers have to function under the discipline of public regulation and community responsibility. There is no escape from this conclusion.

In a growing economy, the role of agriculture is much wider than the problem of meeting the requirements of food and raw materials may suggest. As development proceeds, agriculture and industry come to be more and more closely linked. Increasingly, adequate availability of industrial inputs, such as chemical fertilizers, pesticides and implements and various forms of machinery and equipment becomes a necessary condition for rapid increase in agricultural production. Rise in incomes and the changing needs of the rural population provide the greater part of the demand for the products of industry, specially of consumer and intermediate goods. Industries will be but a relatively small sector of the economy until they spread to the smaller towns and the rural areas and the process of diffusion of the industrial and technical outlook reaches into the daily life and activities of the rural community. In turn, agriculture releases new manpower and enterprise for industrialisation, for the growth of towns and cities and for developing a wide range of processing and other activities allied to agriculture. In time, with a stronger economic base and greater diversification, the rural areas should also contribute increasingly to capital formation and provide surpluses for investment in industry. However, in the first phase, it is essential that there should be transfer of capital from the organised sectors of the economy into rural development. Moreover, there is a strong case for the argument that, to the extent possible, resouces from the villages, gathered through co-operative institutions, small savings, life insurance and public loans, should be channelled back to them as much as possible through projects for the economic and industrial development of rural areas. For, at this stage of planned development, their best use by far will be to strengthen and diversify the rural economy and raise levels of productivity and income in rural areas. This will not come about without a positive national policy, supported by specific programmes and institutional resources. For, in the ordinary course of economic development, the main currents run strongly the other way, towards the widening of the already significant gaps between rural and urban levels of income and productivity, of well-being and opportunity. It is, therefore, a matter of the highest importance that the growth of agriculture and of the rural economy as a whole should be planned for as an organic and fundamental part of the development of the national economy. Without this sense of direction, large numbers in the villages, specially the landless, will remain substantially outside the pale of development, poverty in the villages will persist and deepen, agriculture will remain a source of weakness and continue to be much less than an industry, and the pace of industrial development itself will be far slower than it need be.

PHASES OF AGRICULTURAL DEVELOPMENT

Agricultural development may be conceived of as comprising broadly two sets of processes, namely,

(a) those designed to improve the technical and economic base of agriculture and to develop it as a stable and viable industry, and

(b) those designed to strengthen and change the economic and social structure of rural areas, to integrate all sections of the population into a system of productive relationships based on rising skills and equal opportunity, to diversify rural economic life and relieve the pressure on land, and to create the milieu for a richer community life and culture in the villages.

Each of these two main streams of effort comprises several different elements and activities. These latter are assigned inevitably to a number of different agencies. The institutions and services which have come into existence through community development and the growth of the co-operative movement, including those intended to provide for specialised and technical needs, are common to both aspects of agricultural development. For the greater part, it is through community development, along with rural extension services, dissemination of the results of research and growth of co-operatives, that agriculture has to be transformed into an industry at the same time as a new life is created for the millions in the villages.

It is possible to distinguish at least three broad phases in the development of agriculture. In the first phase, there is a body of accumulated knowledge and experience which the better farmers are able to draw upon readily. They respond quickly to rising demands from the towns through extension of area under cultivation, adoption of improved varieties of seed, use of fertilizers, and employment of improved implements and technology. Partly in response to higher prices, culturable lands which can be brought under the plough without incurring heavy costs of reclamation are taken up for cultivation. The gap in productivity between the small numbers who constitute the better farmers and the general mass of cultivators increases to an extent; this is balanced by the spread effects of the example set by the more skilled farmers.

In the second phase of agricultural development, industrial inputs begin to play a larger role. The demand for fertilizers, pesticides and improved implements and machinery is intensified and outstrips the supply. Limitations of the available results of scientific knowledge of crops, soils and the use of water become apparent. The need is felt for higher levels of skills and more effective organisation on the part of extension workers. The demand for capital and credit increases; so does the supply, but not nearly enough. The pattern of agriculture becomes more varied, specially the cultivation of fruits and vegetables, and dairying and poultry become more significant elements in the economy of an increasing number of farmers. Efficient marketing and stable and remunerative prices become vital elements both in securing the marketable surplus from the rural areas and in stimulating a general increase in agricultural productivity. The second phase is a period of growth in which the scarcities in material inputs and credit and gaps in skill and organisation stand out prominently. Gradually, these deficiencies lessen, the increasing requirements are met and a growing proportion of farmers adopt the practices of scientific agriculture. However, problems of farm organisation and of diversification of the rural economy may only begin to be resolved during this phase.

It is in the third phase that, under the conditions of development in India, these problems should be expected to come right into the centre of agricultural and rural policy. For the economy as a whole to gain the necessary dynamism and to sustain a high rate of growth, a strong agricultural base, reduction in the numbers engaged directly in agriculture, adoption of modern technology and higher forms of organisation in agriculture and other rural activities, are as essential as the development of heavy and basic industries and a varied and fast expanding industrial structure, along with welfare services for the mass of the people. Only when both sets of conditions are realised within the scheme of economic growth, will it be possible to achieve an adequate degree of integration between the rural and the industrial and urban economy.

The present situation in agriculture would appear to correspond more or less to the second phase described above. In working out a strategy for agriculture, therefore, special attention has to be paid to overcoming, as early as may be possible, the shortages and deficiencies which distinguish this phase but are also, from another aspect, a measure of the greater demands which progress itself creates.

PROGRESS IN AGRICULTURE

The small advance in agricultural production during the first three years of the Third Five Year Plan was a clear warning that progress in agriculture could not be taken for granted. The marked increase in agricultural production in the fourth year of the Plan suggested that favourable seasons combined with sustained effort could change the situation for the better over short periods, but did not diminish the force of the warning.*

In looking at agriculture in terms of different phases of development, one can see in clearer perspective the progress in agriculture which has in fact been realised since the commencement of planned development. For this purpose, the study on *Growth Rates in Agriculture*, prepared by the Economics and Statistics Directorate of the Ministry of Food and Agriculture, is a valuable source of information.** The study contains index numbers of area, production and productivity for the period 1949-50 to 1964-65 for the country as a whole as well as for individual States. It also provides some comparable data for other countries. The study has to be followed by closer investigation on a regional basis of areas within India in which there has been marked progress and those in which serious lags have occurred. There should be systematic analysis of the economic,

* The record of agricultural production during the period of the Third Five Year Plan is summarised in the Table below:

	Unit	1960-61	1961-62	1962-63	1963-64	1964-65	1965-66
Foodgrains	Million tonnes	82·0	82·7	80·2	80·6	89·0	72·0
Cotton (lint)	Lakh bales	52·9	45·8	52·3	54·3	56·6	47·6
Oilseeds (Five major oilseeds)	Million tonnes	7·0	7·3	7·4	7·1	8·5	6·4
Sugarcane (gur)	Million tonnes	11·2	10·6	9·3	10·5	12·0	12·1
Jute	Lakh bales	41·3	63·6	54·4	60·8	60·2	44·7
Mesta	Lakh bales	11·3	18·8	17·4	19·0	15·8	12·9
Index of Agricultural production	Agricultural year 1949-50 =100	142·2	144·8	139·6	143·1	158·5	132·7

** The writer wishes to acknowledge his debt to this study, from which the first five tables in this paper have been taken. An earlier version of the paper was based on data up to 1961-62; subsequently, data up to 1964-65 were processed by the Ministry of Food and Agriculture.

5

technical and social factors at work which could be identified in each area at different stages of the developmental effort.

The study by the Ministry of Food and Agriculture sets out data for growth of agricultural production on two different bases, namely, the three years from 1949-50 to 1951-52 and the period of three years from 1952-53 to 1954-55. The linear rates of growth for the periods 1949-50 to 1964-65 and 1952-53 to 1964-65 are set out in the table below:

All India Linear Growth Rates of Agricultural Production

	Base period	Foodgrains	Non-food-grains	All crops
For 1949-50 to 1964-65	Average 1949-50 to 1951-52			
Agricultural production (%)		3·66	4·39	3·92
Area under crops (%)		1·48	2·90	1·72
Agricultural productivity (%)		1·80	1·11	1·78
For 1952-53 to 1964-65	Average 1952-53 to 1954-55			
Agricultural production (%)		2·75	4·79	3·42
Area under crops (%)		1·02	2·56	1·28
Agricultural productivity (%)		1·60	1·79	1·91

Taking the period 1952-53 to 1964-65, with the three years 1952-53 to 1954-55 as the base, the linear rates of growth of agricultural production and food production in a number of countries have been as shown in the table on page 67.

Before proceeding to examine rates of growth in relation to different crops and increases in area and in production and productivity, two broad inferences may be stated. The first is that both for foodgrains and for other crops, there has been increase in area as well as in productivity. The increase in area has been significantly greater for commercial crops. Productivity has also improved in respect of these crops,

Linear Growth Rates of Agricultural Production and Food Production in Different Countries during 1952-53 to 1963-64*

	Country	Agricultural Production (%)	Food Production (%)
Far East	India	3·19	2·55
	Burma	2·34	2·55
	Malaya (Malaysia)	4·63	7·57
	Indonesia	1·41	1·91
	Japan	3·49	3·74
	Pakistan	1·85	1·84
	Philippines	3·93	3·54
	Thailand	6·01	5·44
Near East	Turkey	4·06	4·03
	U.A.R.	4·06	4·72
North America	Canada	1·34	1·25
	United States of America	1·75	2·01
Europe	France	3·13	3·11
	West Germany	2·58	2·65
	Italy	2·07	2·30
	U.K.	3·33	3·39
Oceania	Australia	4·12	4·21
	New Zealand	3·58	2·93

* Except for India, the index numbers of agricultural production used above are those published by the F.A.O. in 'Production Year Book, 1964'. For India, the index numbers as published by the Ministry of Food and Agriculture have been used. F.A.O.'s index numbers for India, which are based on a different methodology, give a growth rate of 2·89 per cent for agricultural production and of 2·73 per cent for food production.

but not much more than for food crops. The index number for area under crops rose steadily from 99.9 in 1950-51 to 116 in 1956-57. The subsequent increases have been smaller. Increases in agricultural production realised in recent years can be attributed to a greater degree to increase in productivity than to increase of area under cultivation. The second broad conclusion which may be suggested is that, while comparisons of agricultural growth between countries present obvious difficulties because of the varying levels from which they start and the diverse conditions under which their economies are expanding, over the period 1952-53 to 1964-65, food production increased in India at a rate lower than that achieved in as many as eleven countries. Of these, six are countries sufficiently advanced in industry to be able to provide the materials and equipment needed for agriculture. In the others, expansion of area under cultivation and a variety of other factors may have operated, including mechanisation of agriculture and expansion of area as in Turkey, institutional changes as in the United Arab Republic and developmental programmes along with price incentives, as in the Philippines, Thailand and Malaysia. Obviously, there is need for closer search into the factors which have proved to be most influential.

Over the period 1952-53 to 1964-65, progress in agricultural production has been uneven as between different crops.

All-India Linear Rates of Growth for Different Crops—1952-53 to 1964-65
(Average 1952-53 to 1954-55=100)

Crop/Group	Production (%)	Area (%)	Productivity (%)
Rice	3·64	1·57	1·80
Jowar	1·99	0·40	1·57
Bajra	1·34	(—)0·20	1·62
Maize	3·08	2·48	0·51
Wheat	3·80	2·57	1·00
Total Cereals	3·05	0·93	1·96
Gram	0·85	1·16	(—)0·24
Total Pulses	0·75	1·42	0·57
Total Foodgrains	2·75	1·02	1·60
Groundnut	5·64	4·40	0·84
Rapeseed & Mustard	3·86	3·34	0·50
Total Oilseeds	3·95	2·90	0·87
Cotton	3·81	1·27	2·25
Jute	5·20	4·01	0·85
Total Fibres	4·60	1·61	2·51
Tea	2·42	0·65	1·67
Coffee	11·65	3·03	6·47
Sugarcane	7·83	4·93	1·93
Total Non-foodgrains	4·79	2·56	1·79
All Groups	3·42	1·28	1·91

Conditions prevailing in different parts of the country need to be examined as thoroughly as possible, so that the right conclusions may be drawn for future planning. This has not yet been done. Similar systematic examination should be extended to the evidence of variations in growth rates in agriculture in different States during the period 1952-53 to 1964-65. The relevant data are summarised in the following table which includes fourteen States and one Union Territory.

Linear Growth Rates of Agricultural Production 1952-53 to 1964-65
(Average 1952-53 to 1954-55 = 100)

State	Agricultural Production (%)	Area under Crops (%)	Agricultural Productivity (%)
1. Punjab	5·56	2·06	2·86
2. Gujarat	5·12	0·46	4·52
3. Madras (Tamil Nadu)	4·91	1·13	3·46
4. Mysore	4·06	0·83	3·03
5. Himachal Pradesh	3·93	0·73	3·00
6. Bihar	3·21	0·71	2·39
7. Maharashtra	3·19	0·44	2·62
8. Rajasthan	3·08	3·23	(—)0·08
9. Andhra Pradesh	3·06	0·27	2·72
10. Madhya Pradesh	2·79	1·35	1·30
11. Orissa	2·72	0·84	1·78
12. Kerala	2·52	1·38	1·00
13. West Bengal	2·07	0·60	1·41
14. Uttar Pradesh	1·82	0·74	1·01
15. Assam	1·25	1·32	(—)0·07
All India	3·42	1·28	1·91

States fall into two groups, seven ranking in terms of increase in agricultural productivity above and eight below the all-India average, which is itself quite low. Within each State fairly wide differences in rates of progress can be observed in different districts and regions. In part, this may be traced to identifiable factors, but more complete understanding of the various elements at work is an urgent necessity. Indeed, a rewarding approach to greater comprehension of recent experience in agriculture and agricultural planning would be to establish the necessary facts by comparing yields in each area in terms of resource endowments such as irrigation, soil, combinations of agricultural practices employed and cultivators with different levels of skill and, in each case, to attempt a careful causal analysis and to seek the elements which, in any given period, have been specially significant. Such analysis would help adapt future development programmes for agriculture to the conditions and requirements of each area.

In comparing experience in India and other countries two important facts stand out, namely, the large differences in yields and the rate of change in yields. For crops like wheat, rice and cotton, between the base period 1948-49 to 1952-53 and 1964-65, there has been in India a sizeable increase in total output. However, in wheat the increase in yields has been small compared to the U.S.A. or France, in rice compared to Japan and the United Arab Republic, and in cotton compared to the U.S.A. Recognising that differences in levels of productivity exist within India as well as between countries, it would be useful for small teams composed of farmers, agricultural specialists and agricultural economists to visit selected countries so as to identify techniques and practices which could be of value in the development of Indian agriculture and could be integrated into the existing scheme of agricultural research and extension. Such an approach has been adopted in recent years as part of the movement for greater productivity in industry and could now be applied to agriculture as well with appropriate modifications.

TASKS FOR THE NEXT DECADE

The development of agriculture, as of the economy as a whole, calls for a long-term plan of development. Among its main elements would be to improve the quality of land as a natural resource through irrigation, soil conservation and afforestation, provision of material inputs, larger capital investment, measures to raise the productivity of agricultural workers and better organisation for transmitting new knowledge to the entire body of farmers, policies designed to raise the efficiency of individual farm units and introduction of new technology in terms of the tools and equipment employed by the bulk of the farmers. Such action requires long periods of effort and intensive organisation. Similarly, institutional and social changes and administrative and organisational measures take time. At each stage, the steps to be taken have to be commensurate in scope and effectiveness with the objectives to be achieved. While a still longer perspective has a great deal of value, perhaps a decade is about the period for which, at each stage, there should always be a fairly detailed and integrated plan for the development of agriculture.

Until recently, such a view of future requirements was not available. However, there are now a number of investigations from which useful guidance can be obtained. Special reference should be made in this connection to the study by the National Council of Applied Economic Research of projections of demand for and supply of selected agricultural commodities, to Dr. P. V. Sukhatme's study of India's food requirements up to 1981, and to studies undertaken by the Institute of Agricultural Research Statistics. In connection with the preparation of the Fourth Five Year Plan, a working group in the Ministry of Food and Agriculture also developed in some detail tentative demand projections for the Fourth and Fifth Plan periods for foodgrains, cotton, oilseeds, sugarcane and jute. Inevitably, many assumptions have to be made in preparing such projections—assumptions as to population growth, growth of national income (in itself dependent in no small measure on the growth of agriculture), consumer

Production and Demand for Agricultural Commodities*

	Unit	1955—56 Production	1960—61 Production	1965—66 Estimated production in Third Plan Report	Base-level production assumed in Fourth Plan Outline†	1970—71 Estimate of aggregate demand	Estimate of production in Fourth Plan Outline†	1975—76 Estimate of aggregate demand
Foodgrains	Million tonnes	66·9	82·0	100·0	90·0	122·8	120·0	152·0
Cotton	Lakh bales	39·5	52·9	70·0	63·0	89·5	86·0	111·5
Oilseeds	Million tonnes	7·1	8·8	10·0	7·5	12·6	10·7	16·0
Sugarcane (gur)	Million tonnes	6·1	11·1	10·2	11·0	13·5	13·5	16·0
Jute and Mesta	Lakh bales	53·9	52·6	75·0	80·0	100·0	110·0	111·5

* Estimates of aggregate demand for 1970-71 and 1975-76 are taken from Ministry of Food and Agriculture, Report of the Working Group on Demand Projections (June, 1964). Data for 1955-56, 1960-61 and 1965-66, are according to information now available.

† August 1966

expenditure, elasticities of demand for different products, norms for consumption of foodgrains and other food articles to be attained over a period and estimates of requirements of raw materials in relation to different levels of industrial output, export demands, etc. Such projections have to be worked out afresh from time to time, but they provide a frame of reference by which the efficiency of measures for the development of agriculture and of industries serving agriculture can be tested. Even more important than the actual estimates and projections are the broader perspectives and guidelines which thus become available.

By way of illustration, the table on page 72 sets the requirements of important agricultural commodities in 1975-76 side by side with the levels of output at the end of the First and the Second Five Year Plans and those taken as the basis for the preparation of the Fourth Plan Outline of August, 1966.

It will be seen that over the fifteen years, 1961-62 to 1975-76, allowing for diversification of output and the growth of dairying, animal husbandry, fisheries and poultry, nothing less than the doubling of the total agricultural production is called for. This implies a cumulative growth rate of about 5 per cent per annum over the entire period. In view of the setbacks which have occurred in recent years, a cumulative growth rate of $5\frac{1}{2}$ to 6 per cent has to be attained over the decade 1966-67 to 1975-76. It is against these dimensions that the present objectives and the means devised to achieve them should be seen.

In quantitative terms, the tasks in agriculture over the next decade are formidable enough. In human and social terms, they are still larger. Therefore, alongside measures for developing agriculture as an industry, it becomes necessary to devise ways of strengthening the agrarian structure, employing the available manpower resources intensively and gainfully, bringing into agriculture, through co-operative farming and other, means, all possible gains from scale, investment and organisation, speeding technological changes in agriculture and taking industry into small towns and rural areas. For carrying out these tasks, all the resources of leadership and organisation within the community and on the part of the Government and the administration as well as co-operatives and Panchayati Raj institutions and other agencies for agriculture and rural life have to be effectively equipped and harnessed.

II

AGRICULTURE AS AN INDUSTRY

One of the main objectives in the Five Year Plans is to transform agriculture from being, what it was traditionally— a way of life for millions of people—into an industry with rising levels of productivity, incorporating the practices of scientific agriculture and making use of improved technology in all the operations of farming. The implications of this change go far beyond the specific programmes of development associated with agriculture. They bear upon the agrarian structure as a whole, the place of the masses of landless labour in the rural economy, the system of farm organisation and the manner in which the rural and the industrial economy should be integrated with each other.

In the narrower sense, viewing agriculture as a field of technical development designed to achieve the maximum crop production under existing conditions of tenure, plans for developing agriculture as an industry will comprise broadly four types of measures, namely,

(a) measures for improving land as a natural resource;

(b) adoption of scientific agriculture, including application of improved agricultural practices, provision of the necessary material inputs, increasing the productivity of labour by imparting greater skill and making more intensive use of manpower, and ensuring greater capital investment per acre of land;

(c) increasing the efficiency of existing farm units through consolidation of agricultural holdings, crop planning and co-operation between cultivators in various farm operations and in arranging for common services; and

(d) speeding technological change in agriculture through the use of improved agricultural implements, introduction of machinery for raising the productivity of labour, and promoting mechanisation of agriculture wherever feasible.

LAND AS A NATURAL RESOURCE

As a resource limited by nature in quantity, up to a point, the area of land under cultivation can be extended. Allowing for increases in area for which agricultural statistics were reported, the area under crops increased during the First Plan by about 13 per cent and during the Second Plan by about 5 per cent. Substantial increases in cultivated area occurred in Rajasthan, Punjab, Assam, Maharashtra, Madhya Pradesh, Mysore and Kerala. Surveys of blocks exceeding 250 acres in area carried out towards the end of the Second Plan by the Committee on Location and Utilisation of Wastelands establish the comparatively small extent to which large blocks of land capable of being reclaimed are readily available. The total area proposed for reclamation in nine States which were surveyed amounted to about 1·2 million acres. On closer study of soils and of costs of development, the area suitable for reclamation and development on economic lines would turn out to be even smaller. It would, therefore, be correct to say that the main approach to land as a natural resource must be in the direction of raising the quality of the soil and increasing its potential for production through irrigation, soil conservation and dry farming and the use of fertilizers and manures. These measures are needed also in respect of areas which have been reclaimed over the past decade or so. In several of these, the yields are still low. The initial effort to bring new land under cultivation has not always been followed by adequate programmes for agricultural development and soil improvement.

The Five Year Plans have placed considerable reliance on irrigation, both through major and medium-sized works and through small works. Irrigation represents one of the most important areas of investment under the Plans. Thus, it is reckoned that major irrigation schemes taken up during the first three Plans have a total potential of about 44 million acres (gross), which would be about 40 per cent of the estimated ultimate potential of 112 million acres (gross) from major and medium schemes. The corresponding potential from minor irrigation schemes is reckoned at 75 million acres (gross). The total area irrigated by works taken up during the first three Plans may eventually be of the order of 30 million acres. Estimates of progress in minor irrigation as reported by the authorities concerned have still to be reconciled with official agricultural statistics. The time lag between the two could be but only one of the explanations. The tentative view that the ultimate irrigation potential from major, medium and minor irrigation schemes may be of the order of 187 million acres (gross) against a total crop area of 376 million acres also calls for more detailed investigation and collection of further data. In this connection, a fact to be marked is that the area sown more than once in the year increased between 1949-50 and 1959-60 from 38 to 49 million acres only, that is, from about 13·5 per cent to 15 per cent of the total area sown.

In addition to irrigation, an important means for improving land as a natural resource consists of measures for soil conservation, dry farming and afforestation. In these, until recently, in the country as a whole (with exceptions like Maharashtra and Gujarat), progress has been slow. The possibilities of extending these programmes through the full utilisation of manpower resources and under proper technical guidance are indeed vast. In particular, soil conservation for agricultural lands and dry farming can be pursued on a large scale as a major item of community action and popular participation. As with reclamation of culturable wastes and extension of irrigation, coordination with other programmes of agricultural improvement and the need for adequate follow-up cannot be too greatly stressed.

A real weakness in the existing system of planning for agriculture lies in the fact that too little attention is being given to the determination of the best crop patterns for each area, both for irrigated and unirrigated lands. Crop planning for an area has to be distinguished from crop rotations for individual farm units. Crop planning implies careful consideration of past trends, of the factors accounting for them, of the directions in which, in the light of past experience, deliberate change could be stimulated towards more productive utilisation of land and improved crop patterns. A crop plan for an area is in the nature of a general design of development in relation to which a considerable part of the local agricultural effort can be organised including, specially, improvements in the distribution of irrigation, supply of improved seeds, adoption of better tools and channelling of larger amounts of credit. Crop planning does not imply that there should be physical regulation of areas to be put under different crops. However, for a general scheme of crop planning to succeed, it is essential that the difficulties inherent in setting up crop patterns for an area as a whole, including those pertaining to irrigation, be recognised and provided for. Once the broad lines have been determined for any area, special steps should be taken to make it possible for cultivators, both as groups and as individuals, to adopt the recommended crop patterns.

INDUSTRIAL AND MATERIAL INPUTS

The key role of inputs in agriculture is now realised much more acutely than in the past. These inputs are among the most important links between agriculture and the rest of the economy. Around such inputs development in a number of different sectors has to be organised so as to subserve the interest of agriculture. Besides fertilizers, pesticides and agricultural machinery, agriculture demands a variety of other goods and services, such as equipment for drilling, processing, demonstration and testing, commodities like steel and cement, and surveys, research and extension. The requirements of material inputs have to be assessed and planned for in the aggregate in relation to individual crops as well as individual areas. Estimates of requirements have to be cross-checked against likely supplies over a plan period and for each separate year. Subject to limitations of supplies, the extent to which agriculture may absorb the various inputs will depend, above all, on the knowledge and receptiveness of peasants, the quality of the extension network, efficiency in distribution and the strength of co-operative agencies. In making use of material inputs such as fertilizer and agricultural machinery, the question of costs and returns is of paramount importance. The inputs have to be brought within the limited means available to the farmer, both through subsidisation and through reduction in the costs of production and distribution. In the next phase of development, subsidisation will have to be undertaken on a larger scale than has been contemplated so far, but the period may be shortened if the rate of growth in agriculture can be accelerated and close attention is given to the lowering of costs.

SCIENTIFIC AGRICULTURE

Increased supplies of industrial and material inputs should be regarded as the spearhead for a campaign for scientific agriculture. The adoption of scientific agriculture implies increase in the productivity of labour, more intensive use of the available manpower and greater capital investment per unit of land. A study undertaken by an expert committee of the Indian Council of Agricultural Research a few years ago showed how much scope existed for adopting improved practices which had been already developed in different parts of the country. It is being increasingly realised that the gap in skills between good farmers and the general body of peasants can be reduced through effective harnessing of the more highly skilled and successful agriculturists. In each area the more skilled farmers have to be brought organically within the scheme of extension services and given opportunities of communicating their experience and extending their influence among cultivators. Differences between the more efficient and the less efficient farmers are reflected not only in their skills and practices but also in the extent of farm investment they undertake. The average investment per acre of land is still too low. For instance, in two progressive districts in the Punjab, Amritsar and Ferozepur, for which farm management studies are available, it was observed that the total farm investment per acre, excluding the value of land, amounted only to Rs. 235. This included dwelling houses, cattle sheds, wells, and implements and machinery. Investment on improved implements worked out only to Rs. 5 per acre.

The problem of increasing the productivity of labour has two aspects. First, to the extent to which irrigation is provided, conditions arise in which there can be more intensive use of labour. In the Punjab, for instance, on irrigated land the labour input per acre came to 23 days of 8 hours each as against only 12 days on unirrigated land. Rapid expansion of irrigation facilities is an essential condition for creating the conditions of intensive agriculture. Secondly, ways must be found of making much fuller use of the available manpower resources. In different parts of the country, periods of anything from three to five months and sometimes longer represent slack agricultural seasons during which one-fourth to one-half of the labour force is available for full-time work at village wage rates. In most areas a large labour force is ready to be put to much more productive use.

Efficiency of Farm Units

The third group of measures for developing agriculture as an industry are intended to raise the efficiency of existing farm units. Apart from crop planning and provision of services, so far the main approach here has been that of consolidation of holdings. Significant results have been obtained in consolidation operations undertaken in Punjab, U.P., Madhya Pradesh and Maharashtra, but progress in the southern parts of the country has been comparatively small. There can be no doubt that if we wish to alter the rural environment, create better living conditions and provide a basis for intensive peasant farming, consolidation of holdings should be given a key place in the scheme of rural development.

Technological Change in Agriculture

Perhaps the most important single lag in agriculture has been in the sphere of improved technology. The average farm unit in India is ill-adapted to rapid or large-scale technological change. Low efficiency in the great majority of farm units is both a cause and an effect of slow technological progress. Every consideration points to the need during the next few years to invest to the maximum in technological change and in increase of labour productivity. It is necessary to think of improved technology more comprehensively, covering such diverse aspects as making more power available for agriculture, better preparation of land for various operations and mobilising science in the service of agriculture. To bring about rapid technological change, a wide range of problems have to be solved. Research has to be intensified so as to determine which implements will serve best under different conditions of soil and climate. There are problems of extension, demonstration and training. There are critical shortages of technical personnel to be reckoned with. Even if experts are able to establish the implements and the machinery which should be widely used in an area, there are serious problems of organisation, including the ensuring of supplies of raw materials, use and development of fabricating capacities, planning of production, organisation of artisans and securing a measure of standardisation and quality control. Technological change is necessarily costly. On the one hand, it is important to ensure that agricultural implements and machinery should be low priced; on the other, until production reaches an adequate scale and key components can be manufactured in bulk, it is difficult to achieve a sufficient degree of standardisation. Provision of credit for agricultural implements has played hitherto too small a part in the scheme of co-operative finance. So far as the more expensive implements and machinery are concerned, within the conditions set by accepted land policies, it is necessary to promote their use on a co-operative basis and to provide for facilities for hiring from panchayats and co-operatives. In respect of small implements, however, it is essential that, in the course of a few years, at any rate in areas in which intensive agricultural work is undertaken, every farmer should be put into possession of the essential improved implements. There is a close relationship between improved implements and improved agricultural practices, and the two should be regarded as parts of a single approach.

INTENSIVE AGRICULTURAL AREAS

We have now reviewed briefly the main facts of the problem of developing agriculture as an industry. Changes of this nature cannot be brought about throughout the country simultaneously, nor can they be achieved without considerable specialisation on the part of the agricultural service. This leads us to two other important aspects of agricultural organisation, namely, the approach of intensive areas and the reorganisation of agricultural administration. When the community development and national extension programme was taken in hand in the early fifties, it seemed difficult to contemplate that for years to come the essential community services should be available for some parts of the country, but should be denied to others. Moreover, community development and extension services were looked upon as vital ingredients in the system of rural administration to be established in all areas. Accordingly, the scheme of community development was extended fairly rapidly to all parts of the country. We find now that even in areas which have had five or ten years or more of development, if there has been no fundamental change in the physical resource base, as through irrigation, electrification, urbanisation or industrialisation, the rural economy still continues to be in the relatively early stages of development. There is indeed greater awareness and some degree of change in the social environment. Certain services have already become available and, within limits, the people of each area have at least some resources and the technical guidance for achieving more rapid development. Yet, in most districts in the country, the proportion of the rural community which has been effectively influenced in the direction of new technology and new occupations and skills is still small. It must be admitted that the period of preparation for rapid and wholesale change in rural areas is much longer than was thought to be a decade ago. Side by side with this appraisal, there is the consideration that rapid increase in agricultural production has now assumed an urgency in the nation's life which calls for radical measures and for departing from some of the assumptions on which work on community development has so far proceeded. There is no gainsaying that in the next phase of development the conflict between concentration and dispersal of resources has to be decided in favour of selection of areas where conditions are more favourable for intensive cultivation and sharp increase in production. These areas may represent about one-fifth to one-fourth of the total cultivated area of the country. This view of development has been strengthened by the experience gained under the intensive agricultural district programme. Work in the intensive agricultural districts has already helped evolve important techniques of development, specially in the extension of improved practices and in the organisation of agricultural services. The intensive cultivation areas which have been marked out in various States are a further step in the same direction.*

Intensive agricultural development involves not only measures directly related to the development of agriculture, but also those concerning the building up of institutions like panchayats and co-operatives, steps to carry assistance and resources to the most vulnerable groups of farmers, schemes for the more intensive use of manpower for creating community assets and improving irrigation and communications, and better organisation of marketing. At every step resources and skills available within each area have to be turned to the best advantage. Yet, intensification of agriculture marks only the first break in the development of the rural economy. In the rural areas, wherever one may begin, it is soon apparent that from agriculture one must go on to rural life as a whole, to the building up of a diversified rural economy with a great deal of industry growing up in

---

* With the introduction of high yielding varieties in 1966, the intensive area approach as envisaged is being greatly weakened, thus going against one of the key lessons of the experience of recent years.

small towns and in the larger villages. Without these the basic character of rural life will remain substantially unchanged.

AGRICULTURAL EXTENSION

To produce the necessary impact on agriculture, specially in the intensive agricultural areas, there have to be important changes in the organisation of agricultural services. This is a large theme, but two aspects deserve special mention. The first is the role of agricultural research and of agricultural scientists in the extension services. Without a large and growing research base and a continuing stream of research findings to be applied in the field, extension workers can hardly promote rapid technological change. Secondly, agriculture demands increasingly specialised and skilled services. When the community development programme was taken up in the early fifties, the principal consideration was that, while the various agencies of Government had sought to reach the farmer independently, none of them was in fact in a position to do so. Therefore, the first step was to provide for a common multi-purpose village level worker to function on their behalf in a group of villages. It was realised that as development proceeded there would be need to provide skills of a higher order. The change should have perhaps come sooner. It has now become imperative that there should be a bifurcation of functions at the village level between those concerned directly with agriculture, including co-operation and animal husbandry, and those working with village panchayats and helping them to take their full share in intensifying agriculture and promoting community action at the village level. The creation of two separate cadres of village functionaries is a necessary reform which has to be carried out first in areas marked out for intensive agricultural development and later in all other areas.

III

AGRARIAN REFORM AND THE RURAL ECONOMY

Size and Distribution of Holdings

In Indian economic literature, the problem of size and distribution of agricultural holdings had for long a central place. Over the last decade, however, this subject has received inadequate attention from scholars and administrators alike. This may be because the task of establishing efficient farm units is so formidable, indeed so fundamental, as to appear to be virtually beyond solution within the existing political and institutional framework. Perhaps, it is felt that, despite existing limitations, through irrigation, extension facilities and more effective price policies and marketing arrangements, a fair measure of advance can still be achieved. Eventually, industrial and economic development may help diminish the pressure on land and facilitate solutions of the land problem which may not be feasible at present. Thus, for one reason or another, our development plans have failed so far to deal with what is still and will remain *the* basic agrarian problem of the Indian economy.

The size of the problem is fairly established in the data obtained in the sixteenth round of the National Sample Survey. In the country as a whole, holdings below 5 acres numbered 63 per cent and accounted for 19 per cent of the cultivated area. Holdings up to 10 acres numbered 82 per cent and accounted for 39 per cent of the cultivated area. Holdings up to 20 acres numbered 98 per cent and accounted for 62 per cent of the cultivated area. Holdings up to 30 acres numbered 97 per cent and accounted for 75 per cent of the cultivated area.

More detailed data were collected with the census of land holdings and cultivation which relates to the year 1953-54. Areas owned, leased and under 'personal cultivation' were separately listed. In some States complete enumeration was undertaken, in a few only holdings above 10 acres were reckoned, and in some sample surveys were carried out. The table on page 87 presents illustrative data for Andhra Pradesh, Madras, Uttar Pradesh and jointly for Gujarat and Maharashtra. For Uttar Pradesh data were obtained on a sample basis, for the others through complete enumeration.

The table bears out the broad trends shown by the National Sample Survey. It also brings out the fact that conditions vary considerably between States and, correspondingly, between different regions in the same State. Within limits, agricultural programmes and policies should, therefore, be adjusted to meet the requirements of the agrarian structure characteristic of each State or region. The data cited here are several years old. They do not allow for differences in the quality of land and other important physical and economic factors. They probably understate the extent of land cultivated by tenants—a tendency which has come to be accentuated in recent years. It is essential, therefore, to provide within the system of land administration for accurate returns at regular intervals concerning the distribution, ownership and cultivation of agricultural holdings. Such returns are not at present available in the ordinary course.

Over the greater part of the country, at least 70 to 80 per cent of cultivators' holdings are less than 10 acres and some 50 to 70 per cent of the holdings are less than 5 acres. Considering the large numbers involved, to ensure the welfare and progress of the rural economy *as a whole*, both policy and administration should be designed specially to raise the productivity of small cultivators. To them, as explained later, we must add the large numbers who are landless labourers and live on the fringes of the agricultural economy.

If data such as have been collected for different States and regions could be broken down in terms of irrigated area, or

Size and distribution of holdings in 1953-54

(*i*) *Cultivated area owned up to* (*acres*)

(*A*) *Holdings* (%)	2·5	5·0	10·0	20·0	30·0
Andhra Pradesh—					
Andhra region	47·5	66·8	82·8	93·0	96·3
Telengana	24·2	40·6	61·2	80·6	88·4
Madras	29·6	46·7	66·4	83·7	91·0
Gujarat &					
Maharashtra	44·9	67·5	85·4	94·9	97·4
Uttar Pradesh	68·6	85·4	95·1	98·8	99·5
(*B*) *Area* (%)					
Andhra Pradesh—					
Andhra region	7·9	18·2	34·7	55·7	67·4
Telengana	1·8	5·7	15·3	32·9	45·3
Madras	3·0	8·3	20·4	41·3	56·4
Gujarat &					
Maharashtra	8·7	21·7	41·6	62·6	72·4
Uttar Pradesh	22·0	43·4	67·4	85·2	91·2

(*ii*) *Cultivated area under personal cultivation up to* (*acres*)

(*A*) *Holdings* (%)	2·5	5·0	10·0	20·0	30·0
Andhra Pradesh—					
Andhra region	47·8	67·4	83·3	93·5	96·7
Telengana	25·1	41·6	62·1	81·1	88·9
Madras	29·7	46·9	66·5	83·8	91·1
Gujarat &					
Maharashtra	45·7	68·3	86·0	95·3	97·7
Uttar Pradesh	68·6	85·4	95·1	98·9	99·6
(*B*) *Area* (%)					
Andhra Pradesh—					
Andhra region	8·3	19·1	36·4	58·4	70·5
Telengana	2·0	6·4	16·8	35·6	48·9
Madras	3·1	8·7	21·1	42·7	58·5
Gujarat &					
Maharashtra	9·4	23·2	44·0	65·5	75·2
Uttar Pradesh	22·0	43·4	67·5	85·4	91·4

in relation to lands of high or low productivity or for different crops, the problem of small and uneconomic holdings and that of fragmentation would loom even larger. Sometimes, to prove that small holdings may not or need not be necessarily unprofitable, the example is cited of small holdings in Japan or of successful cultivation by skilled market gardeners in the vicinity of towns or of intensive cultivators in certain favoured regions in the country. Doubtless, much can be done to improve the economics of small holdings. Farm management studies which are now available for a number of districts for a few years provide useful evidence on the subject. The broad conclusions which may be drawn from these studies in relation to the present argument are:

(1) In terms of gross product and gross return per acre, often small holdings (say, five to ten acres and less) do not compare unfavourably with the comparatively larger holdings; frequently, the labour inputs on small holdings may be proportionately greater.

(2) The larger holdings are able to secure a distinctly higher proportion of inputs which come from outside the farmer's domestic economy, such as fertilizers, pesticides, credit, better tools and improved varieties of seed.

(3) In terms of net return and net capital formation, the larger holdings turn out to be at a marked advantage.

Undoubtedly, it is the foremost task of agricultural and co-operative extension services to reduce the disadvantages to which small farmers are subject, to bring to them all possible gains from improved scale and organisation of supplies, marketing and credit, and to ensure that the industrial and other inputs needed are made available. The question, however, remains whether small farmers will not remain continuously handicapped unless larger and more efficient farm units are created. A large proportion among them are too close to the poverty line. The system of credit and supplies is not yet designed to render adequate service to the small man, and some of the impediments are inherent in

the situation itself. The total resources available for investment in rural development leave at present only a small
margin for rehabilitation finance. Where intensive cultivation
under conditions of controlled irrigation becomes possible,
as in parts of Punjab or in U.P., after agricultural holdings
are consolidated, the disadvantages of small farms are
materially reduced, at any rate, for a period of several years.
While fuller support from agricultural and co-operative
services can make a significant difference, the basic limitations persist, and beyond a point the scope for development
under existing conditions may not in fact be as large as is
often assumed.

LAND REFORM

For nearly fifteen years land reform has been an integral
part of the country's plans of economic and social development, and much store was set by it. The first article in the
strategy of land reform was the abolition of intermediary
tenures, which accounted in the past for some 40 per cent
of the total area, specially in the permanently settled tracts,
in Rajasthan, in the former Hyderabad State and in parts
of Madhya Pradesh, Madras and other States. The call for
land to the tiller rose at first from concern with the rights of
the occupancy tenant who was closest to the soil. Only after
Independence it came to be extended to the tenant cultivator
working on land leased out by the peasant, whether he be
a proprietor or an occupancy tenant. Even to this day,
this wider concept has not been fully appreciated, much
less implemented.

For the tenant-at-will, land reform policies envisaged two
sets of measures—those calculated to provide for security of
tenure and fair and reasonable rents, and those intended to
confer upon him rights of ownership over land directly under
his cultivation. With some important exceptions, legislation

in all States provides for protection from ejectment and a degree of security. However, as several investigations show, there has been considerable evasion. Advantage has been taken of the economic and social weaknesses of tenants and their ignorance of rights conferred by law to enter lands in fact cultivated through tenants as lands under the 'personal cultivation' of owners. The interests of owners, specially the larger ones, have combined with administrative and political failure to deny justice to tenants. It is difficult to say on what scale there has been such failure in implementation and it is equally possible to minimise or to overstate it. However, enough is known to make it imperative for each State to provide for internal checks, within the system of administrative supervision and reporting, to ensure that abuse is detected and the wrong done corrected.

The mischief occurs both in the matter of the right to stay on the land and in respect of rents. In all States, rates of rent much below the customary ones, varying usually from one-third to one-sixth of the produce, have been prescribed by law. The rural community as a whole has not been roused to a sense of social and economic justice as between its constituent elements, and the social objective has yet to be impressed upon those who are placed in positions of responsibility in panchayat institutions and co-operatives. The insistence upon these aspects from administrations and leaders at the national and state level and the effort given to the education of the rural masses in these matters have been quite inadequate. These failures express themselves in the policies and outlook thus far of agricultural departments and of co-operative institutions. By and large, in their concern for output, agricultural personnel have tended to look to the larger cultivators rather than to the involvement of the entire agricultural community and the upgrading of their practices and technology. To many among them, agrarian reform has seemed to be an obstacle to rather than as a means for raising production and yields. Even where rights have accrued in fact to tenants and small cultivators, the support which agricultural extension services have provided to them has been altogether meagre. To an extent, because of limitations of resources, this might have been inevitable and could be mended but slowly. At any event, with the larger effort now under way, it should be possible to give much more effective support in supplies, credit and technical assistance, both to small cultivators and to those who come into possession of land as a result of land reform legislation.

In the scheme of land reform, beyond the protection of tenants, there are two further stages. One is to obtain lands above the ceiling by way of surplus and to make them available to the landless and to the smaller cultivators. The second is to enable those who settle on such lands to become full owners. These measures have been thought of as a necessary prelude to the building up of an agrarian economy in which economies of scale and investment and diversified development are to be realised through a steadily increasing measure of co-operation in production as well as in other activities. Together, they form a consistent scheme of development for the rural economy, keeping in view the need for increasing agricultural production, rehabilitating small cultivators and giving to the landless sections of the population the opportunity to work for a better life and to become equal citizens with others. These larger objectives and their importance for making political freedom meaningful in terms of the lives of the millions are not yet understood widely enough. Perhaps, this may be the main explanation of delays in enacting legislation for ceilings on land holdings in certain States as well as of delays in implementing such legislation as has already reached the statute book. In any event, these delays have served long enough notice to large numbers of landowners to enable them to do away with or to disguise possible surpluses of land. For the time being, the important objective of limitation of land holdings has been largely frustrated. This does not diminish the validity of the objective or its inevitable persistence as a goal in national development but, doubtless, the task will now be accomplished over a somewhat longer period and with greater tension than was necessary or desirable. The ceiling on agricultural holdings was never seen, though sometimes it has been so interpreted, as a ceiling on rural incomes. It is essentially a step in the reorganisation of India's agrarian structure at the very base so that, with rights in land distributed more equitably, the rural economy could be modernised and all those who depend on it might share in the benefits of development.

Along with ceilings on land holdings, the Five Year Plans have also stressed the need for conferring rights of ownership on tenants settled on surplus lands as well as on other cultivators. On the whole, the legislative provisions for this have been inadequate and the extent to which effect has been given to them has been still more so. The minimum condition was to ensure a direct relationship between the Government and two groups of tenants, namely those already on the land and those settled afresh on non-resumable lands. Such direct relationship can be ensured best by means of bonds issued once for all, supported by modest financial allocations under the Five Year Plans for assisting tenants and for making cash payments to certain categories of owners to whom part at least of the compensation has to be paid in cash. Such a provision was not made in the Second or the Third Plan as they proceeded on the assumption that land reform could be an entirely self-financing process. Experience disproves this, and it is important to take the lesson into future plans.

CO-OPERATIVE FARMING

As stated earlier, land reform—with its three essential

conditions, namely, protection of tenants, ceilings on land holdings and rights of ownership for all cultivators—and growth of co-operation in production and other activities, together with general economic development and diffusion of industry, form an integral approach to the re-shaping of the rural economy. There has already been a measure of success in developing co-operation for credit, marketing, processing and distribution of consumer goods. The principle of co-operation has still wider application. In a number of directions, some degree of advance has been made, as in construction, housing and transport. Yet, so far only a fraction of the possibilities of co-operation in the context of India's development has been realised. There is indeed no richer field for constructive effort on the part of Panchayati Raj institutions, voluntary organisations, local leaders and social workers. Sufficient experience has been gained to be able to identify the inherent problems of organisation, method and training and to diminish greatly the chances of failure in co-operation, provided only that the necessary concentration of effort and resources is ensured and that the tasks and objectives to which the co-operative approach is applied are selected with care. However, there is one field in which this claim cannot yet be made, namely, co-operative farming.

Co-operative farming has to be seen, not in isolation nor as a political doctrine, but as part of a practical scheme of development in which the resources and energies of large numbers of small farmers are harnessed, so that they can create, for themselves, by their own effort, a more viable economy based on mixed farming and rural industry, application of science and technology and greater investment. Co-operative farming is often believed to be only a way of rehabilitating the economy of small and uneconomic farmers. While co-operative farming must bring the maximum relief to them and their needs are most urgent, it has also

other and wider aims. Co-operative farming is, above all, a
means for the correction and reconstruction in a fundamental
sense of the pattern and organisation of rural life as a whole.
Since the growth of co-operative farming is seen as a voluntary
movement, which is supported by reasonable incentives
but is dependent essentially on successful demonstration and
practice, even under favourable conditions, many years of
sustained effort will be needed before a substantial part of
the cultivated area of the country can come within its scope.
The necessary conditions for success in co-operative farming
as a popular movement have yet to be established. The
recent study by the Committee of Direction on Co-operative
Farming and investigations of specific instances of co-operative farming experience in the country bring out the several
directions in which effort has been wanting, both at the
level of policy and in administration.

Of over 3000 co-operative farming societies in the country,
about one-half are in what are known as pilot areas and the
others have grown up as a result of local initiative. Commonly, the average area of a co-operative farming society is
too small. In many instances, the forms of co-operation have
been exploited to their advantage by a small number of families with a few others joined to themselves merely to fulfil the
legal conditions for the registration of a co-operative farming
society. Motives such as evasion of land reform legislation,
replacement of agricultural labour by mechanised cultivation
and the desire to obtain assistance from government agencies
account for a proportion of the existing co-operative farming
societies. Frequently, the members bring part of their land
under co-operative cultivation and work on the rest as individual farmers. Even though some useful lessons can be learnt,
such important aspects as organisation and distribution of
work, so as to strengthen incentives for higher output and
for more intensive working on the part of individuals,
families and groups, methods of providing for the return

to ownership and problems connected with diversification of activities, finance and introduction of new techniques and management practices still require closer investigation. In this sense, the pilot projects undertaken during the Third Plan have not served their purpose as well as was hoped for. Here, it is necessary to stress the importance of controlled experiments in co-operative farming, that is, experiments which are undertaken in a genuine way by local groups or communities, with the necessary preparation and partici-pation, and under conditions of systematic observation and evaluation. Many weaknesses which have come to light are capable of being eliminated, and suitable forms of co-opera-tion in agriculture and other activities can be so developed that they become a precise response to the needs, character and potential of each local community and each local area. Conditions vary so widely and elements peculiar to the social structure, psychology and economic needs of the local community play so large a part that the approach of co-operative farming must be ever flexible and its forms and practices must be continuously adapted to local condi-tions, resources and possibilities.

LANDLESS LABOUR

Even if the necessary conditions for the growth of co-opera-tive farming existed, it could only take us some distance towards solving the deep-rooted problems represented by the existence of a mass of agricultural labour of whom some may have tiny fragments of land, but many more are completely without land. The size of the problem varies greatly in diffe-rent parts of the country. In those areas in which agricultural labour represents a substantial population, schemes of econo-mic and social development must provide for them in a far more specific way than has been done so far under the Five Year Plans. The economy of such areas cannot be transform-ed without transforming at the same time the conditions of life and opportunities open to this large mass of population. It is beyond the capacity of industrial development alone to take a sufficient proportion of this labour surplus into non-agricultural activity, leaving the rest to adjust into a stable and progressive rural economy. All evidence points to the harsh effects of increase in population, the slow growth of alternative employment opportunities, decline in the real wages of agricultural labour and some degree of deterioration in living conditions.

A problem of this nature has to be approached simultaneously from several different directions—intensification of agriculture and development of agricultural potentials, change in the system of land management, spread of rural electrification, small industries and supplementary occupations, building up of new nuclei of growth, development of economic and social overheads and training facilities, and a degree of planning in the movement from villages into towns. In other words, not only has there to be a basic approach to agricultural development and to the growth of industry, but also much greater emphasis on expansion of activities within the village and integration between the rural and the industrial and urban economy.

In this context, as developments in different fields are planned and problems of policy and organisation inherent in each sector are resolved, there has also to be much greater stress on two unifying and integrating concepts, namely, the community and the area. At each level, be it a village, a group of villages or a larger area, the community can play a far greater and more continuous role than has yet been realised. How else are resources and energies to be mobilised and concern for the welfare of *all* expressed? Under Indian conditions, the community and the economy have to grow together. The approach of area development becomes specially significant for guiding the different strands of effort for development, both those which are planned and those which are spontaneous, towards common objectives. These different objectives are essentially inter-dependent and are best approached so as to produce a cumulative impact upon the conditions and opportunities of the mass of the people.

4

LAND REFORM AND THE LAND PROBLEM : ISSUES FOR THE SECOND PHASE

THE APPROACH to the land problem embodied in India's
Five Year Plans has reached something like an impasse.
There were two main aspects of this approach: legislation to
change the structure of land rights and land relationships, and
the reorganisation of the rural economy along co-operative
lines, accompanied by the fuller use of manpower resources
and the development of rural industry. Together, these two
facets of agrarian change encompassed persons with rights
to own and cultivate as well as those who were landless and
had only their labour to sell. The essential objective was to
achieve, peacefully and through democratic consent, a social
order with ability to secure continuous change and growth
from *within*, which offered genuine equality for all, broke
away from caste and property in land as sources of rural
power, and created the conditions needed for rapid economic
and technical advance. To attain the goal of a classless society
through the fusion of diverse interests and classes into the
larger good of the community as a whole, as seen from the
angle of the masses and the have-nots, rather than through
violent and bitter conflict between classes, would be in line

with the values of the freedom movement and an assurance for the future.

There are two reasons for recalling these original insights. First, in almost every country in recent history, large changes in agrarian structures have been products of revolution or cataclysm or absolute power. In India, political freedom had been conceived from the beginning as fulfilling itself through economic and social freedom and opportunity for the mass of the people. Therefore, it was hoped to achieve changes, which were in essence revolutionary, largely by persuasion and legislation enacted after full and free discussion and reflecting public opinion as a whole. Secondly, over the last decade, in fact much has been sought to be done in these directions. A great body of legislation has come into being. There are some significant weaknesses in it and, doubtless, there has been much want of will and organisation in giving effect to it. In the course of action, in the exercise of responsibility and in balancing different interests, the energy for change and the capacity to counter the pull of vested interests have lessened, and the vision itself has seemed to recede. What was only the other day a symbol of hope and looked like succeeding has come close to being judged a failure, a prelude to despair. But the goals remain and the laws which have been enacted provide the base for a fresh effort. The gaps in legislation, the obstacles encountered in implementation and the supporting policies required in the future are better known than before. The weak threads can be cast away and a stronger fabric can be woven. The time is ripe for a renewal. The programme for land reform can be improved and accomplished; at the same time, by setting it afresh in the context of the land problem in its present shape and dimensions and learning from the experience of a decade, the movement for agrarian reorganisation and social change can go forward with greater vigour.

I

A combination of circumstances has made these tasks, which were earlier more readily within our grasp, both more difficult and more urgent at the present juncture. The scheme of land reform which was being evolved through the First Five Year Plan reached its concrete and almost complete formulation at the stage of the Second Five Year Plan. Through the proposal for ceilings on agricultural holdings, it sought to reduce disparities in the ownership of land. By assuring protection and security for tenants, followed by acquisition of the rights of ownership, it aimed at establishing a large body of peasant proprietors at the centre of the agricultural economy, with tenants from whom land could be resumed by landowners forming only a small proportion of cultivators. By its emphasis on co-operative farming, co-operative village management, resettlement of surplus lands and the role of village and small industries, it aimed progressively at reducing the chasm between the landless and those who had land, and creating the conditions for greater technical efficiency and diversification within the rural economy. In the design of development for rural areas, in addition to efficient extension services and larger supplies and facilities to assist the whole body of farmers, specially through co-operatives, the central concepts were, those of area and resource development, community organisation and effort at every level, and social change. Effectively implemented, these concepts together formed part of a strategy for carrying all sections of the rural community to higher levels of living and productivity and eliminating wide gaps in status and opportunity.

Over the past decade and more, for reasons indicated later, programmes for agrarian change have not achieved the results expected. While, in a number of directions, important advances have been made through legislative and economic measures, to a considerable extent the former have been evaded and the latter have proved inadequate. Perhaps, even under the best conditions, all the problems of practical implementation might not have been anticipated and provided for in advance though, certainly, much more could have been done. Nevertheless, the fact remains that on the whole the patterns of land distribution and cultivation have not changed materially. The gains in productivity and the adoption of improved technological and other practices are accounted for largely by those farmers whose holdings were above the minimum economic level and, among them, to a still greater extent by the bigger farmers, many of whom are in reality engaged in operating areas considerably larger in size than those bearing their own names in the records of rights.

These gains have become possible through two sets of factors. The first set of factors includes higher prices and improvements in the terms of trade for agricultural commodities, scarcities which have occurred from time to time, widening of the market and, sometimes, a degree of collusion between individual traders and the larger farmers. The second set of factors comprises various forms of assistance which have become available and are being increasingly provided to cultivators through co-operative finance, government loans, supplies of fertilizers, pesticides and machinery and technical advice and other extension activities. Both groups of factors have worked in favour of the bigger farmers. Failure to bring trade in agricultural commodities within the scope of state trading and co-operative marketing has accentuated this trend, besides making the management of the food problem itself more difficult and inducing among influential groups a certain lack of concern for the public interest as a whole. Among these influential groups are to be counted also those co-operatives which have been led by their greater prosperity in the recent past to interpret too narrowly both

their own interest and the role of the co-operative movement
and have been willing to hold supplies off the market.

There is much evidence that, within the rural community,
those better placed and more strongly entrenched have now
begun to evince an outlook of change and innovation, obtaining higher yields and exploiting their resources and
opportunities more effectively. At the same time, the gap
between them and a large proportion of peasant cultivators
is widening. The latter have not been able to make commensurate progress and, under the pressure of numbers, are even
more hard-pressed than before. Likewise, both to achieve
economies in costs and to avoid coming within the purview
of tenancy legislation, there is a growing tendency on the
part of large and medium-sized farmers to adopt labour-
saving techniques. On account of increasing numbers and
for lack of adequate employment opportunities, in most
parts of the country, landless agricultural labourers (and
with them, tenants and petty peasant owners) are now living
under conditions of greater stress than before. This can be
seen in periods of scarcity in the long lines of men, women
and children who walk daily to places of work or where free
food and gratuitous relief are given, for they have nothing
to fall back upon and must live from day to day, seeking
succour from wherever and howsoever it comes.

While the contrast between the so-called 'progressive'
farmers and the bulk of the agricultural community becomes
more marked, the country is faced, at the same time, by a critical agricultural situation, which also presents some immediate
dangers. A certain divergence has, therefore, arisen between
measures to achieve swift progress in agriculture mainly
by giving greater support in supplies and credit and in other
ways to the more favourably placed farmers and pursuing
the goals accepted earlier of land reform, agrarian reorganisation and agricultural advance conceived as a composite programme undertaken within each area and with the support

of local communities. Expansion of the area under high-yielding strains, accompanied by larger supplies of fertilizers and pesticides and more adequate price policies, described of late as a 'new strategy' in agriculture, has pushed this problem to the fore. In fact, it will be unwise to turn what is still a divergence in approach into a more fundamental conflict of interest and policy. On the one hand, there is the undoubted need for speedy and sustained increase in agricultural output for which the technical means now exist. On the other, for a period, there is an unavoidable limitation in the supplies of fertilizers and other scarce resources, a limitation which must be overcome speedily to the greatest extent possible. Without forswearing accepted and declared goals of policy, in the present emergency, it is legitimate to concentrate greater effort in areas enjoying irrigation and assured rainfall where intensive agricultural development can bring quicker gains in production. In these areas, both the larger farmers and the smaller farmers should be enabled to contribute all they can. As other areas come under intensive development, and more supplies and credit can be provided, there too the small farmer can go forward along with the larger farmer, each receiving help in proportion to his need. Intensive development should lead to a stronger and more diversified rural economy and to a fuller use of all the available manpower and other local resources, and all sections of the rural community should be enabled to share in the advance achieved.

Rightly understood, the present crisis in agriculture—which is a crisis both of production and of management and distribution—is an opportunity to hasten greatly the pace of progress in relation to production, in the use of rural manpower and in creating a more adequate and stable rural structure. Steps to implement outstanding land reform legislation as a national programme, to remove the serious flaws which have been observed, to broaden the programme to the extent

necessary and give to it the greater economic support which
is now possible, can go a long way to put the entire countryside to work and give to the rural community a new sense
of confidence and direction. Guided by social purpose, the
second phase in land reform can, thus, consolidate the gains
of the first and, at the same time, help immeasurably towards
resolving the current problems of agricultural production and
food management.

II

Duly enacted laws should be looked upon as solemn
promises on the part of democracy and the governments
and parties which subscribe to them. Laws carry their own
implicit sanction for faithful execution. When a private
individual or organisation fails to keep a bond, certain
remedies are possible. When governments and the political
systems they represent find themselves unable to fulfil their
pledges, whatever the reasons, their ability and even their right
to steer the course for the future comes under doubt. Their
failure may generate new and unpredictable forces, as
different sources of social discontent find ways of linking up
with one another.

Against this and other considerations mentioned earlier,
we may first review the broad circumstances, which have
affected the quality of implementation of land reform legislation over the past decade and then proceed to consider the
various changes and extensions in public policy which
are now required. These include action by way of
restoration of evicted tenants or of tenants who have
been induced to 'surrender' the lands they cultivated,
protection of share-croppers, ensuring effective security
to all cultivating tenants for the future and limiting the
scope for resumption on grounds of 'personal cultivation',

regulation of rents and their commutation into cash, breaking the nexus between landlords and tenants and conferring the rights of ownership upon tenants, enforcement of ceilings on agricultural holdings and provision of the administrative and financial support needed for giving effect to land reform legislation and for building further on the rights secured through such legislation. Land reform is a difficult programme to carry out and some hard decisions are inevitable. It is unfortunately true that much precious time has gone by, and only with great effort will it now be possible to restore confidence in the intentions of the legislation which has been put on the statute book.

Before Independence, the significance of land reform and the range of measures and policies it implied had not been fully grasped. Attention had been given mainly to the position of zamindars and their relationship to hereditary tenants. Little thought was given to the position of tenants-at-will and share-croppers in relation to peasant owners and occupancy tenants, and big landlords received only cursory attention. The concept of ceiling on agricultural holdings had not yet entered into the discussion. The problem of the landless, many of whom were Harijans, was thought of less in terms of employment and economic opportunities and equality and more in terms of civic rights. The role of land in the total social and economic structure was also not sufficiently appreciated. Had it been otherwise and had the implications of food, agriculture and land in relation to economic growth been more completely known at the making of the Constitution, it is conceivable that the precise distribution of functions between the Centre and the States might have taken a somewhat different form. The issues became clearer when the First Five Year Plan was being formulated. From then on, while recognising that States would give due attentions to their local conditions and local needs, it was hoped that they would do so in terms of a broadly agreed and common approach and as part of the national plan. It was in this context that the First Five Year Plan had stated:

> The future of land ownership and cultivation constitutes perhaps the most fundamental issue in national development. To a large extent the pattern of economic and social organisation will depend upon the manner in which the land problem is solved. Sooner or later, the principles and objectives of policy for land cannot but influence policy in other sectors as well.

The advisory and coordinating role of the Planning Commission, of the Central Committee for Land Reforms and of the National Development Council over many years in relation to land reform policies and their implementation has to be understood against this background.

The States took several years to enact the legislation to which they had agreed in principle. Having passed the laws, invariably the process of implementation began slowly and was spread over long periods. There are several instances in which even the preliminary stages of practical action still remain to be completed. In addition to elements peculiar to the legislation of individual States, four general factors may account for the delays which have done so much to weaken the dynamics of land reform. These were:

(i) Much of the period of the First Plan was taken in moving towards the set of policies embodied in the report of the Panel on Land Reform which met during 1955 and with some changes, became part of the Second Five Year Plan. This gave time to many substantial owners to transfer part of their land and escape the impact of legislation passed subsequently.

(ii) Neither public opinion and the administration, nor the people in the rural areas, were adequately informed and educated about the significance of land reform and the rights sought for different sections of the rural community. Even among political parties, to this day, there has been only incomplete formulation of views on land and the future organisation and structure of agriculture. In dealing with the land problem they have shown a degree of ambivalence in their formal statements and still more so in practical action.

(iii) In the traditional economy, tenants and small owners are in a position of peculiar weakness. Their relationship to those whose lands they cultivate is of a personal character, marked in the past by traditional rights and obligations on both sides. In the case of tenants and even more in the case of those with still smaller privileges—the landless labourers—economic weakness has been accentuated by social factors. Working in small, atomistic units, except in situations of exceptional organisation and leadership or under the stress of severe and prolonged discontent, tenants have not been able to organise for their own protection and have given way in silence, as landless labourers too have done in even greater measure. Thus, from the soil, there has not come up the kind of insistent pressure for social justice to which power in its various forms— political, economic and administrative—unless itself so motivated, should have been compelled to respond.

(iv) The new legislation had to be evolved and given effect to by State revenue administrations with the help of land records prepared initially at settlements. In some States, which had been under permanent land settlement, neither established revenue administrations, nor adequate land records were available so that, administratively, only the simplest kind of once-for-all legislation was feasible. Elsewhere, the records of rights had to be brought up-to-date and lacked information concerning tenancies. The revenue administrations themselves were overburdened with much other work. There were two other associated factors. The first was the background of legal complexity and the constitutional issues which arose in respect of several laws passed in the States and in some cases delayed implementation for years. The second arose from the fact that for many decades revenue agencies have worked closely with rural landlords and, until Independence, each supported the other in all acts of administration.

From this analysis, certain conclusions can be drawn which have deep significance for the future of land reform and agrarian reorganisation.

In all new land legislation or modifications of existing legislation, the provisions should be clear-cut and capable of swift enforcement. A less refined piece of legislation, giving perhaps less justice than is due, is to be preferred to elaborate legislation which entails prolonged processes of records, declarations, verifications and appeals on points of law and points of fact before effect can be given to it. From this aspect, a great deal of the existing legislation needs to be simplified and combed out over a period. Meanwhile, of course, effect must be given to the laws already enacted.

Land reform has been treated for many years primarily as an administrative problem. In fact, it raises large policy issues calling for political debate on basic economic and social objectives and clearly defined positions at every level, so that national and State formulations should have behind them the weight of informed political opinion. The findings of research studies which have been undertaken already provide essential facts to draw upon and, for purposes of policy and organisation, it should be possible to weave into them the actual experience and knowledge of conditions in different parts of the country.

Rights in relation to land held by large and medium-sized owners, small peasants, tenants and share-croppers and agricultural labourers (of whom a proportion possess tiny pieces of land) are of varying character. Whatever the changes envisaged under land reform their interests will still be far from identical. Therefore, in the present phase of land reform, if this were to represent the final shape of rural organisation, there is no alternative to what may be broadly described as organisations of *classes*, each pressing for its own interests with whatever sanctions—economic, political or other—it can muster. So far, for a variety of reasons—including weaknesses of political parties and the economic handicaps of small peasants and workers—such organisations have come into existence for short periods and to express specific grievances, not as a continuing feature of rural life. Now, a new stage has been reached. Howsoever it may come about, unless the different segments of the rural community can see their future in the planned development of a common interdependent social and economic framework whose premises do fair justice to their needs and aspirations and, in particular, hold promise of security and opportunity for the mass of workers, separate class organisations will have to develop and acquire what force they can. This is the critical point of departure involved in co-operative village management and *gramdan* and other variants of the co-operative and community approach to the reconstruction of rural life.

Which of the two possible courses will eventually emerge will be, for a time, an open question. The issue will turn on many factors, and specially on whether wider and more inclusive social goals are pursued with the necessary moral force and practical results attained well before separate interests and separate organisations have struck positions of their own and reached, as it were, a point of no return. In all politically dynamic situations, solutions which seem feasible at one stage may pass the opportune moment and, at a later stage, become inapplicable or cease to secure the necessary support.

As with consolidation of holdings, enforcement of land reform legislation now requires separate agencies outside the heavily burdened revenue departments, whose personnel are carefully selected and are trained and motivated to undertake their specific responsibilities with a sense of urgency.

It will be necessary for these agencies to develop their own information and reporting systems as well as criteria for evaluating success and failure. They will also be in a more effective position to secure economic and technical support from other agencies to enable those to whom new rights accrue to develop the necessary strength to stand on their own.

Absence of records of tenancies has come up as a serious obstacle in implementing land reform legislation.The importance of these records, as distinguished from land records or records of rights in general, was specially stressed in the Third Five Year Plan. Action during the past six years has been tardy, partly because of budgetary constraints and pleas by some States for assistance from the Centre (though the amounts involved are modest), and partly because in the past the preparation of land records has been associated with land revenue settlements, which take long periods to complete and cause much commotion. It is desirable to separate the two processes and to treat the preparation of records of tenancies as a specific task to be completed swiftly and to treat these records as supplements to the main record of rights. Methods and procedures for land revenue settlements are also capable of being greatly simplified and accelerated. In particular, policy criteria could be established for States and regions, and settlement operations at the district and local level could be considerably simplified.

III

Action along the lines suggested above should be of help in giving effect to the existing legislation in each State and in drawing urgent attention to the improvements needed.

More than slow progress in conferring rights of ownership or in enforcing ceilings on agricultural holdings, land reform has received a bad name on account of the large number of so-called 'voluntary surrenders' of tenancies which have occurred in all States, failure to bring share-croppers in certain States within the purview of protective legislation, and continued payment by tenants of rents in excess of levels prescribed by law. There are two aspects which require the urgent attention of all State Governments: first, how the existing machinery for ensuring justice to tenants in accordance with the provisions of the legislation may be strengthened and, secondly, modifications needed in the legislation itself.

Even under existing arrangements, where a State Government desires to achieve progress in land reform and revenue officials are suitably oriented, effective implementation can be substantially achieved. This has not generally happened, though some exceptions can be cited. Therefore, the official administrative agency, which should be organised outside the revenue department, has to be supplemented in at least two other ways. The first is to provide for land tribunals. An itinerant district tribunal with powers of investigation, which would also have at its disposal the services of the land reform agency, could provide both a check on violations of the law and a means for redress of grievances. From the district tribunal appeals on certain aspects could be submitted to a State land tribunal. Secondly, there is no reason why State Governments should not themselves promote the formation of tenants' welfare associations and give them adequate assistance in finance and personnel, so that they can represent on behalf of tenants to land tribunals and other authorities, thus bringing justice within their reach. Such associations could also educate tenants concerning their rights and undertake other appropriate services.

There are no statistics to indicate the number of tenants and the areas which may have been involved over the past decade in 'voluntary surrenders', but the magnitudes in question are commonly considered to be disturbingly large.

For the future, it is clear that 'surrenders' should be declared void and that the landlord should not be permitted, without due process of law, to resume land under the cultivation of a tenant. Legislation in some States contains provisions for the regulation of 'surrenders' but these invariably leave loopholes, and more drastic action is now called for. In respect of 'surrenders' which have taken place over the past few years, the wrong done cannot be completely mended. But, at least in a proportion of cases, there should be the opportunity to correct the position. All landowners could be required to report details of the 'surrenders' with which they have been concerned, say, over a period of five years. These should be examined by the designated authorities. Where the landowner is genuinely engaged in personal cultivation, he may be allowed to continue. Where, the tenant who gave up his tenancy has obtained another tenancy he need not be disturbed. But where the tenant, having surrendered his tenancy, has turned into a labourer, if he so wishes, he should be enabled to obtain an alternative tenancy. If, for any reason, this cannot be arranged, then the original owner should be obliged to restore the tenancy. This would seem to be a minimum approach to the rectification of a situation which has done much to weaken confidence in the entire scheme of land reform.

The problem of crop-sharers in West Bengal and their counterpart in Bihar, the *under-raiyats*, has been neglected for too long a period and the only correct course is to give them their due rights as tenant cultivators with full security and opportunity later to become owners of the lands they cultivate. In the same way, in dealing with concealed tenancies which operate under different names throughout the country, wherever the fact of cultivation as tenant is established, the full rights of tenancy should accrue automatically. Those who are in fact cultivating as tenants, but are not so described, should be enabled to submit their claims to district land tribunals, whose decision should be final.

Research investigations into the working of rent and tenancy legislation bring out the fact that, as at present placed, without positive and continuous administrative and political support, tenants are not able to keep their payments to levels prescribed by legislation, and customary rentals still hold the field. In some instances, rents have risen even above the customary levels. The relative economic position of tenants, the lack of other employment opportunities and the bias even on the part of small owners in favour of traditional levels of rent together lead to this result. In several States, the rents now fixed are clearly excessive, but it is to be hoped that pressure of opinion aided by the organisation of tenants may lead to their reduction. In a few States the procedures for relief against excessive payments are so complex and costly as to defeat the object itself. This is another area of reform. The main issue, however, is that so long as rents are payable in produce, it will be difficult to prevent high rents. With cash rents, while vigilance will still be required, receipts in lieu of payment can be enforced. Cash rents also provide for greater flexibility. If they are fixed as multiples of land revenue and the total rent to be paid is thus limited, as was proposed in the Third Plan, there would be greater encouragement to tenants to invest in improvements.

In the execution of land reform legislation, considerable mischief has arisen because of provisions under which landowners are permitted to resume land from tenants for 'personal cultivation'. Experience over the past decade shows that a satisfactory legal definition of 'personal cultivation', which is also capable of being enforced, is extraordinarily difficult. So far as tenants of holdings above the ceiling limit are concerned, old tenants or tenants who are newly settled on non-resumable lands should be granted

8

ownership rights over their lands forthwith. This is the only course available. In the case of holdings below the ceiling, it becomes necessary to reconcile the interests specially of small owners and of tenants cultivating under them. In certain categories, legislation already allows for exemptions, as for defence personnel, widows or minors. Under existing conditions the facility of leasing in and leasing out lands is of help to many small owners. Various formulae indicating the minimum areas which must be left with tenants and setting limits to the amount of land which may be resumed have not worked satisfactorily.

A measure of rigidity in relation to land relationships is difficult to avoid even in respect of small owners. However, it is necessary to take note of certain developments which have occurred throughout the country in the wake of legislation conferring greater security on tenants-at-will. The total volume of leasing has diminished on paper, but there is still a considerable measure of concealed leasing. Entries in revenue records concerning tenancies are frequently incorrect. Those who serve as tenants themselves become parties to such entries, for otherwise they would not be able to get land to cultivate and would find themselves driven to work as field labourers, a way of life much more precarious and less desired than that of tenant cultivators. Even where it becomes necessary to lease out land for a period for reasons which may be valid on social considerations, resort to some form of subterfuge tends to be the rule rather than the exception.

There is, thus, a contradiction between the law and the principle on the one hand and practice and day-to-day experience on the other. This contradiction has introduced an element of falsehood into rural life which has its demoralising aspects and needs to be considered objectively from the standpoint of public policy for the future. The choice is by no means an easy one, for there are important considerations to be set against one another. Any relaxations which are made may weaken the principle that land should belong to the tiller without materially altering the present practice in rural areas. On balance, it seems desirable to permit leasing freely to the extent of a basic holding, which is commonly taken to be one-half of the family holding. Thus, any one may be allowed to lease out or lease in land up to a basic holding. Beyond this, the provisions of tenancy legislation should be enforced after due scrutiny.

In some States, legislation distinguishes different classes of tenants (for instance, protected tenants and ordinary tenants) and differentiates between the rights given to them. The distinctions are essentially historical and social and not in any sense functional or economic. In terms of the reconstruction of the land system and the development of agriculture, there is no case for continuing to maintain them. The proper course, therefore, would be to apply the same set of terms to all those who fall within the broad description of tenants, whether or not in the past certain distinctions have existed amongst them.

As we move beyond essential provisions for security for tenants to the question of the structure of land rights to be built up in the future, it is clear that, unless otherwise stipulated by law, the status of tenancy is essentially of a transitional and interim character. It must lead on to ownership. In this respect, much of the existing legislation is quite inadequate and calls for drastic changes. Rights of ownership have to be conferred on at least two groups of tenants, namely, those on non-resumable lands under owners with holdings above the ceiling limit and those cultivating lands belonging to owners with more than one family holding but below the ceiling. The first category of tenants should be given priority in conferring ownership rights. At the next stage the second group of tenants can be taken up. There are three main propositions to be advanced. First, the landlord-tenant nexus has to be broken at the earliest stage and, pending transfer of rights to tenants, ownership should come to vest in the Government and rents should be collected by it. The compensation to be paid to owners should be laid down under the law as also the payments to be made by tenants in appropriate instalments in lieu of ownership rights. Secondly, tenants should be given assistance through land mortgage banks to purchase the rights of ownership. Thirdly, an alternative approach, which should also be provided, would be to compound the payments on account of ownership rights and rent so that, after a period of years, ownership devolves automatically on the tenant. In this context, it may also be urged that, in areas in which intermediary rights have been abolished, appropriate arrangements on these lines should be worked out and all occupancy tenants enabled to obtain the full rights of ownership. As in the matter of security of tenures, so also in relation to grant of ownership rights, distinctions between different classes of tenants are now only a vestige of the past and should be done away with.

We turn, finally, to the question of ceilings on agricultural holdings. Although there are variations between States, and some serious weaknesses have crept into the legislation, in fact considerable care and thought have gone into the determination of levels of ceilings, valuation of different categories of land, exemptions from ceilings and rates of compensation. Except in one State, the concept of ceiling has been correctly applied. But, in several States, provisions concerning transfers of land above the ceiling, prior to enactment of the legislation and in some instances even subsequent to it, have done much to nullify the effect of the reform and to reduce greatly the area of land which may still become available as surplus for settling landless labourers and for augmenting the holdings of petty peasant owners. This has been a source of failure which, with the passage of time, has become specially difficult to remedy.

Transfers to avoid the incidence of ceilings on agricultural holdings are made either to those who will be entitled in due course to inherit the land or to third parties. Though they do entail deferment of the application of the legislation to a later period, from practical considerations, it will now be difficult, retrospectively, to reopen transfers which have been effected in favour of future heirs. It is, however, feasible to discriminate between these transfers and transfers which are of a *benami* or fraudulent character in favour of persons without any intrinsic concern with the land now or in the future. These latter must be subjected to the most careful scrutiny and brought to an end, whether they took place before or after the enactment of the legislation. As for the future, the existing legislation should be amended so that all *unauthorised* transfers will become void, whether these are to prospective heirs or to other parties.

A comprehensive approach to the land problem would include discussion of such features as provision of credit and other assistance to those who benefit from land reform, resettlement of landless agricultural workers, consolidation of holdings, prevention of fragmentation, creation of minimum holdings, co-operative farming, and institutional developments such as co-operative village management and *gramdan*. Our object here is, however, more specific, namely, to point to those essential measures which are required at the particular juncture reached in the progress of land reform, so that the sense of disillusionment about land reform as serious policy and as an integral part of national development may be ended and the growth of agriculture and the rural economy correspondingly hastened. Though the damage done cannot be altogether repaired, if the relevant issues are laid bare and widely grasped, it is still not too late to secure significant and lasting benefits from the measures

which have been already enacted and to undertake the
further improvements necessary in keeping with the principles
which gained general acceptance more than a decade ago
and continue to be valid and of great importance to the
future of India.

5

CO-OPERATION AND ECONOMIC ORGANISATION*

As A principle of economic organisation, co-operation plays a small part in the present structure of production in India. It has a varying place in the economic life of different countries and only in a few branches of economic activity does it make a substantial contribution. In the perspective of the past two hundred years, except perhaps in the Scandinavian countries, co-operation has had only a meagre share in stimulating the process of economic and social development. For the greater part, co-operative activities have stood on the outskirts of the mainstream of economic life or they have been like pockets in a system based mainly either on the principle of community ownership or on that of individual property. It would, therefore, appear that, as a method of economic organisation, co-operation has so far exerted only a limited influence on economic thinking and practice. Yet, weakness in action does not seem to have impaired the hope which the idea

*Adapted from an address at the University of Rajputana (now University of Rajasthan), Jaipur, on March 13, 1955. See Indian Journal of Public Administration, Vol. I, No. 1, January-March, 1955, pages 25-32.

of co-operation has always inspired, specially among intel-
lectuals and social workers in countries with low standards
of income and consumption which have a great deal of
leeway to make up.

There is, thus, a certain contradiction between theory
and practice, between the experience of the past and expectations of the future. It might, therefore, be of interest to
consider, specially from the aspect of under-developed
countries seeking a rapid rate of economic progress, what
the precise place of co-operation as a principle or as a method
of economic organisation could be and the conditions
which would need to be met if co-operation is to fulfil the
role assigned to it. Until recently, the process of economic
growth and the conditions which determine its rate and
form were not a subject of close study. Although important
beginnings have been made in dissecting the experience of
different countries, perhaps conditions in various parts of
the world have varied to such an extent that it is still not
easy to present general principles of economic development.
Both in the national and international sense, political conditions provide the setting for economic aims and practice
and, in turn, economic factors help in shaping the political
trends.

In the middle of the twentieth century, few countries
are able to leave their economic development to chance
and circumstance or to the unaided enterprise of their
citizens or to the advice and assistance of countries
more favourably placed than themselves. In different degrees,
therefore, the expressions 'economic development' and
'planned development' have become almost synonymous.
In a society in which, in an increasing measure, an attempt
is made to prescribe the goals to be achieved and to organise
human and material resources for achieving them, methods
of economic development turn upon the place given in the
scheme of planning to four main ideas or concepts. These

concepts and the manner in which they are interpreted in practice provide the framework within which co-operation, viewed as a principle of economic organisation, can function. Within such a framework, again, there are other conditions which will determine the form which the principle of co-operative organisation may take and the range of activity which it may encompass. The four concepts are: Freedom, Property, Technology and Incentives. We may consider each of these briefly in turn.

Freedom is an absolute value, even though under certain conditions it may be difficult to preserve it. There could be many tests of freedom. Perhaps among the most important are whether there is freedom of information and expression and freedom of association. In societies in which freedom in this sense does not exist, there may be activities based on the principle of co-operation, but their role and functions are of a subordinate and non-independent character. Those activities which cannot be organised equally well by the State or which are of altogether minor importance may be left to the co-operative sector.

The system of property relations which exists in a community has considerable influence on the manner in which its economic development will take place. Where freedom exists in the sense described above, changes in property relations are likely to take place continuously until gross inequalities due to inheritance or on account of wide disparities in the scale of rewards for different classes of work largely disappear. The aspect to emphasise is that in the conditions of freedom, whatever their scope, changes in property relations are brought about through a process of law and, even though the effects may be revolutionary, the methods adopted are democratic and evolutionary. In a community in which there are gross inequalities in wealth, income and opportunity, co-operation as a method of economic organisation cannot play any significant part.

Nor can it contribute much in a community in which the means of production and distribution are mainly in the hands of the State. Changes in property relationships achieved democratically leave small units intact. By bringing these into group or co-operative organisations, it becomes possible to maintain and develop the structure of production and distribution even through the difficult period of transition.

Technological change is of the very essence of economic and social development. In any economy which is expanding, changes in technology can be introduced with much less social strain than when the rate of economic progress is low. This holds for all types of societies. A system of enterprise based on private property and a system of State ownership are alike favourable to technological change. The problem of technological change has, however, wider implications. In a society in which property and income relationships are in the process of democratic change, there is special emphasis on human values and on the welfare of the community as a whole. As inequalities diminish, the problem is one of combining small units into sizeable groups so as to obtain the advantages of combination, scale and organisation. The small units may be farmers working on their own land, artisans serving the village community or working for merchants, labourers felling trees for forest contractors, or consumers seeking to eliminate the middleman. In each case, in the immediate future, it may be possible for a well-organised larger unit or for a powerful individual to adopt improved techniques and drive out the small man. Co-operation, on the other hand, enables a democratic society to adapt changes in technology from the point of view of the interest of the community as a whole and, more specially, for meeting the needs of small men. The principle of co-operation enables small units to organise themselves. In this manner, over a large sector of the economy, the community may achieve technological change by stages, each stage leading to the next, but never at the cost of the welfare of large numbers of small and relatively helpless people for whom the community is in no immediate position to offer alternatives. This is a point of special importance in countries like India.

Finally comes the question of incentives. As human beings are constituted, given a fair measure of equality of opportunity, it may be that the maximum results are secured through a system in which social and individual incentives are blended together. In countries in which the means of production belong altogether to the community, the incentive of additional reward for additional work plays an important part in securing production. There are limits to which individual incentives can be successfully established in a structure whose dimensions are such that the individual worker is rather apt to be lost. This applies as much to a large factory as to a State farm or to a big collective farm. On the other hand, the appeal to the individual incentive alone may soon degenerate into anti-social forms. Within the limits which may be set by basic technical and economic conditions, there is little doubt that in a society marked by democratic change co-operation offers opportunities of achieving a combination of incentives which are good for the group as well as for each individual participating in it. This analysis suggests, therefore, that in a society seeking freedom and social change along democratic lines, co-operation as a method of organisation can help in achieving a rate of technological change and a system of incentives which will contribute to the welfare of the community as a whole.

Given a favourable climate of opinion and policy, the limit to the range of activities to which the principle of co-operation can be applied is set by the fact that a co-operative group has to be reasonably small for its members to know one another as individuals and as fellow workers and to trust one another. It may well be that for certain purposes a number of small groups may combine into larger organisations. These organisations derive their strength and vitality from the fact that they are based on small and fairly homogeneous groups which are functioning actively. Thus, it is easier to organise co-operative activity where the means of production are of small size or of a simple character than where they are based on complex technology. A co-operative farming society for an area of 50 or 80 acres can be brought into existence more easily than a society which takes in the entire land of a village. A group of artisans working individually or in small groups on relatively simple equipment, may be able to organise their work co-operatively with less difficulty than if, because of the equipment involved, work could not be easily divided between them. A farm worked altogether by mechanical equipment takes on the character of an enterprise in which there may be a considerable distance between the position of the manager and that of the workers. Similarly, in the field of trade in which middlemen control operations, whether as buyers or as sellers, given some assistance, a small and compact group can organise its buying and selling activities more successfully than one whose members are bound to one another only tenuously. In other words, the size of the group and the character of the tools employed have considerable bearing on the extent to which co-operative activity at the primary level may be organised. It may, of course, happen, as suggested earlier, that strong primary units at the base will make possible the organisation of a strong super-structure, each layer in the organisation being then able to take on functions which the layer below cannot. Thus, a body of co-operatives concerned with agricultural marketing may be able to undertake, at one level, processing of agricultural produce; at another, wholesale trade in foodgrains; and, at a third level, foreign trade in processed industrial raw materials. Within the co-operative structure, strength lies at the roots, and therefore, the sectors of economic activity which co-operative organisations can best take over are likely to be mainly those in which the elements of strength lie at the roots, in the size of the primary group and the kind of tools and resources it uses. From this aspect, fields such as agricultural production, agricultural marketing and processing, trade in all commodities produced or used in rural areas, consumer co-operative stores and co-operatives of industrial artisans are specially amenable to the co-operative method. In these and other like fields, it should be the aim to enable co-operation to become increasingly the principal basis for the organisation of economic activity. This implies not only that new activities in these fields should be co-operatively organised but also that existing activities should be taken over, step by step, by co-operatives.

In large industrial or transport undertakings, which entail heavy capital investment and may be appropriate for public or semi-public enterprise, the principle of co-operation can be expressed to some extent through participation in management on the part of workers. This is, however, an extension rather than an application of the idea of co-operation as it has been known in the past and is intended to achieve a somewhat different object, namely, avoidance of bureaucratic control and involvement of workers in the sharing of larger responsibilities.

The fields in which *prima facie* co-operation should become the leading principle of economic organisation will not be developed along these lines unless, in a system of planned development, co-operation is *assigned* certain sectors as a matter of public policy. The report of the Committee on the Rural Credit Survey suggests two conclusions which

are significant in this connection.* The first conclusion is
that there has to be a partnership between the State and
the co-operative movement if co-operation is to succeed
and that such partnership has to extend directly or indirectly
to all levels of organisation. The second conclusion, reached
with reference especially to the problems of co-operative
credit, is that the credit system of the country has to be
reorganised so as to subserve the needs of the rural population. It is implicit in the study carried out by the Committee and in its recommendations that, not merely has
there to be State partnership for promoting co-operative
development along certain lines but also, as a matter of
State policy, certain fields of economic activity have to be
developed into a co-operative sector.

In building up the co-operative sector of the economy
as part of its scheme of development, the community would
have to provide for those elements which are specially
lacking at present. These are: (a) clear demarcation of the
field which has to be progressively organised along co-
operative lines, (b) resources, and (c) managerial personnel
and training facilities.

Even under favourable conditions, in the short run, it
is much more difficult for the co-operative form of organisation to succeed than it is for a completely socialist enterprise or for an individual entrepreneur. The human factors
involved are more complex. On the other hand, if success is
attained, the gains to the community are much larger. It is,
therefore, necessary for a democratic community to make
special efforts to enable co-operation to succeed as a method
of organisation in the fields assigned to it. For co-operative
farming to succeed, for instance, in a country in which there
is heavy pressure of population, it is essential that when
a number of small men pool their small holdings into a

---

*All-India Rural Credit Survey, Report of the Committee of Direction,
Volume II, the General Report, Reserve Bank of India, Bombay (1954).

co-operative, they should get additional land for cultivation as well as additional capital resources. Secondly, both in the field of production and in trade, in the co-operative sector managerial personnel have to be trained and provided by the State. While such personnel will be deputed to serve with co-operatives, responsibility for making them available at all levels will largely rest with the Government.

To consider the place of co-operation in planned economic development mainly as a matter of demarcating a sector of activity for co-operatives would be to take a wholly inadequate view. The point may be illustrated from co-operation at the village level. With the economic structure of the country rooted in the village, it is necessary to think of co-operation not merely as a series of activities organised along co-operative lines, but even more as a system of co-operative community organisation which touches upon all aspects of life. Within the village community there are sections of the population who do not yet enjoy equality of status and opportunity in any significant degree. Co-operation would have failed unless it meant a sense of obligation towards all families in the village community and the development of land and other resources and social services in the common interest of the village as a whole.

To sum up, therefore, in a society built upon freedom, economic development has to be viewed as part of a process in which property and income relationships are being steadily and continuously modified in favour of the small man. Small men, whether they are farmers or artisans or labourers, can hold their own and gain in strength and opportunity only if they combine along co-operative lines. Co-operative organisations permit the adaptation of new technology in stages which are in tune with the interest of the community as a whole. Through them it is possible to achieve a balance between the social and individual incentives which will benefit the community as well as the individual. There are important fields in which co-operative organisations can play a distinctive part in building up the economy and in eliminating existing agencies such as moneylenders or middlemen whose contribution to the economy is marked by certain undersirable features. As an extension of the idea of co-operation in large enterprises, workers' management can help in preventing the growth of bureaucratic and impersonal methods of control and in giving a sense of sharing to the workers. The development of a co-operative sector as part of a scheme of planned development, how-ever, requires that the aim be accepted as a matter of national policy and that, in addition to managerial personnel and facilities for training at all levels, the resources of the banking and credit system as well as resources such as additional land derived through land reform and improved equipment be provided to those engaged in different forms of co-operative activity. These various steps have to be taken, not merely because they are a condition of practical success, but because the idea of co-operation embodies the essential values of the new society which we seek to create.

6

THE CO-OPERATIVE VILLAGE*

THE VILLAGE has held a central place in social and economic thinking in India. Surveys of villege life, of which there have been hundreds since the twenties seldom penetrated deep enough to the elements which provide the motivations, the cohesion and continuity and the conflicts and tensions in the life of small and once largely self-contained communities. Nor did these studies throw much light on how villages in any area functioned in relation to one another, as part of a larger rural society or in relation to urban centres. In recent years fresh interest has been focussed on the village because of the community development programme, land reform, the *bhoodan* and *gramdan* movements, the enunciation of co-operative village management as the objective of agrarian reorganisation, the place assigned to village panchayats and the stress on village industries. Under the impact of these developments, basic questions concerning the future of the village are now beginning to assume a concreteness which had not previously existed and to suggest the need for fresh analysis.

*Adapted from a contribution to the Economic Weekly Annual, Vol. X No. 4, 5 & 6, pages 143-148, January 1958.

When we speak of the village or of village society we are, of course, aware of the fact that there are enormous differences between villages in different parts of the country. There are differences in size and population, in the way homes and hamlets are located, in the internal social structure and in the influence on the traditional village and on the various social groups of new developments such as irrigation, growth of towns, progress of large-scale industries and the decline of small industries. With all these qualifications, it is remarkable how, through the length and breadth of a vast country with such complex and varied cultures, there yet emerges the picture of a pattern of society, of living, called the village, which has vitality and is adjusting itself to new conditions.

The village no longer stands alone. From within and without powerful forces bear upon it. We are beginning to see more clearly the interaction of many cultural, economic, technological and political factors, but we need to know much more. The village community may not be so closely bound by a sense of mutual interest and obligation as to be described as an extended family. But it is much more than a mere agglomeration of families with diverse interests which may be expected sooner rather than later to fall apart completely under the impact of new forces. The truth is that in every part of the country, often in each village, one may witness two sets of competing influences, those that bind and unite and facilitate adaptation, others which divide and disintegrate. If we understand the nature of the influences which are at work, we shall soon see that some, such as technological development, have to be absorbed and integrated into the village structure, others like the growth of individualism have to be guided and tamed.

Planned economic development is but another side of planned social development; both aspects have to be seen

together, not only at the village level, but right through
the entire social order. The reconstruction of the village
involves, not only a concept of the village but also at every
point a view of rural society and its relationships with
the national economy as a whole.

Perhaps, it is because such a perspective does not yet
exist that national programmes like community development, increase of agricultural production, co-operation,
land reform and village and small industries lack real focus,
an inner unity, and fail to give strength to one another.
To the extent this statement is judged to be correct, each
of these programmes contributes less to national well-being
and to economic growth than has been hoped for. The time
has, therefore, come to define with some precision our conception of the village and of the village community, the
directions in which various forces of change may be guided,
and the place of the village in the future economic structure
of the country.

Specific proposals can be traced often to assumptions
which may have been accepted implicitly or instinctively.
This is true of those who approach the village with a view
to its preservation much as it is; it is also true of those
who would absorb individual villages into larger units,
for instance, for panchayats or for co-operatives. Unless
it is transformed from within and integrated fully into the
wider economic structure, the present day village cannot be
easily sustained. On the other hand, if its entity as a unit
of development is given up, the resulting structure may
well prove to be weak and lacking for a long time in cohesion
and stability. Where there is economic progress, the village
will inevitably pass through great changes. Where these
changes have in fact led to the discarding of the village
unit, as in USSR and in some ways recently in China,
much of the initiative and responsibility for change pass
out of the hands of the local community to the State, to

political party cadres and to technicians. There is need, therefore, for a clear concept of change concerning the village structure and the village community.

For centuries, in the absence of economic progress, caste, property in land and occupation combined to give a certain character to the village community. Differences in status and opportunity were part of the accepted pattern.

We see the village of the future as a community composed of equal citizens, in which the have-nots have full opportunity no less than the haves, and everyone in the community has similar values and aspirations. Reaching a goal such as this involves fundamental changes in the ownership and management of land as well as in the pattern of employment. It also involves a reorientation of the outlook of all sections of the community concerning their own situation as well as their relationship to others.

If these are the objectives, it is necessary to work out appropriate processes and institutions for attaining them. This is a large theme and in this short paper it is not possible to do more than touch briefly upon some aspects of the problem. Three preliminary premises may, however, be stated. Firstly, rural society cannot be expected to be much more integrated and classless than the larger national community of which it forms part, although necessarily rural areas will have a less differentiated social and economic structure. It is, therefore, an essential assumption that although there will be differences in application, fundamentally similar social principles will be brought to bear on changes in rural as in non-rural society. In the second place, the goal of a classless society may be reached through class conflict and the victory, as it were, of the have-nots over the haves, or by removing disparities, giving greater opportunity to those who have been handicapped in the past, and stress on the fusion of various elements in the community. The latter is the way of democracy and of co-operation. Elements of conflict are recognised and, in the interest of the community as a whole, steps are taken to reduce them as rapidly as may be possible, both as a matter of social policy and in response to new demands and challenges from those adversely affected. In the third place, while individual claims and incentives are allowed for, the larger emphasis has to be on instruments of a social character. For the greater part, these turn on the nature and functions of community organisation and the obligations placed upon it.

The objective of change at the village level may be summed up in these words: to develop the village structure as part of a wider economy, largely through the initiative and resources of the local community, by assuring equality of social status and economic opportunity to all sections and all individuals in the community, and achieving levels of production and employment as would lift each village community out of its present state of poverty, ignorance and ill-health.

The question may be asked whether the efforts now being made in different directions are likely in the course of a few years to reach the objective defined above. It is true that the development of irrigation, power, communications and industries can do a great deal to strengthen the economy of an area. A large part of the justification of the community development programme lies in its stress on local resources and initiative. Programmes such as land reform and welfare schemes for backward classes are intended to reduce social and economic disparities. The object of the various agricultural programmes is to raise the productivity of land and increase production, even as it is the aim of education and health programmes to ameliorate the condition of the people and to extend educational facilities to the limit of the resources available. If the experience of the past few years is any guide, these various efforts are likely to take rural areas only a small way in the direction of the objective we have indicated. In part, this may no doubt be due to the very complexity of the process of development and the gulf which inevitably arises between the aspiration and the reality. In considerable part, however, the inadequacy of much that is being undertaken arises from a certain absence of synthesis in our approach to rural planning. The main local resources in a rural area are land and manpower. To get the best out of them, we need appropriate institutions, improved technology and capital investment which would supplement local resources.

In each area, conditions have to be created in which there is the necessary organisation and leadership to realise the full value of the manpower resources available and to apply improved technology to agriculture and other activities. If our efforts were concentrated to a larger extent on this essential task, much greater progress might be achieved in rural development. Without minimising the value of what is being done, it will be readily granted that at present we do not succeed in using manpower resources or harnessing other local resources to any great extent. This may be largely because we have not clearly identified the instruments for achieving the changes that we desire. In development blocks under the community development programme, we think less of the economic and social structure we are creating and far more of the various development schemes which government agencies are to sponsor and execute.

Similarly, at the village level, we fail to see the village community as a whole, how its resources are to be developed, how much, as a community, it can do for itself, and we give much more attention to odd schemes for which assistance is provided from public funds—schemes which seldom go to the heart of the problem. Again, at the village level, the entire programme of co-operative development now being undertaken is little more than a series of somewhat isolated activities, not related sufficiently closely to the well-being of the community as a whole and to the development of its total resources.

The land reform programme has begun to correct immediate injustices and to ensure security to the tiller, but its other aspects, which are related to the building up of the desired agrarian structure, have yet to be taken in hand. The net effect of the drawbacks mentioned above is that there is not enough purposeful and coordinated activity by each community at the local level in developing its land and other resources, using its manpower to the best advantage, assuming new obligations and responsibilities and creating a milieu in which every member of the community has a contribution to make and a future to look for. Proceeding on these lines, the pace of social and economic development is likely to be relatively slow and uneven and, for large sections of the rural community, the gains will not be appreciable.

It is from this aspect, more than from any other, that there is need to build up co-operative villages as the effective base of the entire rural economy. The co-operative village is to be regarded as a direction in which to move as rapidly as each village community finds possible. In moving towards the co-operative village, the various programmes for which government agencies are responsible under the national plan can help a great deal if, in pursuing their specific aims, they are all guided by the same basic social objective. In that event, they will reinforce one another and will also strengthen the village organisation. The co-operative village should not be viewed as a rigid pattern of relationships, of land management or of employment, for there is no limit to the growth of a community which organises its work on co-operative lines and also co-operates in larger tasks with other similar communities in the area.

We may attempt here a brief statement of the conditions

under which a village community may be able to work for the goal of the co-operative village. The first condition is the acceptance of the obligation of the community as a whole for the welfare and livelihood of each of its members. To discharge this obligation, a community has to function through two main village institutions, the village panchayat and the village co-operative. With the pressure of population that exists in many areas, individual village communities can only plan for increasing their productive resources and assuring work to everyone if their plans are linked with the plans of the area of which they form part, just as the plans of different areas have to be linked with the plans of the State.

The second condition, therefore, is that village planning and area planning should be undertaken as essential parts of the same process. This would make it possible for each area, as for each village, to assess its requirements and its resources and to put forth the maximum effort of which it is capable in realising the potential that exists. Programmes such as agriculture or village industries or social services, for which there have to be different government agencies, could thus become integrated into fully coordinated programmes and acquire much greater value in terms of the development of given village communities and given areas. Close to the soil, they would cease to be mere 'schemes' run by different agencies.

In the third place, in moving in the direction of the co-operative village, it is to be clearly understood that land belongs to individual peasants and it is their right and privilege to choose to cultivate it either as individuals or as co-operative groups. The land reform programme has been conceived so as to strengthen the peasant base of the rural economy and to reduce disparities. If this programme has failed so far to release new energy in most rural areas, this is to be attributed in some part to the fact that, apart from the pressure of powerful interests, it leans too heavily on administrative and legal processes and is not designed at present to operate as a community programme in which each village community has a direct stake and a clear responsibility.

Land reform will be a creative force in the development of the rural economy if it is conceived as a vital element in the building up of co-operative village communities. In so far as it makes for a more homogeneous village society, land reform should therefore facilitate the development of co-operation in farming as well as other activities. Viewed thus, it becomes the aim of public policy and of village planning to encourage, assist and guide co-operative farms which are established voluntarily by local groups. Naturally, the pace at which co-operative farming develops will be determined by its working in actual practice, the results achieved and the manner in which problems of human relationships are resolved. During the progress towards the co-operative village, therefore, there will be in varying proportion co-operative farms as well as individual peasant farms. Both sets of farms will be units within the village plan and the scheme of land management accepted by the community.

The fourth condition for progress towards the co-operative village is that, besides individual peasant holdings and co-operative farms established as voluntary associations, there should be an area of community ownership in each village. Such community ownership would partly be in the form of land, partly in the form of shares in economic enterprises in the village and in the area in which the village is situated and partly also by way of social services provided by the community, such as the village school and the health centre. Lands derived through *bhoodan*, or gifts made by individuals, from the application of ceilings on existing agricultural holdings or through contributions made during consolidation of holdings and common pasture lands would all come into the pool of community ownership. If managed well, even a small proportion of the area of the village under the ownership and operation of the community can have much social and economic significance. For one thing, such an area can provide the resources to each village community to attain a state of universal literacy and education—an aim which at present seems so difficult of achievement. Those sections of the community, which have suffered in the past from special handicaps, can be brought to a level which gives them equal opportunity with others.

Areas owned and managed directly by the community will need to be worked with improved methods, including the use of agricultural machinery, and can be developed as mixed farms with ancillary enterprises. The value of such development in terms of local employment potential and for creating new forms of work and services cannot be over-estimated. What the relative proportions of areas worked individually, co-operatively by groups and by the community as a whole may be in course of time will depend upon the judgement and the experience of the people, but we could certainly look for a steady expansion in the co-operative and community sectors of the rural economy. In developing the community sector, the social philosophy of *gramdan* has a rich contribution to make. A village in which *gramdan* is adopted to any considerable extent (even if the entire area is not made available), takes a leap forward in the reconstruction of its economy whose full implications may not yet by easy to perceive. In the conception of the co-operative village, therefore, *gramdan* enters as an ingredient of the utmost importance equally with all the programmes now undertaken under the scheme of national planning.

The fifth condition for rapid development towards the co-operative village concerns steps to be taken for cooperative reorganisation of marketing, distribution and processing activities. These represent an area in which the peasant and the village have long been the weaker parties. Rural capital formation can be greatly enhanced if, on the one hand, local manpower resources are fully mobilised and, on the other, in the course of a few years, through deliberate planning, private merchants, traders and entrepreneurs are largely replaced by co-operative institutions. Co-operative marketing and processing units, where they are of any size, should bring together not only individuals who subscribe capital but also village communities as organised, participating units.

The resources of villages and of individuals could be further supplemented by the State in those fields, in which Government have a special contribution to make by way of guidance in policy and planning, management and capital. Co-operatives alone, left to themselves to face the existing competition of the local trader and the entrepreneur, cannot get very far in bringing marketing, distribution and processing into the co-operative sector. These are activities in which the State as representing the overall national interest, co-operative associations and village communities and individuals have all to function as partners. These activities enable each village to become an organic unit in the total economic structure of an area. In this way, such problems as the securing of the marketable surplus in foodgrains, maintenance of agricultural prices and the distribution of foodgrains and other supplies can be resolved fully in accordance with public policy and the needs of the community as a whole.

The reorganisation and development of the economy of a large country is a highly complex and varied undertaking. All manners of institutions, incentives and programmes have to find their right place in the scheme of planning. Therefore, we must be careful not to overrate the role of any one set of institutions, policies or methods. At the same time, it is difficult to escape the conclusion that in the coming years the most important single element in the progress of the Indian economy will be the rate of growth in the rural sector. Here we have far greater advantages on our side than in many other fields, for the resources needed are in essence already with us. Today, these resources are being utilised to an extent which can only be regarded as meagre. The main hope of vitalising the rural economy, of greatly increasing the impact of development which is already under way in rural areas, lies in harnessing all agencies to the tasks of integrated area planning and village planning. In this context, the co-operative village, conceived as the base of a large co-operative rural structure, becomes a major goal of policy and progress towards it an essential means of social and economic advance.

7

APPROACH TO CO-OPERATIVE FARMING*

WHEN WE consider the problems of co-operative farming in the mid-sixties, we do so against the background of considerable experience in many countries. We are no longer discussing assumptions and expectations on their own. During the past fifteen years or more, there has been experience of economic and social planning in many countries. We have seen how different political systems function in face of problems which are similar. We have more insight today than a decade ago into the problems, conflicts and tensions of changing and developing societies. We also know much more than we did before about the functioning at the practical level of different types of farming co-operatives. Therefore, it is possible now to assess in a balanced manner the contribution which co-operative farming could be expected to make and the conditions under which this contribution might be best secured.

I

The description 'co-operative farming' covers a wide

*Based on an introductory lecture at the F. A. O. Regional Seminar on Co-operative Farming for Asia and the Far East at New Delhi on May 2, 1966. See *Indian Co-operative Review*, Vol. III, No. 4, July 1966, pages 1078-1086.

range of possibilities of organisation and cuts across different political systems. Therefore, it is useful to define the frame of reference within which the subject is discussed. For this purpose, we may envisage three broad propositions. First, the right to choose whether an invidical cultivator will or will not join a co-operative production unit belongs to him. Any steps that cultivators may take towards forming farm co-operatives should be the result of voluntary decisions on their part. Secondly, through planned development, institutions and facilities are created for achieving continuous agricultural and industrial progress and enabling all available agencies—public, co-operative and private—to participate in the developmental process. These institutions and facilities are available equally for co-operative units in agriculture and for individual farmers and the dice is not loaded either against the co-operative or against the individual peasant. Thirdly, public policy accepts in principle the need to enlarge the sphere of co-operative activity among peasants, including co-operation in production, and seeks to promote and create conditions which favour the growth of farm co-operatives. While these three conditions may be said to be broadly fulfilled in many countries, circumstances vary a great deal. The nature of political power, the sanctions on which it rests, the purposes of public policy, the political and administrative machinery at the disposal of government, the attitudes and motivations of the people and objective economic conditions differ widely. For this reason, in discussing co-operative farming, it is necessary to be specially cautious in putting forward propositions of a general nature.

As a method of organisation in a basic field of human activity like agriculture, co-operative farming has undoubtedly great social significance. It is, however, important to recognise that the social value of co-operative farming depends altogether on its capacity to attain its economic and production objectives. If these objectives are not realised,

the larger social purposes to which we relate co-operative
farming will not be served. Therefore, it is best to concentrate on those elements of the economic structure and of
policy and operations which bear specially on the ability
of farm co-operatives to achieve their economic aims.

II

Before considering the specific problems of co-operative
farming and the policies and measures which these suggest,
it is useful to place co-operative farming in a wider perspective from four different points of view. These are:

(a) the character of the agrarian and economic system in relation to which
the scheme of co-operative farming is designed;

(b) the overall objectives of economic and agricultural development which
have to be accomplished;

(c) policies, institutions and facilities which come into existence as a result
of efforts to carry out planned development and their impact on the
rural economy; and

(d) co-operative farming viewed as an aspect of total co-operative development and of the growth of the co-operative sector in the national economy.

The economic and agrarian structure of each country has
its own distinctive character. One may distinguish between
countries in three different ways. First, we have countries
which are densely populated, in which pressure on land is
heavy and is increasing and small agricultural holdings
predominate. In these countries there may also be sizeable
sections of the rural population who are landless and suffer
long periods of under-employment, so that low income
farmers and the landless together constitute the most important problem within the agrarian system. As against
this, we have countries in which there are few landless
workers, the available land resources are significantly larger
than the requirements of the present population, and higher
living standards can be attained through moderate increases
in productivity. Secondly, we may distinguish between coun-

tries in which the development of industry and trade is proceeding or may be expected to proceed sufficiently rapidly to provide the relief needed within the rural economy, and other countries in which, though there is considerable movement from the rural to the urban areas, pressure on land continues to increase, and the agricultural economy has to absorb larger and larger numbers each year. In the third place, we may distinguish countries in which low income farmers constitute a relatively small proportion while the bulk of the farmers are able to participate actively in the dynamic processes of growth, from other countries in which low income farmers constitute by far the greater number. Even within the same country, there may be regions in which the various contrasting situations described above are found to exist side by side.

On the whole, India falls within the group of countries which are densely populated, in which the vast majority of farmers are within the low income group and where a significant proportion of the rural population is accounted for as agricultural labourers. In India, the average per capita agricultural land is less than an acre, 82 per cent of the holdings are less than 10 acres and 98 per cent less than 20 acres. Holdings up to 10 acres represent 39 per cent of the cultivated area and those up to 20 acres 62 per cent of the cultivated area.* Agricultural labourers account for 19 per cent of rural workers although the proportion varies much in different parts of the country. Even so, there are regions in the country marked by the opposite set of conditions, namely, potentially large land resources and low density of population.

We may conclude from this discussion that the place which co-operative farming may hold in the strategy of agricultural development and the results which it may bring

*Chapter 3, pages 85-88.

will vary greatly with the nature of the overall economic and agrarian structure in a country or in its different regions.

In all under-developed countries, by far the most important objective of planned development is to raise the level of agricultural output. Growth of population, urbanisation and industrial development, development of animal husbandry, and the need for exports lend urgency to this task. In India, we are called upon to raise our foodgrains production from about 89 million tonnes in 1964-65 to about 120 million tonnes in 1970-71 and to about 150 million tonnes in 1975-76. Similarly, over this period, cotton production has to be raised from about 6 million bales to about 11 million bales, and oilseeds production from about 8·5 million tonnes to 16 million tonnes*. In other words, over the next ten years, nothing less than the doubling of agricultural production has to be achieved. It is, therefore, necessary to make co-operative farming meaningful and urgent in terms of such an overall objective, which must be achieved from the point of view of the national economy as a whole. Somewhat similar tasks have to be accomplished in other countries, depending upon their conditions. The FAO study on projections for 1970 for different agricultural commodities brings out the wide gap between production and demand for foodstuffs and raw materials and other commodities in the case of low income countries and the implications of this gap for their economy and living standards and for future economic relationships between low income and medium or high income countries. It is in the measure in which co-operative farming can contribute to the fulfilment of the total agricultural programme formulated for a country that it is likely to find its due place in the scheme of planned development.

In the thinking on agrarian problems, considerable stress

*Chapter 3, pages 70-74.

has been placed for many years on the problem presented by the size and distribution of agricultural holdings. One consequence of the expansion of facilities like credit, marketing and processing, the widening of markets, development of extension services and the building up of new institutions is to make farm size beyond a certain minimum level a somewhat less consequential and less urgent factor in production than in an earlier phase. These institutions and facilities are able to reach out to a growing number of farmers, specially in the middle range and the higher range of holdings. They are less able to serve very small farmers, at any rate, not without a great deal of effort. Depending upon conditions prevailing in a country or a region, there may be said to be a critical point below which small farmers must be brought together and organised if the institutions and services developed through planning are to serve them effectively. Whether cultivators are organised in co-operative farms or function independently, they are affected by such common factors as prices, market conditions and conditions of supply, but the impact of these on different groups of farmers varies greatly. If opportunities for very small and low income farmers are to be enhanced, some additional measures and policies have to be devised to serve their special interests.

Problems of the rural economy and of agricultural development extend beyond the traditional sphere of agricultural policy. Industrial inputs are a major element in the progress of agriculture. Similarly, education and social services and markets and communications are important ingredients in the scheme of rural development. Just as agriculture cannot be thought of in isolation from the other sectors of the economy, so also co-operative farming cannot be pursued in isolation from measures to develop co-operative institutions on a wider plane. Since co-operative activities shade into and supplement one another, there has to be a broad approach to co-operative farming. At each stage, it is necessary to identify and discover points of advance and points where different activities will link up with one another, so that the whole becomes larger than the sum of the parts.

III

In what has been said above by way of introduction, an attempt has been made to place co-operative farming in the perspective of overall growth and development. Against this background, in terms of experience gained in India, it is possible to consider the future approach to co-operative farming. A preliminary issue to be cleared is whether the pooling of lands is an essential element in co-operative farming. This question may be looked at from the point of view of what constitutes a production unit. By definition, a production unit has to have an integrated scheme of investment and returns and has to be so organised that the economies of scale and economies available in the use of labour, livestock and other resources may be obtained to the greatest extent possible. In a production unit the risks are spread over the operations of the unit as a whole. From this aspect, activities which fall short of the pooling of land, while being important in themselves and deserving of as much support as can be given, do not add up to co-operative farming. The holdings which together make up a co-operative farm should constitute a single organic unit for purposes of planning, investment and management.

The next issue to be considered is whether co-operative farming is intended only for very small and uneconomic farms or whether this is a concept with a wider application. In the thinking thus far under India's Five Year Plans, the approach has been that co-operative farming is required not merely for small and uneconomic holdings but, more comprehensively, for reorganising and strengthening the agricultural economy as a whole. There is a reason for this. Unless holdings of different sizes—large, medium and small—can come together, it is not possible to achieve a proper balance between the labour force and the land available. The additional land required may come from such sources as surplus land derived from the enforcement of land ceilings or through reclamation and development of waste lands. Where land is already under cultivation, there has to be encouragement for farms of different sizes to come together into co-operative production units. If we think of co-operative farming as being designed only for very small units, then it becomes essentially a welfare and rehabilitation measure and its economic significance in relation to the total agricultural objective and the total land surface on which crops are grown will be diminished.

In many parts of India, consolidation of holdings, that is, bringing together fragmented plots of land belonging to a farmer through an agreed scheme of exchange based on valuation of different classes of land in the village, is already a fully accepted idea. It has not been carried through in every part of India, but in some States much progress has been achieved. Looked at operationally, co-operative farming is but one stage beyond consolidation of holdings. It is only when the average farmer begins to think of co-operative farming as a method of organisation which he adopts because he feels that it will help him, will some of the overtones associated in the past with co-operative farming begin to disappear. Through the experience we have gained, one of our main tasks now is to make the idea of co-operative farming as simple and as logical and acceptable as the idea of consolidation of holdings has already become. Indeed, the scheme of consolidation of holdings should itself be regarded as a necessary element in the development of co-operative farming. Co-operative farming for any large proportion of farmers may take time to arrive. However, if fragmented holdings are consolidated and the principle is accepted that during consolidation operations those who wish to bring their lands into the same production unit may have them put together, subject to a fair deal for all, this would give strong support to co-operative farming.

If we look at any economy undergoing development, we shall see that many different kinds of organisations come into existence and function side by side, for instance, in industry and transport. Thus, there may be public enterprises, large private corporations, small units functioning on their own and others linked with larger units. A similar differentiation in patterns of organisation is to be expected within the rural economy once the process of development begins to go forward fast enough. There are two different lines of advance that we can anticipate. Firstly, within each area, a series of linkages develop between individual villages or groups of villages and the growing urban centres. Secondly, we may expect that, within the land area of each village, while many of the agricultural holdings will be cultivated by their owners, there are others whose owners will combine into co-operative production units. The first group will consist of peasant holdings, the second of co-operative units. Thirdly, planned development leads to the strengthening of local institutions such as village councils and similar bodies at higher levels. These function as civic authorities within certain defined fields and are also entrusted with economic and social responsibilities. Thus, at the village level, we may see functioning side by side the individual peasant sector in the rural economy, the co-operative sector and what may be called the community sector. Through the promotional and other efforts of village councils and higher level bodies and the working of various institutions and facilities, voluntary effort in the direction of co-operative farming can have a significant role as a spearhead in the scheme of agricultural advance for raising yields and introducing new technologies. For, we have now a frame of development and a set of developmental institutions capable of responding to the needs of the people at the local level. This makes co-operative farming, not merely a distinctive activity, but one which grows with the progress of community development and is itself an important means for enlarging community action. Into this wider effort fit village programmes, for instance, for the fuller use of rural manpower in the development of agriculture, in afforestation, soil conservation, adoption of improved techniques, local fuel plantations and extension of welfare services.

It is of the utmost importance that co-operative farming should not get isolated from the main stream of agricultural development. In fact, it should be looked upon as an important element in achieving new advances in agriculture, such as introduction of high yielding varieties, improvement of techniques, intensive use of manpower and others. In intensive agricultural areas, where conditions for agricultural growth are considered specially favourable, co-operative farming should come naturally and organically into the scheme of development. However, in co-operative farming, targets set from above have all the disadvantages and there is little to be gained in resorting to them. To grow to significant proportion, co-operative farming has to become a movement, with roots in the soil, which meets the genuine needs of the land and the people.

Pilot projects have an important role in the growth of co-operative farming. But they should be small enough in number to receive close attention and to become a method of solving practical problems and not merely a way of obtaining additional resources under the cover of some general schemes of assistance for the co-operative form of organisation. Pilot projects should truly involve the people and should become task-oriented, so that they can help find answers to specific questions which may otherwise prove baffling.

While there may be some personnel at a higher level taking specialised interest in co-operative farming, on the whole, the requirements of co-operative farming will be better met if the extension machinery at the field level serves simultaneously those farmers who work as individuals along with those who come together into co-operative units. The desirable course would be for all persons working on extension, whether in agriculture or co-operation or other allied areas, to go through a period of orientation in the methods and problems of co-operative farming as part of their training in general extension and in working with groups and individuals. Extension workers concerned with co-operative farming should not be merely advisers. They should be people living and working with cultivators. The notion of advisory and extension services in western countries was somewhat different, because there they were concerned with limited numbers of farmers who could read on their own, discuss their problems and indicate what they needed. In under-developed countries, extension workers must come very close to peasant communities and spend a great deal of time with them, understanding them intimately and educating and preparing them for the future. The more they themselves learn about and share life with the people, the more effective they will be as extension workers.

As stated earlier, co-operative farming is not merely meant for very small land holders. We may go further and suggest seven broad situations in which, at the present juncture, co-operative farming deserves to be placed in the forefront of agricultural development programmes. These are:

(1) areas in which new lands have been brought under irrigation for the first time. In such lands there is a call for new agricultural practices and new cropping patterns. If consolidation of holdings could be taken up simultaneously, ground would be prepared for an expanded co-operative effort. Co-operation in farming could then grow out of the experience of co-operation in many allied fields;

(2) areas in which sizeable land reclamation operations are organised;

(3) areas in which tenants and landless cultivators and small farmers are being brought together and organised for the first time in new communities;

(4) sizeable farms which may come into the possession of Government on account of the enforcement of land reform measures, as in the case of land belonging to sugar factories in Maharashtra;

(5) areas in which the man-land ratio is favourable to technological change, and small farmers and middle-sized owners may, through co-operative farming, obtain the benefits of rapid technological change which, in their individual capacity, only large farmers are in a position to secure for themselves;

(6) lands donated as *bhoodan* and *gramdan* under movements for the reconstruction of villages sponsored by Acharya Vinoba Bhave; and

(7) densely populated areas in which co-operative farming is not a development programme by itself, but part of a wider scheme for the strengthening and reorganisation of a weak and precarious rural economy. In these areas the development of agriculture and rural industry and the infra-structure constitute a single composite programme.

In the situations listed above, co-operative farming can be given a central role in agricultural development plans. In the measure in which success is attained in these areas, extension to others would become feasible. The contribution of co-operative farming can be further enhanced if, in drawing up plans for agricultural development in any region, close attention is given to its physical and agro-economic characteristics as a basis for crop planning and crop specialisation. Co-operative farms could help evolve appropriate crop patterns and agricultural practices as well as methods and techniques for the effective use and development of local resources.

IV

Once we are clear about the directions in which co-operative farming is likely to contribute best towards the speeding up of agricultural development, certain problems of public policy and of internal organisation and management become specially important. The Report of the Committee of Direction on Co-operative Farming has recently provided valuable guidance on questions of public policy.* Of these, one of the most important concerns is the provision of finance for co-operative farming societies on the part of co-operative institutions as well as on the part of Government. Other questions of great importance concern the nature of advisory extension services to be provided and the training to be given to workers and farmers. The need to link up social education programmes and programmes of vocational training for rural youth with co-operative farming should also be stressed. The Committee of Direction on Co-operative Farming has given close attention to conditions pertaining to membership, minimum size, accounting system and other aspects with a view to ensuring a framework of law and regulations within which abuse of facilities given to co-operative farms can be prevented.

Two other points should be stressed here. The first is that co-operative farming in any country cannot come about through the efforts of national and regional authorities alone. It is in the measure in which co-operative farming becomes an accepted part of the thinking and the practice of development at the local level that it will succeed in creating its own support from within the community. It is at this point that its roots have to be specially strong. Secondly, programmes for utilising rural manpower through rural works and provision of additional employment opportunities in the slack seasons, both for men and for women, are an essential condition for the success of co-operative farming.

Turning to the subject of internal organisation and management of co-operative farms, a few problems may be briefly mentioned. The first question to be considered is the

*Government of India, Ministry of Community Development and Co-operation, *Report of the Committee of Direction on Co-operative Farming*, (1965) pages 183-204.

manner in which rights of ownership are to be compensated for. Legislation for controlling rents provides some kind of upper limit to the amount which a co-operative farm may pay out by way of return for ownership. While such an upper limit is desirable and necessary, it is important to create incentives for diverting incomes derived from ownership to the maximum extent possible into investment in the development of the co-operative farm.

The next question concerns the manner in which work is to be rewarded. On paper it is possible to evolve elaborate systems of norms for different farm operations even where these are not mechanised. However, in many kinds of agricultural operations, it is difficult to provide for the elements of quality and personal attention through a system of work-norms to which remuneration for work done may be related. It is, therefore, a matter for serious consideration and for experiment whether groups of households could not be assigned specified areas of land to work on for which they would have responsibility for the entire range of operations. Frequently, plots of land falling within a co-operative farm are not situated at one place. Allowing for differences in soils and crop patterns, there might well be scope for suitable work units being marked out within the co-operative farm for operation by designated household groups. A great deal of adaptation and flexibility will be needed. What is certain is that anything like allotment of work from day to day or from week to week, without responsibility being clearly defined and a continuing link over the season or the year between work and reward being provided for, may prove to have strong disincentives built into it. Where responsibility for operating on an area of land is assigned to specified household groups, it should be possible for them to give almost as much attention to various operations as if the land belonged to them. Because of larger investment and more scientific agricultural practices, frequently they should be able to achieve higher levels of productivity and income than they might on their own. Inevitably, there are many problems of internal human and social relationships within a co-operative farm for which effective answers have yet to be found, and we have as much to learn from success as from failure. Three different series of studies of experience in co-operative farmings in India are now available. These and other examples should be probed more deeply. Concentrated attention to problems of internal management and operation in co-operative farms will throw up rewarding opportunities for creative and systematic experiment.

One of the dangers in any co-operative farming society is that the bulk of the members may come to be dissociated from running the affairs of the society. Much attention should, therefore, be given to ways in which members can be involved in various aspects of management. It is important that everyone should have some share in the running of one or other activity within the co-operative farm. For, ultimately, it is only under such conditions that the capacity of the community as a whole to manage its own affairs and reach higher levels of development and productivity can be raised. Co-operative farming societies undoubtedly require technicians, secretaries and other functionaries, but it is desirable that they should be chosen as far as possible from within the community and trained for specific tasks. To designate certain functionaries as *managers* is a course better avoided.

By its nature and purposes, a co-operative farming unit involves longer-term planning of production and measures to improve the land and, therefore, a higher rate of investment than could be achieved by most farmers on their own. Production plans for individual co-operative farming societies are best prepared and implemented within the framework of production and development plans for the local area and for the village as a whole. This would also make it easier for higher financing institutions like co-operative central banks and land mortgage banks to deal with the problems of finance in a more satisfactory manner and to meet the special requirements of co-operative farming units.

It should be observed, finally, that in approaching farmers and in bringing them together to form co-operative production units, it is essential to understand well the nature of the society we are dealing with and the nature of the economy of the area. While working at the village level, special attention should be given to the wider problems of the area such as those concerned with marketing, communications, credit and provision of supplies and inputs. Similarly, programmes for the development of education and other services should be an integral part of the scheme of work. When the people are drawn into co-operative activity, and specially into co-operation in production, they should be enabled to feel that they are not merging some agricultural holdings with others merely to constitute a co-operative unit, but are in fact entering upon a new course intended to strengthen their entire social and economic fabric and upon a larger scheme of effort of which they are and will continue themselves to be the masters.

8

ROLE OF THE COMMUNITY IN RURAL ECONOMIC GROWTH*

THE PROCESS of economic growth in the under-developed countries proves in practice to be much more complex than was assumed in the earlier stages of planning. There are no ready-made answers and many premises have to be modified as experience is gained and new problems arise. The first anticipations of the costs of development and estimates of the skills and organisation needed are found to be inadequate, and the period needed for basic changes in levels of living and of income and productivity frequently turns out to be longer. It is, therefore, of some importance to discover, test and give more definite shape to whatever elements in social and economic life may have a dynamic and forward-looking content and may be capable of bringing about greater mobilisation of the available resources. From this aspect, it is useful to explore whether, against the background of rural economic growth in India over the past decade, the 'community' at the village and local level could

*This paper was prepared for the meeting of the UNESCO Expert Working Group on Social Prerequisites to Economic Growth held at Kyrenia, Cyprus, in April, 1963, and is published by special agreement.

contribute more effectively to the acceleration of economic progress and, if so, under what conditions.

India has now completed a fair period of planned development. These years have been marked by considerable continuity in policy and approach and each important step has been broadly in sequence with the earlier steps though, necessarily, there have been changes in emphasis and fresh innovations have been introduced from time to time. From the beginning it has been stressed that the development of agriculture and of the rural economy was fundamental to overall economic progress. In principle, the priority for agriculture has never been in doubt. The connection between agriculture and industry has also been emphasised: without rapid agricultural development, industrial advance cannot proceed far, and without industrial production increasing, for instance, in steel, fertilizers and pesticides, the progress of agriculture is greatly impeded.

The community development programme, which was introduced in the early fifties, was symbolic of the value attached to the concept of 'community' in India's development plans. The basic assumption was that an integrated view of all aspects of rural life should be taken and that, organisationally, the life of the people should not be seen or dealt with in compartments. The rural development programme had, therefore, to be sufficiently composite to include both economic and social aspects. Secondly, an important role was assigned to community or group values at the village level, although it was realised that, as the peasant had to work and take risks largely on his own, individual incentives could not be ignored. It was thought that through the village panchayat the obligations of the community to the individual would be expressed with increasing coherence and that unutilised local resources could be tapped with greater effect. In the third place, the community development programme sought to provide a network of rural extension services for each development block (roughly 100 villages with a population of 60,000 to 70,000) supported by a group of village level workers.

To begin with, community development programmes were operated by teams of extension specialists at the block level under the leadership of a block development officer working with the local people and the local non-official leadership. During the past four years a new process has been at work, namely, the transfer of *responsibility* for development in each district and development block to democratically elected bodies, the Zilla Parishad and the Panchayati Samiti, with the village panchayat providing support at the base. This structure of democratic rural administration, along with the network of administrative and technical services established by the Government and voluntary and popular organisations like the co-operative movement which may be functioning in each area, are together described as Panchayati Raj. The introduction and extension of Panchayati Raj marks a major transformation in the scheme of administration within the district, assigns to the local people and the local leadership a clear and positive role as agents of social change, raises directly the question of harmonising local, State and national priorities and, finally, points sharply to the issue whether, under the conditions now envisaged, the local community will in fact be able to mobilise resources by way of manpower, organisation and capital formation which may otherwise be but thinly drawn into development. Would these developments, for instance, speed social change or would they retard it by giving greater influence to the existing leadership in rural areas ? Would they help achieve more comprehensive and continuous area development and greater interaction and impact *inter se* between rural and urban development in each area ?

The process of planning has brought with it new action

and policies over a wide front. Thus, it has involved attempts to reform the agrarian system, the primary aim being to establish a peasant economy shorn of feudal vestiges and capable of development along co-operative lines. The extension services which have been established are the means for transmitting improvements in technology, imparting skills and carrying the results of research to the field. New resources go into development from the side of the Government and, with its aid, also through the co-operative movement. Moreover, there is a qualitative change in farm management. Community development and extension throw open new opportunities to the local leadership. Such leadership may function on behalf of the entire group or may at first represent mainly greater initiative and a new outlook on economic development on the part of a small section of farmers. The institutions through which local leaders work have, however, a wider purpose and their concern becomes steadily larger in scope. The ethos of community development and of rural democracy is also in favour of extension from the notion of individual responsibility to that of social responsibility.

The characteristic 'village community' in India is a small and fairly homogeneous group composed of peasant cultivators, with some but often quite limited differentiation among them, and of smaller groups undertaking ancillary or even subordinate functions within the village economy, such as landless labourers, artisans or traders. There is interdependence between these various groups and, partly for this reason and partly from traditional ties, the village community can be often regarded as a social entity which may respond to new tasks and new opportunities by acting together in the common interest of all its members. At any rate, this is a major assumption in community development. It is not, of course, suggested that the village is not being influenced by powerful forces from within and without, or that there are not quite considerable differences between and within villages in different parts of the country. What is hoped for is that these differences will be taken into account in adapting the pattern of development to conditions in different areas and that elements in the traditional structure which are favourable to economic development will be further strengthened. In the early stages of development, factions in village life are found to be an obstacle to growth but, as these are essentially a facet of stagnation and backwardness, the hope is entertained that, with greater dynamism in the rural economy, their significance will diminish. Moreover, as the concepts of leadership and community organisation are broadened beyond the village to include larger areas such as groups of villages and development blocks, the civic aspects become more important, and some at least of the traditional distinctions will come to have less meaning.

With greater community action and responsibility at the village and local level, the stimulus to growth may arise in four principal ways:

(a) enabling each group (whether farmers or landless workers or artisans) to equip itself to share more fully in the benefits and opportunities which development offers;

(b) enabling small men in the community, specially when organised in co-operative and other associations, to obtain greater benefits from development;

(c) enlarging the total effort through the exploitation for accelerated development of the real resources of the community and, in particular, of manpower and unutilised time; and

(d) securing a higher rate of savings.

Greater capital formation, both in real and monetary terms, and wider transmission of developmental opportunities, would make for more rapid and broad-based economic growth. Systematic analysis, both of actual experience and of the precise steps and processes involved, would go some

11

distance in suggesting techniques and motivations for achieving these aims to a greater extent through integrated development at the village and block levels as part of the general scheme of planned development.

One of the conflicts met with in planning concerns the relative emphasis on the individual and the social approach. The latter is more difficult and there are resistances to be overcome; the former frequently promises early and noticeable results, specially in economic terms. In the provision of social amenities, differences between the two approaches are less marked, and community efforts are more easily mobilised. However, this itself may become a factor in diverting attention from productive efforts to perhaps less urgent social considerations. It has yet to be seen whether, by broadening rural democracy, it will become more difficult or less difficult to secure the degree of adherence to national priorities which constitutes an essential basis for economic planning.

Some elements in the problem of enlarging the role of the community for rural economic growth can be seen from four areas of development which have considerable significance, namely, (a) utilisation of irrigation facilities from newly constructed projects, (b) extension of credit to small farmers, (c) crop planning and (d) extension of technological improvements in agriculture. All these are among the urgent conditions of economic development in rural areas and in practice they have been met only partially. In each case, the primary conditions are: firstly, a clear recognition of the relative obligations and claims of the individual and the community; secondly, the role of public policy and administration, including extension; thirdly, a well-knit scheme of complementary investments by Government, the local community and the individual; and finally, utilisation of the manpower resources available. Moreover, it is essential to work out the specific methods and techniques which are most likely to achieve each given objective. Thus, evaluation of existing experience, analysis of the assumptions implicit in the stated objective, their translation into concrete administrative and economic terms, creation of the necessary social environment and some provision for experimenting with alternative approaches would all be important for formulating and carrying out schemes for enhancing the contribution of the community to rural economic growth. On these and other processes which are involved, those concerned with economic planning could benefit greatly from field studies and theoretical analysis undertaken by social scientists.

9

THE VILLAGE PANCHAYAT AND THE PATTERN OF VILLAGE DEVELOPMENT*

THE ATTEMPT to place the village panchayat at the centre of village development is in fact an effort to establish a new institution under an old name. The new panchayat and the old belong to different social settings and their aims, functions and implications are also different.

The village in which the old panchayat flourished was a more or less static society with few economic links beyond the nearest market town or fair. As a rule, it found its own food and materials for clothing and the bulk of its wants were met from within the neighbourhood. Its social structure comprised several strata, each distinct in its status and duties within the community. The various strata were, however, bound in a relationship of continuing inter-dependence and *at each level* there was a large degree of equality. This social pattern was accepted implicitly by all the sections within the village, including those who filled a subservient position. Because of this acceptance, in practice the institutions of the village remained in the care of those favoured by caste and property. They were the effective

*Adapted from a contribution published in *Economic Review*, All-India Congress Committee, New Delhi, Vol. VII, No. 15, December 1, 1955, pages 13-16.

village community. They functioned as a homogenous body with a common outlook and with values which had all the semblance of permanence.

It was this homogenous community which the village panchayat served for hundreds of years. The panchayat preserved the village from within, represented it to the ruler, chieftain or official who held for the time being the authority to impose the land tax and the power to punish. The panchayat was constituted informally as a matter of custom. Its members were the village elders whose word no one questioned; their numbers perhaps varied according to the needs of the occasion. The institution was rooted in the soil and served well the needs of a society sustained by custom and caste and largely autonomous in character.

Now that the village panchayat is being created afresh, the nature of the transition through which village society is passing should be appreciated. For several decades, as a well-knit *social* organisation, the village community has been slowly but steadily declining. As the pursuit of individual interest within and outside the village has become more common, the influence of the community over its members has diminished. The growth of inequality in the ownership of land, transfers of land to non-cultivators and migration to towns are evidence of these trends. Relatively to their population, villages in India are now more predominantly rural in their occupational structure than they were fifty or even twenty years ago. With the growth of population, the lack of continuous and full-time work opportunities has become more pronounced and some sections of the village community, such as small owners, tenants, labourers and artisans have suffered more severely than others.

Recent land reforms have sought to reduce inequalities in the ownership of land, but have yet to become effective. The old leadership in the village has been losing its position and influence without substantial signs of a new leadership stepping into its place. The institution of caste has less of its social incidence, but it may well be that the economic incidence of caste, being due to lack of independent means of production and lack of alternative opportunities for employment, is being accentuated, especially for the scheduled castes and other backward classes. There are some signs of increase in the productivity of land, but scarcely enough to make much difference to the problems of rural poverty. The economy as a whole has gone forward, but the gap between population and production has not yet noticeably narrowed.

In this situation, conflicts of interest within the village community have sharpened and the process continues. There are now few values which can be said to be common to the whole community, and certainly there is no common purpose which inspires all the sections equally. Many innovations benefit some, hurt others. As instances, one may cite the landlord's tractor and the electric connection which provides energy to the village entrepreneur's rice and flour mill. Progress and enterprise on the part of some proceed alongside greater pressure on others. The community as such seems to exert little influence over either trend.

Thus, the new village panchayat comes into being in a community which has lost much of the old belief in its unity and interdependence, whose members are becoming increasingly aware of their diversity of interests. It would seem that at the present time the foundations on which a structure of village democracy might be built are far from secure. In these circumstances, how far will the panchayat succeed as an instrument of economic and social development for the village?

Whether one thinks of the village panchayat as the first step in village development or as a spearhead of change and reconstruction, it will succeed in the measure in which

(a) it can function within a more or less homogenous social structure, in which different sections of the community are moved by common loyalties and urges, and (b) the economic basis of village life is expanded and strengthened. The first condition follows from the past history of panchayats and the demands now made upon them, the second from economic developments and growth of population over the past several decades. The essential issue, therefore, for those who wish to use panchayats as instruments of village reconstruction concerns, not so much their form and organisation (which are doubtless important) as the manner in which the two conditions mentioned above can be secured. What, then, are the principles of change which are inherent in the concept of village panchayat and constitute conditions for its fulfilment in the present day village ?

For the village panchayat to carry out the functions proposed for it, village society has to be transformed so that, on the one hand, it offers equality of status and opportunity to all its members and, on the other, it offers gainful employment to individual workers. Clearly, large disparities in the ownership of land are not consistent with these objectives, and limitation of individual holdings is a necessary condition of advance. Even if this aim were met, the distinction between those who have land and those who are without it, poor as many of the former might be, would still continue. The bulk of those who now cultivate land as owners and tenants would continue to do so although, as land reforms are implemented, an increasing number of tenants might become owners. By itself, redistribution of the lands of the larger owners, to which there will be no lack of claimants, can therefore make only a marginal contribution to improvement in the living conditions of the landless, especially the scheduled castes and other backward classes. To achieve this result is a larger and more difficult task than the corrrection of disparities; it calls for close integration of planning at the national level with the pattern of change in the rural economy in different regions.

A growing section of the rural population has inevitably to move to towns to take up new work. If, in the location of new industrial units, the need for a balanced economy in thickly populated regions is given proper consideration along with other relevant factors, the impact of industrialisation on the rural economy might be highly beneficial. In that event, movement out of villages, manpower training programmes as well as several other features of the process of development could be largely planned *pari passu* with the growth of industry. Even if the planning of the urban and rural economies were closely integrated, which is not yet the case, there would still be heavy burdens on the land. The vast majority of existing and potential workers in the villages would still have to find employment on land and in occupations which could be developed in the rural areas.

The role of the village panchayat and other village agencies in raising agricultural production is now appreciated, but there is no clear perception yet as to how and by whom new forms of work and service are to be developed within the village economy. New work opportunities in the village will not come by themselves or arise to any extent as a result of urban development and the enterprise of merchants, contractors and small entrepreneurs operating in rural areas. If, therefore, diversification of the village economy is not to be dependent merely on the secondary and indirect effects of industrialisation (for the most part concentrated in large towns remote from the average village), the village panchayat must take upon itself responsibility for creating and maintaining sufficient work opportunities.*

---

*In this context, in view of later developments, it would now be more appropriate to speak of Panchayati Raj institutions as a group and not only of the village panchayat.

In other words, in the development of resources and employment in various forms for the utilisation of locally available
manpower, local institutions have a crucial role.

At any time, even under favourable circumstances, such
an aim would be extremely difficult to achieve. Certain
external conditions would need to be at least congenial
to such local development. In the main, these are related
to the basis adopted for the location of industry, implementation of common production programmes for related
large and small industries, and the acceptance of co-operative
and public management as normal forms of organisation for
industries closely allied to the rural economy. Difficult as it
may be to bring about these external conditions, by themselves they will not be sufficient. Certain conditions internal
to the village economy also need to be created. These
concern organisation, technical change and property relations and can be briefly indicated.

Although, for many purposes, groups of villages rather
than individual villages constitute the appropriate planning
units, the concept of joint or co-operative village management is important for the further development of the rural
economy. It means that the land and all the resources of
the village are to be managed and developed in the interest
of the entire village community. That is to say, the village
as a whole is an economic unit in which agriculture and
other occupations are organised by or on behalf of the
community with the object of securing the maximum output
and employment. Within this unit, there should be room for
individual producers as well as for co-operative groups and
for positive planning for the community as a whole. At
present, whether an individual from a village has or is
equipped for gainful work or not depends largely on inheritance, accident of caste and/or other similar circumstance.
Under co-operative village management, the community
accepts responsibility for providing opportunities for gainful

work to all those workers who are in the village, are in need of work and are prepared to do whatever work can be made available. Such a responsibility entails also corresponding obligations on the part of individual members on which the community has to insist, the chief of them being hard and conscientious work.

To be able to provide a diversity of occupations, it is essential that the village economy should accept and develop new techniques. Rapid technical change, including the utilisation of power and of equipment involving larger quantities of steel, is basic to further progress. Technological change should, however, be conceived as an intrinsic and integrated aspect of social and economic change. This is quite different in principle and in social impact from the adoption by individual landlords or entrepreneurs of labour-saving devices in their own limited interest without concern for the well-being of those adversely affected by the more advanced technology. In other words, the application or extension of technology, itself a subject for planning and forethought, has an intimate connection with the development of local resources and the productive employment of village manpower.

Thus, in its wider sense, social change includes material changes in organisation and techniques and the rapid development of new work opportunities. In an under-developed country with a large amount of disguised un-employment, in which the institutions of the past frequently impede economic progress, social change can be greatly stimulated through changes in property relations carried through as an element in national planning. The possibilities of this idea have to be worked out and tested with care, but the action it implies is relevant in several fields of economic life. In relation to the ownership and management of land, for instance, such propositions as the following may be involved:

(i) Property held by any individual has to be limited. At what level the limit is set is determined by a variety of social, economic and political considerations;

(ii) Property is held by individuals on conditions laid down by the community. Thus, land may be held so long as it is cultivated by the farmer and his family, is not sub-let, and is managed in accordance with prescribed standards;

(iii) Land not cultivated by an owner and his family would ordinarily pass into the co-operative management of the village community; and

(iv) Besides individual farms and voluntary co-operative groups, within the economy of each village, there may be a sector of community ownership and community operation. The extent of the community interest and the manner in which it is expressed would vary with the nature of the activities which are undertaken.

The sector of community ownership and community operations could include (a) a proportion of the land of the village, and (b) common village undertakings such as a dairy, a fruit preservation plant, flour and rice mills, tube-wells, power distribution, small workshops and worksheds. Peasant farms under the cultivation of their owners have a place along with co-operative farms in a developing economy based on the democratic principle. They are, however, inadequate as a source of capital formation on any scale; in any event the majority of them have to struggle for their very existence. Without steadily increasing resources from within the village economy itself, even with some assistance from the State, it will be difficult to develop many new forms of work and service needed for employing the labour force of the village, which must remain an acute and growing problem even with rapid industrialisation. The community's pool of land might include, for instance, common lands, lands above any ceiling which is prescribed, lands not worked by their owners which might be acquired by the community, and lands which are gifted for the benefit of the landless. If those holdings which are altogether uneconomic are consolidated, they could also be worked together as part of or along with the community's pool of land.

The land which is owned and worked in common may have a great deal of significance, depending upon factors such as the quality of village management, the direction of land policy, the place assigned to rural industries in the scheme of national and regional planning, the manner in which large industries are located, the technical and financial assistance provided by the Government for the village, and the rate of growth of the national economy as a whole. In the first place, the co-operatively owned land of the village should be a source of capital formation and further investment. Secondly, since it will be necessary to secure the utmost economy in its operation and to maximise the net receipts, in working the co-operatively owned land, improved techniques and equipment should be adopted in keeping with the level of development of local skills. Thus, the large holdings represented by community lands and co-operative farms may become important means for technical change, taking the place, though with different results for the economy, of the substantial farmer. Technical improvements in one field call forth similar improvements in others. In the third place, the operation of co-operatively owned lands on behalf of the entire community should, on the one hand, give greater authority and initiative to the village panchayat in raising agricultural production and working out the scheme of co-operative village management and, on the other, it should provide some of the initial capital resources and incentives for developing new work opportunities within the village economy. Expansion of employment, introduction of new skills and new techniques and the strengthening of the village community will go a long way towards eliminating those disparities in status and opportunity which are already ceasing to be merely a social or economic problem. Thus, to get adequate results from the establishment of the new village panchayat, it is essential to view the institution as part of a larger process, namely, the fundamental reconstruction of social and economic relations within rural society and between rural and urban society.

10

THE LANDLESS LABOURER AND THE PATTERN OF SOCIAL AND ECONOMIC CHANGE*

I

AMONGST THE most critical problems which face several under-developed countries is the position of that section of the population commonly described as landless or agricultural labourers. Conditions in different countries are not of course identical, but many of the processes at work and the problems of policy are common enough to permit a fairly general analysis of the nature of the conflicts involved and the possible directions in which development could occur. In this paper some illustrative facts are taken from India, but the experience from which inferences are drawn extends over a wider field.

The 'level of development' of a country is a complex of several different social, economic and political elements and, just as there are vast dissimilarities between one under-developed country and another, within the same country also several different levels of development are to be found side by side. The problems of landless labourers are related, therefore, both to the growth of the economy of which they form

*Adapted from a contribution to the Third World Congress of Sociology, Amsterdam, 1956. See *Transactions*, Vol. II, pages 278-88.

part and to the existence of varying levels of development within the economy. The factors which determine the overall rate of economic development and those which influence relative levels of development within a country are in part independent, in part dependent on one another. In the past there was little conscious attempt to relate the two. In the conditions of India and other countries similarly placed, it is the purpose of planning to achieve a high rate of economic growth and, at the same time, to ensure that various sections of the population do not long remain at such varying levels of development and standards of living and culture as to render the entire social structure unstable.

This is the crux of the problem of development in South Asia. There may be several measures of success or failure, but from many points of view the future of landless labourers will serve as one of the surest tests and may well prove to be a decisive factor in determining the approach and methods which will eventually prevail. It is not generally appreciated how large a stake the community as a whole has in what becomes of landless labourers in the next few years. Many of the major challenges with which India and several other countries are confronted express themselves in their most concentrated form in the conditions and immediate prospects of landless labourers. Current challenges may be better understood if seen against the background of the social processes which have been in operation over several decades. These could perhaps be grouped conveniently under four heads: impact of the west, development of indigenous capitalism, growth of population and increasing disintegration of the rural social structure.

II

In relation to landless labourers, all these processes together converge at two principal points—place in the social structure and employment opportunity. The impact of the west upon the village came slowly and indirectly. Western goods, supported as they were by the prestige of alien rule, gradually broke down the self-sufficient and interdependent character of the village economy. New goods introduced into the village through the pedlar and the merchant reduced the demand for goods produced in the village, thus taking steadily increasing proportions of artisans into the ranks of agricultural labourers. Western ideas of property, born of nineteenth century laissez-faire and competition, along with the growth of the money economy, introduced something new into the village—the acquisitive spirit, the element of exploitation, under legal cover, of the weak by the strong, wealth and income as the scale of values, and a decline both in the sense of social obligation and in the claims of the community upon the individual. Seeds sown under the influence of the west flourished through indigenous agencies and developed a life of their own. New towns sprang up and old towns expanded through export of raw materials and import of manufactured goods, development of communications and the growth of settled administration. In these conditions, an internal capitalism emerged, its three main elements being foreign interests engaged in trade and industry, Indian merchants who took to industry and found steady support in nationalism, and rural capitalism expressed through the growth of money-lending as well as landlordism. Establishment of oil mills, rice mills and flour mills in rural areas and trade in the products of new industries seeking out the rural market reduced both full-time and part-time traditional work opportunities. Rural capitalism reinforced feudalism and turned sections of peasant owners into tenants and tenants into casual labourers.

The growth of population accentuated the economic effects of western economic influence as well as of indigenous capitalism. During the past sixty years or more, the population dependent on agriculture has increased, not diminished. Between 1931 and 1951 the population dependent on agriculture is estimated to have increased from 193 to 250 million.* The growth of trade and industry has fallen considerably short of increase in population. New techniques destroyed existing work opportunities to an extent greater than those they created. In this phase, the classes benefiting from change were largely different from those injured by it, who were more numerous and stood lower in the social and economic scale. For a long time this aspect was not clearly perceived, and even scholars placed greater emphasis on the benefits of the new developments. Mahatma Gandhi had the insight to see through the situation, but its leading facts had not been adequately ascertained by social scientists. In India, information showing the present position first became available through the Agricultural Labour Enquiry carried out by the Ministry of Labour in 1950-51, which entailed the study of conditions in about 800 villages of 104,000 families, of whom 11,000 were agricultural labourers. A few facts thrown up by this enquiry may be cited briefly to illustrate the social and economic situation which now exists in India's villages, a situation which has parallels in varying degrees in several other countries in Asia.

The size of a problem turns in part on the definitions which are followed, and few definitions are altogether complete. In the Agricultural Labour Enquiry, an agricultural labourer was a person who for more than one-half of the total number of days on which he actually worked during the year worked as an agricultural labourer. On this definition, of the rural families studied, 30·4 per cent were agricultural labourers, one-half of them being without land, and the rest being in possession of some land. As many as 85 per cent of the agricultural labourers had only casual work,

*By 1961, this rose to about 310 million.
12

mostly in connection with harvesting, weeding, preparation
of the soil and ploughing. The average annual income
per family was Rs. 447, which was eked out in various
ways. The average per capita income was Rs. 104 per annum,
compared to the national per capita average in the same
year of Rs. 266. The extent of employment varies under
different conditions in various parts of the country, the
average being 218 days in the year, 189 days in agricultural
work and 29 days in non-agricultural work. Thus, there
was work for wages for about seven months in the year,
total unemployment for rather more than three months
and some kind of self-employment for less than two months.
As 15 per cent of the 'attached' agricultural workers had
employment for 326 days, the average for the rest was
only 200 days in the year. The reason given for being
unemployed on more than 74 per cent of the days on
which casual workers had nothing to do was merely 'want
of work'. Some 16 per cent of the agricultural labourers
had no wage-earning employment at all during the year.
This is a measure of the chronic unemployment which exists
in addition to the under-employment mentioned above.*

The Agricultural Labour Enquiry was concerned primarily
with certain economic aspects, but the social disabilities

---

*In the Second Enquiry into Agricultural Labour in India (1956-57), an
agricultural labour household was defined as one for which the major source
of income during the previous year was agricultural wages. On this definition,
against 66·6 million rural households, 16·3 million or 24·6 per cent were
agricultural labour households. Of these, 57·1 per cent had no land and
42·9 per cent had some land, owned or leased. Of the agricultural labour
households, 73·4 percent were engaged in casual labour and 26·6 per cent
were attached labourers. The average annual income per family in 1956-57
was Rs. 437. The average income per capita was Rs. 99·4 per annum, compared to the national average in the same year of Rs. 283. There was no
improvement over the employment situation revealed in 1950-51, although
the data are not easily comparable. The quantum of average employment
available to casual adult male agricultural workers in 1956-57 was 197 days
compared to 200 days at the earlier enquiry.

and the subordinate social position of the bulk of agricultural labourers are in themselves no small part of the
problem. A proportion of agricultural labourers are dis-
possessed peasants and artisans partially or wholly without
work in their own trades. The vast majority, however,
belong to castes which have long been in the lower rungs
of the social structure and were expected to stay there
permanently. Gradually, as a result of reform movements
and changing attitudes to caste, the social handicaps have
tended to diminish. This trend has, however, served to throw
into sharper relief the economic problem of finding adequate
work opportunities for the mass of the people in the villages.
Elimination of social disabilities remains only a partial and
incomplete process unless employment can be found for
all who are willing to work. As at present organised, the
village economy is incapable of fulfilling this condition.
A substantial section of farmers live on the margin of
subsistence. The obligations which bound farmers and
village servants and labourers together in the traditional
village society have disappeared to a considerable extent.
Old values are under constant challenge and traditional
occupations which implied a low social status, such as the
removal of carcasses or scavenging, are often given up
by castes associated with them. Thus, the bulk of agricultural labourers are no longer an intrinsic and essential
part of the scheme of production and of social life in the
village. This brings the whole social order to the point at
which radical departures become inevitable, although the
direction is yet far from certain.

III

What new relationships will take the place of the old ?
On what basic principles will the new scheme of society be
based ? What will be the instruments and processes through

which the change-over will take place ? What manner of transition to a new social and economic order will it be possible to achieve ? These are open questions in India and several other countries in Asia. They do not admit of simple answers, and the course of events may be shaped to no small extent by a whole range of factors beyond the scope of planning. Yet, fundamental issues are involved, and they need to be uncovered. The surprises of history are only sometimes the result of our inability to see the elements of a situation in time; more often, they flow from failure to take the practical steps needed.

In India and other countries in South Asia, the solution of most problems, whether social, economic or political, will turn on the measure and the manner in which the conditions of an expanding economy come to be established. The experience of western countries since the early nineteenth century and the more concentrated economic development in the Soviet Union and in countries in Eastern Europe have valuable lessons, and the technical and scientific knowledge of the west is an important asset, but much of the philosophy of social action has to be thought out afresh. Institutions and incentives cannot be transplanted, and there has to be conscious effort to fuse the techniques built up in the west with the cultural background and the aspirations of the common people. Problems of mass poverty in India and other countries in similar circumstances can be traced to various factors many of which have been at work over a long period. They can be solved only through sustained and continuous endeavour, through patiently building up new institutions serving the welfare of the entire community, and through the harnessing of modern knowledge. More prosperous countries can no doubt assist, but in each country the effort and the bulk of the resources must come from the people themselves. Concepts such as class war will gain force if the effort ends in failure; at this stage, however, they are not indispensable tools of social and economic change.

The requisites for the solution of a problem as large and complex as that of landless labour in circumstances such as prevail in India are, therefore, peaceful and continuous development, a rapid rate of economic growth and early changes in the social structure. The attempt to achieve these three aims at the same time through democratic means lends to India's planning special interest and significance and also puts the entire approach to test under circumstances which, though difficult enough, are yet favourable if considered against the background of the rest of Asia. The approach and the methods are still no more than an outline; as concrete problems are faced, out of the clash of opinion, clearer definition emerges, sometimes as doctrine, more often by way of empirical programmes undertaken in the spirit of experiment. Behind many of the problems around which the method of democratic planning is taking shape are the following basic issues:

(1) Economic growth requires technical progress. Unless the economy is expanding sufficiently rapidly, technological progress leads to unemployment, not only among those following the traditional techniques but also in organised and established industries. To integrate technological change into the scheme of development and to ensure that inequalities and disparities are not created by it are problems of primary importance.

(2) A high rate of economic development demands a high rate of capital formation. In some western economies private savings—the savings of private firms who are free to make large profits and of private individuals who are free to earn large incomes—account for a considerable proportion of the capital formation which takes place. To create these conditions in South Asia or to let them continue to the extent they exist would lead, in the judge-

ment of experienced observers, to such reactions as would reduce seriously the possibility of democratic methods being given time enough to prove themselves. On the other hand, complete ownership of the means of production and State control of all trading activity provides no doubt for a great deal of capital formation but exacts a stern price in other ways. In South Asia, a middle way is to be sought— expansion of public savings, building up of a large co-operative sector, mobilisation of the savings of peasants, workers and other persons of small means, and a degree of direction of the savings which arise in the organised private sector. Where precisely is the line to be drawn now and in the future between the different elements of this composite approach? The question bears on the magnitude of capital formation and, more pointedly, on the agencies chosen for achieving economic development. What should be the relative place of the public sector, the co-operative sector, the organised private sector and the small, independent entrepreneur? The proportions are not static, but ordered development implies a firm sense of direction and steady progress towards the accepted goals.

(3) In a relatively static society, for most individuals their occupation is a way of life. In the making of a progressive society, incentives have a vital role. What makes an individual give of his best ? Every social system has to evolve its own scheme of incentives according to its cultural background and its leading aims. Incentives constitute a complex subject, but in practical terms one could perhaps think of them as falling into five main categories, namely (i) the incentive of property, (ii) the incentive of income, (iii) the incentive of social recognition, (iv) the incentive of power, and (v) the incentive of social obligation and philanthropy. In different fields of activity, one or the other combination of these incentives may be found to produce the results which a community desires. What should be the

place of each of these incentives in the pattern of social and economic development of India and other countries similarly placed?

(4) Equality of opportunity is a feature common alike to the free enterprise system of North America, the welfare state which has grown up in Western Europe and the socialist economies. This characteristic is yet missing in India and in most other countries in Asia. Equalisation of opportunities depends no doubt to some extent on the rate of economic growth and the size of the national income, but it cannot wait until a country is rich enough to afford, according to its circumstances, a fair chance to all its citizens. The responsibility for bringing about equalisation of opportunity rests squarely upon the State. There are several aspects of this process which could be distinguished such as, for instance,

(a) changes in property relationships, as in land reform and other measures aiming directly at redistribution of existing wealth;

(b) transfer of resources from the more well-to-do sections of the community to the less well-to-do through expansion of social services, taxation and other means;

(c) measures to ensure that a relatively larger proportion of the addition to the income of the community goes to those sections of the population who are at present in a position of disadvantage; and

(d) changes in status and human relationships through the operation of political, social and economic forces.

IV

The questions which have been posed above can admit of a variety of answers. Certain strands may be observed in most of the developed economies, but historical factors and the cultural and economic background have played a large part. They furnish an explanation of differences in emphasis and in the rates of economic change, for instance, in North America, Western Europe and the Soviet Union. India and many other countries in Asia, now set on the path of development, have an opportunity to create social and economic patterns suited to their own needs and conditions. They have a more difficult task than the western countries because their problems are more complex and they have less time in which to solve them. Their primary aims are, firstly, to secure economic growth and social change through peaceful and democratic methods and, secondly, so to organise the process of development that landless labourers, small peasants and others of small means receive early relief and have a creative, positive role in the building up of the economy. One cannot say how far these aims will be realised. It may, nevertheless, be possible to suggest the lines on which, in view of the economic, social and political problems which face countries in South Asia, the latter are most likely to fulfil their object. The economies of these countries are vulnerable in many ways, above all from within, so that they need to conserve their resources in personnel and social goodwill no less than in material terms. They can neither spread their development over too long a period, nor see it taking place in a cycle of jerks forward and backward. From this aspect the paths which India and other countries might choose, in so far as the choice lies with them, could be briefly suggested.

These countries seek development, not in isolation, but as parts of an interdependent world economy. This very fact has important implications for them as well as for the more advanced economies of the west. Secondly, since so large a proportion of their population lives in villages and depends on the land, increase in agricultural production and reorganisation of the rural economy have for them a significance at least equal to (and in fact much greater than) that of industrial development. In the third place, for these countries, the development process represents not only the pursuit of economic objectives but also a choice of the methods of social change. The process will succeed in the degree in which social and economic aims are in harmony with one another and are effectively supported in terms of political and administrative action. These considerations will largely determine the answers to the various questions which have been suggested earlier.

The problem of landless labour, because of its very magnitude, is symbolic of the lack of adequate employment opportunities which marks under-developed economies in Asia. Fear of increasing unemployment, therefore, exerts a dominant influence on the approach to technological change. It is recognised that technical progress lies at the root of economic expansion and technical and scientific knowledge has to be fully harnessed for basic industries and large construction works as well as in the service of the small man, be he peasant or artisan or independent organiser of small-scale enterprise. The utilisation of new techniques has, however, to be a process conceived and planned so as to keep in view the community's limited capital resources. The pace and direction of technological change have to be so guided and regulated that those following the older techniques have time and opportunity to improve their methods and organisation and are not merely thrown out of work with little else to turn to. In the sector of modern industry, the presumption must be in favour of advanced techniques except where overall policy calls for protection for a transitional period in the interest of those engaged in village and small industries or where sudden displacement of labour is likely to upset labour-management relationships and even affect the total volume of production.

To the extent the public and the co-operative sectors expand, the gains of technical progress go directly to the community, thus increasing its ability to undertake further investment. An important factor in the psychological resistance which technological changes frequently arouse comes from the fact that they intensify the conflict of interests within the economic structure. Instead, in a planned society, they should be undertaken so as to enlarge the economic base and increase the production potential of the community as a whole and, therefore, its capacity to create greater employment. This view of technological change involves apparent compromises which are less easily understood in the west, but are in fact an essential aspect of public policy for minimising social tensions in the interest of ordered development.

Forms of economic organisation which grow up in one period are often challenged in the next. In a democratic society, as new interests begin to express themselves, economic institutions have to respond to new claims. In India, as in several other countries, until political freedom was gained, many of these claims were held back mainly because the interests they represented were not sufficiently organised. Once the urgent political problems of freedom are out of the way, the scene shifts and economic and social questions come to the forefront. There are at least two tests which economic institutions such as the managing agency system or the joint stock company or the entrepreneur have to satisfy in respect of past performance as well as promise for the future. Have they brought about or will they be able to bring about a rate of development sufficient to meet the growing needs of the economy ? Will their operations lead to greater equality of opportunity or to greater disparities in wealth, income and status ? On these tests, despite such contribution as they have made, the indigenous capitalistic systems which have developed during the past several decades have been found to be wanting. It is, therefore, necessary to re-examine the fundamentals of economic organisation in relation to the problems of mass poverty, growing population and widespread lack of work.

It is common judgement that while private enterprise has a part to play, especially in the development of small and medium industries, the State has to undertake or initiate heavy industries, the manufacture of a great deal of machinery and the development of natural resources. As the years go by, over a large field, social forms of management may be expected to replace private management. Although the role of the State is central to all planned development, it is hoped to build up an economic system in which forms of organisation are diversified and there is a great deal of decentralisation of initiative and resources. Changes in the existing pattern will necessarily be in the direction of an expanding public sector. The combination of economic and political power which occurs when most activities in which men engage are under the control of the State is to be avoided. Instead, between the public sector and a re-organised private sector, a large co-operative sector has to be envisaged. The latter should embrace much of agriculture, rural trade and village and small industries and should be large enough to account for one-third to one-half of the national output. Closely allied to the co-operative sector is the establishment of institutions to provide credit, technical advice and common services to assist small and medium-sized activity in industry and trade. In this scheme of organisation, there is perhaps enough internal balancing between different kinds of social and private management and the relative claims of individual initiative, group organisation and State control.

The direction of investment and the distribution of income resulting from such a structure may well be on the lines desired. It has, however, to be seen whether, taking all aspects together, a mixed economy with the balance strongly tilted in favour of the public and the co-operative sectors, can provide a sufficiently high rate of capital formation, call forth the degree of effort associated with a system based on profit, and ensure such increase in national production as will succeed in eliminating the spectre of poverty and unemployment. Before these questions can be answered, more experience of working the new institutions is needed, but it is useful to remind ourselves of the test of practical achievement to which all ideas and institutions must sooner or later submit. At present, too little is known, for instance, of the role of incentives in relation to economic development—incentives not only for entrepreneurs and men of property but for rural and urban workers, for consumers and for technicians and managers, all of whom have a vital share in building the future.

The question of incentives comes close to the foundations on which an economic system rests. In the life of a community all the incentives which were listed earlier—property, income, social recognition, power and social obligation and philanthropy—are needed, but the institutional structure in different countries could place greater emphasis on some than on others. Property and income are related concepts, one being convertible into the other. In the rural sector, with the progress of land reform, there is expectation of a degree of redistribution of property and, consequently, of incomes. In the villages, one expects to see steady growth in economic activities undertaken not only on the basis of mutual aid but also in terms of community ownership and operation of land and other resources. Under certain circumstances, redistribution of land could affect large numbers of persons in the rural areas. The question, however, arises whether changes in property relationships do not have to be extended also to the urban sector. Here the forms of property are more varied and the problem is much more difficult to handle; there is also a greater degree of hesitation. On the whole, although detailed steps need to be worked out, it is difficult to avoid the broad conclusion that the principle of limitation of property or wealth which any individual can hold has to apply equally to the rural as to the urban sector.

The strength of the incentive to property may diminish as development proceeds, but the incentive of income or of reward for work done is likely to become more important and more potent. Of all the incentives, income is the most universal and requires a well-considered approach. In a society which lays stress on equitable distribution, the higher incomes cannot be too far out of step with the average. The principle of limitation has, therefore, to apply to all incomes, but the means of enforcing it are likely to be indirect rather than direct. Of the other incentives, social obligation and philanthropy need to be specially stressed. They are both important because they are the basis of co-operative self-help and voluntary service, which are among the leading social values of a truly democratic society. In an expanding economy, along with changes in property relationships, nothing is so important for the welfare of peasants and landless workers as the organisation of co-operative community effort. The value of social recognition as an incentive is much greater than is commonly appreciated, and here useful lessons can be drawn from the experience of the Soviet Union and of countries in Eastern Europe since the war.

For the mass of the population and, specially for those who count among the have-nots of society, all public policies are ultimately reflected in the measure in which in practice equality of opportunity comes to be realised. Extension of social services and, in particular, of educational opportunities is the positive side of the programme. Without reduction in disparities in wealth and income, however, progress in the direction of equalisation of opportunity will be slow, probably much too slow to be felt. Limitation of property and incomes is also necessary if more equal human relationships are to be brought about and barriers between man and man reduced. There need be no conflict between the democratic approach and essential reforms in the social and economic structure. Indeed, in the conditions of India and several other countries in Asia, they are both essential aspects of the same process.

Planned development places a great deal of initiative and responsibility on the State and its administrative apparatus. In any under-developed country, social forces, economic policies as well as political pressures turn largely on one or the other aspect of the developmental process, and various aspects are inter-related. The key to the solution of any major problem is continuity of action at every plane. This is specially true of a problem like landless labour whose far-reaching implications have been briefly set out in this paper. Continuity of action turns largely on the working of the political system, so that a crucial test of the democratic approach in India and other countries in South Asia lies in its ability to sustain over many years, with the general support of the people, adequate developmental effort and stable policies for economic and social change. It is not possible to say yet whether this test will be met successfully but, while the endeavour proceeds, especially in India, it is well for students in the more advanced countries to appreciate the differences in the pattern of development and in the outlook upon technological change and upon property, enterprise and incentives which flow from conditions which exist in South Asia, and to consider how the search on the part of countries like India for economic stability and rapid social change as part of a well-knit world economy can be best assisted.

11

HARNESSING LOCAL RESOURCES*

IN EVERY endeavour, from time to time, it is necessary to go back to first premises, to the original insights and expectations. This is specially important where the drive and stimulus have come largely from without, from compulsions which have been given form and substance by the government or by external agencies. It is in the nature of such action that the end should tend to gain primacy over the means adopted and over the process through which development actually occurs. Of the steps initiated during the past decade and more, none has greater or more wide-ranging significance for the future than the expansion of community development and extension services to cover the entire countryside. Yet, reflecting over this period, one cannot but feel disturbed that community development should have become so much more a pattern of rural administration than a movement with roots in the hearts and experience of the people, bringing out their best by way of co-operation and mutual self-help.

The value of community development as the nucleus for local planning and for coordinated action on the part of all

---

*Adapted from a contribution to *Building From Below: Fiscal Policies and Economic Growth*, 1965, Sarva Seva Sangh, Bombay.

agencies, official and non-official, is not to be under-
estimated. But, by itself, this will not ensure the continuance
of community development or its fulfilment as a living
concept with seeds within it of growth and capacity to serve
the social, economic and emotional needs of local communities. The question may, therefore, be asked how best
community development, which has increased so greatly
in size and range of operations, may now be helped to look
inward, to seek new strength from the soil, to become a
deeper, more real, more satisfying approach than we know
it to be at present. A social idea has vitality in the degree
in which it has both inner content and physical proportion.
From now on, if community development is to grow in
significance, the place given to it by the State or in planning
will count for much less than the quality of service it comes
to represent and its ability to motivate and inspire individuals
and groups to new effort.

The intrinsic and continuing appeal of community
development will depend, perhaps more than on any other
circumstance, on the manner and measure in which it grows
on the basis of self-reliance and succceeds in harnessing
local manpower and other resources within the community. Harnessing of local resources is a familiar thought
which needs to be spelt out. We should visualise the problem
for a local community, whether rural or urban, for an area
such as a development block or groups of blocks and,
finally, in the larger context of regional and national
development.

In the vast majority of Indian villages, local resources
may take primarily the form of (a) land, including flora and
fauna, (b) water, (c) manpower, (d) cattle wealth and (e)
wastes and by-products of different kinds. At a given
moment, under the technology and organisation in vogue,
these local resources may have developed to a certain level
of productivity and efficiency. They may or may not be

fully employed even in terms of this level of productivity. There may be large variations in the levels of productivity attained by different farmers or groups of farmers in the community or for different classes of land or even for lands in the same class. Thus, within the existing and known levels of efficiency and technology, the village community may have a considerable 'reserve' to draw upon. But the scope for *raising* the level of productivity may be very substantial. This may imply fuller development of natural resources, of higher skills, of improved technologies, of better organisation. The extent to which local resources are harnessed should then be thought of in relation to these higher and attainable levels of productivity. Both in terms of the existing and the potential levels of productivity, the *utilisation* may fall short of what is technically possible. This is another form of 'reserve' which can be drawn upon.

Thus, in the abstract, in respect of any local resource, be it land or water or manpower or animal power or technology, there is (a) considerable scope for growth and development and (b) considerable scope for fuller utilisation, firstly, in terms of the existing levels of productivity reached within the community and, secondly, in terms of potential and progressively attainable levels of productivity. To get to higher levels of productivity will involve many changes in economic and social organisation, will call for new and large investments and, above all, will demand education in the widest sense. That is to say, within the local community, all the processes of social change and development of resources and skills have to be brought into focus simultaneously, in unison, and in terms of cumulative growth. For these processes to succeed, there has to be continuous interaction between the skills and resources available to a local community from within, and technical knowledge and capital resources which can be introduced from outside the community. Since there are limits to what a few hundred, or even a

13

few thousand persons can do for themselves, the notion of
'local community' has to be broadened to cover a larger area,
for instance, a development block or a group of blocks or
a district. For many purposes, though not for all, such an
area may provide an adequate unit for the development of
local resources and by way of skills and technology. Even so,
it would be necessary to attract from outside still higher
levels of expertise and technology and to secure larger investment resources. In other words, on the one hand, it is
necessary to envisage the local community and the area of
which it forms part as self-reliant entities and, on the other,
there is the deliberate effort to enlarge local skills and resources and achieve high levels of productivity through the
injection of resources in skill, technology, capital and organisation from without. In the measure in which the two sets
of processes are firmly established and go forward largely on
their own momentum, as movements rooted in the capabilities and motivations of the people, the objectives of
community development can be more fully realised.

Though man is the key to the harnessing of local resources,
first a few words may be said about land. Efforts to transform
agriculture have relied hitherto largely on the spread of
irrigation, on the development of the potentially available
water resources. Substantial gains in productivity have
come from this source. Farming under conditions of controlled irrigation facilitates changes in cropping patterns
and greater diversification. Differences in yields between
irrigated lands are necessarily narrower than those between
irrigated and unirrigated lands. Many improvements in the
system of cultivation can only be realised if there is assured
irrigation. However, even with irrigation, the really high
yields will come only if, at the same time, local resources are
fully harnessed. These may take the form of fuller use of
manpower, for instance, for digging field channels, for more
scientific irrigation or for more intensive working of the

soil; or they may take the form of more efficient use of village wastes for building up the fertility of the soil. Just as the productivity of land and the productivity of man can be progressively enhanced so also, within wide limits, there is increasing scope for fuller and more productive utilisation of local manpower and other resources.

Perhaps the most difficult part of the problem of rural change consists in the fact that the existing land system, the size and distribution of agricultural holdings, the fragmented nature of agriculture, the dependence on land and the existence of sizeable populations who are landless and are dependent mainly on operations ancillary to agriculture together make for relatively low levels of productivity for land and labour, leave considerable reserves of idle time, and limit the extent to which the available wastes may be productively utilised. The task of harnessing local resources has, therefore, to be approached from many sides. At the very centre we must place measures to raise the productivity of land, through extension of irrigation, more efficient use of water, application of fertilizers and scientific methods of agriculture and building up of the fertility of the soil. These measures must be supported by steadily improving technology and better organisation of credit and marketing as well as by better communications.

The existence of disguised unemployment on a large scale makes it imperative that, along with efforts to strengthen agriculture and, over a period, to build more non-agricultural activity into the rural setting, there must be intensive programmes for utilising the available manpower, specially during the slack agricultural seasons. Through such programmes agricultural development can be accelerated, rural communications improved, community assets created and the rural environment changed, for instance, through planting of trees and provision of better living conditions. In thinking of manpower and devising programmes for the better utilisation of human resources, it is necessary to consider not only what men can do but also what women can do in or nearer the home. At first one may see the problem of manpower, more or less, in terms of hours of labour available for gainful employment but, more and more, the utilisation of manpower resources must be conceived of in terms of rising skill and productivity. Therefore, the more efficiently we seek to use manpower, the greater will be the proportion of investment in equipment, technology and organisation.

To harness local resources, it is not enough to consider only land and manpower. Through the better organisation of the rural economy, the development of animal husbandry, dairying and milk supply and the promotion of ancillary and processing industries, there is also enormous scope for enlarging cattle wealth, making cattle far more productive, and reducing the burden of inefficient and unprofitable animals. Similarly, the problem of utilisation of village wastes, specially of animal manures and human manures, is also primarily one of organisation. Once the standard of agriculture begins to rise, all forms of waste materials become too precious to throw away. Through planned planting of trees and supply of soft coke, it should be possible largely to eliminate the use of cow-dung as fuel. Through a widespread movement for rural latrines, not only could living conditions be improved, but valuable manures could be conserved for use on the land.

To sum up, to organise effectively for the harnessing of local resources should be regarded as the essential foundation of all rural planning. The tasks involved go far beyond marginal improvements in the use of land or of manpower and other resources. Step by step, they entail reorganisation of the land system, greater understanding on the part of the people of each village and area of what they can do for themselves, the linking of local efforts and the intensive use of local resources with wider schemes of area and resource development, introduction of new techniques and practices, and capital investment on a large scale. Community development and the patterns of rural change embodied in our national plans will succeed in the measure in which development of local resources—land, manpower, skills, cattle wealth and wastes and by-products of all kinds—becomes an organic and purposeful element in the entire scheme of planning within each area and each community.

12

RECONSTRUCTION OF TRIBAL ECONOMIES IN THE HILL AREAS OF ASSAM*

THE COURSE of history, specially since the Partition of the sub-continent and even more during the past few years, has given to the north-east region of India and its people a crucial role. The region may be said to comprise Assam, including both the hill districts and the plains, Nagaland, Manipur, Tripura, NEFA and the districts of Darjeeling, Jalpaiguri and Cooch Behar in West Bengal. It has a population of 17·5 million or about 4 per cent of India's population and an area of about 265,000 square kilometers or about 8 per cent of the country's total area.

---

*This paper is based in large part on the findings of a Joint Centre-State Study Team which toured the hill areas of Assam early in 1966 and with which the writer was associated. The observations of the Team were reported at a meeting of the Members of the Assam Legislative Assembly at Shillong in March, 1966. They were also presented by the writer in a paper on Development of Tribal Economies at a seminar in Calcutta in December, 1966, devoted to the Hill People of North-Eastern India. The work of the Study Team formed the basis of the plan of development for the hill areas of Assam which was formally acccepted by the Planning Commission and the Government of Assam for the period 1966-67 to 1970-71. For implementing the plan, the State Government set up a special Planning Board. See, *A Common Perspective for North-East India* (1967), ed. Pannalal Das Gupta, pages 200-208.

The challenging problems and the opportunities which the region presents are far greater than these statistics may suggest. The setting in which nature has endowed the region with its hills and plains, the relationship between these in physical and ecological terms, the vast natural resources waiting to be developed and the cultural richness and diversity of the people, constitute fascinating features. The hill areas of the region, in particular, raise urgent problems of economic and social development and of political justice which have still to be resolved. These too are products of the facts of geography as well as of culture and history, and it is imperative to lose no time in taking all steps necessary to bring the economic and cultural needs and the political aspirations of tribal communities living in the hill areas into complete harmony with the needs and aspirations of the country as a whole. While the broad answer lies in an integrated and intensive approach to the economic and development problems of the north-east region as a whole, accompanied by the maximum opportunity in political terms to the people, more specific solutions have to be found for individual tribal groups. The Assam hill districts—Mizo Hills, Garo Hills, Mikir and North Cachar Hills and Khasi and Jaintia Hills—which together account for about one-half of the area of Assam and 11 per cent of its population, have to be seen not merely in their relationship to the Assam plains but also in the larger perspective of the north-east region as a whole. This context brings out their political and strategic importance as well as the need for the entire region to work towards an integrated approach in transport, power, irrigation and flood control, management of forest resources and supply of food and essential consumer goods. General statistics on development such as revenue, extent of road mileage, progress in education and others, which are often cited, do not bring out the nature of the problems with which tribal areas in the hills are confronted. It is no injustice

to whatever efforts may have been made in the past to say
that so far even the surface of the problems of development
has not been scratched.

I

The economic problems of the hill areas in Assam, as in
the other tribal areas in the north-east region, need to be
understood in terms of five principal factors. First comes
geography, the terrain, the topography and the resources
which nature provides—land, forest and others—and what
the hand of man has done or can do to utilise these resources.
It is interesting to observe how, within the same district,
from the geographical and physical angle, there is enormous
variation from one area to another.

The second important factor is the people, with their
cultural heritage and social structure, their land tenures and
their skills and occupations. In the tribal areas, it is essential
to know much more about the people, to understand their
cultural and other traditions and to study closely the problems of change and adaptation in their human, social,
economic and other aspects. For, whether we consider the
more advanced or the less advanced areas, ultimately it is
the people who have to be transformed and who have to
undertake the tasks of development.

Next to geography and the people, the aspect which strikes
one most is that of transport and communications. During
the period of British administration, the policy followed
in the hill areas was one of isolation and studied neglect.
Something has been done since Independence, but what it
adds up to is quite meagre. As transport facilities begin to
develop, the gaps are more keenly felt and the desire for
further development becomes more intense. The manner
and quality of implementation of plans for constructing
roads and creating transport facilities are as important as
the size of the development programme.

The fourth aspect is that of markets and outlets. The main economic links before Independence of large parts of Garo Hills and Khasi and Jaintia Hills were with market centres now falling within East Pakistan. These links came to be broken, but effective substitutes have not yet been established, so that a degree of avoidable suffering and impoverishment has occurred. Although there has been significant progress towards the integration of the national economy of India as a whole, in the hill areas of Assam elements of isolation are much more marked than those of composite growth. Therefore, in undertaking development, it is necessary to proceed as swiftly as possible towards creating substantial outlets *within* the Indian economy for the products of the hill areas, thus bringing their production and distribution system within the wider regional economy in relation to which they continue to remain at the very fringe.

Finally, in considering development in the hill areas, the fact has to be faced that these areas are deficit in food, and supplies have to be brought from other areas over long distances and at heavy cost. Therefore, the manner in which supplies are arranged, the prices at which they become available, the regularity and efficiency with which they reach the population and how the basic needs of the people, specially for food, are met, are matters of paramount importance.

The hill areas are sparsely populated and for the most part they are dependent on a single crop. For several months in the year, both men and women are without work. During these months we encounter the more extreme forms of poverty and under-nourishment in these areas. Yet, as in other parts of the country, this slack period and the labour resources available are a potential asset to be harnessed towards the building up of the local economy.

As the population has grown, the traditional economy has

become much less able to supply the essential needs of the people. The reconstruction of tribal economies in the hill areas, therefore, calls for a more basic strategy of advance than has been visualised in the past.

Whatever the scheme of development, certain elements will be common, such as the need for greater investment, provision of social services, training in new skills and the development of natural resources. How the administration and the various agencies address themselves to these tasks makes a great deal of difference. Too often, the schemes and programmes sponsored in the hill areas follow the general patterns of planning familiar to government departments and are not directly relevant to the problems thrown up by the real struggles which mark tribal life. Despite some little contribution they have made, community development blocks in the hill areas are a source of dissatisfaction. The real meaning and purpose of community development, namely, to enable the people of each area to grapple in their own way, with the problems of which they become aware, with such know-how and resources as the administration can bring to their assistance, has neither been put across nor even grasped. Therefore, much that is done through the community development blocks is not directly pertinent to the requirements of the hill areas. In other words, in these hill areas, the task of orienting plans of development to the needs of the people has yet to be undertaken.

II

Plans for future development are best formulated in each hill district through the adoption of an area approach, that is, in terms of the geographical, social and economic character- istics of different areas. Where extensive hilly tracts are involved, a district is too large a unit for development, even as a block by itself forms too small a unit. It is, therefore, necessary to envisage the physical environment and the human resources and the problems of the district in terms of a limited number of Development Areas. Even apart from long distances, reorganisation of the existing pattern of the agricultural and forest economy calls for different methods and approaches according to the conditions of each Development Area. The average tribal block has a population of about 25,000 which is much too small for arranging for several of the services needed. Programmes of development like communications, irrigation, forestry, processing industries and vocational and secondary education can gain much from being planned in relation to somewhat larger, yet reasonably homogeneous, areas.

Thus, it should be possible to work out systematic plans for each Development Area within the framework of a five year plan as well as a longer term view of developmental needs. These plans would take into account, on the one hand, the physical features, communications, social structure and economic needs of each Development Area and, on the other, the experience, judgement and aspirations of local leaders and workers and those associated with traditional as well as new local institutions. Keeping these considerations in view, the Joint Centre-State Study Team, which visited the hill districts of Assam early in 1966, recommended increase in the number of tribal and community development blocks from 42 to 55 and proposed 13 Development Areas in the hill districts.*

The scheme of community blocks and tribal blocks, suitably reorganised, links up with the concept of Develop-

*These Development Areas were as follows:

Mizo Hills

1. Aijal, Saitual and Mamit blocks.
2. Area east of Seling-Lungleh road, mainly comprising the Champai block.
3. Hnahthial and Serchhip blocks.
4. Pawi-Lakher region.

ment Areas. It provides an essential means through which, to a considerable degree, the people at the village and block level can assume responsibility for their own development. The necessary pre-conditions for this exist, for many of the tribal groups in the hill areas have on their side vigour and eagerness to go forward, are burdened with few inhibitions and possess a keen sense of community. These are assets of incalculable value. The distinction followed in the national community development programme between two different stages of the programme, each representing a certain order of resources, is not appropriate to the conditions in the hill districts and in the tribal areas generally. To reduce the volume of resources before development has got even seriously under way and the initial handicaps have yet to be cleared, is to hinder continuous progress. Therefore, on the suggestion of the Joint Centre-State Study Team, it has been agreed by the Central and State Governments that each block should be able to count upon pre-determined resources steadily for the next ten years. The total allotment proposed

Garo Hills

1. Western area comprising Resubelpara, Dadenggiri, Selsella, Rongram, and Betasing blocks.
2. Southern area comprising Dalu, Chokpat and Dambukaga blocks.
3. Eastern area, comprising Songasak and Sambarangjing blocks.

Mikir Hills and North Cachar Hills

1. Eastern Mikirs.
2. Western Mikirs.
3. Diyang Valley block and part of Jatinga block.
4. The rest of Jatinga block.

Khasi and Jaintia Hills

1. Jowai subdivision.
2. Border areas of Khasi Hills to the south.
3. Plateau areas of Khasi Hills.
4. Areas of Khasi Hills to the north of the plateau.

The proposed demarcations were tentative and were to be defined further after closer study on the ground.

is Rs. 17·6 lakhs for the period 1966-67 to 1970-71, comprising Rs. 10 lakhs under the scheme of tribal development and Rs. 7·6 lakhs under the scheme of community development. These allocations are intended to form a nucleus to be supplemented by additional resources to be provided in accordance with development programmes in different sectors.

The concept of area and block development would remain incomplete without the addition of two other basic elements. The first concerns the need to utilise the manpower resources available for several months in the year in productive works for strengthening the rural economy. For this reason it has been proposed that a financial provision for a rural works programme should be built organically into the scheme of development at the block and area level. Secondly, the completely agricultural character of the economy of the tribal areas is a source of great weakness. A project for carrying at least modest-sized industries into the towns and key centres of the hill areas, such as they are, has to be an essential component of the plan of development. Industries which could be developed would include the processing of agricultural, horticultural and forest produce, industries using traditional skills, as well as others capable of meeting the essential requirements of the population or utilising the new skills which are now being imparted in vocational training institutions.

In every district and Development Area, communications have a primary role and may well serve as the starting point for planning. Without them, no other aspect of development can be undertaken successfully. Roads are both costly and difficult to build, and their maintenance is also expensive. In many hill areas, with the best effort, it will take a decade or more to provide even the essential communications needed. A carefully worked out road plan is indispensable. This should include roads to be constructed and maintained by the Public Works Department as well as by local authorities. Within such a framework, there should be programmes for the construction of village roads and feeder roads during slack agricultural seasons by utilising the manpower resources which are waiting to be put to work in all hill areas.

The core of reconstruction for a tribal economy consists in road and road transport development, forest development and changes in the pattern of agriculture being thought of as parts of a single well-knit programme, each part being executed in terms of a joint plan of operation covering all the related sectors. Development of education and new skills and housing and several other activities can also be usefully related to such a scheme of combined operations for communications, forests, agriculture and soil conservation. This approach is best undertaken for fairly sizeable areas, specially where shifting cultivation systems prevail at present, so that the productivity of land can be increased and isolated hamlets brought together into villages where a fair number of households can be located. Small irrigation works and the development of animal husbandry, including piggery and poultry, can also be closely related to the requirements and progress of the forest-based agricultural economy.

The strategy of land development has to be worked out for each area separately in accordance with its natural conditions and possibilities. The first step, therefore, is a careful survey of land use with the object of selecting promising areas and marking out lands suitable for forestry, pasture, settled agriculture, shifting cultivation and horticultural crops.

A scientific scheme of management of forest resources is of crucial importance. It will involve both institutional changes and developmental schemes. Thus, *reserved* forests in the hill areas, which are already under technical State management, have to be re-stocked to the extent possible with valuable fast-growing species. From the forest areas held by local authorities such as District Councils, it will be necessary to demarcate areas to be declared as *protected* forests and to evolve working plans for them. Where conditions permit, cash crops such as arecanut, rubber, pepper and cashew could be introduced as means for increasing the productivity of land.

Perhaps the most critical aspect of agricultural development is the treatment of lands now subject to the practices of shifting cultivation. There must be much careful experimentation before all the solutions needed can be established. As a first approach, the Joint Centre-State Study Team visualised a series of possible prophylactic and preventive measures to minimise soil run-off from lands under shifting cultivation where the slopes are specially steep, say, 45° or more. These measures might include, for instance, provision of catchwater drains, fire-tracing of the area under shifting cultivation prior to burning, piling of unburnt debris along the contours, contour-wise strip-cropping practices for arresting soil erosion, development of suitable areas as pasture-cum-fodder reserves, training schemes for minimising gully erosion, and use of chemical fertilizers and organic manures to improve fertility and to prolong the cultivation cycle. The latter has tended to become shorter in consequence of the agricultural practices which have been followed over many years. Lands with slopes which are not too steep for settled agriculture could be terraced and systematic terracing practices could be promoted. In the valleys, steps could be taken to prohibit the felling of trees and grazing and burning within, say, a hundred feet on both sides of every river or stream. On settled lands special efforts could be made to grow cash crops, specially of non-perishable varieties.

III

In every aspect of the growth of the tribal economy, the issue of education has critical interest and takes many different forms. The approach hitherto adopted in the expansion of education involves more or less mechanical repetition of what is being done elsewhere. A considerable amount of effort is being made by the tribal communities themselves but, because the system as a whole is ill-suited, much of their labour and expenditure runs to waste. There are many obvious gaps, notably those concerning the education of girls, high proportion of drop-outs from school, absence of central schools with hostel facilities, poor quality of teachers and of textbooks, teaching materials and other facilities, specially in science and mathematics, and lack of facilities for vocational instruction. The long distances and the scattered nature of village homesteads greatly reduce administrative efficiency in the field of education. In any community, education best fulfils its purpose if it is closely related to the requirements of economic and social development. In the tribal areas, from the beginning, there is an opportunity to develop educational systems and practices which can meet this test, so that education and development may proceed together, each supporting and stimulating the other. On the success attained in devising and implementing the correct solutions in education will depend how far two essential needs of the tribal areas are met. These are, firstly, the availability of trained persons from within the tribal milieu in the numbers needed for undertaking development and, secondly, growth of leadership among tribal communities which will command influence and respect among them, will secure their increasing participation in the developmental effort and will be able to take them towards a larger scheme of regional and national unity and integration.

Different tribal communities are at varying stages of economic and cultural development. Frequently, between them, there are significant differences in the skills they have attained and in the technology they employ even in the traditional agricultural systems. Therefore, each group and the area in which it lives have to be studied closely, and suitable patterns for the future have to be evolved in co-operation with the people. It is in terms of such a design of development that educational programmes, institutions and priorities need to be worked out. Because this has not been the approach in the past, such facilities as have been developed have inevitably produced mixed results. Products of existing institutions often face not only difficulties of employment but also those of social and personal adjustment within the society to which they belong and from which, for the vast majority, there is no escape. Besides dealing with the deficiencies mentioned above, it is necessary to introduce vocational and technical courses within the system of secondary schools, so that school-leavers may fit into the agricultural and other programmes of development, which alone can provide work for the bulk of the young people. From secondary schools, boys and girls need to be picked out for instruction in vocations requiring long periods of training and, with the aid of special coaching facilities such as they must have, they can be helped to come out as skilled and trained workers equipped and motivated to serve their own people.

IV

While the reorganisation of forest-based agricultural economies in the tribal areas, communications, and education are fundamental, certain other aspects of development which are of great importance should also be mentioned briefly. Tribal communities are favourably placed for the development of co-operatives. The greatest need is for co-operative organisations for credit, marketing, supplies of agricultural inputs and supplies of food and essential consumer goods such as salt, kerosene oil and sugar Credit and supply can be best developed around marketing of produce, whether of agriculture, horticulture or forests. In the hill areas, it is

14

essential to interpret the concepts of co-operative organisation with the utmost flexibility and freedom from set patterns,
the real tests being those of practical working and accept-
ability to local communities. In view of the place assigned in
the hill districts, under the Sixth Schedule of the Constitution,
to District Councils, which also have ultimate control over
the use of land, the need for these Councils not only to promote but also to become major share-holding partners in the
co-operatives is worth emphasising. Since there is already a
tradition of working together on the land, co-operatives for
production also present a fruitful possibility, but some
measure of study and experiment, with the participation of
local communities, would be necessary, in this context
drawing specially upon work practices associated in many
areas with shifting cultivation.

Rural and small town electrification has a very real
contribution to make to tribal economic development. Partly
because of the need to subsidise for an initial period, and
partly because the urgency of stimulating the growth of small
industry in the tribal areas has not yet been recognised,
power development in the hill districts has been almost
overlooked. The failure here has been one of policy and
approach, for the issue is generally seen by electricity
authorities in unduly narrow terms.

V

In the last analysis, the pace of development turns not only
on the resources available but on the quality of personnel,
their competence in carrying out tasks assigned to them and
their sense of identification with and intimate knowledge
of the tribal communities among whom they work. Hill areas
and tribal areas are invariably short of personnel. The gaps
in personnel which are observed in practice in schools, dis-
pensaries and other services are a matter for deep concern.

Since tribal communities frequently live in remote and inaccessible areas, and conditions of work among them are arduous, even apart from unfilled positions, the turnover of personnel is heavy and transfers take place at short intervals. Therefore, in most fields, it is essential to build up special cadres to work among the tribal people. By their training and opportunities of living and working with tribal communities, public servants who belong to these cadres can, in the manner of the best missionaries, establish bonds of sympathy and understanding with the aspirations and desires of the people.

Although the conclusion should itself be obvious, in the working arrangements which have prevailed hitherto, the contribution which local institutions and local leadership have to make towards the reconstruction of tribal economies has been bypassed. District Councils, despite their formal status, have been allowed to stand apart from the work of community and tribal development blocks, and responsibilities for development have not been entrusted to them. With such strengthening and streamlining of arrangements as may be required, there can be no question as to where responsibility for development at the district and area level now belongs. It is essential that problems of planning in the hill areas should be conceived of in an overall way for each district and Development Area as well as for the hill districts considered together as a planning region, which has links with the Assam plains as well as with India's north-east region as a whole. The knowledge and association of those who belong to the region and have a personal perception of needs and possibilities will be the best assurance that changes and adjustments will be made in time and in accordance with the genius of the people.

Even with the fullest association of local institutions and local leadership, it has to be admitted that in dealing with problems of tribal reconstruction there are no ready-made solutions. In many fields the first effort must be to identify the key problems and work out appropriate methods and strategy for dealing with them with the fullest co-operation of the people. This thought led the Joint Centre-State Study Team to propose the establishment of a network of Development Institutes in the hill districts. It was envisaged that one of the institutes might concentrate on the study of selected problems of the entire region, while the others could devote themselves to the particular problems of different areas. Each institute would have a small team of experts in fields such as agriculture, animal husbandry, forestry, co-operation, social education and cultural development. The specialists and extension workers would work with local institutions on problems which are encountered in different areas and help find the answers. It is expected that the Development Institutes would also serve as centres for the training and orientation of workers, both official and non-official, and in time they could build up a stock of knowledge and experience which would be of real value in ensuring development at the grass roots.

Rapid and purposeful development and sustained work on the reconstruction of tribal economies in the Assam Hills, as elsewhere in the north-east region of India, is essential both to the solution of economic and social problems and to the evolution of equitable and satisfying political relationships. Altogether, the task presents difficult tests at every point of implementation at the same time as it offers unique opportunities for constructive and creative service both to workers from within the hill districts as well as others drawn from the rest of the country.

13

RURAL RESETTLEMENT IN THE PUNJAB AFTER PARTITION*

VILLAGE LIFE in the Punjab had long been marked by harmony and good relations between the different communities. Irrigation works brought new life to large tracts in the western districts, but the prosperity was shared in generous measure by colonists from the eastern and the central districts.

Service in the army, a more or less similar way of life and outlook between the main agricultural tribes, respect for one another's prowess and tradition, long-standing friendship between the leading families, and an administration which laid stress on the province rather than on its different regions had helped to bring about a feeling of unity.

*Between September 1947 and December 1949, the writer served as Director General of Rehabilitation in the Punjab and was closely concerned with the rehabilitation of displaced persons in the rural areas. The paper is based on four articles contributed to the *Statesman*, New Delhi, of July 18 to 21, 1950. Fuller details are given in Tarlok Singh: *Land Resettlement Manual for Displaced Persons*, 1952, published by the Punjab Government. The *Manual* describes at length the various operations connected with the resettlement of displaced persons on land and the principles of valuation, allocation and allotment which were followed.

In 1947, between March and August, in less than six
months, the best part of a century's work was destroyed.
On August 15, 1947, when the province was partitioned into
East and West Punjab, with the withdrawal of officials,
minority populations could no longer live with safety or
honour. The movement of population between East Punjab
and West Punjab began in the last days of August, 1947.
By the middle of September, 1947, the movement had grown
into a flood, and bore the ominous signs of a permanent
transfer of population.

At this time no one knew how wide the sweep of this
transfer would be, what numbers were to be expected, how
soon they might come, and what could be done for them.
Before the end of the year, the transfer of population had
been more or less accomplished. Two and a half years later,
many of those who had lost their all were engaged throughout the countryside of East Punjab and the Patiala and East
Punjab States Union (PEPSU) in obtaining possession of
land which they could call their own.* They are now cultivators and farmers in their own right. They have borne
grievous wounds which will take time to heal, but their lives
are set upon a fresh course. The story of rural resettlement
in the Punjab is a record of this transformation. The conclusion of resettlement operations in East Punjab and PEPSU is
an event of some significance for the country, and in some
ways the experience has a deep, abiding interest.

I

The manner and method of resettlement of the rural
population in East Punjab and the East Punjab States, as the

---

*Under the States Reorganisation Act, 1956, the territories first included in
the State of PEPSU were merged with those of the Punjab. Ten years later,
in October 1966, out of this composite State, two separate States, Haryana
and Punjab, were constituted; at the same time, certain areas were merged
into Himachal Pradesh and a new Union Territory, Chandigarh, was created.

territories were then known, bears the stamp of August
and September, 1947. The problems emerged with bewilder-
ing suddenness. The new Government of East Punjab, still
barely on its legs, was unprepared and unequipped, but the
situation was handled on the whole with cool courage and
ability to improvise. There were no facts or statistics on which
a scheme of resettlement could be based. The first problem
was to send the people into the villages. The Muslim population from the Jullundur Division of East Punjab and non-
Muslims from the Lahore and Rawalpindi Divisions in
West Punjab were on the move, but in the Ambala and the
Multan Divisions only the first portents were to be seen.
The East Punjab States were separate entities and, except
for Patiala, their policies were by no means certain or beyond
question. The districts of the Jullundur Division had long
been linked with the canal colonies and, therefore, colonists
from these districts bent their steps homewards. This became
an important feature of the scheme of allocation of areas in
East Punjab and PEPSU for displaced persons from different
parts of West Punjab, which was announced on September
15, 1947. In the moment of emergency, the issue whether
refugees could be re-established on the pattern of West
Punjab districts was judged once for all.

A rough and ready scheme of distribution of land for the
first harvest was drawn up. Land was allotted in groups to
owners as well as tenants. Agricultural refugees were advised
to proceed to the headquarters of tehsils as far as possible in
groups in which they had lived or in groups in which they
wished to settle. To each person the area cultivated by a pair
of bullocks, sufficient for a worker assisted by a family of
average size, was to be allowed. If a family had more male
adult workers than two, additional area was given for the
third, fourth and fifth worker. A group allotment having
been taken, the members of the group were expected to
divide the land amongst themselves for cultivation. The

scheme of group allotment was designed to ensure quick distribution, to enable refugees from particular villages and areas to remain as much together as possible and to enable cultivators to pool their resources for the sowing of the rabi and to share the standing kharif crops equitably among themselves. These objects were largely secured and, within two months, two million acres of land were occupied.

The idea of group allotment and of allotment to owners and tenants alike, however, frightened many people. It went against the common notions. Some thought it to be a collectivist experiment. The fact that there was at the time no alternative to it was admitted, but soon the urge for a permanent settlement based on rights held by individuals in Pakistan gathered force. On the whole, as rural society was constituted in the Punjab, the idea that land abandoned by Muslims in East Punjab and PEPSU should be allotted only to those who had abandoned lands of their own was a necessary basis for any scheme of land resettlement. Even within this framework, it might have been possible to achieve a measure of reform. But influential opinion favoured a settlement on lines familiar to the people in which each man got his own bit of property and his own separate fields. The aim of the resettlement operations was, therefore, to rehabilitate refugee landholders (and through them other rural refugees) by allotting to them lands abandoned by evacuee Muslim owners. One cannot say whether this was the best course to take, but it is important to recognise that the settlement sought to restore a way of life known to the people rather than to build new patterns.

The fact that the objective of the settlement was a limited one did not diminish the size of the task to be handled. Four circumstances made the task less difficult than it might have been. During the first few months of 1948, an increasing measure of coordination was brought about between East Punjab and the East Punjab States, so that all the evacuee land in these separate territories came to be treated as a single pool. Secondly, the Government of India agreed that all displaced landholders from West Punjab and those of Punjabi extraction from other parts of West Pakistan would be resettled on evacuee lands in East Punjab and PEPSU. This gave a definite shape to the problem of resettlement, so that the land which was available for allotment could be matched with the claims of those who had to be settled. In the third place, and most fortunate of all, the East Punjab and the West Punjab Governments undertook to prepare copies of revenue records on an agreed basis for one another's use. Accurate land records alone could ensure a sound settlement. The exchange of records began towards the end of November, 1948, and was completed during the winter. Finally, at considerable sacrifice in other directions, the Governments of East Punjab and PEPSU placed almost all the revenue staff at the disposal of the rehabilitation authorities. Fifteen months of intense work at a central camp, in which at one stage more than eight thousand revenue officials lived and worked under canvas, made it possible to accomplish what might otherwise have taken perhaps three years or more.

II

When the problem assumes large proportions, resettlement of displaced persons on land is a process which falls into five phases, namely, (1) immediate settlement, (2) consolidation of temporary allotments, (3) permanent settlement on land, (4) restoration of the rural economy, and (5) reconstruction and development of the rural economy. In East Punjab and PEPSU the third phase has been completed and efforts are now being concentrated on the fourth.* While steps towards a permanent system

*This refers to the stage in land resettlement reached by the middle of 1950.

of settlement on land were being taken, it was necessary to devote as much attention as possible to the second phase, that is, consolidation of the temporary settlement. This phase was marked by three main features. The first of these was the creation of the necessary administrative organisation. The second was the elaboration and filling in of the initial scheme of settlement, which included the drawing up of a more complete scheme of allocation of areas, dispersing the rural population from relief camps in accordance with the scheme of allocation, restricting future temporary allotment of land to displaced landholders, and giving somewhat bigger allotments to the larger holders than to the smaller holders by means of a scheme of special leases. The third feature was the organisation of financial assistance for displaced persons. Between September, 1947, and September, 1949, Rs. 2·12 crores were spent to this end. This included loans for purchase of food (Rs. 80 lakhs), for seed (Rs. 56 lakhs), for bullocks (Rs. 56 lakhs), and also some assistance for fodder and implements and for the settlement of rural artisans and village servants. Loans and grants for repair of houses and repair of wells were also sanctioned, but in the absence of a stake in the land they were not a success.

Until issues relating to evacuee property are resolved between India and Pakistan, ownership in each country of property abandoned by evacuees continues to rest with them.* This had led to the use of the expression 'quasi-

---

*Even in later years these issues remained unresolved. Under legislation enacted in 1954, the Government of India were empowered to acquire evacuee properties and to compensate displaced persons, through permanent transfer of land and, otherwise, in lieu of properties abandoned by them in Pakistan. In the case of evacuee properties which were in dispute or had composite ownership, after the settlement of disputes or the separation of evacuee interests, such properties became part of the compensation pool which had been instituted. So far permanent rights have been transferred to 284,116 persons in respect of 2,028,816 'standard acres'.

permanent' as the key word in the scheme of land resettlement introudced in East Punjab and PEPSU. 'Quasi-permanent' allotment of land entails a number of complex processes. A scheme for distributing five million acres of land on the basis of rights claimed by more than half a million individuals in territories now falling within Pakistan cannot be evolved without elaborate land statistics and without careful rules for valuing different classes of land and rights and assessing the worth of each man's claim. If it is established how much land a person has abandoned and how much is to be allotted to him, the next step is to allocate his 'claim' to a particular village. Holding land in a village is not like holding any other piece of property. One becomes part of the village community and accepts its way of life and the rights and obligations that go with it. In the allocation of claims to villages, therefore, considerations of the quality of land as well as social considerations supervene. When it is known that certain claims are allocated to a particular village, if the distribution of fields is left to the individuals concerned, in a system of agriculture based on small holdings, it may lead to years of conflict. The allotment of fields on an impersonal basis is, therefore, one of the major tasks in a scheme of land resettlement such as that adopted in East Punjab and PEPSU. Finally, a land resettlement on such a vast scale could scarcely be free from errors and defects and it is necessary to provide machinery and procedures for review and revision of allotments in the light of the principles on which they were based. The operations have to be rounded off by completing new revenue records.

In East Punjab and PEPSU, parallel legislation governs the rights and obligations of those receiving land in quasi-permanent settlement. The expressions 'allotment' and 'lease' are used so as to correspond respectively to 'quasi-permanent' and 'temporary' grant of land. Allotment on the basis of entries in revenue records or other equivalent proof is described as 'quasi-permanent', while grant of land on any other basis is described as 'temporary'. The allottee comes as near to being an owner of land as is possible at present. He pays land revenue, can exchange his land with another allottee, and can lease it for periods up to three years. A longer lease requires the consent of the custodian of evacuee property. Even though the vast majority of allottees have received possession of land from kharif, 1950, their rights under the law take effect from kharif, 1949. From this harvest they became entitled to receive a prescribed rent on account of land allotted in their names.

III

A scheme of land allotment has to be built around certain basic statistics. These relate to area abandoned by displaced persons and area available for allotment to them. Information about area abandoned by displaced persons is obtained by adding up the verified claims of various individuals. In turn, this requires a considerable body of decisions about rights which are eligible for allotment and those which are not considered to be so eligible.

Information about areas abandoned by evacuees is obtained from the revenue records and here it is important to distinguish between rights which can and those which cannot be the basis of allotment. The central problem is to assess the claims of different individuals, but to be able to frame a scheme of resettlement it is necessary first to obtain the total figures on both sides of the account.

Altogether, the claims of 617,401 displaced landholders from Pakistan were assessed; of these, as many as 606,879 were from West Punjab. The total area abandoned outside towns was 6,729,050 acres, of which 1,464,281 acres were uncultivated land. Against this, the total area abandoned by evacuees in East Punjab and PEPSU was 5,015,616 acres, of which 894,795 acres were uncultivated land. There were marked differences in the relative fertility of land in East and West Punjab. For a long period, the resources of the composite province had been devoted largely to the development of waste tracts in the western districts so that, against 4,306,558 acres of irrigated land abandoned by displaced persons, only 1,325,853 acres of irrigated land were now available for them. The proportion of perennial irrigation available was even smaller, being 433,829 acres in East Punjab and PEPSU, compared to 2,555,844 acres in West Punjab.

Before a scheme of resettlement could be framed, it was necessary to devise a unit of value in terms of which different classes of land and rights could be reduced to a comparable basis. The value of a claim is a result of three separate factors—the rights held by an individual, the area held by him under each right, and the class of soil pertaining to each separate item in his area statement. The unit devised for land resettlement operations in East Punjab and PEPSU has been given the name of *standard acre.** The comparative value of land may be judged by criteria such as the amount of land, revenue assessed per acre, value of gross produce, net profit, sale value, lease value or average yield.

After some trial and error, the yield of wheat assumed at settlement for each class of land in each assessment circle in the various districts of West Punjab, East Punjab and PEPSU was taken as the starting point. Wheat is a well-nigh universal crop for which the requisite yield data were available in settlement reports. Where wheat was of rela-

*In subsequent years, the idea of *standard acre* and the approach embodied in it were found useful and adopted more widely in the practice of consolidation of holdings and in the application of measures for land reform, specially ceilings on agricultural holdings.

tively less importance, a rough equivalent was established
between wheat and the local cereal crops. A soil valuation key, setting the value at so many annas against so
many maunds of yield per matured acre assumed at settlement was adopted. The key gave an approximate value
according to conditions prevailing at the time of settlement.
This was then considered with reference to changes in
cropping, developments in irrigation, and other factors such
as higher cost of production on land irrigated by wells.

The final valuation of each class of land in each assessment
circle was fixed after examining other comparative data
and after detailed discussion. Sixteen annas of value were
described as a 'standard acre'. As a unit of value, therefore, the standard acre can represent different areas according to the type and situation of the land valued. Similarly,
full ownership rights were rated at sixteen annas and allowance was made for lesser rights of a continuing character,
such as those of occupancy. Something like 2500 valuations
of land in about 400 assessment circles and group of villages
and a very large number of different classes of rights under
colony and non-colony tenures were successfully dealt
with through the concept of the standard acre. Calculations
were generally made to 1/64th of a standard acre.

IV

The final reckoning showed that displaced persons due
for settlement in East Punjab and PEPSU could receive in
quasi-permanent allotment 2,448,830 standard acres against
3,935,131 standard acres abandoned in West Pakistan.
Evacuee land in East Punjab amounted to 2,101,829
standard acres. The gap of 1,486,301 standard acres (about
38 per cent) had to be spread amongst displaced land
holders after considering the distribution of land between
holders of different grades of holdings in Pakistan. It was

found that more than 80 per cent of the claimants had less than 10 standard acres, 95 per cent had less than 30, and more than 98 per cent less than 60 standard acres. The proposal to give every displaced landholder a uniform proportion of the area abandoned by him was, therefore, rejected as being harsh to the vast majority. The second course was to put a ceiling on the area in standard acres which could be allotted to any displaced person. To pursue the logic of such a ceiling, the notion of 'floor' would also have to be added. It would have become necessary to give additional land to a very large number of petty holders (many of whom were non-cultivators) and to reduce the allotments of a great many peasants who had better holdings and, through their enterprise and skill, had built up progressive farms in West Punjab. A middle course was followed. A scheme of graded cuts was devised from which no one was to be exempt, but whose incidence would be less severe in respect of small holders and middle farmers and more severe for higher grades of holdings. It was felt that the class of farmers holding, say between 10 and 30 to 50 standard acres, representing the best skills of the Punjab farmers, should not be hit too hard. The scheme of graded cuts, which works on a slab system like income tax, was as follows:

	Grade (in standard acres)			Rate of cut (%)	Net allotment at maximum of grade (in standard acres)
1.	Up to 10			25	7·5
2.	More than	10, but not more than	30	30	21·5
3.	,,	30, ,,	40	40	27·5
4.	,,	40, ,,	60	55	37·5
5.	,,	60, ,,	100	65	51·5
6.	,,	100, ,,	150	70	66·5
7.	,,	150, ,,	200	75	79·0
8.	,,	200, ,,	250	80	89·0
9.	,,	250, ,,	500	85	126·5
10.	,,	500, ,,	1000	90	176·5
11.	More than 1000			95	

Above 1000 standard acres, an allottee received 50 standard acres for every thousand abandoned by him. This meant, for instance, that a displaced landholder who had abandoned 4000 standard acres could get only 326·5. The cuts were based on practical considerations and had no political or reformist objectives. Nevertheless, they put an end to the very large holdings which were so conspicuous a feature of rural life in West Punjab.

The scheme of graded cuts provided a formula for ascertaining how much land in standard acres was to be given to each claimant on the basis of the valuation of his lands in Pakistan. The next step was to determine the district in which his claim was to be met. Quasi-permanent settlement was not being written on a clean slate. It had been preceded by two years of temporary settlement in the villages. This temporary settlement had been based on the allocation of areas for resettlement in East Punjab and PEPSU to colonists and non-colonists from different districts of West Punjab.

There were some who felt that the population of each district from West Punjab should be settled together, so that continuity with the past could be maintained. Many urged that a similar principle should be applied also to the population of individual villages of West Pakistan. To upset the settlement which had been effected already and to set whole populations moving again from district to district seemed a hazardous undertaking. The distinction between colonists and non-colonists had been drawn in September, 1947, and it was inconceivable that colonists who belonged originally to the districts of East Punjab should be settled without regard to this consideration. In the temporary settlement the principle had been extended to colonists from East Punjab as well as from West Punjab districts. The final scheme of allocation of areas aimed at settling the population from West Punjab according as they were colonists or non-colonists in as homogenous and compact a manner as was consistent with the desire to reduce the volume of movement of persons who had already been settled in villages. According to this scheme, it was possible to determine fairly definitely the district to which each claim had to be allotted. If a person were a temporary allottee in a district, unless the allocation scheme provided for his settlement in another district, he could continue in that district.

Every district in East Punjab and PEPSU which sent out colonists to West Punjab has received them back. The bulk of the population of the Rawalpindi Division has been settled in Ambala and Ludhiana districts and in the adjoining areas of PEPSU. Most of the people from Gujranwala and Sheikhupura, which once formed a single district in joint Punjab, are settled in Karnal and in PEPSU. The greater part of the population of Jhang is in Rohtak district, of Multan in Hissar and Karnal, of Dera Ghazi Khan in Gurgaon, and of Muzzaffargarh in Rohtak and Hissar. The bulk of the non-colonists of Lyallpur are settled in Jullundur and Karnal and of Lahore and Montgomery in Ferozepore district.

V

For each individual claimant, after the district in which he was to be settled had been determined, the next task was to indicate the village in which land was to be allotted to him. In the first few months of temporary settlement, displaced persons tried everywhere to move into good villages. There was always a struggle for good villages in which, quite frequently, money and influence played a part.

Those who had abandoned irrigated lands felt sore that others who had owned inferior lands should be able to seize upon the better lands. If the existing temporary settlement continued without change, those who had taken no land so far would be adversely affected. It was not enough to evaluate each person's claim in standard acres. To

15

ensure fairness, schemes of sub-allocation and grading of villages were drawn up.

A broad distinction was made between irrigated areas, riverain areas, hilly tracts, and sandy and insecure tracts. Within an area of allocation, for these different types of tracts, the first preference was to be given to those who had abandoned land in villages situated in similar areas. Ordinarily, no one was to receive land markedly superior or markedly inferior to that abandoned by him. All villages in West Punjab and East Punjab and PEPSU were placed in four or five grades. In West Punjab, the grades were based on assessment circles and the proportion of different classes of land in them; in East Punjab and PEPSU, in some districts this basis was followed, in some others, on a consideration of various factors, each village was graded separately. In advance of quasi-permanent allotment, every village had been inspected. There was also a scheme of grading specially applicable to colonists as between one another, since colonists from different areas competed for good lands in their parent districts.

In the allocation of villages, the first principle was that a person temporarily settled in a village within his area of allocation was entitled to allotment in that village if its land was not markedly superior to that which he had abandoned. Holding markedly superior land meant as a rule having temporary allotment in a village which was more than one grade above the grade of land abandoned in Pakistan. This criterion applied to all grades of land in PEPSU. But, in East Punjab, it was laid down that in the allotment of Grade I land, Grade II holders could not be considered unless there was a surplus after meeting the claims of Grade I holders. Although this was a rule of fair distribution, it led to the shifting of a proportion of the settled population. The distinction was made under strong pressure from agriculturists from colony areas.

Amongst displaced persons, there was a strong sentiment in favour of village-wise allotment. In principle this had much to commend it, but to recompose villages as they existed in West Punjab could not be a practical undertaking. Some attempt was, however, made to assist settlement with the people of their own village of those who had expressed this wish, or had received land for the first time, or were required to move from the village of temporary allotment. Practical decisions become difficult when a number of different principles have to be watched simultaneously. To bring together the areas held by an individual in different districts and villages into a single claim, to grade the consolidated claim, and to consider a person's wishes in the matter of allotment as well as his status as a temporary allottee were complex operations.

These operations were being performed simultaneously through the agency of several thousand revenue officials some of whom, as might be imagined, were prone to abuse their responsibilities. As the work of allotment of villages progressed, there was criticism that close relations were not receiving allotment together. This led to an additional principle. Close relations were defined so as to include specifically parents and children, husband and wife, real brothers and widows and minor sons of real brothers. These relations were to be treated as a single group and could receive allotment according to the grade in which the major portion of their area was situated, even at the risk of moving some who were temporarily settled. The rules of allocation of villages thus became extremely elaborate, and this factor made the operation even more difficult than it might have been otherwise. However, social cohesion and strength meant a great deal to the displaced person and it was well that some remedial measures were introduced at an early stage in the resettlement operations. Even as it is, there must have been numerous instances in which the allocation has failed to afford reasonable satisfaction.

The general principles of allocation of villages which have been described were not, however, found sufficient to deal with all types of cases. Special rules were made, for instance, for institutions. Widows were permitted under certain conditions to take land with their parents or their in-laws or others according to their convenience. With a view to avoiding dislocation of tenants-at-will, especially those who had cultivated for long periods for evacuee owners, displaced landholders to whom more than 60 standard acres were due were obliged to take one-half of their land in villages in which a proportion of the area was with resident tenants-at-will. Land situated close to towns, being more valuable than ordinary rural land, was given additional value and was allotted under special rules. Similarly, those who had abandoned suburban land near towns which had a population of 15,000 or more at the census of 1941 were allotted suburban land near similar towns in East Punjab and PEPSU. Evacuee gardens of any substantial size situated in East Punjab and PEPSU have been allotted to displaced garden owners from West Punjab. About fifty villages were earmarked in East Punjab and PEPSU for the settlement of defence and ex-defence personnel. Finally, about 19,900 acres of land were allotted in the form of co-operative garden colonies, the area allotted being reckoned against the land due to each person. It was hoped that these garden colonies would grow into prosperous rural settlements with fruit preservation industries of their own.*

The resettlement of a displaced person on land is not just one act, but rather a series of interdependent acts.

---

*In retrospect, a few of the garden colony villages took up horticulture on a significant scale, but the majority devoted themselves to ordinary agricultural operations, although frequently on progressive lines.

The land due to a person may be correctly calculated and his village determined to his satisfaction. Yet, unless he is satisfied with the fields given to him, the settlement may prove a failure. The task of allotting fields to more than half a million individuals was a formidable one, and some even doubted if it could be accomplished. It was felt, however, that if fields were not specified, the allotment would remain incomplete and there would be greater scope for delay, corruption and injustice. The methods evolved for the allotment of fields, although not free from criticism, have broadly stood the initial test and ensured impartiality. They may be said to constitute a new chapter in the experience of revenue administration.

The foundation for the allotment of fields was a careful system of records prepared as part of the resettlement operations. For all villages of East Punjab and PEPSU, in which there was evacuee land, statements concerning area, rights and source of irrigation for each individual field which could be allotted were prepared and carefully checked. The next step was to arrange all the persons due to receive land in each village in a certain order. To eliminate the element of discretion, the alphabet was followed in arranging allottees by province, district and village of origin, care being taken to bring groups and relations together, so that their fields should be close to one another's. For the actual allotment of plots, the order in which the names of various individuals were arranged in the list of allottees had to be followed; it could not be altered, upset or departed from.

The third step in the operation was to determine a mode of partition for the evacuee area of each village. The land of each village varies in quality, and good and bad land has to be distributed fairly among all. Generally, land was classified in two grades, sometimes even in three. Very small holders, to whom less than three standard acres were due, were given land in one grade. For others, for each village, there was a uniform proportion in which land of different grades was to be given. Thus, the mode of partition fixed the proportion of land of different qualities which could go to any individual. In the demarcation of fields for each individual, the order in which the names of allottees were shown in the village list had to be followed strictly. The order in which fields could be taken up for allotment was also fixed. There were other rules designed to ensure that, as far as possible, the holdings which emerged should be convenient for farming.

The final allotment order given to each person is a complete document. It gives the details of the land and the rights abandoned by a person in different villages in Pakistan, the value set by the rehabilitation authorities against each separate item, the area to be allotted to him, the village in which allotment has been made, the rights held by or against him by other displaced persons, the area, class of land and rights pertaining to each field and the area in ordinary acres of different classes of land allotted to him. On the basis of his allotment order, a person receives possession of land and thereafter his name is brought into a new revenue record.

Further, a careful procedure for review and revision of allotment has been provided, and all the instructions and principles on which the allotment has been made are set out in the Land Resettlement Manual which has been prepared. Thus, so far as circumstances permitted, the endeavour has been to give to each person a complete basis for the action taken and a clear remedy should substantial injustice have been done.

VI

The bulk of displaced persons to whom land has been

allotted in East Punjab and PEPSU have already obtained possession and they have made arrangements for cultivation. The completion of land allotment marks the end of a critical stage in the resettlement of the rural population. It paves the way for the administrative effort required for the restoration of the rural economy.

In a number of ways, the partition of the Punjab and the transfer of population to which it led has dislocated the economy of East Punjab and PEPSU. The countryside has been denuded of a large proportion of its artisans and village servants, specially weavers, blacksmiths, potters, dyers, and those who lived by the slaughter of animals and sale of hides, skins and bones. As evacuee villages regain prosperity, some gaps will be filled, but it is not unlikely that the coming years will see a marked diminution in the self-sufficiency of the peasant village and increasing concentrations of artisan groups in the towns and in the larger villages.

The movement of population was accompanied by some destruction and loss of property, but even greater ravage was caused in the subsequent period. Houses and wells suffered extensive damage. Sixteen months after the partition, 34 per cent of evacuee houses in East Punjab were beyond repair, 19 per cent were considered fit for repair, and only 47 per cent were intact. Of the wells left by evacuees, 62 per cent were in working order, 26 per cent stood in need of well gear, and 12 per cent required both repair of masonry and new well gear. It will be a considerable period before the rural economy is adequately restored. There are other serious shortages also to be met. Among these are the displaced cultivator's shortage of bullocks and of milch cattle. The health of displaced persons from Pakistan who have been resettled in villages was generally good, but the past three years could have some long-term effects, specially on the very young. This is particularly true of the poorer sections of the population, such as Harijans and others who live by their labour.

In a number of districts, the outgoing population, which had a high percentage of peasant workers and agricultural labourers, has been replaced by a population, of whom many have never worked on the land. These non-cultivators, particularly from the districts of the Rawalpindi and Multan Divisions, had their lands tilled mainly by Muslim tenants. They had developed for themselves a kind of composite economy in which they engaged in small trade and money-lending, mainly in the service of Muslim peasants and landlords. Their own holdings were as a rule exceedingly small and had only an ancillary value. Even if, following partition, they had remained in Pakistan, they would have lost their place in the economy, and impoverishment would have followed. They have now received small allotments of land in villages in East Punjab. Some may take to cultivation, but many will not find it possible to do so. The rural economy of East Punjab will not provide sufficient scope for their traditional skills, so that it will be difficult for them to make an adequate living.

In certain parts of East Punjab, such as Hissar, Karnal, Rohtak and Gurgaon, in the first phase production is likely to suffer. Whole villages, consisting of small owners, few of whom have ever cultivated with their own hands, are a new feature in the economy of these areas. The effects on production will be marked in riverain areas and in insecure tracts, where conditions of living and production are difficult, except for those who are determined enough to adapt themselves to the environment. It may well be that of the new population who have settled on land, a proportion at least will be unable to carry on the struggle and will move to other occupations in urban areas. At different stages in the evolution of the scheme of resettlement, there were a few who advocated the allotment of economic holdings to cultivators. This meant distinguishing somewhat arbitrarily between cultivating and non-cultivating owners from Pakistan. To have denied land to the non-cultivator and the petty holder would have been to deny, in the absence of other compensation, the prospect of some kind of home and location which the scheme of land resettlement offered. There would have also been serious misunderstanding of a communal character. On balance, therefore, the just course was to give at least an opportunity to all those who had land, whether much or little, to make a new start in life and to merge with the rest of the population. It could be left to future policies to deal with questions such as uneconomic holdings and small non-cultivating owners.

VII

It is probably correct to say that, given the assumptions on which land resettlement in East Punjab and PEPSU was based, technically and administratively, not much more could have been done. A tragedy such as that which overtook the Punjab might have led to the emergence of new values and new social impulses, to an awakening to the need for a major effort on the part of the people as a whole to rebuild the life of the province. Much of the thinking, however, was in familiar grooves, and many who might have guided events along progressive lines were absorbed in small conflicts.

It has, therefore, been necessary to be content for the time being with relatively modest aims—the restoration of the damaged rural economy and the assimilation of the new population with the old. These tasks are essential and have to be performed if the newly settled population are to be able to move forward with their own skill and enterprise to a better future.

Skill and enterprise will take them part of the journey.

But they cannot bring back the lost prosperity unless the entire economy of the province is placed on stronger foundations. At present the foundations are far from stable. In the immediate future, for making good the minimum agricultural capital, lack of finance is the most serious impediment. Means of irrigation must take the first place in any programme of reconstruction, and in this respect much will depend on the progress achieved in the execution of the Bhakra-Nangal Project. Four-fifths of the new allottees have holdings in the lowest grade of ten standard acres and less, and many of them have completely uneconomic holdings to work upon and will not be able to find the subsidiary occupations on which they could subsist. At least a third of the evacuee land in East Punjab and PEPSU has gone to small rural traders from predominantly Muslim districts in West Punjab. They have intelligence and resourcefulness, but they will need assistance and encouragement to venture out into other parts of the country while perhaps leaving their families at home, and build for themselves a new composite way of life intertwined with interests in their own province. Tenants-at-will and landless labour are now far more conscious of their situation than they were ever before. The traditional system in which they functioned as the lower strata of rural society at the goodwill of others cannot long continue.

Altogether, reduced holdings and poorer lands, a fall in the number of actual workers on the soil, insufficient irrigation facilities, slender capital resources and the rise of tenant interests, combine to produce a picture of increasing economic pressure. As early as may be possible, it is necessary to give attention to these developing features.

The migration has brought to East Punjab and PEPSU a peasantry uncommonly rich in experience and progressive in outlook, whose record of achievement over sixty years of colonisation is truly remarkable. They are unlikely to accept the state of relative poverty which Fate has thrust upon them. New means of irrigation, reform in the management of land, investment of capital in agriculture, and the growth of new occupations are certainly necessary but, in the short run, economic pressure may be relieved by schemes of colonisation for the small holders and the landless within and outside the province. The allotment of land which has been completed was indispensable to further progress, but it will be wise not to regard it as being by itself sufficient to ensure the effective rehabilitation of the population uprooted from West Pakistan. In so far as the settlement pays primary attention to displaced landholders, it represents an approach to the larger problems of rehabilitation which must be supplemented by other programmes. Opportunities for gainful employment for the landless and for the large mass of traders who have a hard struggle ahead to make the two ends meet have also to be found.

14

CATTLE AND CATTLE POLICY DURING FAMINE*

A FAMINE is a crisis in the life of a rural community which severely tests all its strength and weakness. Famines were an outstanding aspect of India's economic life until the beginning of the present century, and in some guise or form they can still stalk the land. Reports of Famine Commissions give valuable information about the assistance rendered to men, women and children at famine works and in their homes. Yet, through the entire range of famine literature, little information is available concerning the effects of a period of famine on cattle which, with land, constitute one of the two main foundations of the rural economy.

An inquiry into rural economic conditions conducted at the end of 1940 in the Hissar district, which had been

*This paper is based on a field investigation undertaken by the writer in 1940 at the end of eighteen months as a famine official in the Hissar district, which now forms part of the State of Haryana. The results of the investigation were first described in two articles on *Cattle Policy During Famine* in the *Eastern Economist*, New Delhi (April 28 and June 2, 1944). Subsequently, there were opportunities of reviewing the broad conclusions reached in three other famine situations—in the Hissar district in the early fifties, in the Jodhpur district of Rajasthan in June, 1964, and in the Gaya district of Bihar in April-May, 1966.

then gone through two years of a severe famine, may help fill this gap to an extent and suggest some of the essentials of a carefully conceived policy for cattle during a period of famine.

As an aspect of the investigation, which itself had a somewhat broader purpose, it became possible to study the effects of famine on (a) plough animals, (b) milch animals and (c) young stock, as also the problem of replacement of animals lost during a famine.

The district of Hissar was known widely for its cattle wealth. Before the war every year ten cattle fairs were held; in 1936, 144,459 animals were brought for sale and transactions valued at Rs. 2·3 million were concluded. In the territories by which the district is surrounded, a score or more fairs were held each year and these were popular specially with villages lying within a range of 20 to 30 miles. At the cattle census of February, 1935, there were in the district 101,016 bullocks, 42,036 camels, 119,460 cows, 89,957 buffaloes, and well over 250,000 young stock. Five years later, in February 1940, while the district was still under the impact of the famine, the next cattle census returned 58,137 bullocks, 26,556 camels, 67,218 cows, 46,871 buffaloes and about 117,000 young stock. Cattle census data may be far from accurate, but the comparison is at least instructive.*

Next to land, cattle are the greatest wealth and in some areas the annual income from livestock contributes more to the support of the people than land itself. When crops begin to wither, the problem of cattle becomes even more urgent than that of men. *Tinkal* or fodder scarcity has

---

*In the recent past, thanks to irrigation and other developments, the Hissar district has been one of the more rapidly advancing rural areas in the country. In 1961, the population was 1·54 million compared to 1·05 million in 1951 and 1·01 million in 1941. In 1966, the district had 149,791 bullocks, 66,802 camels, 141,479 cows, 192,923 buffaloes and over 350,000 young stock.

always been the first of the three phases of famine described by the word *trikal*, the other two being food and water.

The account which follows is based on data for 1055 families living in 8 unirrigated villages. These included 719 families of peasant owners and 336 from 'non-agricultural' castes and groups. When the famine set in around August-September, 1938, the families studied had in all 837 bullocks, 246 camels, 845 cows, 623 buffaloes, 294 male calves, 471 female calves and heifers, and 375 buffalo calves and heifers. At the end of the famine, more than two years later, after allowing for losses and replacements over the period, compared to the number before the famine, they had about three-fifths of the bullocks, three-fourths of the camels, about a fourth of the cows, buffaloes and male calves and about a third of the female calves and heifers. While there is no suggestion that the sample of families investigated was statistically representative, the problems thrown up were illustrative of situations known to be widely prevalent at the time, so that it was permissible to draw at least some broad conclusions for the future from this study of a period of distress which had engulfed the bulk of the population of the district of Hissar for more than two years.

Of all animals, camels were the easiest to preserve because of their hardy character and the possibility of using them for hire and, in some areas, also for petty trade. A camel in the hands of a man who is not a stay-at-home is a good piece of famine insurance. One-fifth of the camels were lost through death. Nearly a third were sold and an equal number were acquired in the course of the famine. At the end, the number was still 74 per cent of the pre-famine figure.

Despite the Government's effort to save bullocks, specially during the first part of the famine, over 30 per cent were lost by death and 37 per cent by sale for cash. At kharif, in 1939 and in 1940, the urgency of cultivating the land compelled peasants to bring in new animals, and in many cases ornaments were sold, new debts were incurred and the favour of friends and relatives was eagerly sought for buying plough animals. By the second year of the famine, the families studied were left with only 50 per cent of their bullocks though, through fresh purchases, the number increased later to 60 per cent of the pre-famine figure.

A famine always tells hard on cows, which are kept in Hissar more for breeding than for milk. For every 100 cows at the start of the famine, more than 40 died, 23 were sold, 8 let loose or sent away to *gaushalas* and four or five lost in other ways. There was scarcely any replacement, the new animals being only 7 per cent of the number lost during the famine. At the end the peasants had little over a quarter of the number they possessed in August, 1938.

Deaths among buffaloes amounted to 22 per cent, but more than one-half were sold for cash and about 8 per cent were disposed of on credit. Buffaloes are very expensive to maintain and hence few peasants attempted to get new buffaloes. At the end of the famine, the families studied possessed only one-sixth of the number of buffaloes they had two years earlier.

Out of 100 male calves at the beginning, about a third died, 3 were let loose or sent to *gaushalas*, 41 were sold for cash and 9 were disposed of otherwise. At the end of the famine, the families studied possessed hardly one-fourth of the male calves they had before the famine. Deaths among female calves were even heavier than among male calves, being about 40 per cent of the pre-famine numbers. One fourth of the female buffalo calves were sold for cash at an early stage in the famine. After allowing for the small replacements which occurred, barely one-third of the original number were to be found at the end of the famine.

The number of plough animals was never allowed to fall

much below 60 per cent of the pre-famine figure. On the other hand, the position of milch cattle and of young stock continued to deteriorate with the result that the supply of milk and milk products dwindled to at least a fourth of the normal. Similarly, for a cattle-breeding tract, diminution in young stock was a matter for great concern.

About 95 per cent of the camels and 89 per cent of the bullocks sold were given for cash. Money-lenders readily accepted whatever animals they could possibly get at the outbreak of the famine and often gave them what were, for the period under study, fancy book prices. Whereas 93 per cent of the buffaloes sold were given either for cash or credit, the proportion in the case of cows was 88. Some milch cattle were even given away as gifts, mainly to daughters living away from the parents' village. Of the animals which were disposed of, sales for cash amounted to 81 per cent in the case of male calves, 65 per cent in the case of buffalo calves and heifers and 45 per cent in that of female calves and heifers. Generally, 25 to 30 per cent of the animals were disposed of outside the district. Cattle fairs accounted for the largest sales in the case of camels and male calves; buffaloes, as in normal times, continued to be purchased by itinerant cattle merchants directly from the villages. Cows and heifers were scarcely sent to fairs.

The data on prices are limited and may not be quite accurate. It seems that the first effect of the famine was to depress the prices. The price of bullocks fell relatively less than the price of camels. The price of bullocks did not recover materially until 1940, but the price of camels began to recover in the spring of 1939 and reached the pre-famine level in the autumn. In the case of bullocks, the rise in prices was due to their scarcity; in the case of camels, it was due to the realisation that the camel was a good earner in bad times. The price of camels might have risen earlier if it had been anticipated that the famine would be something more than a short year's stress. Taken as a whole, prices of plough animals remained steady, despite the severity of the famine. Some of the best buffaloes were sent to Bombay or Calcutta at what seemed then to be very high prices. Prices of cows, male calves and other young stock fell very sharply.

To sum up, therefore, when a famine deprives the farmer of his capacity to maintain his cattle and throws him on to his meagre margins, his impulse leads him to sell such of his animals as he is not obliged or able to maintain. The impulse is sound but, as mortality figures show, the farmer feeds on hope from one harvest to another, and the waiting process itself involves heavy losses. While camels largely find the means for their own maintenance, bullocks need special assistance. With some effort, on the whole, the plough animal position may be maintained, but milk supply deteriorates seriously at the very moment when the reduced and inferior diet to which a famine drives the rural population makes the need for vitamins and essential foods greater than ever before. Buffaloes, being readily realisable assets, are sold at the first opportunity and, in the case of cows, as we have seen, losses are heavy and come swiftly. There is little incentive or ability to maintain young stock, so that the future development of the cattle economy is jeopardised.

During the famine 52 per cent of the camels and 46 per cent of the bullocks lost by the people were replaced, but there was very little replacement in respect of milch cattle and young stock. Some attempts were made in June, 1939, and again in June, 1940, to provide loans for the purchase of bullocks, but the extent to which peasants obtained plough animals on their own made government aid an almost unimportant factor in the situation.

From this analysis of the effects of a typical famine situation on different classes of livestock, the main conclu-
16

sion to be drawn is that a complete famine policy must take account of the part played by each class of cattle in the economic life of the people, the manner in which each category is affected by the catastrophe and the resources available to different sections of the population. The policy envisaged in the famine codes, which were adopted at the beginning of the present century, may be summed up in five propositions:

(1) encouraging greater production of fodder in canal-irrigated tracts and through the sinking of temporary wells in the areas affected;

(2) importing fodder, mainly through private enterprise;

(3) arranging for grazing facilities in state pastures;

(4) assisting removal of cattle to the hills; and

(5) opening cattle camps under veterinary supervision for selected cows and bulls, the chief object being to preserve valuable breeds.

As a policy, these propositions have proved inadequate on more than one occasion in different parts of the country. The prospect of increasing the supply of fodder and of resorting to State pastures is negligible in an area prone to famine. Migration of cattle has been attended frequently by heavy losses, mainly due to death and starvation. Moreover, in order that the migration of cattle may be a source of relief, it is not enough that the areas to which they move should provide sufficient natural grazing by hillside or riverside; there must also be work for men. Experience bears out that import of fodder through private agencies, accompanied by public distribution, often gives rise to abuse and misallocation of available supplies. Finally, more than once we have known cattle concentration camps wound up hurriedly in the middle of a famine because they failed to achieve their purpose and proved costly to run. As one famine code wisely points out, it is far more effective to bring the fodder to the cattle and to keep the cattle in the village. The best way of preserving cattle is to help their owners in the villages.

When a famine occurs and supplies of fodder are no longer available, cattle-owners are thrown in the first instance upon their fodder reserves brought over from the previous season and upon their ability to purchase such fodder stocks as may be forthcoming. On both counts the majority of farmers are in a weak position. The rations which they are able to allow, for instance, to bullocks, cows and calves become more and more meagre and, within the first few months, there may be heavy losses through death accounting, in the investigation in Hissar, to well over a third of the total number. It would, therefore, be sound policy to advise all farmers and more particularly the poorer ones to sell in the neighbouring non-famine areas at least a proportion of their animals at an early stage in the famine. No small farmer need retain more than one milch animal; young stock should be maintained chiefly on grounds of quality by those who can bear the expense; the number of bullocks can also be reduced on the whole by about a third. Animals which can no longer be maintained with advantage or which are not absolutely essential for the farmer's personal needs, whether for milk or cultivation, should be sold at cattle fairs while they still retain strength and vigour. To sell them in a semi-starved condition, when they are nearer death than life and their owners have reached a state of distress, is to incur a double loss. Loss of this character has been a constant feature in famines; timely guidance can help cultivators to avoid it.

Apart from such fodder as a certain number of farmers may have in storage, fodder supplies in a famine have to be obtained mainly through the agency of government. It is, therefore, the duty of public authorities to arrange for supplies of fodder on a scale commensurate with the needs of the famine area. To use these supplies to the best advantage, the problem of maintaining cattle should be seen from three points of view. These are, firstly, the extent to which a particular class of cattle must be preserved in the immediate interests of health or agricultural efficiency; secondly, the extent to which it is necessary to preserve a particular breed; and thirdly, the extent to which different classes of cattle can 'earn' their own keep. In other words, as soon as the character of a famine has been fairly assessed, the objectives and targets should be determined in terms of different classes of cattle. Having done so and agreed upon the measure of relief to be given, it should be the task of the famine administration to ensure that help is given in an efficient and continuous manner. Care should be taken to work out a ration which will provide all the necessary food constituents at minimum cost over the *entire* period of stress. Often, the fodder provided during a famine is poor in quality and ill-suited to the health of the animals to whom it is served. The needs of animals maintained in this manner and the seasonal factor should be kept in view. Although these may seem elementary cautions, it is easy to lose sight of them.

What, then, should be the objectives for different classes of animals ? A few broad considerations derived from the investigation in Hissar which, with appropriate modifications, may have interest also for other areas affected by famine conditions, may be put forward.

In areas in which they are important as plough animals and beasts of burden, camels are an earning asset during famine and may be left entirely to themselves; their owners will either sell them or earn a small livelihood with their help.

Buffaloes make it possible for their owners to pull through the famine by selling *ghee*. But they are expensive to maintain and when money is short it is tempting to sell them. Sales of buffaloes on a large scale were the main cause of the reduction in milk supplies during the Hissar famine which, in turn, had adverse effects, specially on the health of the children. If small farmers are enabled to maintain their buffaloes during dry periods, provided these are otherwise worth keeping, fewer sales are likely to take place and the supply of milk will be kept up to a considerable extent.

In the case of bullocks, even in the worst periods, there is fairly extensive replacement at harvest time. The real danger lies less in reduced numbers and temporary insufficiency for ploughing, as in the fact that very largely inferior animals take the place of superior ones. The longterm effects of this change on the economy of the affected area deserve more attention than they have so far received. The remedy lies in assuring adequate and continued assistance to good animals owned by those who would not be able to keep them without special help. It has been observed that during famine veterinary doctors tend to recommend assistance to animals who conform to their standards for a particular breed. In doing so, they overlook the fact that the strongest animals often belong to those who are probably able to keep them on their own. Such a policy sends the poorer owners to the wall. The quality of the animal and judgement of its owner's means should both be taken into account in determining the measure of help to be rendered on behalf of the government; in the past, much injustice and loss have occurred through concentration only on the first factor.

In the case of cows, breeding is often a more important aspect than milk yields. In deciding upon a policy, the first place should be given to the requirements of breeding. If a large proportion of peasants carry the burden of maintaining cows longer than they have the strength to, death takes a heavy toll and the animals which remain over are but poor assets.

For young livestock, policy has to be guided wholly by considerations of breeding value.

It would be desirable to propose some specific goals on a regional basis even within a single district, so that the varying circumstances of different sections of the population can be taken into account. It is difficult to lay down general guide-lines for different classes of animals but, broadly speaking, much could be gained if it were possible to assure at least one bullock to every farmer holding, say, more than 5 acres, and a milch animal to as many families as possible. In the tract as a whole, a minimum objective may be to preserve at least one half of the cows and a third of the young stock. For buffaloes and bullocks, the preservation of at least two-thirds of the total number may be considered to be reasonable objectives for a period of prolonged famine.

However complete the policy may be, during a period of famine, plough animals are bound to fall short of demand. It is best on such occasions to advance small public loans for hiring animals. Through a combination of the policy of preservation of plough animals and assistance for hiring, it should be possible to ensure that all land will be ploughed. Loans for purchase of plough animals have been found to be both costly and ineffective.

During famine, the administration of fodder assistance is exposed to a number of obvious dangers such as corruption, inefficiency and waste. There are, in addition, three fundamental errors which those in charge of a famine should take special pains to avoid. The first error is that of regarding fodder permits as favours to be distributed to owners of animals according to the preference of subordinate officials. The second error is the failure to preserve a proper balance between value for breeding, the owner's means and the place of each category of animals in the economic life of the people. The third error is the failure to give consistent and continuous support to animals selected for preservation. It has been observed that, although large sums may be spent, the numbers supported by way of fodder assistance may change so fitfully from month to month that the survival of such animals as remain in the end can be hardly attributed to help rendered by the government. Many mistakes are avoided if the conception and execution of fodder policy are under a single administration, and care is taken to define and follow objectives clearly with reference to the essential needs of the people.

The cattle policy which has been described above is designed to answer the needs of the present rural economy. If peasant owners could be organised into larger co-operative farm units, a great deal more should be possible at small cost. It would become feasible, for instance, for these farms to carry perhaps a year's supply of fodder in store, to adjust more easily to changing conditions, and to pursue dairy farming and the manufacture of milk products as wholetime occupations, so that even imported fodder supplies may be a source of gain. There will be scope also for promoting suitable rural insurance schemes which could enable farmers to replace cattle without carrying debts into the future. With cattle policy, as with every other aspect of our rural economic life, the first need is to re-organise the very basis upon which our agriculture is conducted.

PART TWO
PLANNING AND PLAN IMPLEMENTATION

15

JAWAHARLAL NEHRU AND
THE FIVE YEAR PLANS*

THE SETTING up of the Planning Commission, with the
Prime Minister as Chairman, was announced towards
the end of February, 1950, within a month of the pro-
mulgation of the Constitution. Jawaharlal Nehru's decision
to associate himself with planning in this way was more
than a symbolic act. Years of preparation through identification with the problems of the masses and the work of
the National Planning Committee lay behind this association. In the fourteen years and more which have since
elapsed, Jawaharlal Nehru's association was of decisive
significance at every important juncture, both within
the Planning Commission and outside. Whether it was
in the Cabinet, in Parliament, in relation to States, in
moulding and educating public opinion, or in projecting
the country's economic and social goals abroad, he remained
the greatest support and inspiration behind India's planned
development. His last meeting with the Planning Commis-

*Adapted from a contribution to *Yojana*, Vol. VIII, No. 11, June 7, 1964,
pages 5-9. Jawaharlal Nehru passed away on May 27, 1964. The paper
points to the nature and significance of his personal association with each
of the three Five Year Plans which carried his name.

sion took place on May 10, 1964 when he said that he would be glad to give as much time as was needed because he was deeply interested in planning. Since the informal meeting, which Jawaharlal Nehru attended on March 12, 1950, and the first official meeting on March 28, 1950, and until the closing period, he visited the offices of the Planning Commission on an average twenty times a year or more, his visits being specially frequent during periods when intensive preparation of successive Five Year Plans was under way. At such times, he followed the discussions on major issues intently and, where there was a vital principle or departure involved, he listened carefully and gave a direction for the future. Sometimes, his mind was already made up and the issues were quickly resolved.

Tasks for the Planning Commission

When Jawaharlal Nehru assumed office as Vice-President of the Interim Government on September 2, 1946, no one knew the shape of the future. Within a few weeks, he took two steps which were to prove important later. The first was the appointment of an Advisory Planning Board which recommended the setting up of a Planning Commission. The second was the constitution of a Scientific Manpower Committee whose work prepared the ground for the remarkable advance of scientific and technical education in subsequent years. At this juncture, Jawaharlal Nehru also gave the utmost support to the programme for establishing a chain of national laboratories, for which plans earlier conceived in outline were now greatly enlarged.

Through the political turmoils and uncertainties of 1947 and the terrible aftermath of Partition and the new anxieties which Kashmir brought, for a period little could be done in pursuit of planning. However, from around the middle of 1949, Jawaharlal Nehru's mind turned more and more to the solution of the food problem and to economic planning. Towards the end of 1949, he gave a great deal of time to a foreign expert, who prepared a memorandum setting out his ideas concerning economic planning and the machinery required for it. This memorandum was considered by senior government officials whose approach to planning the Prime Minister found halting in the extreme. Soon, he travelled alone far beyond their thinking and, if one's belief is correct, in January, 1950, at a meeting of the Congress Working Committee, the decision was taken to ask the Government to constitute a Planning Commission. Two days after the Finance Minister announced the composition of the Commission, with Mr. G. L. Nanda as the Deputy Chairman and a distinguished membership, the draft of a Government of India Resolution setting out the terms of reference came up for consideration. Jawaharlal Nehru re-wrote a considerable part of the draft and, in particular, in the words cited below he linked up the work of the Planning Commission directly to the Fundamental Rights and to the Directive Principles of State Policy embodied in the Constitution:

"The Constitution of India has guaranteed certain Fundamental Rights to the citizens of India and enunciated certain Directive Principles of State Policy, in particular, that the State shall strive to promote the welfare of the people by securing and protecting as effectively as it may a social order in which justice, social, economic and political, shall inform all the institutions of the national life, and shall direct its policy towards securing, among other things,

(a) that the citizens, men and women equally, have the right to an adequate means of livelihood;

(b) that the ownership and control of the material resources of the country are so distributed as best to subserve the common good; and

(c) that the operation of the economic system does not result in the concentration of wealth and means of production to the common detriment.

Having regard to these rights and in furtherance of these principles as well as of the declared objective of the Government to promote a rapid rise

in the standard of living of the people by efficient exploitation of the resources of the country, increasing production, and offering opportunities
to all for employment in the service of the community,
The Planning Commission will...."

Thus, though the accent was more marked in later years, from the very beginning, India's planning was rooted in the concepts of Democracy and Socialism and the objective of giving equal opportunity to and creating the conditions of good life for the masses of the people.

Since India accepted the approach of planned development, many other countries have also formulated and implemented their own economic plans. Perhaps what has distinguished India's plans from those of other poor countries is their sense of continuity, going back to the insights and inspirations of the days of the national struggle, the widening horizon and the greater depth from one plan to the next, and the involvement in the plans, though still far from complete, of millions of people at all levels of national life. The significance of India's plans lies not merely in the economic expansion which might be achieved but, even more, in the transformation of the social order, the emergence of a broad-based leadership at the level of the community, and the creation of the institutions of democracy through which the people everywhere could harness their energies to the solution of their common problems, improvement of living conditions and the development of human resources. These trends became possible because of the outlook which Jawaharlal Nehru and a long line of national leaders before him, from Dadabhai Naoroji to Mahatma Gandhi, brought to bear on the movement for national freedom. Their total impact is not easy to measure, nor can it yet be fully assessed.

Each of the first three Five Year Plans was presented by Jawaharlal Nehru to Parliament. He regarded the beginning and the end of a Five Year Plan as vital dates in the nation's history. His speeches in Parliament on each Plan traversed far beyond the dimensions and priorities of the Plan and conveyed to the nation a series of vistas into the future, some in sharp focus, others in outline.

BASIC GOALS AND APPROACH

Although the First Five Year Plan laid the foundation for many important developments of later years, and in the life of a nation its first Plan will often be its most important, to Jawaharlal Nehru India's First Plan somehow seemed always less than adequate in its total comprehension. However, among its contributions he set great store by the idea of community projects which, he said:

is something which is basically revolutionary, if worked well...We have not paid enough attention to these rural areas in the past and, unless we bring them up to a certain level, we shall always be weighed down by them.

Jawaharlal Nehru read through several chapters of the Plan and even wrote in a few paragraphs himself. Yet, the Plan seemed to him to be wanting in the perspective for the future and in placing sufficient emphasis on basic objectives. It was also weak in its scientific and industrial content. These thoughts were much in his mind through 1954 and 1955.

At the meeting of the National Development Council on November 9, 1954, held immediately after his return from China, in the course of an opening address, Jawaharlal Nehru offered some of his current reflections. Planning, he said:

is not putting down just as you want, planning is not merely giving priority to all things which you wish to do. Planning is something wider and deeper ... Now, the first thing I should imagine about planning is to have a definite picture of where you are going to; one cannot frame vaguely, just doing good deeds from day to day like the boy scouts, or putting up good enterprises which are good, of course, but we have to have some definite picture. I do not mean to say it should be a rigid picture; it may be a changing picture as we gather experience, information, etc. Nevertheless, we have to plan for something.

Then he went on to describe the problems of 'under-developed countries and poverty-stricken people, more or less, chiefly agricultural, trying to industrialise themselves.' He said:

> the mere fact of dealing with these vast populations is an exacting operation —changing them not at the top, not by laws passed by Parliament here, but changing the human will, and taking them out of that static condition of mind and social habit which has been their lot for a long time.

He continued:

> I wish to lay stress on that. The Planning Commission is of no use at all if it has a static outlook. That way, we sit, we sleep, we rest. One must have that dynamic outlook of change, change of every kind—political, of course, economic and social.

A moment later, he came to his central theme:

> The picture I have in mind is definitely and absolutely of a socialistic picture of society. I may not be using the word in a dogmatic sense at all, but in the sense of meaning largely that the means of production should be socially owned and controlled for the benefit of society as a whole.

In this picture, Jawaharlal Nehru saw plenty of room for private enterprise, provided the main aim was kept clear. The dominance that private enterprise had throughout the world during a certain period seemed to him to be out of date; indeed, any system based on acquisitiveness was also immoral.

From this perspective and approach, Jawaharlal Nehru went on to speak of industrialisation and industrial growth:

> We as an under-developed country, industrially under-developed, have continually to fight trying to cross that barrier of under-development, so that we may be able to go a little faster.
>
> Now, if we think in terms of building up our industry, me must give up the idea of continually getting machines from abroad. We must build them here. I see it is just obvious ... We must aim at producing machines, the basic things here.

Thus, in a single speech Jawaharlal Nehru brought together the main strands of Parliament's Resolution of December, 1954, on the socialist pattern of society, the thinking in the Indian National Congress at Avadi, the Industrial Policy Resolution of April, 1956 and a considerable part of the strategy of development towards a self-reliant economy proposed in the Second and the Third Five Year Plans.

SOCIALISM AND INDUSTRIAL GROWTH

These trends in thinking influenced the formulation of the Second Five Year Plan and indeed became an organic part of it. In retrospect, it is possible to see why, without being committed in detail, Jawaharlal Nehru was greatly attracted to the scheme of development outlined in the draft plan frame prepared by Professor P. C. Mahalanobis. Jawaharlal Nehru saw the approach in this document as marking a turn towards acceleration in economic growth, towards basic changes in the industrial and technological structure, the application of science and scientific method on a larger scale, and promise of a self-reliant economy which would itself possess the means to achieve rapid economic progress and solve urgent social problems. This was a period of intense debate and criticism, but Jawaharlal Nehru adhered throughout to all his fundamental propositions. He expressed them most completely in two important addresses, one delivered to the Standing Committee of the National Development Council on January 7, 1956, and the other to the National Development Council on January 20, 1956. In these, he declared that it was our firm policy to go towards a socialist structure of society. 'Taking India as it is,' he said, 'I think we have the background here, the urge and the necessity for going in that direction.' This would be a long term process. For this purpose, long-term planning was essential, so that we have some clear idea of what in 15 years' time we hope to achieve. Shorter plans must be fitted in with the broad general scheme. Ultimately, we should develop that structure of society which encourages the right impulses and not the wrong impulses, the right

17

trends and not the wrong trends.' Jawaharlal Nehru believed
in our capacity in India in winning over people rather than
fighting them. He said:

> We can bring about social changes and developments, under pressure of
> events, by the pressure of democracy and also by a friendly co-operative
> approach, rather than the approach of trying to eliminate each other and
> the stronger party winning. I think we can do that, even in the industrial
> field.

Perhaps, it is in this phase that Jawaharlal Nehru's views
on the general concepts of planning came to be most clearly
defined. He emphasised that planning and, specially democratic planning, meant consultation with as large a number
of people as possible from all over India. The approach to
planning depended more and more not only upon the
broader objectives, but had to be based on statistical data,
sample surveys and calculation at every stage of the results
of the action we contemplate. Planning meant the inter-
locking of production, consumption, employment and a
large number of other things, like transport, social services,
education and health. In seeking the objective of socialism,
there should be some precise content about the goal, about
the methods and about the means by which we seek to
achieve the goal.

Jawaharlal Nehru did not wish merely to nationalise and
waste resources in compensating private parties, but certain
fields of activity should be sacrosanct for the State, and
the public sector should be given much greater scope.
Subject to these, there should be every opportunity and
freedom for private enterprise to grow, and we should increase and encourage every element to produce and help
in nation-building.

There should be much greater stress on heavy machine-
making industry, as that was to be the basis of industrial
growth. He declared:

> You must go to the root and the base, and build up that root and base on
> which you will build up the structure of industrial growth. Therefore, it is

heavy industries that count, nothing else counts, excepting as a balancing factor which is, of course, important. We want planning for heavy machine-making industries and heavy industries; we want industries that make heavy machines, and we should set about them as rapidly as possible because it takes time.

These thoughts led directly to the revision of the Industrial Policy Resolution of 1948 and to the new Industrial Policy Resolution of 1956, which has since held the field. The approach to industrial development set out in this Resolution was applied successively to steel, coal and oil, in each case after a degree of controversy. In steel and oil, in particular, without strong personal support from Jawaharlal Nehru, it would have been difficult to proceed very far. These trends were helped decisively by what was at the time a new factor in India's development, namely, the offer of economic and technical aid by the Soviet Union.

Co-operation and Panchayati Raj

Jawaharlal Nehru saw planning as a movement, in thinking and action, from the political to the social and the economic plane. As he observed in the National Development Council in May 1956, when the final draft of the Second Five Year Plan was being discussed, the more one considered the complexity of planning, the greater was the fascination for it. 'The new problems which arose at every step,' he said, 'gave confidence in ourselves and the ability of the people to achieve development.'

Already, at this stage, Jawaharlal Nehru's mind had begun to turn from industry to agriculture and the rural economy. Emphasising the great importance of food production for the Second Plan, he said, in a sense, the whole Plan depended upon food being relatively abundant and the price of it not being high. Community projects and the national extension schemes were of great importance, for they were changing the minds and, to some extent, the habits of the people in the rural areas, apart from the material benefits which they brought. But they should devote greater attention to the production of more food, for this was the primary purpose for which they were started.

In the three years that followed, Jawaharlal Nehru's influence and direction led to a number of important decisions in the rural sector. In November, 1958, the National Development Council adopted a Resolution on Co-operative Policy. For the development of co-operation as a people's movement, the Council declared that it was essential that co-operatives should be organised on the basis of the village community as the primary unit, and that responsibility and initiative for social and economic development at the village level should be placed fully on the village co-operative and the village panchayat. At the same session of the National Development Council, the decision was taken to introduce State trading in foodgrains at the wholesale level. The policy was worked out in detail in the succeeding months but, for reasons upon which it is not necessary to dwell here, it remained substantially unimplemented. Earlier, in January 1958, with the fullest support of Jawaharlal Nehru, the National Development Council had taken a major step in deciding upon establishing a system of democratic institutions at the village, block and district levels which later came to be known as Panchayati Raj, a name provided by the Prime Minister himself.

At this stage in the country's development, Jawaharlal Nehru also felt concerned at the slow progress in carrying out co-operative farming and in implementing the programme for land reform. On both issues, there had been considerable discussion at the highest level when the Second Plan was being formulated. Jawaharlal Nehru had thrown his weight decisively on the side of co-operative farming and agrarian reform. The Second Plan had envisaged such essential steps being taken as would provide sound foundations for co-operative farming, so that over a period of ten years or so, a substantial proportion of agricultural lands could be cultivated on co-operative lines. Similarly, proposals in the Plan for agrarian reform represented a broad common approach to be adopted and pursued in each State as part of the national plan with due regard to local conditions and in response to local needs. The principles of change and reorganisation on which the scheme of land reform was being based were conceived as part of the wider social and economic outlook which must surely apply in some degree to every part of the economy. These were basic approaches to fundamental national problems. They were accepted by the States and at the political level but, on account of weaknesses in political organisation and in administration, action had lagged far behind. It was natural, therefore, that the resolutions of the Indian National Congress at Nagpur early in 1959 should be devoted to these and other agrarian problems.

ISSUES FOR THE THIRD PLAN

By this time, Jawaharlal Nehru was thinking again of the future and specially of the Third Five Year Plan and beyond. In a long series of meetings in the Planning Commission, in November and December, 1958, and early in 1959, Jawaharlal Nehru explored the question of basic objectives which should be set for the future. It was now less necessary to stress the need for building up a strong industrial base and an economy capable of self-sustained growth, for these concepts had come to be integrated into India's approach to planning. The issues which arose in relation to industry had to be dealt with primarily at the technical, administrative and financial level. Action for economic and social change in the rural areas lay largely in the States. Jawaharlal Nehru felt more and more concerned with lags in education, with the need to ensure certain minimum amenities to the mass of the people in the rural areas, with the problem of slum clearance and slum improvement in the cities and, more keenly than ever before, with the welfare of children. The emphasis in the Third Five Year Plan on these aspects of development was strongly influenced by the views which Jawaharlal Nehru urged repeatedly within the Planning Commission and in other forums.

As work on the Third Five Year Plan progressed through the Draft Outline to the Final Report, three questions came to the fore and drew Jawaharlal Nehru's personal attention. The first concerned the targets for steel and coal and, through these, for the development of heavy and basic industries. The Prime Minister left no doubt in the minds of his colleagues that these, along with power and rural electrification, were essential objectives, that the Bokaro steel plant should be given the highest priority and that the target for steel should not be less than ten million tons.

The second issue concerned the size of investment in the Third Plan, specially in the public sector. There was a significant gap between the financial requirements of programmes accepted for the public sector in the Third Plan and the resources which were indicated. The Plan adopted the approach which Jawaharlal Nehru had proposed, namely, that the physical programmes to be accepted for implementation over the five year period should not be altogether limited by the financial resources immediately in sight at the stage of drawing up the Plan, although the outlays incurred would have to be regulated with reference to the actual resources mobilised from year to year. Behind this was Jawaharlal Nehru's confidence in the future and his view of the nature of planning. He held that the programme for industrial development, including power, transport, technical education and scientific research, should proceed in a connected manner in accordance with the approved scheme of priorities so that, as the requisite foreign exchange became available, corresponding internal resources were also found and rapid progress was assured. Whatever we could do ourselves by way of advance action or otherwise should be done, for the costliest thing in planning was time lost to action. Opportunities should be seized upon as they came and there should be readiness to take a measure of risk in speeding development.

The third issue, which exercised Jawaharlal Nehru, was the need to set forth the social objectives of planning as clearly as possible. The Planning Commission, the Central Cabinet and the National Development Council gave a great deal of time to the section in the Third Plan on 'objectives of planned development', but it did not yet have Jawaharlal Nehru's personal touch. Accordingly, at the request of the National Development Council, he took the draft to the hills, worked upon it paragraph by paragraph, adding substantial portions and improving upon others and, thus, emerged the final statement which forms the first chapter of the Third Five Year Plan and comes close to being his final testament. In this, Jawaharlal Nehru linked present developments to the aspirations and outlook of the leaders of our national movement, drew the economic progress and welfare of each country into the larger context of efforts to build up a liberated humanity, brought out the intimate connection between national objectives and the maintenance of world peace, and ended, finally, on the following note:

Planning is a continuous process and cannot be isolated for short periods. Thus, the Third Five Year Plan is a projection and a continuation of the First and the Second Plans, and it will lead to the Fourth and subsequent Plans. Planning is a continuous movement towards desired goals and, because of this, all major decisions have to be made by agencies informed of these goals and the social purpose behind them. Even in considering a five-year period, forward and long-term planning has always to be kept in view. Indeed, perspective planning is of the essence of the planning process. As this process develops, there is a certain rhythm of expansion in the development of the people, and a sense of enterprise and achievement comes to them. They are conscious of a purpose in life and have a feeling of being participants in the making of history. Ultimately, it is the development of the human being and the human personality that counts. Although planning involves material investment, even more important is the investment in man. The people of India today, with all their burdens and problems, live on the frontier of a new world which they are helping to build. In order to cross this frontier they have to possess courage and enterprise, the spirit of endurance and capacity for hard work, and the vision of the future.

DEFENCE AND THE PLAN

In the second year of the Third Plan, with the attack from China, came a critical moment for planning. Some said that the Plan would have to be heavily pruned, even set aside, and some agencies and some responsible officials in the Government began to give a low priority to the Plan. However, at the height of the crisis, early in November, 1962, Jawaharlal Nehru set his face firmly against any attempt to nibble at the Plan from within. We are at the crossroads of history, he said to the National Development Council, and are facing great historical problems on which depends our future. The Plan was the warp and woof of our national life and it was the war effort itself that requires the Plan. The basis of the Plan was to strengthen the nation, to increase production. Of course, non-essential expenditures should be kept down and too much must not be spent on big buildings and construction, but the basic objective of the Plan was to strengthen the nation and, therefore, the Plan should be looked upon as an essential part of the national effort. The support which Jawaharlal Nehru gave at this stage and in the succeeding months made it possible not only to continue the Plan, but also to enlarge its scope in some vital directions.

A NATIONAL CONSENSUS

Planning in a federal and democratic structure necessarily brings up difficult problems from time to time. Jawaharlal

Nehru was always conscious of these. As far back as 1951, he had decided to set up the National Development Council. The influence which this Council acquired over the years was in large measure his personal contribution. At the very first meeting in November, 1952, and in many subsequent meetings, Jawaharlal Nehru stressed that the Chief Ministers of States bore intimate responsibility for the Plan in all its phases. As Chief Ministers, they shouldered heavy responsibility for their States and naturally had to think of their States but, at the same time, as members of the Council, they had to shoulder responsibility for the whole of India and had to look upon every question from a national point of view. In addition to building up a continuing partnership between the Centre and the States in the formulation and implementation of economic plans and policies, Jawaharlal Nehru stressed at every stage the need to achieve a national consensus, to seek the counsel of various political parties and other groups and to bring to bear the entire weight of the nation in support of the Plan. Jawaharlal Nehru succeeded to a very large extent in both the aims he had set himself. It is perhaps permissible to add that, on its part, from the beginning, the Planning Commission endeavoured equally to translate Jawaharlal Nehru's outlook into appropriate working relations with the States and to function in all matters as an institution wholly committed to the national good.

16

ECONOMIC GROWTH AND DISPARITIES IN LEVELS OF DEVELOPMENT*

IN THE recent past, there has been growing concern over two aspects of India's economic development. The mid-term appraisal of the Third Plan brought out the critical role of increase in agricultural production and suggested that the achievement of sustained growth demands a scale and intensity of effort and a quality of implementation far exceeding performance in the past. Questionings concerning the means to more rapid growth have been accompanied by equal anxiety over increase in disparities in income, and wealth and in levels of living and opportunity. The underlying issues have not yet been laid bare, but two broad

*Adapted from the Brij Narain Memorial Lectures, 1964, delivered on February 7 and 8, 1964 at the Punjab University, Chandigarh. The first lecture was devoted to a broad analysis of the principal economic factors and the general approach, and the second to outlining some implications by way of policy and planning for the next phase in India's development. Long before India attained freedom, there was a great deal of pre-occupation over the problems of poverty and the shape of the future social and economic structure. Among scholars who devoted a life-time of study to these problems, one of the best known was Professor Brij Narain of Lahore. He was a man of learning and a dedicated teacher, sincere and fearless in his convictions and in dissecting the ideas of others. One of his last works, published less than a year before Independence, was entitled *The Economic Structure of Free India*.

views appear to be emerging—the view of those who stress the paramount need for stepping up the rate of economic growth even at the cost of having to pass through a period of widening disparities, and the view of those who give priority to social and institutional changes in the hope that, in turn, these will create a sounder basis for economic advance. Behind much current discussion lies one basic issue: the nature of the interaction between economic growth and economic disparities in the context of India's development, the extent of conflict between them and the terms upon which that conflict may be resolved.

I

Disparities in levels of development in an under-developed country should be distinguished from the situation of poverty in plenty which is found in many developed countries even after a long period of advance towards the welfare state. In these countries, sections of the population are, as has been well said, still enclosed in pockets of poverty, but means and resources to attack the problem are at hand and the conscience of the community is now being aroused to bring about speedy and substantial changes in living conditions and opportunities available to the less privileged groups. Our present problem should also be distinguished from the disparities which characterise a static society.

Where changes in the volume and pattern of economic activity and in techniques are so gradual as to be almost imperceptible, disparities persist and harden. But, in their origin and functioning, the dominant elements in these disparities are social, feudal and largely agrarian. Periods of widening disparities and of deepening clash between today's realities and tomorrow's aspirations are nearly always periods of economic change and transition. What gives special significance to the problem of economic disparities in present day India is that, while these bear a strong heritage from the past, increasingly economic development and consequences flowing from it have become the main causal factor underlying the new disparities. India's economic development is taking place under the conditions of a mixed economy, within a framework of democracy and freedom, and in the context of an overall national plan. Those who disagree with the present approach call into question, at the same time, the concept of planned development, of social democracy and of responsibilities falling upon the private sector within the national economy.

In this situation, unless the basic conflicts are resolved to the satisfaction, not merely of the elite and the organised groups, but of the common man, who is bound to judge all policies and plans from the reality of his own living conditions and the problems encountered by him from day to day, there can be no consistent and continuing pattern of development. Moreover, the gap between declared purpose and the actuality can itself become a growing source of discontent and dissatisfaction. The dichotomy comes out most sharply in differences in approach which may often mark decisions concerning the current management of the economy and the principles on which development plans are based. Over a period, such differences can greatly weaken the nation's sense of direction. It is, therefore, essential that the premises of economic and social development and the possibilities to be explored by way of policy and action should be widely appreciated.

In speaking of disparities in levels of development, at the very beginning, one may counter the suggestion that in a large and comparatively under-developed country like India, there could be more or less uniform levels of development between different groups in the community and between different regions. The essential question relates to the range of disparities and the directions in which they may be increasing or diminishing. It is also necessary to define the concepts employed, bringing them to the extent possible, within the scope of measurement and appraisal. The expression 'level of development' represents three related notions: firstly, the average level of living; secondly, per capita income and its rate of change; and, thirdly, the pattern of production, services and economic activity generally. These elements in the level of development could be assessed, both separately and jointly, for different regions, for urban and rural areas and for different social and economic groups. This is a fruitful field for study and research and in future the extent of development at the national and regional levels could be judged more and more in these terms.

Corresponding to the concept of level of development, one might explore areas of greater or smaller economic change within the economy. The process of economic development will remain incomplete until the bulk of the population comes under the influence of economic change, not passively or through secondary effects, but actively as participants, at rising levels of skill and productivity, in applying new techniques and creating new goods and services. The analysis of disparities accompanying economic growth could perhaps be best undertaken through a study, on the one hand, of changes in levels of development and, on the other, of sectors and regions within the economy which come within the influence of economic change.

It would, probably, be fair to summarise the main features of progress under the Five Year Plans, in so far as they bear on economic growth in relation to disparities, in ten broad propositions:

(1) Significant increases in production have occurred in several basic industries and in regions where new resources have been developed.
(2) Increases in agricultural production have resulted from marked improvements in some areas accompanied by relatively small improvements spread over wider areas; some areas are still stagnant.

270 TOWARDS AN INTEGRATED SOCIETY

(3) The effects of large investments in industry, both at existing centres and at new centres, have been largely limited to these centres. So far 'the spread effects' of these investments have been comparatively small.

(4) The growth of the private sector has led to marked expansion in the range of operations of well-organised business houses, accrual of high incomes in certain categories, specially on account of capital gains, speculation, trade and evasion or avoidance of taxation, and expansion of small and medium-sized industries, mainly in cities and towns.

(5) Considerable development has taken place in a number of large cities and towns. This has intensified the problems of housing, health, water supply and education in urban areas, with which State and municipal administrations have been unable to cope effectively. Worsening of living conditions in many towns is an important aspect of disparities in levels of development.

(6) On the whole, development in areas under heavy pressure of population which were otherwise relatively backward, has barely kept pace with the growth of population, and the existing framework of services and levels of agricultural production are not sufficient to support rapid economic growth. These areas present the problems of poverty, under-employment and low productivity in their acutest form. The growth of population has borne with particular harshness on large sections of the landless population in these areas.

(7) Generally, and more specially in rural areas, benefits of new services and institutions have been availed of much less completely by the weaker sections than by those at the middle or higher levels or who have been already drawn into the development process.

(8) Greater progress in agriculture and greater stress on social services, specially education, and on the utilisation of manpower, would have helped limit disparities in relation to large sections of the rural population.

(9) Increases in price levels accompanied by changing patterns of consumption and demand have affected the lower fixed income groups adversely.

(10) Development of a character sufficiently intensive and far-reaching to counter the trends towards the widening of disparities has not yet occurred in any part of the country or in any branch of the economy.

While the gains and limitations of progress secured thus far could be stated in these terms, it would be a mistake to minimise the present significance or the potential value of the processes of economic transformation which have been initiated or to seek lightly to depart in a basic sense from the objectives and policies set out in the Plans. At the same time, we have to recognise that, even after a decade and more of planning, we are yet in the early stage of economic development. The economic and social problems confronting the country are much too deep-rooted and have dimensions which call not only for a far higher order of national effort but also for constant evaluation of experience, for the forging of new techniques and instruments, and for a much more integrated approach to development. Often, in the way plans work out in real life, problems described in familiar terms are in fact new problems, revealing new facets. Indeed, there are many aspects of our economic and social life and institutions of which our understanding and perception are still quite meagre.

II

Each of our Five Year Plans has set forth its aims under two broad heads, namely, (a) expansion of agriculture and industry and the resulting increase in national income and (b) other objectives, notably utilisation of manpower, expansion of employment, establishment of greater equality of opportunity, reduction in disparities in income and wealth and securing more even distribution of economic power. In the actual implementation of plans, these two sets of objectives have tended to remain too far apart. For this reason, action bearing on the broad social objectives has been diffuse and halting, in effect giving to these objectives an inferior status. Yet, an important premise in our plans is that social objectives are not only essential in themselves but are also a vital means to greater production and attainment of higher levels of productivity. This gap between the plans and their implementation may be partly ascribed to the fact that the goals of economic planning are sometimes interpreted too narrowly or in too simple a way. For instance, by themselves the objectives of self-reliance and modernisation seem to place much greater stress on certain aspects of industrialisation than on resource development, regional or area development and utilisation of manpower resources and on crucial social and welfare components of the developmental process.

It is, therefore, necessary to consider how Plan objectives are in fact translated into action through the scheme of investments, the sources from which investments are financed, decisions bearing on location and technology, relationship between agriculture and industry, and the machinery through which such decisions are implemented. It will be seen that the results outlined earlier are a direct consequence of giving effect to one important part of the Plan, but not to its entire scheme. The results would be significantly different if the investments and the various techniques and instruments employed could fully reflect the concepts and philosophy of the Plan as a whole. The argument here goes beyond the question of priority given to social services as against economic development. The provision of social services is an integral part of economic development. The essential point is that the economic plan itself can and should be so devised and operated as to provide *over a period* both for economic growth and for a range in levels of development between different income groups, between different regions and between urban and rural workers, which a democratic community will accept as fair. This takes us to the basis on which investment decisions in the economic plan are made and the means by which they are implemented.

Investments under the Five Year Plans have to be determined of necessity against the background of overall inadequacy in relation to the needs and possibilities of efficient use. There cannot be too much emphasis on measures to achieve the maximum capital formation feasible and on laying out investments in a manner calculated to provide substantial resources for development in the future. But the task of allocating resources is an exceedingly complex one. Both the Second and the Third Plan represent a stage in the development of the economy during which gestation periods have been relatively long, specially in industry. Larger burdens have, therefore, had to be borne in the present, and returns have tended to be deferred, sometimes considerably more than was foreseen in the blueprints. Secondly, on account of pressing demands for development in different branches of the economy and the difficulties inherent in selection, there has been a tendency to spread resources too thinly. Even within the limitations under which the plans are formulated, there would be a strong case for greater selection and concentration. Thirdly, in many fields of development, the efficiency of the investments undertaken could be enhanced if all the related and complementary investments and other action were undertaken at the same time. Finally, while different objectives of development have to be viewed together, it is of particular importance for a country with meagre resources to assess costs and benefits with the utmost care and, when making decisions which might involve comparatively lower returns, to do so with precise knowledge of gains and sacrifices. The fact that in each of the directions indicated there have been deficiencies in the past accounts, firstly, for the total resources mobilised through development falling below attainable levels, and, secondly, for the smaller spread of benefits in terms of area and by way of multiplier effects across other sectors in the economy.

Even under favourable conditions, investments which do not bear fruit early enough or are not adequately supported by complementary action in related fields would tend to enlarge existing disparities. This result becomes even more probable because of four other factors; namely, the circumstances under which foreign exchange resources have to be obtained, the technology which is adopted, the

18

degree to which conscious and well-conceived policies for locating economic and industrial enterprises are followed and, finally, the limitations of the administrative machinery and of the apparatus available for implementing various plans.

External assistance and credits are indispensable factors in carrying out an important segment of our industrial plans at the present stage of development. Adequate external resources have to be secured for ensuring development in certain key areas. It has, however, to be recognised that in a variety of ways this dependence on external resources, while helping to achieve overall economic growth, also strengthens the trend towards enlargement of disparities. This can happen for two main reasons. Firstly, specially in fields of development assigned to the private sector, credit and collaboration arrangements are reached much more easily by large established undertakings, which are in a position to draw upon extensive resources and facilities on their own account. The Third Five Year Plan envisaged that means would be devised to enable small and medium-sized units and co-operative undertakings to obtain greater advantage of possibilities of foreign collaboration as well as larger credits from public and private financial institutions. So far very little progress has been made along these lines. Secondly, agreements with foreign parties for collaboration in industrial enterprises tend to enlarge disparities, not so much because of the terms and conditions upon which credits are obtained, as because our own approach and policies for import substitution, development of technology appropriate to conditions in India and location of industry have not yet been worked out systematically. With clearer formulation and more effective implementation in these fields, not only could foreign exchange resources help fulfil the objectives of growth and development more completely, but recent trends towards widening of disparities and concentration could be countered to a significant extent.

Over the past decade, industrial capacities have been established and the foundations of scientific and technological research have been laid to an extent which should now make it possible to incorporate a distinct technological dimension in working out all our plans of development. In the earlier phases, it was necessary to set up plants based wholly or largely on foreign designs and calling for extensive use of imported components and raw materials. If the resources and personnel now available for research and investigation are turned to the effective utilisation of indigenous materials and the solution of specific problems, and existing productive capacities are employed in a planned and coordinated manner, dependence on foreign exchange resources can be considerably reduced. This would make it possible to evolve a strategy and a programme, both short-term and long-term, for more rapid technological change suited to the conditions of different branches of our economy.

Against the background of limited resources of capital and foreign exchange and large reserves of manpower, industrial development has to be based on units of different sizes, functioning at varying levels of technique but gaining continuously in efficiency, and coordinated so as to produce goods and services needed by the community. In other words, large-scale, intermediate and small-scale technologies should be viewed as parts of a single dynamic industrial structure, closely related to one another and functioning under a common overall plan of production and development. The absence of a well-worked-out scheme of technological development, inevitable in some measure until recently, has tended to create a bias in favour of large units and large-scale technology which has, in turn, contributed to the widening of disparities. Given time, this trend could be substantially reversed through a systematic approach to technological change. This approach might also make it

possible to undertake intensive and purposeful experimentation at the technical, economic and organisational level
for carrying industry away from metropolitan concentrations
into medium-sized and small towns and into rural areas.

As a result of advances under the Five Year Plans, it has
now become possible to develop a comprehensive approach
to the location of economic activity, specially of industrial
enterprises. Industry is often described as a leading sector
in a developing economy. Within limits, this is a correct
description but, for industry to fulfil this role effectively,
certain essential conditions need to be ensured. Firstly,
it should be an important aim of location policy to secure
external economies appropriate to the size of the unit and the
technology being established. Secondly, where large enterprises, whether public or private, are being set up for the
first time, each such location should be developed as a
complex of related industries. In other words, land acquisition, town development, economic and social overheads
and training facilities should be designed to meet requirements not merely of particular enterprises established in
the first instance but also of other related industries which
it is proposed to develop over a period of five to ten years.
Much detailed study needs to be given to the planning
of such industries by the appropriate agencies of the Central
nd State Governments in co-operation with the major
enterprises. Once certain industrial centres have come to
be established, they should be used effectively as growth
points for future industrial expansion, care being taken
not to spread all at once to too many new locations. Thirdly,
for such a scheme of industrial location to become meaningful and to yield full benefits to the national economy, it will
not be sufficient to let enterprises move to various locations
without a measure of guidance and even direction. This
may take the form in part of restriction against expansion
in congested cities, and, in part, of offer of facilities at a

limited number of approved locations to which entrepreneurs may be required to restrict their choice.

Finally, an important aspect of disparities is the growing difference in wage levels between urban centres and rural areas. The existing trends lead to the development of what is sometimes described as a dual economy which implies a widening gap in levels of development between urban and rural areas and has large social, economic and political implications for the future. This constitutes a difficult problem, but a step forward would be to extend location policy to include a considered approach to regional development. Thus, according to its size and character, each industrial location should be viewed as the nucleus of a wider region, whose development is taken in hand *pari passu* with the development of facilities at the industrial centre. Such a composite approach to development would involve the strengthening and adaptation of the agricultural economy of the area, intensification of agricultural production plans, provision of communications and other services, and schemes for training and orientation which could, in time, help integrate the economy of the rural region with that of the industrial centre. Action along these lines is indispensable for countering recent trends towards greater disparities between urban and rural areas.

III

Although some of the conditions for carrying out the measures suggested here did not exist earlier, if our concepts of policy and development had been clearer and were better supported by concrete action, the economic development of the recent past might not have led to undue enlargement of disparities. It has to be admitted, however, that neither our plans in their detailed working nor the machinery for implementation could fully sustain and fulfil such concepts.

There has been inadequacy at all levels—national and State, in individual enterprises, in city and district administration and in the institutions responsible for co-operative development. Planning is an aspect of implementation, even as implementation is an extension of the process of planning, and much detailed planning can only be undertaken in the course of execution by those who are attuned to its philosophy and method. The factor of machinery and organisation, therefore, acts as a drag, not only on the rapid growth of the economy but also on the success of policies and measures designed to prevent disparities widening as a consequence of economic development. There exists today a large chasm between the requirements of our plans in terms of administration, techniques of implementation and quality of leadership at levels close to the community and the instruments available for carrying our the extraordinarily difficult tasks to which we are committed. Under the best conditions it would take time to bridge this gap. But it is necessary to mark the fact as one step in devising a large-scale programme for the training and re-education of workers in all fields, both official and non-official, harnessing local leadership and knowledge, and developing more effective methods of implementation, specially at the regional and the local level.

IV

We may sum up the argument thus far. The considerable efforts which have gone into the economic development of the country under the Five Year Plans have yet not been on a scale sufficient to ensure rapid enough growth, specially in agriculture and in social services, nor have they reached far enough to counter some of the stubborn facts which lead to the widening of disparities. The objectives of the Plans are broader than the programmes of investment embodied in them but, in practice, both public authorities and private enterprise take a view of development and of their role in it which is often limited and parochial. The overall limitation of resources calls for much more precise and careful formulation of investment priorities and programmes than has been achieved. With greater concentration and integration of investments and avoidance of unduly long gestation periods, economic growth could be speeded. At the same time, with better husbanding and direction of the available foreign exchange resources, both in the public and in the private sector, a systematic plan of technological development in each branch of the economy, carefully worked out location policies and regional and area plans aiming directly at the development of resourcs and the utilisation of the available manpower, income levels and productivity for large sections of the population could be raised to a greater extent than has been possible so far. In other words, provided the objectives and the means by which they are to be fulfilled are spelt out in concrete detail and are in accord with one another, there need be no inherent conflict between economic growth and social and economic integration, whether of different sections of the population or of different regions. Even when the objectives are consistent, in any given period, their impact will not be equal for all parts of the country, or for all sections of the community. However, with the foundations already laid, it should be possible to formulate and implement plans in depth and to develop a set of supporting strategies for different branches of the economy and for different regions which could in time help achieve the twofold objective of economic development and social justice.

V

It was an element of strength in India's development plans that they sought both economic and social objectives and there was readiness to undertake institutional changes in support of these objectives. If, in practice, the two sets of objectives have often remained in separate compartments, amongst others, two explanations may be important.

Firstly, there has been a tendency to regard the overall growth of the economy as the principal and sometimes as the only dependable approach to more equitable distribution. A corollary to this proposition is that possibilities of so organising the forms, processes and institutions of development as would ensure rise in levels of income and productivity for large sections of the population have tended to be neglected. Self-reliance has been viewed more as an *end* and less as a *means* of economic development. In the light of India's own experience, it can be stated that unless, in increasing measure, the approach of self-reliance becomes a conscious and active principle of economic organisation, the achievement of a self-reliant economy will be pushed further into the future.

The second and perhaps the more fundamental reason for economic and social development not keeping pace with each other is that our development plans have not yet provided a sufficiently clear picture of the social order to be built up through planned development. There are, of course, numerous hints and suggestions and many of the practical steps required have been at least initiated. Yet, the picture as a whole remains somewhat blurred and wanting in detail. The transformation of the economy through planning and the creation of the desired social structure are essentially two sides of the same scheme of development. There should be no basic contradiction between them although, at particular junctures and for limited periods, the priorities may need to be adjusted. In the ordinary course, unless the pattern of economic development itself is so conceived that a considerable measure of harmony is achieved during each phase, eventually there may come about a degree of divergence between the structure of the economy and the social objectives which, within its own assumptions and without serious convulsion, a democratic polity may not have even the capacity to resolve. The questions to be posed, therefore, are: in what directions, in the light of experience, our plans should be reoriented, what supporting strategies would have to be evolved and, in consequence, what kind of limitations might have to be accepted in any realistic scheme of planned development? Essentially, these questions are intended to make more explicit and to give concrete form to many suggestions and inferences which derive from the Directive Principles of the Constitution and are already embodied in our Plans, and more specially in the Third Five Year Plan.

In a scheme of development which aims simultaneously at economic growth and reduction in disparities in levels of development between different economic and social groups, between urban and rural areas and between regions, the emphasis on securing a high rate of growth and achieving a self-reliant and self-generating economy through the expansion of basic industries would be no less than in the past. The first priority, which is rightly assigned to agriculture, would need to be translated into action far more boldly and radically by way of material inputs, investment and credit resources and, above all, in terms of the quality of technical and managerial personnel and the leadership and knowledge which are drawn into the development of agriculture and the rural economy. Thus, in the reorientation which now appears necessary, the departure in respect of industry and agriculture and in the development of economic overheads would be one of degree rather than of kind. However, for a plan of development to involve and motivate the bulk of the population, specially in rural areas, and to influence their levels of living decisively, it would be necessary to bring at least three other elements organically into the scheme of basic objectives.

In the first place, the stage has reached when the minimum consumption standards to be ensured over a period should be determined and declared quite specifically. Consumption standards conceived from the point of view of the mass of the community lead logically to certain priorities in production. Restraints in consumption, specially in respect of luxuries and semi-luxuries, and the enforcement of social criteria, for instance, in respect of urban housing and urban services become a necessary element in planning. Secondly, the plans should provide purposefully for securing a strong social base by ensuring education, health services and minimum amenities and extending a measure of social security to increasing numbers within the community. However, consumption patterns conceived from the point of view of the community as a whole and a stronger social base will not by themselves be sufficient to ensure a minimum to any considerable proportion of the community, at any rate, not until the economy has greatly developed and can make available large surpluses to aid the weaker sections of the community.

A national minimum calls, above all, for the fullest possible deployment of the country's manpower resources and a much larger expansion of employment opportunities than has yet been visualised in our plans. Limited efforts are being made through community development and rural works to utilise manpower resources in the rural areas. On the whole, however, in the formulation and implementation of plans, manpower has been regarded more as a reserve to be drawn upon to the extent necessary and less as a resource to be harnessed, developed to higher levels of productivity and utilised to the greatest advantage.

The effective employment of manpower holds the key to a national minimum, not by itself, but as part of a plan of development which seeks to diversify the rural economy, carry opportunities of industrial work into smaller towns and rural areas, integrate large and small units of industrial production, and develop the natural resources and potential of each area to the maximum. Such a plan would need to mobilise all the available agencies, both public and private, and would place special stress on the development of co-operatives as a primary agency for organising the resources and meeting the needs of the community. The next important objective of reorientation in planning would, therefore, be to link up development in different sectors in the economy more closely with the development of different regions in the country. When new productive capacities and services are established and new goods and services become available, in larger or smaller degree and, as a rule, with some unsuspected distortions, area development also occurs, but systematic area development has not been hitherto a significant aim in the design and execution of plans. There has been little regional planning and seldom has conscious effort been made to integrate the development of the industrial and the urban economy with that of the rural economy.

VI

A plan of development which brings the objectives outlined above into an organic structure would have assimilated some of the major lessons of experience of the past decade and would also articulate more clearly the social values and assumptions which lie behind India's Five Year Plans. However, to give practical effect to such a plan would call for several supporting strategies and for technical, administrative and organisational leadership of the highest standards attainable, specially at the area and community level. Material for such leadership exists and by far the most important step now is to provide creative opportunities to existing and potential leaders in all spheres of activity, give prestige to their work and greatly enlarge their ranks, and enable them to accept ever larger responsibilities for planning and implementation.

The Third Five Year Plan referred to a broad strategy of economic development which would ensure that the economy could expand rapidly and become self-reliant and self-generating within the shortest possible period. This strategy emphasised specially the inter-dependence of agriculture and industry, of economic and social development, of national and regional development and of the mobilisation of domestic and external resources. It also stressed measures for scientific and technological advance and for raising the general level of productivity, as well as policies relating to population, employment and social change. Many of the economic, financial and industrial aspects of this general approach have become clearer through the actual working of our plans and we are now better aware of their possibilities as well as limitations. There are, however, other aspects which still remain to be worked out and it is for these that supporting strategies are now needed. Here, it is not possible to do more than invite attention to them. In this context, agriculture should be considered first because the most important single test of the effectiveness of India's plans and the fundamental condition for overall growth is rapid progress in agricultural production.

In this brief compass, it will be sufficient to make two points on agriculture and the rural economy. First, community development and the network of extension services established over the past decade have given to each area a minimum but by no means an adequate framework for economic development. This network serves the purpose, as it were, of holding a vast rural front lightly and providing in most areas a jumping off ground for fuller development. But, generally, it is not sufficient by itself to bring about rapid and substantial gains in production. These can only be secured through a great deal of intensification of existing efforts, with considerable freedom in the use of resources and personnel and without needless administrative constraints. In the next phase, such intensification has to be undertaken first in areas with a marked potential for production on account of irrigation or assured rainfall. These may account perhaps for a third of the total cultivated area of the country. It is in these areas that the strategy of intensive agricultural development should be applied systematically and with the kind of organisation and support by way of resources and personnel which mark out times of war and crisis from other years.

Vital as intensive agricultural development is to the growth of the economy and the raising of living levels for the mass of the people, it is yet only one side of the scheme of rural development and reorganisation. The other side of the scheme on which, beyond a point, the success of plans for intensifying agriculture will also turn, is the building up of a co-operative rural economy. The completion of the land reform programme is but one important step towards such an economy. During the past several years, a number of significant measures have been taken for the development of co-operatives and a series of new institutions and facilities have come to be established. Given the necessary local leadership and determined support from public authorities at different levels, the essential apparatus now exists for developing a strong co-operative sector in India's economy, specially in the rural areas. There is, however, still too large a gap between the scale of present efforts and the declaration in the Plans that, in a planned economy pledged to the values of socialism and democracy, co-operation should become progressively the principal basis of organisation in many branches of economic life, notably, in agriculture and minor irrigation, small industries and processing, marketing, distribution, supplies, rural electrification, housing and construction and the provision of essential amenities for local communities. And further, in medium and large industries and in transport, an increasing range of activities should be organised on co-operative lines. More and more activities assigned to the private sector should take the form of co-operative effort. These challenging and urgent tasks have been long recognised in principle, but without their full implications being sufficiently grasped or followed up. Yet, they are well within the country's capacity to accomplish, provided we are clear in our social concepts, will work towards them with purpose and direction, and are prepared to devote adequate resources to developing citizen leaders and evolving the necessary techniques and organisation.

VII

The central idea underlying the acceptance in the First Five Year Plan of community development as the method by which social and economic life in the villages was to be transformed was the perception that the peasant's life was not cut into segments in the way government's activities were apt to be and that the approach to the villager should be a coordinated one, comprehending his whole life. Intensification of the agricultural effort should on no account run counter to this thought. Such intensification is of course indispensable and should itself be regarded as the single most important aspect of integrated area development. The area might be a district or a development block or a resource development region or a market or an industrial town serving as the nucleus for the surrounding region. The strategy of area development has been accepted in a general way for several years but, for want of systematic experimentation and study, the relevant techniques of organisation have not been fully worked out. Many of the elements for making area development a creative base in the process of planning exist already in the shape of community development, district and block plans, Panchayati Raj institutions and the co-operative movement. In some parts of the country in which considerable development of resources has occurred in recent years and which have become areas of marked economic change, the prospects of integrated area development are quite favourable. In these, it should be possible to secure rapid progress in the diversification of the rural economy and there should be greater scope for using manpower resources effectively. Intensification of agriculture, accompanied by expansion of communications and other services, creates conditions in which extension of industry into smaller towns and rural areas becomes increasingly feasible.

The significance of area development consists in the growth of the rural economy as well as in its integration with the economy of urban areas, giving to both a distinctive place in a composite plan of development. The economic possibilities of integrated area development are greater in the measure in which, as has been suggested earlier, there are well-defined policies for locating economic and industrial activities, and large-scale, intermediate, and small-scale units, with varying but progressive technologies, function as parts of a fully inter-related industrial structure. On these assumptions, it becomes both necessary and possible also to implement a clear cut concept of urban development as part of the total plan. This itself will serve as a supporting strategy of considerable value for the future.

VIII

The first two Plans went some distance to provide a base

both for the development of the economy as a whole and for purposeful integrated development in selected areas. Given the limitations of resources, specially in personnel, intensification of effort implies selection and, therefore, a degree of what may be thought to be discrimination between different areas. More correctly, this should be regarded not as discrimination, but as priority in time for reasons of overall economic and social advantage which can be fully explained and openly justified. Such priorities will sometimes present difficult political choices especially if they involve postponement of programmes of massive development in areas which are backward and have deep-rooted problems of unemployment and under-employment. Backward regions may be divided broadly into three groups. There are, first, those regions which are rich in natural resources, whose development follows directly from the implementation of economic and industrial plans. Areas with undeveloped coal, iron or water resources may be cited as an illustration. Secondly, there are areas which are under-developed and have no significant resources, but are not also under heavy pressure of population. In these areas, progress towards a reasonable minimum could be secured in part through agricultural and other development at the local level and in part by measures for training in new skills and facilities for stimulating mobility of labour. Thirdly, there are backward areas which are both poor in resources and under intense and growing pressure of population. At the present stage of development, these areas represent one of the most critical features in the country's economy. They call for a comprehensive strategy of development which would provide, at the same time, for the location of carefully selected industries, extension of basic communications and services, intensive agricultural development and planned mobility on the part of the labour force. Their resources and economic and social needs should be carefully considered with a view to working out such plans. It should also be possible to identify more precisely the vulnerable sections and the pockets most exposed to poverty, to prepare each area, according to its conditions and possibilities, for more rapid advance by multiplying skills, providing the essential infra-structure, utilising manpower and ensuring more rapid economic progress. These efforts will still not go far enough. The problems of densely populated, low-income regions, which often face the deepest forms of poverty, are indeed serious. They can be resolved only over a period through a combination of intensive industrial and agricultural development within the regions with accelerated efforts for freer movement of workers and potential workers within the national economy as a whole.

IX

The propositions advanced thus far can now be briefly restated. It has been suggested that at the stage of development in the Indian economy which has been reached and in view of the growth of population and other considerations, there is need to reformulate to some extent the objectives of planning and to institute more adequate techniques of implementation. In addition to the expansion of basic industries and a more urgent and far-reaching effort in agriculture, it is also necessary to work towards specified consumption standards for the community as a whole, to restrain consumption of certain kinds of goods and services, to raise the productivity of manpower not only in selected fields but in the mass, to utilise manpower resources more intensively, and to link up the development of different sectors of the economy with the development of different regions in the country. This approach has certain important implications for investment policy, use of external

19

resources, development of technology, location of economic and industrial activity and integration of large and small industries.

To give practical effect to this approach, besides the broad strategy of development towards a self-reliant economy which forms an integral part of the present scheme of planning, there is need also for certain supporting strategies. In particular, over the greater part of the country the present community development and extension approach could be made more effective and agricultural development could be greatly intensified, specially in areas which have a high potential for increased production. This will demand not only larger investment and material inputs, but also leadership and personnel, both official and non-official, of higher quality. Intensive agricultural development is not by itself a sufficient approach to the rural economy. It is fundamental that the rural economy should be speedily reorganised along co-operative lines, and the building up of a strong co-operative sector should be pursued as a major national aim.

Aided by the economic policies outlined earlier and on the basis of intensive agricultural and co-operative development, it is possible to ensure integrated development in each area. Area development implies a concept of rural as well as urban development, viewing them both as parts of a composite scheme. There is scope for integrated area development in larger or smaller degree in all parts of the country. Priority in time for intensive development should be given to areas which have undeveloped natural resources and areas in which major industrial and economic enterprises have been located or may in future be located. In some measure, within the resources available, the approach of area development can be applied within every district and block. For this reason, a systematic approach to planning at district and block levels and, to the extent feasible at the village level, should receive special attention in the preparation and implementation of plans in the States. An important application of the approach of area development is to be found in those parts of the country which are markedly under-developed and, while lacking in resources, have heavy pressure of population and a high degree of unemployment and under-employment. The development of these areas has to be conceived on a long-term basis and, in addition to exploiting their development possibilities and promoting mobility of labour, it would also be essential to identify the sections of the population and the pockets which, during the period of transition, call for special action by way of rural works and other schemes for utilising manpower.

Planning along lines described above appears to offer the largest opportunity during the coming years of assuring a reasonable minimum to an increasing proportion of the population, specially in the rural areas. Compared to the prevailing pattern, such development is likely to call for a larger total investment and the allocation of resources will need to be better balanced between longer and shorter periods of gestation. At the same time, the fuller utilisation of manpower resources, greater emphasis on development of agriculture, strengthening of the social base, integration of the rural with the industrial economy and the wider spread of industry are calculated to provide for greater mobilisation of resources and a larger national output. These aspects have to be worked out necessarily in quantitative terms and with reference to different branches of the economy.

Reduction in disparities in levels of development between different regions, between urban and rural areas and between different economic and social groups is undoubtedly a process spread over time. A measure of redistribution through the provision of community services and special facilities and assistance for those in the lower income

brackets are essential aspects of social policy. The expansion
of the public sector and measures to prevent concentration
of economic activities in a small number of hands are
important as means both for ensuring the growth of the
economy and for giving command over larger resources to
the community. However, in an under-developed economy,
with the problems and compulsions which exist in India,
neither redistribution of income through fiscal and other
measures, nor the growth of the public sector, will by themselves be sufficient to narrow the disparities between the
fully employed and the unemployed or under-employed,
the skilled and the unskilled, workers in towns and those
in villages, and regions whose economy and resources are
developing rapidly and those which are lagging behind. If
these disparities are not to widen in excessive degree and a
large proportion of the population, specially in the villages,
are to be enabled to secure a reasonable minimum, the
strategy and pattern of development have to be conceived
more broadly than has been possible so far. Moreover,
they have to be so designed and executed in detail that
progressively all parts of the country and all sections of
the population can come in a positive way within the influence of economic change.

17

INTEGRATION OF ECONOMIC DEVELOPMENT PLANS*

THIRTEEN YEARS have passed since the setting up of the Planning Commission and the formal acceptance of planning as the key to India's economic and social advance. During this period, vast numbers of persons have shared in the processes of planning, the inter-dependence of national, state and local plans has increased, the common economic problems of the public and the private sectors have assumed greater importance, and the managerial and administrative implications of planning have begun to claim urgent attention. As planning has penetrated more deeply into different fields, the responsibilities of those concerned with it at every level have increased. At the same time, since the test of results must be applied, the line between planning and implementation has become thinner. Those concerned with planning have to feel assured that the concrete form in which the plans are expressed conforms to

*Adapted from the Laski Memorial Lecture, 1963, delivered in March, 1963, at the Harold Laski Institute of Political Science, Ahmedabad.

Harold Laski was a teacher with deep social convictions and sense of values. Large numbers of students from India owed a personal debt to him for his inspiration and understanding. India's freedom was a cause dear to him and he worked for it through all his life.

the intention and is adhered to in actual implementation. Those concerned with execution have the intimate knowledge and experience without which future policy and plans cannot be evolved. The functions of planning and implementation come closer together as two facets of the same task.

THE PLANNING PROCESS

Many complex elements go into the making of a plan of development for any given period. There has to be a careful appraisal of past experience and performance as well as analysis of the main problems of the economy. Each period forms part of a longer perspective to which it must be related. The present and the future are linked together through certain basic objectives which the community places before itself and by which it would wish to test its progress. This is its conception of the good life for the entire body of citizens. In setting forth this conception, there is inevitably a large element of rationalisation and aspiration for, in real life, conflicts of interest are much less easily reconciled, and the social and moral premises of a plan gain greater acceptance only as they meet and overcome fresh challenges. The limitation of resources—natural, material, human and financial—provides the chief compulsion for planning, for choosing between the present and the future, for balancing between different claims during each plan period. The central focus of a plan has therefore to be on resources, on their correct assessment and rapid development, on their allocation and use between different sectors and regions and, within each of these, on the specific projects and schemes to be undertaken. The planning process has to be so designed that in each phase the scheme of allocation and use of resources will take the economy and the community farthest along the road it has chosen to travel. How far the essential scheme of a plan will in fact achieve this result depends on the institutions and the techniques developed for carrying out the plan and adapting it to changing conditions and demands. Planning demands more and more exacting measurement of resources, requirements and costs. Both the planning process and the institutions through which different parts of a plan are fulfilled require increasingly accurate statistical, economic and technological data and techniques of analysis.

Over the past decade and more, the planning process has become more comprehensive, the institutions through which plans are implemented have grown in number and responsibility, and there have been distinct improvements in data and in analysis. However, during this period, the economy has also grown greatly in size and complexity, its relationships with the economy of the rest of the world have changed, the aspirations of the people and essential national objectives have become more sharply defined, and the demands on the available resources have assumed such dimensions that only with the most effective and continuing integration between the various economic development plans can the basic goals of planned development be realised. The present national emergency makes it all the more necessary to analyse our experience and practice and to suggest possible directions in which there may be need to strengthen the planning process, the institutions and the instruments through which it is undertaken and the techniques which are adopted.

We may assume broadly that when a plan is presented, as in the case of the Third Five Year Plan, after labours extending over two or three years, it is a fairly integrated piece of work though, doubtless, not without its blemishes and loose ends. The expression 'integration' is used here to describe certain leading characteristics expected of a plan, namely, consistency between economic and social objectives and priorities and between long-term and medium-term goals, the scheme for mobilising internal and external resources, allocation of resources between different sectors consistent with the rate of growth and physical targets stipulated in the plan, selection on objective criteria of projects to be undertaken under the plan, complementary character of national, regional and local plans in relation to the approved goals, and harmonisation of the private sector within the overall plan. Some parts of a plan may be more fully elaborated than others and more detailed studies may be needed in certain areas but, as a basis for implementation, the broad dimensions of the plan are presumed to be in balance in relation to one another. Such a plan having been adopted, the next question is how, in the course of actual execution and adaptation to changing conditions, its principal parts will remain integrated or in unison with one another. This leads us to a review of the processes, the institutions and the techniques employed in planning and plan implementation. Some of the issues involved may be projected with reference to four important areas of planning: (1) coordination in planning between industry, transport and power, (2) private industry under planning, (3) public enterprises and (4) planning at the State level in relation to national objectives.

Coordination in Industry, Transport and Power

Industry, power and transport accounted for 55 per cent of the investment in the Second Plan compared to 40 per cent in the First. The proportion of 56 per cent set in the Third Plan may be exceeded. The Third Plan conceives of the programmes for industry, along with power, transport, scientific research and technical education as a connected set of tasks stretching over a fairly long period which are to be implemented in successive phases. At the time of the formulation of the Second Plan, the importance of coordinated planning in the sectors of industry, transport and power was stressed, specially with reference to uncertainties in the supply of steel and equipment and availability of foreign exchange. It was urged that there should be careful priorities within which adjustments could be made rapidly and expenditures so phased that each group of projects yielded the maximum return. Experience in the closing years of the Second Plan, more specially in relation to the transport of coal and the shortages of power in certain regions, suggests that integrated planning of industry, transport and power calls for a wider approach.

In drawing up a five year plan for industry, a great deal of study is devoted to the estimation of demand for the products of individual industries, the extent to which capacity should be developed and the likely requirements of capital, foreign exchange and raw materials. An attempt is also made to work out roughly the likely demands for power and transport. However, in the past the picture on the industrial side has become available too late to be of use in laying out plans for power and transport. These have had to be based on preliminary conjectures. Invariably, implementation of the plans for transport and power commenced later than was desirable. But for the fact that many of the industrial projects, whether in the public or in the private sector, also commenced considerably later than first anticipated, shortages in transport and power might have been felt even more acutely, at any rate, in the major industrial areas. An important lesson of experience would, therefore, seem to be that plans for the development of transport and power, which involve numerous long-term projects, should not depend unduly on the completion of detailed blueprints of individual industries. This points to certain changes in the present approach to the planning of industry.

Both during the Second Plan and the Third, it has been

apparent that demands for transport and power tend to be under-estimated and that anticipations of shortage, no less than actual shortages, inhibit the growth of industry. Frequently, the demands for power and transport which in fact materialise may not be as large or may or may not occur as rapidly as first visualised. In relation to industrial development to be undertaken over a given period, it would be desirable to accord a certain priority in time to the development of power and transport. In other words, the development of these basic utilities should proceed continuously and ahead of detailed planning for their utilisation.

Hitherto, planning in industry has been much too fragmented and piece-meal. Development programmes for individual industries which have been drawn up in association with each of the five year plans have not been sufficiently inter-connected and dovetailed. This has led to the foreign exchange requirements, both for capital equipment and for the maintenance of production, being somewhat higher than was necessary. Perhaps, in the early stages this was difficult to avoid. However, with the development which has already taken place and the knowledge and experience now available, it should be possible to project an integrated picture of the industrial structure as a whole. This would show the relationships by way of supply and requirements of raw materials, intermediate products and equipment as between different industries and in relation to the final products consumed by the community. Such a design of the industrial structure as a whole may be built largely around the major industries. For the smaller and more miscellaneous branches of industry, working assumptions may be made on the basis of the available technical knowledge.

This outline of the industrial plan would provide some guidance in drawing up long-term plans for the development of transport and power, and details could be filled in progressively. However, since both transport and power call for action at the regional level and in relation to specific areas, along with the outline of the industrial plan, it is essential also to evolve a general pattern of industrial location. This is a difficult task and one involving close study of the raw materials and other resources of different parts of the country and an appreciation of various technological possibilities which could in due course assist each important region in the country in developing a complex of industry suited to its conditions. The preparation of the long-term plan of industry and of a broad scheme of industrial location are difficult undertakings which can only be completed through close and continuing collaboration on the part of the best available talent drawn from the Central and State Governments, from major public enterprises and the national laboratories and from the technical and managerial cadres of private industry.

The third important step for securing the integrated development of industry, transport and power would be to ensure coordinated planning for different media of transport. In the main, the planning of transport in relation to industrial and economic development is still limited to the railways. Programmes for road development and for the development of road transport, both public and private, continue to be treated as independent efforts and are nowhere linked into well-knit regional transport plans which would include both railways and other means of transport. An integrated approach to transport in which the requirements of each region in relation to its development perspectives are assessed systematically and met through coordinated planning and development of different means of transport is likely to make for substantial economies in investment in the future.

Finally, it is already being realised that various forms of energy have to be viewed and planned for together. Some studies have been recently initiated, but these are only a beginning, and considerable economic and technological data will need to be brought together before an integrated plan for the development of energy resources can emerge.

Given the general design of the industrial structure to be built up over a period of years and a broad guide map of industrial location, along with advance planning for transport and power, it should become possible to simplify and make less rigid some of the existing procedures connected with planning and licensing of individual industrial units. Economy in foreign exchange and the test of overall priority will of course be essential, but certain other considerations could be taken care of more effectively through the general industrial plan.

PRIVATE INDUSTRY UNDER PLANNING

Much of the investment undertaken by Government in transport, power, training of manpower and the building up of social overheads assists the organised private sector in developing new productive possibilities and adding to national wealth. At the commencement of planning, this assured place for private industry was seen as part of a wider scheme. The Draft Outline of the First Five Year Plan stated:

> Economic development in India has to be based on the existence, side by side, of a public and a private sector. But the system of private enterprise would have to be very different from that which now exists; industry will have to accept not only the social and economic policy but also its own obligations to the worker, the investor and the consumer. Private industry will have to fit into the scheme of national planning equally with other sectors of national economy and will have to be so conducted as to satisfy the public at large, that it meets the social needs adequately and avoids misdirection of national resources as well as exploitation or corruption.

The theme has been reiterated in the Third Five Year Plan:

> In the context of the country's planned development the private sector has a large area in which to develop and expand. It has to function, of course, within the framework of national planning and in harmony with

its overall aims, and there must be continuous stress on undertakings in the private sector acting with an understanding of obligations towards the community as a whole. At the same time, it is essential to ensure that the opportunities available in the private sector do not lead to the concentration of economic power in the hands of small numbers of individuals and businesses and that disparities in income and wealth are progressively reduced.

It is necessary to keep these social premises in view while establishing the means by which the private sector may fulfil more effectively the tasks set in the national plan. With the establishment of Development Councils for a large range of industries in accordance with the Industries (Development & Regulation) Act of 1951, there came into existence a machinery for planning in relation to the private sector from which it should have been possible to obtain substantial results. The main purpose of Development Councils was first stated in these words:

> There is at present no machinery for enabling private industry to play its part in planned national development. The question of development and regulation of industries has, therefore, to be considered not so much from the point of view of how Government should exercise certain powers in relation to industries as of the kind of machinery which can work from within each industry and help to bring about a steady improvement in the standards of productivity, efficiency and management. It is only by establishing a system of management which is efficient in itself and is seen to function in the interest of the community as a whole that a system of private enterprise can, in future, gain the confidence of the public.

It was thought that Development Councils, as bodies set up under the law and drawn from amongst owners, technicians and workers, would exert a great deal of progressive leadership in the development of each industry, and thus avoid excessive bureaucracy and rigidity on the part of Government agencies in dealing with individual industrial units. With this in view, the Second Schedule of the Industries (Development & Regulation) Act, 1951, visualised that Development Councils would not only recommend targets, coordinate production and review progress from time to time, but would also carry out such functions as suggesting norms of efficiency, recommending measures for securing the fuller utilisation of installed capacity and improving the working of industry, particularly of the less efficient units, promoting arrangements for better marketing and distribution, standardisation of production, training schemes, improvement and standardisation of accounting and costing methods and practice, promoting or undertaking the collection of statistics, and investigating possibilities of decentralising stages and processes of production with a view to encouraging the growth of allied small-scale and cottage industries. These aspects have failed to receive the attention due to them.

It was thought at the time that by providing an organic link with individual units or groups of units in the private sector, Development Councils would facilitate the achievement of production targets as well as other objectives of the national plan. Admittedly, the problems faced by industrial units are complex and varied and many of them may need governmental assistance or intervention. Nevertheless, organisations within each industry such as Development Councils can play a larger role, and it is worth considering how the machinery created for industrial planning under the Act of 1951 could help individual industries to develop with greater initiative and leadership at the local level in subserving the larger aims of planning.

On the purely economic plane, there are certain problems which need further study. It has been customary with each five year plan, largely in consultation with representatives of individual industries, to propose targets and capacities to be realised by the end of the plan period and to work out estimates of investments and foreign exchange and other essential requirements. Thereafter, it has been left to individual parties to come forward with proposals for setting up new units or expanding existing units. The shortage of foreign exchange and the necessity of finding foreign collaborators has increased the uncertainty of achieving many targets in the private sector or, at any rate, of achieving them in time. Since the original targets were related to estimates of requirements for the economy as a whole, in varying degree, an important element of imbalance is thus introduced. The existing arrangements and methods for reviewing progress and for setting and defining further tasks in co-operation with industry need to be improved. There is need also for fixing more firmly obligations of parties whose projects are approved and of watching and reporting on progress in implementing projects in the private sector.

In the nature of things, the aggregate programme accepted for the private sector entails investments and foreign exchange costs and requirements of scarce materials somewhat larger than the magnitudes provided for in the plan actually permit. In other words, planning in relation to the private sector is still somewhat estimational in character. Therefore, from the point of view of the economy as a whole, it becomes necessary to adopt a scheme of priorities as between industries in the allocation, for instance, of foreign exchange and of other scarce resources. It is not enough to introduce priorities in the licensing of new capacity. The scheme should also extend to the effective utilisation of the capacities presently available and their future development through marginal additions. On account of the development which has already taken place, planned and combined use of available capacities in different units will have a considerable contribution to make in the future in meeting the requirements of essential goods. The system of industrial planning should therefore provide not only for licensing or other action by Government in relation to individual units, but also for close collaboration between Government and Development Councils and other organisations serving individual industries and for the maximum degree of co-operative planning within each industry.

Finally, in a planned economy, without disregarding essential considerations of costs and returns, there should be scope for more purposeful direction and planning of location of industry. The suggestions offered earlier on the subject of industrial location should assist in developing the resources and the industrial potential of different parts of the country so as to give to each large region a better balance between industry and agriculture and prevent over-concentration of industry in large metropolitan areas. Industrial development involves such massive investments in transport, power and other services that through appropriate complementary action in different fields special efforts should be made to enlarge and broaden its total contribution to the growth of the economy and to the diffusion of economic opportunities in different regions.

PUBLIC ENTERPRISES

Activities carried out directly by Government under the five year plans may be divided broadly into enterprise, extension and administration, training and research, and creation of the desired social environment. Each of these has its own special implications for planning, policy and implementation. The field of public enterprise is already considerable and will continue to grow rapidly in the future. If we consider public enterprise and activity in its wider sense to include irrigation, power, transport, industry and minerals, and training, research and other facilities created or sponsored by Government, it will be seen readily that the importance of public enterprise in giving shape to the entire social and economic fabric will go on increasing. This large and growing influence over the economic and social structure entails corresponding obligations. It will not be enough in the future to think of public enterprise in terms of what each individual undertaking is able to do or is unable to achieve. The horizon is a much larger one and, without under-estimating the need for efficient management and financial success, a larger perspective would have great value in relation to the national plan and the balanced development of the economy.

The Industrial Policy Resolution of 1956 has so far provided guidance in determining the role of Government in industrial development. During these years, the industrial structure has grown both in range and in depth. The crucial points at which public enterprise may make the most effective contribution in the future to the growth of the economy and give to the Government an effective role in production and development should now be assessed after a much closer study of the structure of each industry or group of industries than may have been necessary in the past. In other words, the tests prescribed in the Industrial Policy Resolution should be supplemented by a longer-term view of the development of the industrial structure as a whole and of the changes needed in the scope and organisation of each of the major industries. This would help ensure that public enterprises not only have a large share in investment and production, but become a positive factor in transforming the character of the industrial structure and the national economy as a whole.

There are a number of possibilities which deserve consideration. Until recently and even at present, in several fields, the detailed planning of projects is often assigned to foreign consultants. In a few enterprises, technical teams which can undertake the investigation and design of projects have been built up. Besides working out proposals for the various components of the main plant, the planning of a project involves specialised studies of raw materials, power, transport and distribution, and raises a series of problems calling for scientific investigation. While the main project teams must be built up in association with leading public

20

enterprises it might be useful for each of the Central Ministries concerned to build up and maintain a corps of project specialists in its respective field. Persons drawn from such organisations could function from the start as members of project teams which are set up for preparing new project studies. Project teams, so constituted, will be able to anticipate many problems which may arise later and provide well-integrated plans worked out in detail which will eliminate possibilities of subsequent delay. Also, from the beginning, project specialists from the appropriate national laboratories could function as members of the project teams, providing thus a link between the laboratories and the projects and carrying to the laboratories problems which, given time and resources, will be frequently within their capacity to solve. So many of the operational problems of projects and time-lags and increases in cost estimates can be traced to initial failures in planning that, with the experience which has been gained and the knowledge available, it should be possible now to give a more favourable start to public enterprises in most fields. The dependence on foreign knowledge in the preparation of projects exists in even greater degree in private industry, for few private units in India can have the resources to build up their own technical and research organisations. It is worth considering whether technical organisations for investigating and designing projects, which are built up in large public enterprises, should not also equip themselves deliberately for providing consultancy services to the entire range of Indian industry in their respective fields.

In comparison with much existing industry, major public enterprises are not only conceived on a big scale but have the prospect of becoming still bigger in the years ahead. This has certain important implications for development. In the first place, each such enterprise is or should be the nucleus of more broad-based industrial and other economic development. The industrial plan and the map of industrial location, to which we have referred earlier, could serve as a starting point for determining the network of industries which could be best developed as part of the complex. This would have a bearing, secondly, on the land acquisition and housing and urban development policies which are adopted from the beginning by each major enterprise. The social consequences of company towns, with which we are now familiar, could be avoided, and part of the investment on land and the township could be treated as falling outside the economics of the main project. In the third place, since new major public enterprises are frequently sited near hitherto undeveloped sources of raw materials or of power, they entail the creation of new industrial centres. Each such centre has a wider regional aspect. The region of each project should be carefully studied from the social and economic aspects and an attempt made to evolve for the area a regional plan of development which can be brought into action as the project proceeds. Such a regional plan would be designed to bring about the reorientation of the agricultural economy of the area and its communications and changes in the occupational pattern and the educational system, and thus help create the right balance between a large enterprise and its environment. The regional concept has not been embodied so far in any major public enterprise. To that extent, the contribution of many projects towards the growth of the national and the regional economy has been smaller. The interweaving of industrial and regional development on the lines here suggested will not be easy, but presents a challenging and fruitful possibility. If a few public enterprises can integrate their development with the development of the region, it should be possible eventually to extend the concept generally to include large-scale enterprises in the private sector equally with those in the public sector.

STATE PLANNING AND NATIONAL OBJECTIVES

A feature of India's planning which has struck many students is the manner in which the Centre and the States have drawn together in evolving and carrying out development plans. The national plan embraces the whole field of economic and social development and crosses over the lines of distribution of subjects provided for in the Constitution. The National Development Council has in practice embodied and given informal sanction to the underlying concept of partnership and co-operation between the Centre and the States over the whole range of development. The Central Government's initiative in proposing to the States far-reaching policies and measures is balanced by the States' own growing concern with and influence over general economic policy and the development of industry and transport and the assumption by them of responsibilities for execution even when the resources come wholly or largely from the Centre.

This partnership between the Centre and the States has been facilitated through the interposition, at the national level, of the Planning Commission, a body which endeavours, within its limits, to assist both Central Ministries and State Governments and, despite important links, remains somewhat apart from the normal executive machinery of the Central Government. The idea of partnership has been expressed for some years through three main institutional arrangements—the State Plan, Central assistance for the State Plan, and procedures and patterns relating to the release of Central assistance. Briefly, State plans comprehend agricultural and rural development, village and small industries, irrigation and power, development of roads and road transport, education and social services and some measure of industrial development. The role of State plans is now exceedingly important in relation to the development of the national economy and achievement of a high rate of growth, the welfare of the mass of the people and the realisation of major objectives of social policy. Without the plan of every State succeeding to a high degree, efforts at the national level can bear only meagre fruit. The nation as a whole and the Centre have a large and growing stake in the efficient execution of the plans of individual States.

For this reason, as part of the scheme of finance under each five year plan, large sums are assured by way of Central assistance for development in each State. The assistance is made available by way of allotments for implementing annual plans which are given final shape by the States in co-operation with the Central Ministries under the auspices of the Planning Commission. Assistance is given for a wide range of schemes, for which special patterns are prescribed. In recent years, there has been some simplification and liberalisation in arrangements connected with the administration of Central assistance, and a great deal of initiative and responsibility in the proper deployment of Central resources, equally with those contributed by the States, now rests with the latter. Correspondingly, the responsibility of State Governments for realising the main targets and objectives accepted by them in their five year and annual plans is beyond question.

The tasks which States are called upon to accomplish are amongst the most difficult that could be conceived of. For instance, to name a few, programmes for increasing agricultural production, implementing land reform, development of co-operative farming and co-operative credit, marketing and processing, measures to bring landless workers to higher levels of living, rural industrialisation, urban and regional development and family planning, involve such complex administrative and social processes that they would strain the resources of any government. There are also large undertakings in the field of irrigation, power, transport and industry for which State Governments are responsible. Moreover, in each branch of the economy, the efforts of the States and the Centre have to integrate so that the total impact on national development may measure up to the intentions of the plan.

With the establishment of Panchayati Raj institutions at the district and block levels, effective coordination between them and the organisations which function at the State level becomes a most important factor in realising the major objectives of planning. While there would doubtless be variations in emphasis, and experiment and innovation must be encouraged, in many fields a common scheme of priorities, continuity in implementation and complementary action at different levels are necessary conditions for success.

The tasks envisaged in the States in the Third Plan are considerably larger and more difficult than those in the Second. Planning at the State level now calls for technical and economic study of a high order. The total effort required for implementing a State plan by way of raising resources, training manpower and organising various services is large by any standard. From time to time, the State plan must be viewed as a whole and adapted to changing requirements. It would also be necessary for States to be prepared to take on additional responsibilities in development without the tasks already in hand being allowed to suffer. In the preparation of the long-term plan for the country, each State is expected to have an important share. Panchayati Raj institutions at the district, block and village levels need and expect authoritative guidance in formulating plans, determining priorities and finding ways of enlarging the local effort. For these and other reasons, it has become a matter of considerable urgency for all States to strengthen their planning machinery. It is in this context that the Planning Commission's proposal for setting up State Planning Boards assumes importance. These Boards are conceived of essentially as expert advisory bodies whose assistance will be available to the State Cabinet at the level of policy and plan formulation. Since State Planning Boards will not be charged with day-to-day duties in administration, their reviews of progress, advice to Panchayati Raj institutions and technical and other studies can go a long way in raising the quality of planning in the States. Moreover, they will be able to build up a pool of specialised personnel whose experience will be invaluable for national development.

It is a feature of the departmental approach to planning that it tends to take the form of individual schemes. While the efficient execution of each individual project or scheme is indeed essential, the greatest gains in development, specially at the regional and local level, are likely to accrue from the cumulative impact of a series of measures taken together. An integrated approach towards area planning and regional development, therefore, holds a large promise. Through the years, in terms of development planning, an unnecessary barrier has existed between towns and villages. Instead, the time is ripe for schemes of composite development through regional plans which will include both urban centres and the regions influenced by them.

The goal of enabling all regions in the country to realise their potential for economic development and attaining levels of living not far removed from those of the nation as a whole has been accepted, but if this is to be realised over the next fifteen or twenty years, most strenuous efforts must be made at the national, State and local levels. It is from this aspect that the integration of economic development plans, whether undertaken by the Central or State Governments or in the nature of private effort, has to be viewed as a major objective of policy and administration.

18

PLANNING FOR INTENSIVE AREA DEVELOPMENT

FOR A number of reasons intensive area development has become potentially one of the most significant ideas in India's development. In several sectors the impact of development has not gone deep enough to touch more than a fraction of the population or to draw upon more than a small proportion of the energy and the capacity or of the intrinsic resources which local communities can mobilise. Secondly, experience has shown that in such varied fields as agriculture, community development, health, education and tribal development, while it is difficult to hold back from rapid extension of coverage, this itself causes the resources in manpower, materials and finance to be spread so thin as to make meagre results inevitable. For the quality of performance to improve in substantial measure, a period of consolidation and concentration of effort has become essential. In the third place, more specially in agriculture, the prospect of obtaining a large increase in output depends on the ability to turn areas with favourable conditions for growth to good account by concentrating resources by way of personnel and supplies, speeding changes in organisation and technology and creating all the economic and social conditions for rapid increase in production in the immediate future. While advance in agriculture provides the main focus and precondition for intensive area development, the possibility of progress in different branches of activity being achieved in a cumulative and inter-dependent manner, both within rural areas and as between rural and urban areas, also adds greatly to the value of development at the area level being planned and undertaken as an organic and composite process.

I

The concept has been implicit for many years in proposals for district, block and village plans. Efforts to implement such plans have not gone more than half-way in any part of the country, but lessons of value can be drawn from whatever experience has accrued. While district, block and village plans and plans for intensive agricultural development in selected areas provide the largest field for intensive action at the area level, the concept has a vital role in all regions in which the physical resource base is being developed, new industry and technology established or a new pattern of skills created. Wherever a major centre of activity takes root, whether on account of new enterprise or the growth of population, there comes into being a dynamic element ready to be used as a force for intensive development. To harness together all the possibilities of the natural and human resources of an area and its material advantages is the crux of development. It is this task which provides both the justification and the opportunity for the agencies which government establishes and for the new social and economic institutions which are created as part of the scheme of planned development. These agencies and institutions have to meet increasingly exacting tests as development proceeds and must constantly seek to renew themselves by improving and refining their techniques and setting fresh goals.

The main assumptions which lie behind intensive area development take us to the roots of the working of India's democracy, of the capacity of the administrative structure inherited at Independence and the efficacy of the changes which have been since made or envisaged. In the measure in which the assumptions are or can be realised in practice, they provide a test equally for the political and administrative system and for the scheme of economic and social development embodied in the five year plans. There are perhaps five important premises to be specified. The first is that the process of development should reach out to one and all. The entire people should participate in it and be enabled to contribute towards it. In the two-way stream of what is given and in turn received, every member of the community has his place. The common purpose is that each should contribute according to his capacity and, within the limits of the resources available, receive according to his need. There will be constant pressure, sometimes for good reasons or to achieve immediate results, to favour a few at the expense of the many, and the balance may not be easily struck, nor without a measure of strife. But it is important to stress that, within any community, both strength and weakness are apt to become cumulative and, while some areas may have to be given priority in time over others for reasons of wider public interest or public policy and in frank recognition of overall limitations, in the areas selected for intensive development, the weight of policy and institutions should be on the side of generating an all-embracing effort in which all the people can be involved.

The second premise of intensive area development is that the outlook, attitudes and the skills of the people and their capacity to use the natural and economic potentials lying within their grasp are the single most important factor for economic progress. Whatever stands in the way of the growth of such capacities has to be removed. The obstacles may come from feudal relationships in land, from attitudes embedded in caste, from low productivity and lack of employment opportunities. They may persist and even grow because many failures and shortcomings are apt to be interacting. Therefore, determined action on the part of the mass of the people and the majority of those who lead and represent them to press for basic social change, to seek to establish equality between man and man, to strengthen and transform the human and social base, is an essential part of any scheme of intensive area development. Such development is, therefore, both a process of change and a process of education, bringing the entire community within its fold. Progress through democracy implies continuous and unremitting action from within towards the elimination of inequality and injustice in all its forms. When the pace of change slows down and distinctions harden, democracy loses ground and confidence in its capacity to solve social problems may well be destroyed.

The third assumption in intensive development is that each area and its people will put forth the maximum effort of which they are capable. Such effort will take the form of mobilising whatever local resources and possibilities are available—manpower, land, savings and others. From outside the area, only such assistance and supplies will be sought as will enable the local communities to maximise their own contribution. This contribution includes both what individual workers, as individuals, can do, and what can be done through large groups and through community institutions. The main purpose and basis of development of the network of institutions established in recent years, such as co-operatives and panchayat organisations at the village, block and district levels, as well as of voluntary organisations to which public support is extended, is to assist each area to enhance its total contribution up to the limits of its capacity.

In this effort, the role of different popular institutions and administrative agencies functioning at the area level is seen as being one of responsible partnership. Thus, acting alone, neither the administrative cadres working directly under the government or deputed for service with local institutions, nor the panchayat organisations and the co-operative and other agencies, have the competence to carry out all the tasks implicit in intensive area development. The various agencies are complementary to one another, and each has its place in the total structure. The authority and resources vested in each agency and institution are intended to subserve a wider purpose common to them all and governing their respective actions. This view of the functions of different agencies and institutions is not often stressed and the obligations flowing from it are still insufficiently understood, but they are essential to the concept of intensive area development.

Finally, intensive development has the major implication that, within each area, action for development will be related directly to its own conditions, needs and problems. Knowledge of the resources of the area and its requirements, therefore, becomes the starting point in local planning. It is not uncommon for agencies at the national and State level to put forward their proposals and schemes and to expect them to be accepted and implemented literally in the districts and the blocks. This mistaken approach is buttressed by administrative and financial procedures which are marked by a great deal of rigidity. It is necessary to emphasise that schemes formulated at higher levels should be no more than guide-lines and assurances of certain minimum financial and technical resources and supplies which can be drawn upon for intensive development at the area level. The plan of action in the area should be autonomous and flexible, and closely related to its own needs and potential and, within a wide range, it should be possible to transfer resources from one activity to another. In the process, mistakes will be made, but this is not something to be deplored or resisted, and there should be fair opportunities for the leaders and workers of each area to gain their own experience of making and implementing responsible and autonomous decisions. Following from this, there is the further inference that personnel and institutions at higher levels have to assist those at the lower area levels in planning, implementing and evaluating, in solving problems and evolving techniques beyond their present capacity, and in supplementing their efforts by way of resources and supplies. Thus, intensive area development has important implications not only for the method and pattern of development, but also for the functional relations which should subsist between different levels of development and administration.

For many years, in terms of policy, institutional developments have proceeded along the assumptions outlined above. The emphasis on co-operatives and Panchayati Raj institutions and suggestions for the formulation of district, block and village plans had these very objectives. However, administrative structure and practice have greatly lagged behind and the educational effort has been altogether inadequate. At the State level, as among many agencies at the national level, development has not been seen as a total effort, whose many strands supplement one another, so that the approach has been invariably segmented and departmental. In practice, district plans have remained loose collections of schemes sponsored by different departments with little practical scope for alteration and interchange. An organic link between plans at the district and block level has been lacking. In both, no conscious effort has been made to integrate the mobilisation of local manpower and other resources with resources flowing in from outside, and there has been excessive dependence on financial allocations from the State level. Financial and administrative arrangements within State administrations have compelled each area to look for authority from above without drawing on their own initiative and responsibility. Failures in coordination between allied activities at one level have accentuated failures at other levels. Action on known gaps in development, which it is within the ability of personnel and institutions in districts and blocks to undertake, has had to wait for approvals and sanctions of specific funds from higher authorities, so that the administrative process has been on the whole a stultifying one. The fact that efforts along the lines of district, block and village plans have not so far achieved the results hoped for may not be entirely due to administrative factors, but these have a large share. Therefore, while defining the priorities and directions and the method and organisation of intensive area development, the need for reform in the administrative sphere cannot be too greatly stressed.

II

In considering the priorities and approach of intensive development in some detail, it is convenient to assume the framework of the district and its constituents, namely, blocks and villages. This is already the common pattern of rural administration and, despite possible variations here and there, it may be expected to continue. It may be assumed, secondly, that it is an agreed objective of policy to place development in the district in the hands of representative Panchayati Raj institutions, which will be supplemented by co-operative institutions and voluntary organisations to the extent these are developed. Whether decentralisation provides for greater authority at the district or the block level is a matter of administrative detail rather than principle. But it is recognised that these two levels and the village level are complementary to one another and that even those areas of development which are at present outside the sphere of Panchayati Raj institutions will be passed on to them until the entire scheme of development within the district comes to be their responsibility. Thirdly, at a time when the interaction between town and village is much greater than in the past, development at the area level must envisage a great deal of joint and coordinated action between local self-governing institutions serving urban and rural areas, and the efforts of both have to be related to a wider plan of action which underlines the points of contact and influence and the contribution due from each set of institutions. Thus, viewing the problems of area development as a whole, in terms of the needs and resources of the entire population, there will be, on the one hand, separate plans for each urban area as well as rural plans corresponding to the district, the block and the village and, on the other, a joint plan emphasising the links between urban and rural development which will need specific attention within the scheme of development with clear indications of phasing and responsibility for action.

III

Fundamentally, area development is focussed on the resources and population of rural areas, though necessarily the dynamic influence of urban centres has also to be brought to bear on rural conditions to the utmost extent possible. Growth in agricultural production on a significant scale, with the bulk of the farmers participating in its achievement, is the principal condition not only for increasing employment and raising levels of living but also for simultaneous advance in social services and in rural industry. All the main components of intensive area development can be set out in terms of their significance for a rapid increase in agricultural production and it is best to develop area plans with agriculture as the pivot and the point of concentration. Though the different components are closely interconnected and must be built up together to the greatest extent possible, it is convenient to group them, both for planning and action, under six broad heads:

(1) Planning, supplies, personnel and extension;

(2) Strengthening the physical base;

(3) Strengthening the economic infra-structure;

(4) Accelerating technological development;

(5) Strengthening the social base; and

(6) Community effort and utilisation of manpower at the village level.

The principal activities comprised under each head in the effort to achieve the intensive development of an area, with the central emphasis on agriculture, and how they can best integrate with one another can be briefly described. It is common to prepare proposals and schemes for development in terms of the fields of interest of different agencies and departments. The conditions and needs of various areas and regions and the manner in which efforts in different spheres must be harnessed to support one another are aspects which do not receive the close attention they deserve; from this fact flow many lags and inadequacies. The merit of the area approach is to bring within a common frame both technical programmes which are sponsored and drawn up by different agencies and the resources and capacities for leadership and initiative which exist and can be further developed in local communities, so that the welfare and development of the entire population serves at every step as the unifying objective.

IV

Planning, supplies, personnel and extension represent key functions which raise the question of organisation and administration of intensive area development. What began as an effort to establish a team of extension workers at the block level has developed in later years into democratic and representative institutions. However, the Panchayat Samiti in the blocks is not yet quite certain of its role, and in many States its functional relations with the representative body at the district level, the Zilla Parishad, and with the various technical departments at the State level are not sufficiently clear. Experience in several areas suggests that the Panchayti Raj organisation, specially at the district level, is not equipped to plan for the district as a whole, and its tasks in relation to State level departments in such crucial matters as assessing the requirements of inputs and supplies and receiving and distributing them are not clearly defined and are therefore poorly executed. Three aspects appear to be specially important. Firstly, at the district level, the Zilla Parishad should be made effectively responsible for all aspects of district development and planning and, in turn, a similar responsibility must be cast on the Panchayat Samiti for block development and planning. The Zilla Parishad and the Panchayat Samiti should be able to function as institutions, as corporate bodies, responsible for their complete range of functions, in relation to the State Government and its various agencies. Secondly, at the district level, within the Zilla Parishad, there should be a competent planning unit under a trained functionary who can coordinate in detail the planning exercise in different branches and can guide those assisting the Panchayat Samiti in preparing block level plans. Thirdly, the Zilla Parishad needs a full-time and experience functionary to act as a team leader for the technical officials assigned to different fields of development. In States like Maharashtra and

21

Gujarat, the chief executive officer can fill this role, but such a functionary is required in all States. His field of operations should be the district as a whole, but where a part of the district is at first treated as an area of intensive development, this would claim his special attention.

Supplies, credit and personnel represent the critical link between planning at the State level and planning at the area level. The framework into which area plans fit has to be provided by the planning organisation at the State level. The fact that the operations of planning in the States are at present left largely to different departments, with little more than financial coordination being provided by the State planning department, is a real impediment to systematic planning in the districts and in the areas selected for intensive development. Developing an effective planning organisation at the State level is an essential step for planning and development to be undertaken in depth in the districts. Along with this, systematic forward planning of materials and supplies, such as fertilizers, pesticides, implements and machinery, steel and cement for agriculture and of requirements in other fields like education, health and family planning, has to be undertaken in step at the State and the area levels. Where supplies are limited because of overall constraints, priorities for distribution are a matter for careful planning. Ad hoc distribution or short-term priorities accentuate shortages and reduce greatly the impact of the total effort which may be made. Similarly, in relation to personnel, the shortages, which are frequently observed in districts and blocks when development becomes more intensive and the coverage increases, can be anticipated and provided for through more careful long-term planning at the State level, accompanied by similar action at other levels.

In what is commonly described as extension, there are three different strands which need to be kept in view. The first is that extension workers at the block and village level represent a form of technical assistance to local communities and to individual farmers to enable them to reach higher levels of productivity and to increase their output. The quality of extension workers has to be continually raised through special training and facilities for gaining new knowledge. In any area selected for intensive development, a programme for the re-training of extension workers at every level is, therefore, a necessary element. Secondly, while extension workers have to advise individual farmers to the extent they can and should be always available to them, communicating knowledge and experience and pursuing specific proposals for technical change is a social process, in which village institutions such as the panchayat and the co-operative have a vital part. These institutions are as much part of the extension system as the trained personnel who are formally described as extension workers. In the intensive areas, in particular, there should be special emphasis on the panchayat and the co-operative making a large and increasing contribution. The third strand in the concept of extension is that of team approach on the part of workers drawn from different fields and functioning at the district and block levels. Frequently, they are not themselves fully conscious of the interdependence which subsists between their diverse activities, and they tend to function as if they were accountable only to the heads of the departments they represent and not so much for producing results on the ground by working with the people and enhancing their capacity and initiative. The educational aims of extension are realised best when the extension workers at the district and block levels are able to see how the work of each contributes to the total effort and pay close attention to the specific areas in which they can supplement one another.

To achieve intensive area development, one other element has to be actively incorporated within the concept of extension in addition to the three described above. Even more than other industries, agriculture demands leadership from those with high skill in the profession, whose own performance and ability to improvise and innovate serve as an example to the community as a whole. Within the intensive area, good farmers should be enabled to play a central role in the development of agriculture. This, rather than the right to exploit others or to expand their holdings at the expense of the smaller peasants, is their social function in the scheme of development. The holdings of the more skilled farmers should serve as demonstration farms, and the operational agricultural programmes to be implemented in the intensive area and the practices and cropping patterns to be recommended by extension workers for general adoption should be derived largely from their experience and practical achievement.

V

In the apparent attempt to gain quick results, often insufficient attention is given to measures to strengthen the resource base in the intensive area, first, by making more efficient use of existing assets and, subsequently, by creating new physical assets. Thus, it is rare for the existing irrigation systems and arrangements for the distribution of water to be functioning so as to yield the maximum advantage. Complaints about maladministration and maldistribution in irrigation often contain more than a core of truth and even small improvements in the prevailing arrangements for the distribution of water can contribute significantly both to production and to the lessening of tensions. Frequently, at modest cost, it is possible to supplement large irrigation works with small works, whose supply of water is under the farmer's own control, and thereby to promote more intensive irrigation and the attainment of high yields. Therefore, one of the most rewarding beginnings in an intensive area is to work with the people to identify possible improvements in the irrigation supply system serving groups of villages and to involve them directly in a practical programme for giving effect to the changes proposed, at the same time using improved irrigation as the spearhead for increasing agricultural productivity.

An important element which tends to be missed currently is the need for a personal relationship and a sense of identity between plans of development for an area and the people who belong to it. In part, this may be due to lack of knowledge and understanding. In part, this is due to the wide gap which has come to exist between the people living in the villages and the elite and the professional classes and those engaged in study and teaching in colleges and in high schools in towns and cities. That these latter groups have a wider social role than the pursuit only of their own vocations is seldom stressed as a matter of public policy, nor is there any real effort on the part of the administration, including Panchayati Raj institutions, to seek their help and co-operation in the study and solution of specific problems, in the survey of human and material resources and in the education of the people. Such an effort, supported by even modest facilities for transport and in other ways, would win wide response both from individuals who have knowledge and experience and are imbued with a feeling of social responsibility (itself an important attribute of the democratic way) and from those associated with academic and educational institutions at school and college levels. With the great expansion which has occurred in the numbers of teachers and students, these institutions represent a most important and still largely unutilised resource for development, specially in the regions in which they are situated. There are now only a few districts in India where it is not possible to draw into the developmental effort and the study of resources the knowledge and leadership of those associated with agricultural and engineering colleges and schools and with the teaching of economics, geography and the social and natural sciences generally. Such persons would receive no less than they give and could do much to enrich and diversify leadership within the community and enlarge the ranks of citizen leaders, whose understanding of public issues and sense of direction could greatly advance intensive area development as a worthwhile and satisfying cause for the young and the dedicated.

Guided by such citizen leaders and aided by the expertise available both in government agencies and in academic institutions, and drawing upon students, teachers and others, it should be possible to make a rapid survey of the land and natural resources of the intensive area. Where there is so much to be done, it is necessary to select but, even with limited resources, often useful processes can be initiated and then carried through over a period of time. In measures to strengthen the physical base, the first place should be given to plans for the best use of land and for improving cropping patterns, specially where irrigation is available and the farmer has some measure of choice of crops. Close study of the changes which have occurred within the area in the pattern of land use and in the scheme of cropping and the experience and practices of the more skilled farmers would provide useful guide-lines for the general body of cultivators, which must of course be supported by supplies and services to enable them to increase their yields and farm incomes. Land use directly related to agriculture has to be supplemented by other steps, more specially, survey of waste lands, forest areas and areas subject to soil erosion, followed by plans for reclamation, afforestation and soil conservation. Implementing these plans will provide for a vast potential over many years for utilising the manpower resources which are readily available and now run to waste.

A plan for the completion of consolidation of holdings over a specified period will do much to promote both agricultural productivity and improved living conditions in the intensive area. Where the programme is already under way, it could be speeded up. If consolidation of holdings is undertaken in terms of sub-basins of rivers and streams and the drainage and flow of irrigation, the programme can be executed more swiftly and will make for bigger results than in the ordinary course. Its value as a step in support of co-operative farming, undertaken voluntarily as peasant owners feel ready for it, should also be stressed.

In a country in which crops fail so frequently because of the vagaries of rainfall, the development of irrigation, and specially of underground supplies, which the farmer can use at will and establish quickly, becomes naturally the most important single measure for strengthening the physical base for greater production. The progress of rural electrification has greatly enhanced the scope for such irrigation. Other improvements—in techniques and practices, in labour utilisation and by way of increase in farm investment—are closely related to irrigation and have to be implemented as a combined programme at the level of the community.

VI

In large part, programmes of development undertaken over the past several years have served to strengthen the infra-structure and created conditions for increase in production in industry as well as in agriculture. However, as we look beyond the metropolitan cities, the larger towns and a few favoured regions in which there has already been considerable resource development and economic change, we are struck less by the facilities available and more by the weaknesses in the economic and social overheads which still exist. The most notable of these concern communications, availability of facilities for marketing and the spread of electrification. Facilities for vocational and technical training are also often inadequate, though in this respect there has been a marked advance in recent years, and skilled workers are able to move into permanent employment from one area to another more readily than unskilled workers. In the intensive area, from the standpoint of agriculture, the main concentration has to be on creating a network of communications for rural areas, establishing regulated markets with all the needed facilities, and carrying electricity to villages in accordance with a carefully worked out plan for the expansion of rural electrification and the use of power. In this context it has to be emphasised that development of industrial centres in small towns and large villages is important not only as a means to the diversification of the rural economy and increase of employment opportunities, but also as a direct and immediate stimulus to increase in agricultural production.

Adoption of improved technology is as much a question of providing the requisite knowledge and equipment as of inculcating the outlook of change and increased productivity. In other words, educational and technological developments in the intensive area have to proceed together, the former creating the desire for change and the latter the means for fulfilling it. Too little attention is given at present to the aspect of conservation and avoidance of loss of produce in various forms. This is an objective capable of being achieved at small cost. Similarly, not only in the agricultural stations, but in the experience of skilled farmers, there are agricultural practices which can be spread widely by extension workers and local institutions among the agricultural community as a whole and as a rule with very little investment. The main thrust of technology has to be, on the one hand, in the adoption of improved varieties of seed (specially the high-yielding varieties) and the application of optimum quantities of fertilizer and, on the other, in the introduction of better agricultural implements and machinery. In extending technological improvements, the economic capacity of the farmer is a severe limiting factor. Frequently, this is associated with the size of the agricultural holding—a limitation which bears in India on the condition of the bulk of the farmers. It is, therefore, essential to develop a strategy of technological change, so that the benefits of new technology will not be confined to the larger farmers, but will make an increasing impact on small farmers.

VII

Although the existing social weaknesses of the rural economy are freely admitted and policies at the national level have sought to take account of them, practical action directed towards their elimination receives scant attention in the strategy of development in districts and blocks and in intensive areas. This failure has marked community development programmes from the beginning and has also persisted in intensive agricultural districts as well as in intensive agricultural areas. It is to be explained by the erroneous belief that in avoiding difficult social and structural problems it becomes possible to secure a more widely agreed approach in carrying out programmes relating to agriculture and other activities of general interest. For the same reason, however difficult the situation of small and uneconomic cultivators, co-operative development and in particular co-operative farming do not receive the emphasis due to them.

The social base in an area selected for intensive development has to be strengthened through action in five principal directions:

> (a) effective implementation of the programme of
>   land reform mainly in accordance with legislation
>   already enacted;

(b) development of co-operative credit, marketing and processing;

(c) promotion of co-operative farming on a voluntary basis;

(d) expansion of adult education and development of skills among rural youth; and

(e) family planning, village water supply and sanitation programmes.

The plans now in progress give fair scope for action under each of these heads, provided there is active leadership at the community level and the administration, including those associated with Panchayati Raj institutions and the co-operative movement, put their weight behind social change. Their apathy in this respect is due as much to failure on the part of those responsible for public policy at the national and State levels as to ignorance among the people and the economic weakness of large sections of the rural population. Indifference to basic social problems or hesitation in dealing with them and intensive area development cannot go together.

The extent and manner of mobilisation of community effort in support of agriculture and allied activities are decisive for the success of all plans for intensive area development. The main elements have been identified for many years, namely, village organisation, village planning and utilisation of manpower. However, in the recent past, less stress has been given to them at the Centre and in the States than might have been expected. Consequently, extension agencies in the districts, specially agricultural officials, have tended to provide more definite support to individual farmers than to community and group effort. The village panchayat and the co-operative are correctly conceived institutions and can serve the community as a whole much more effectively than they seem to have done. It is true that factions affect their day-to-day working as they do with other institutions, but the only answer to local factions is a work programme in the rural areas of such sweep and comprehensiveness as will involve the bulk of the people and make those seeking their own narrow interest appear altogether out of place. Such an approach is essential in any area selected for intensive development.

Village plans have been spoken of for many years, but the main stress in intensive agricultural development districts and elsewhere has been on individual farm plans as a means of obtaining credit and other assistance. Thus, the real objectives of planning at the village level have come to be obscured to some extent. Rightly understood, there is no conflict between village plans and farm plans of individual farmers. A village plan should provide, firstly, for those activities which the people of the village can themselves undertake, using their manpower and other resources to the maximum and, secondly, for supplies and credit and technical help which the village needs from outside. In the former category, we may include specially those works which require labour on the part of the people, usually functioning in groups, with some technical and financial help. Such works may be for minor irrigation, maintenance and renovation of tanks, soil conservation, reclamation of land, or village fuel plantations. Where it is necessary to ascertain the requirements of individuals and to meet them to the extent possible within the limited resources available, as in the case of credit and supplies, the village plan has also to include specific farm plans of individuals. These latter would identify the problems and needs of individuals. The village plan would not only specify the works to be carried out on a group basis, but would also have some broad concept of a crop plan and of production goals for the community as a whole. While the principal accent of the village plan must be on agriculture, other aspects of the life of the community would also fall within its purview, notably, the minimum amenities needed by the people, such as water supply and sanitation, approach roads, primary education and education for adults, and welfare measures for women and children and for the weaker sections. Village plans on these lines and the block plans, of which they form part, have to be organically related to one another.

Where peasants cultivate separate holdings, many of which are small and fragmented and far from economic, the struggle for subsistence in which they are engaged leaves little or no room for group activities undertaken as part of the total effort for agricultural production. A rural works programme can provide the necessary leaven and flexibility for community and group activities in support of agriculture and should be regarded as an essential component in planning for intensive area development.

VIII

Plans for intensive area development are not an isolated effort and cannot be formulated and carried out except as constitutents of wider schemes embodied in national and State plans. This is because, for all the ground they may encompass, area plans cover only a part of the total activity. The national and State five year plans determine the overall economic and social policies and goals, the framework of prices and incomes and the limits of resources within which intensive development can be undertaken in particular districts and areas. Nor, in terms of their time horizon, can area plans look beyond the span of national and State plans. Fundamental problems, whose solution has yet to be approached, such as the future of landless labour, the growth of population and extreme dependence on land and the pattern of property relations, fall within the larger world of economic and social planning. Towards these goals many other activities and measures have to contribute besides those directly associated with intensive area development and planning at the district, block and village level. These latter have, however, great vitality and potential for the future, both as instruments for giving effect to the policies and measures envisaged in the national plan and as means at the level of the community by which the people can give shape to and labour for their own aspirations for welfare and enhance their capacity for social action.

19

PLANNING AND THE STUDY OF NATURAL RESOURCES*

As THE years have gone by and one five year plan has succeeded another, it has become possible to see many problems of development in greater depth. Analyses and solutions which seemed fairly certain at first have called for more probing. The gap between the values and objectives of planning and the ability to attain them has proved to be much larger than was anticipated. At every step, the need for fuller understanding is being felt. To plan for the development of a nation like India is, at the same time, to mould the minds and motivations of men, to reshape institutions, to build upon and explore the endowments of nature, and to draw all the resources of science and technology into the service of the future.

These are demanding tasks for which we have been inadequately equipped. Our perceptions of the nature of many of our major problems are far from complete. Over the next

* Based in large part on addresses to the National Geographical Society of India at Varanasi (February 10, 1965), and the Geographical Society of India at Calcutta (February 12, 1966). An opportunity in May, 1967, to learn at first hand about the progress of studies in natural resources and regional planning in USSR and about the contribution being currently made in these fields by Soviet geographers and other scientists was also of much help.

decade or two the shape and dimensions of several of these problems will change calling, in turn, for new policies and instruments to meet the larger challenges of the future. Such challenges arise, for instance, in relation to each of the principal natural resources—land, forests, water, mineral and energy resources. They arise in the development of each region and, indeed, of each district or block or area. They arise also in the development of human resources and in the effort to raise the level of productivity. In each case the challenge involves both a change in physical volume and a change in qualitative terms. Moreover, as we look forward, even for a period, we see the striking degree to which different problems interact with one another as well as the interdependence of various disciplines and approaches. There is no question that if we are to succeed in the attack on poverty, all that social studies and science and technology can contribute must be brought together to bear on the problems of each region and of the country as a whole. In identifying problems, applying the results of social and scientific research and seeking solutions, the need for team work and for a concerted approach becomes apparent at every step.

I

The terms of reference laid down for the Planning Commission at its inception in 1950 had stressed the assessment of the material resources of the country, along with its capital and human resources, as the basis of plans for the most effective and balanced utilisation of resources. During the first few years of planning, efforts were made to strengthen several organisations concerned with the study or development of natural resources such as the Geological Survey of India, the Indian Bureau of Mines, the Indian Council of Agricultural Research, the Central Water and Power

Commission, the Council of Scientific and Industrial Research, the Oil and Natural Gas Commission, the Atomic Energy Commission and others. As a result of the work of these national organisations, our knowledge of the country's natural resources has greatly improved. Yet, certain weaknesses in the situation are to be observed and attention should be drawn to some of them in their broader aspects.

In the main, the various organisations concerned with natural resources have tended to approach their task with what may be described as a project or programme orientation. Only as possibilities of developing particular projects came in sight, investigations into available or potential resources were undertaken or speeded up. Thus, the study of natural resources has been rather less systematic, less complete and coordinated than was called for in the circumstances of the country.

In the second place, though the surveys have helped establish a number of tasks in qualitative terms, an adequate quantitative picture has yet to be built up. Thus, while it is known that, with the growth of population, cultivated land per head has already diminished from a little over an acre to less than three-fourths of an acre, and there are severe limits to the new area which can be brought under cultivation, the extent to which uncultivated areas are capable of being reclaimed is far from certain. In our knowledge of soils, to a large extent, we still make do with traditional administrative and settlement data. Scarcely 5 million acres have been covered by detailed soil surveys and less than 70 million acres by soil surveys of the nature of reconnaissance. A great deal of systematic work must be undertaken before crop planning and land use planning in keeping with the physical characteristics and possibilities of land in different regions can be attempted on any scale. To increase the productivity of land, besides irrigation and soil conservation, precise and tested knowledge of the soils in each area should be a valuable working tool for agricultural extension and development.

The problem of low productivity runs through every aspect of the use and development of natural resources. In relation to forest resources, data concerning the yield of wood and other forest produce are extremely meagre. It has been stated, for instance, that the productivity of accessible forests in India, at present reckoned at 0·3 tonne per hectare, can be raised to 5 tonnes per hectare or 16 times the present level.

In the investigation of mineral resources there have been marked advances in recent years. Yet, on closer study, several customary estimates have proved to be optimistic and it has been difficult to prepare precise and worthwhile projects speedily. Obviously, more critical and objective appraisals were essential. Because knowledge of the country's mineral resources has not been as complete as has been sometimes claimed, even for many basic industries, we are not yet in a position to provide an adequate design of location over the next ten or fifteen years such as might serve as a basis for detailed industrial planning in accordance with the possibilities of different regions in the country.

Weaknesses in quantitative assessments of natural resources can be traced to a third factor, namely, failure to link up work on natural resources with carefully worked out and interrelated projections for demand and economic growth.

We are not yet in a position to present national balances for key resources based on closely studied information. The economic dimension in studies of natural resources needs to be greatly strengthened in all fields though, it should be added, in a few areas significant progress has certainly been made in recent years, as in relation to the development of energy and of water resources. Studies and projections of requirements and availability of key resources over a period of ten to twenty years can be prepared best by bringing together all the knowledge and expertise available within

22

public agencies as well as in academic and research institutions. They provide a most promising area for co-operative scientific work. Their value lies as much in the greater precision they make possible as in the stimulus they furnish to the formulation of considered judgements on long-range social and economic policies and specific action programmes related to them. Hitherto, in many fields, even where the policies needed were broadly known, action has lagged behind and, more often than not, the shorter term view has prevailed over the longer term view, and policies which were correctly conceived have been pursued half-heartedly without the support of adequate resources in personnel and organisation. There is no gainsaying that success or failure in relation to major resources turns entirely on the extent and quality of action on the ground, and this will be influenced decisively by accurate knowledge in advance of how demand and availability are likely to change over a long period of years.

II

Experience under the five year plans has brought with it greater appreciation of the nature of the developmental processes in relation to different categories of natural resources. These processes are by no means identical for land, forest or water resources or for minerals and energy resources. Up to a point, through the inexorable pressure of population, land may be reclaimed and brought under the plough even under conditions of primitive technology. Similarly, to meet elementary needs, under such conditions, forest resources may be exploited or, as is often the case, increasingly denuded. Within certain limits, through simple techniques, water resources and minerals may also be utilised. However, without the growth of technology and the application of science on a large scale, natural resources can neither become fully known, nor can they be effectively put to productive use. In the development of resources, yield and productivity are of paramount importance. Depending upon the aspect under study, productivity may take the form of output in physical terms per unit of land or per unit of labour or per unit of capital. In the process of development, at the same time as existing resources are put to fuller use, their productivity must increase so that, in a real sense, new resources are created and multiplied.

The presence of resources in any region in a physical sense does not necessarily make for their development in an economic sense. It is the object of planned development, viewing the resources of the country as a whole as well as of its different regions, to bring together the physical and the economic into a common framework of policy and action. At each step, this common framework has to extend over a fairly long time span, the precise periods varying for different parts of the country. The entire infra-structure of development and the state of economic and social overheads enters into the picture. Above all, development has to be achieved at a time and in terms of social costs and benefits which must fit into an overall assessment of needs and resources related to each given period. Each of the main elements involved, be it technology or organisation or transport, facilitates growth and is also conditioned by it. Costs of development have to be reckoned and short-term and long-term considerations and considerations of national and regional growth have to be balanced against one another in the light of the prevailing social and political judgements. In other words, knowledge of natural resources and possibilities of technological development have to go hand in hand with the criteria of social action and the economic calculus, so that national and regional development may be achieved most rapidly and, having regard to all the relevant factors, at minimum cost to the economy.

In seeking to achieve balanced regional development within a framework of steady growth of the national economy as a whole, one recognises both the importance of the objective for economic and social integration and for meeting the minimum needs of the people and the conceptual and economic difficulties inherent in it. The expression 'region' itself has diverse meanings. For crop planning and agricultural development, the appropriate regions might differ greatly from those adopted in planning for the development of water resources, for transport or for power, or for guiding the growth of metropolitan cities along rational lines. Further, whatever the purpose in view, the requirements of regional planning, conceived in physical terms, have to be brought into harmony with political and administrative jurisdictions, specially the States and, within each State, with units such as districts and blocks. If districts and blocks are thought of as 'area units', perhaps the use of the expression 'region' could be related to such aspects as resource development, the development of power or transport, and metropolitan and urban growth. It is unavoidable that in all definitions of regions there should be an element of arbitrary choice; it is therefore all the more necessary to identify areas of overlap and of mutual influence.

For many years, the need has been felt for a classification of India into regions based on physical characteristics. A number of useful attempts have been made to evolve regional classifications which may serve as tools in the strategy of national and regional development. None of them has yet been put to such practical use. In a scheme of resource development regions worked out in the Planning Commission an effort has been made to take advantage of earlier classifications and to bring together some data on physical conditions and agricultural resources as well as economic information gathered at the 1961 census and in other recent enquiries. The scheme divides the country into 15 regions and 63 divisions.* In another scheme prepared by the Census Commissioner for India, the country is divided into 7 national regions, 31 sub-regions and 89 divisions.** Both schemes carry information down to districts.

Any scheme of regional classification is essentially an attempt to comprehend the physical and economic characteristics of different parts of the country and to relate them to plans and perspectives for the future. Allowing for variations to meet different purposes, schemes of regional classification provide a useful starting point in obtaining clearer appreciation of some of the physical and economic factors which may be of special relevance for development. To take one instance, in agricultural development, and specially in the planning of land use and cropping patterns, accurate knowledge of physical and economic characteristics of different regions and sub-regions would be of great value. But the concept of agricultural regions has yet to emerge in a clear way in Indian studies. There are certainly hints to be gathered from studies of individual crops and of land utilisation, but no definite formulations are available so far of agricultural regions which could serve as a basis for the study of developmental measures required to achieve high levels of agricultural productivity under particular conditions. In 1964, an attempt was made at the Massachusetts Institute of Technology to identify policies for increasing agricultural productivity in relation to four major ecological regions in the under-developed world, namely, the wet rice region, the rainforest tropics, the monsoon-tropical region and the high-altitude region.*** In this exercise, since the regions

---

* The Planning Commission, Committee on Natural Resources, *Resource Development Regions* (1965).

** Census of India, 1961, *Levels of Regional Development in India* (1965).

*** Massachusetts Institute of Technology, Centre of International Studies, *Policies for Promoting Agricultural Development* (1964), being the Report of the Conference on Productivity and Innovation in Agriculture in the Under-developed Countries.

were based on a world view, the findings had to be some-what generalised in character. However, where agricultural regions are demarcated within a single country, as in USSR, it is possible to bring to bear greater and more accurate knowledge of programmes and policies and to point more closely to gaps in existing information and in the quality of implementation which need attention. This is a task of national importance for teams of experts working together, including geographers, agricultural specialists, economists and planners, and is likely to yield considerable dividends in terms of developmental potentials.

With greater understanding of agricultural regions and a broad national design for building up agriculture as an industry and developing land as a natural resource, it would become easier to formulate systematic agricultural development plans at the area level, that is, for districts and blocks and groups of villages as well as for regions where water resources are being developed for the first time. Area level plans are of great importance because the various factors of development—physical, economic, human and technological—have ultimately to be harnessed together on the ground in terms of districts, blocks and villages and the groups, communities and individuals who live in them. At several points, area level plans call for local surveys, for in-stance, of soils, land utilisation and cropping, underground water resources, sources of drinking water, communications and marketing. Invariably, such local surveys have to be derived from or related to surveys undertaken on a wider regional basis. As a rule, administrative agencies are not equipped in personnel and organisation for carrying out the various surveys required at the area level. Therefore, it is necessary that academic and research institutions and others specially equipped for work in the field of area planning should supplement administrative agencies and bring together geographers and other specialists.

III

When new irrigation is opened up or new industries are established, the development which occurs is of the nature of a 'complex', involving the working together and mutual interaction of a number of factors and the association of several kinds of specialists. Among these latter, the role of economists and geographers is to see the 'complex' as a whole from their specific angle. In the development of natural resources and in all regional planning, along with economics, the contribution of geography as an integrative or unifying scientific discipline is of great importance. With the work done in the past few years through a number of national organisations concerned with the survey and development of natural resources, studies sponsored by the Planning Commission's Committee on Natural Resources, investigations undertaken by the National Council of Applied Economic Research, the Energy Survey of India and others, the stage has come when geographers and other scientists and specialists can participate most fruitfully in a comprehensive programme for the study and development of India's natural resources. Their contribution in bringing to bear an analytical and critical approach to available information and in developing concepts and objective criteria for policy decisions can be of special significance. The start made a few years ago in the use of geographical techniques in the preparation of an Atlas of Resources for Mysore and of a Diagnostic Survey of the Damodar Valley Region, which includes a new Planning Atlas, has to be carried much further through the closer association of geographers and other specialists in the universities with the formulation of national, State and regional development plans.

The need for utilising the techniques of survey developed by geographers should be stressed not only for large resource regions, but also for smaller areas. Wherever intensive development of agriculture or water resources or other local activity is undertaken, there is scope for drawing on many forms of expertise. If a small expert group comes to be organised, this itself prepares the way for associating large numbers of students and voluntary workers with local knowledge and a strong motivation in the exploration of the natural resources of the area. This will be a useful way of creating in the local community an awareness of the existing resources and potential for growth and of the need to conserve and develop the natural wealth of the area. Similarly, in the development of transport and industry and in city development plans, the geographer has a valued role.

Thus, taking a broad view, geographical studies and applications of geographical techniques now extend far beyond the customary view of the subject. Human, economic, regional and physical aspects of geographical investigations blend together to make an original and exceptionally significant contribution to economic and social planning. To draw this contribution fully into the scheme of development, besides giving opportunities to geographers and other scientists from the universities to take part in studies of interest to them, a great deal may be gained by establishing a new National Institute of Geography. At such a centre, scientists from different disciplines can come together, develop basic concepts, undertake studies in depth and evolve new and bold approaches to the development of natural resources.

IV

The role of correct social and economic policies in the conservation and development of natural resources should also be stressed. Such policies are easier to evolve where decisions have to be taken at a high technological level, as is frequently the case with mineral and energy resources. However, in dealing with land resources, forest resources, water resources and urban development, there is the greatest need for public understanding and community participation. In these areas, decisions are widely dispersed, large numbers of individuals are involved, insistent local pressures have to be overcome, and whole groups and communities have to be educated at the grass roots and organised to place common and long-term objectives above individual and short-term interests. Nothing short of a widespread movement for effective conservation and management, supported by the necessary legal and other sanctions, will help preserve and enrich further the heritage which a community receives, for instance, in the form of its land and forest resources.

In relation to natural resources, there is an intimate connection between long-term plans of economic development and long-term social policies. Both call for continuous collaboration between governmental agencies at the Centre and in the States and leading institutions engaged in scientific, economic and social research. Organisations functioning within the orbit of Government have their limitations and can accomplish only a part of the task. There is need also for a wider forum outside the structure of Government, perhaps a National Council for Natural Resources, with nucleus technical personnel of its own. From time to time, such a body could endeavour to bring together influential groups of specialists and scholars, geographers, economists and men of public affairs, who are committed to the conservation and development of natural resources, and seek to create wide understanding of major problems at all levels within the national community. The work of the Council, of the National Institute of Geography and of other leading organisations within and outside the Government should go some distance to ensure that public policies and programmes as well as the response of individuals and groups will accord increasingly with the country's permanent interests.

20

PLANNED DEVELOPMENT AND THE NATIONAL SYNTHESIS: THE APPROACH OF JAWAHARLAL NEHRU*

DURING THE period of the national movement, next to Gandhiji, Jawaharlal Nehru was most exercised over the economic and social content of freedom. The national movement threw up many great figures, but what marked out Jawaharlal Nehru was his concern with the problems of poverty and planned development in their larger political and economic context and the social philosophy and values which he evolved to deal with them. The years before Independence can be seen in retrospect as a long period of preparation for practical action. When the opportunity came, the transition from the role of freedom fighter to that of gifted statesman was, therefore, easy and altogether natural.

I

During his lifetime, the leading ideas which Jawaharlal Nehru held and his social and economic outlook were

_____
* Adapted from a lecture delivered on November 7, 1967, under the auspices of the Nehru Memorial Museum and Library, New Delhi.

expressed concretely through a series of national plans which followed one upon another. These plans provided the basis of work and thinking for millions of persons throughout the country and in all spheres of activity. This integration of an outstanding individual's philosophy with national plans whose significance penetrated far into the life of the community gave to Jawaharlal Nehru's ideas the quality almost of a national synthesis. Without these plans, his ideas would have been judged by common tests such as might apply to other leading social thinkers or reformers. For the future, too, the strength of his ideas and their interest for posterity will depend on how far they continue to form the basis of India's national plans and their implementation close to the people. Through history, the influence of the ideas of those who have combined thought with action, to whichever school they belonged, has depended on the nature and effectiveness of the medium through which they came to express themselves and the basic problems which their thought helped resolve. Take away the instruments of action and the reality with which the ideas were associated, the latter may still add to the sum of human wisdom, but their influence on welfare and progress will be either remote or strictly limited.

There are two features which distinguish Jawaharlal Nehru's thought from that of contemporary students in India, whether of economics or other social sciences. Some of them had greater knowledge and learning and understanding of detail. But none had his wide range, his perception and wholeness of outlook. Secondly, few of them had the same close identification between personal and social values and outlook. In whatever he said and did, wherever he was, Jawaharlal Nehru was ever revealing his own mind and heart, his whole being. The forum scarcely mattered; it merely determined the way he would get to the central themes; he was not acting a part, he was himself. This is the reason why in the things that mattered most, where a man's words and actions are but a mirror of his inner self, Jawaharlal Nehru was able to get at the core of what was true and lasting, could see beyond the moment, and was invariably consistent on fundamentals.

Jawaharlal Nehru's thought in matters which touched social and economic life or the ethos of democracy was not merely honest and a reflection of his personality. It was, at the same time, a considered response to the objective conditions, limitations and possibilities of India as a nation. It largely coincided with the precise needs of the time and fitted well into the historical epoch during which he lived and worked and India gained her freedom. It reflected the conditions and thought of this period, and also contained within it the seeds of growth for the future.

In his own time, both Jawaharlal Nehru and the country would have gained from a more discerning consideration of his ideas. Their possible weaknesses, specially in terms of practical action, would have been recognised and provided for. Instead, they met with almost too ready acceptance. Since his departure from the scene, they have been questioned and doubts are beginning to be raised almost equally un-critically and often on false grounds, and as a cover for current weaknesses and failures. Of course, no man's thought is complete in itself. Some part of it is of continuing value, some directly related to the special conditions or tasks of the contemporary scene. Later, as circumstances change and new problems emerge, both his thought and action have to be supplemented, enlarged and even modified. In this sense, because of the sources on which it drew and the quality of comprehension which it possessed, while Jawaharlal Nehru's thought and the action through which it expressed itself are by no means a complete answer to the next phase in India, there is no better anchor to which we can hold,

nor a greater assurance that the paths pursued are right
and well-conceived.

II

Jawaharlal Nehru had many occasions to put across his
thinking and his ideas are best conveyed as far as possible
in his own words. His speeches in Parliament, specially
when presenting the first three Five Year Plans and during
the debates on the Industrial Policy Resolutions of 1948
and 1956, his addresses to the National Development Council
at important junctures, and observations made before many
gatherings contain his main thoughts on how India should
go forward. His basic premises and values led him to a certain
social approach for the fulfilment of which planning was a
necessary means. In turn, planning led him to define his
priorities and his concepts of economic policy and structure.
Behind his thinking on economic problems lay a pervasive
belief in the possibilities of science and technology. In
reviewing briefly Jawaharlal Nehru's value premises, outlook on society, approach to planning, and view of economic
policy and structure and of the role of science, at this distance
of time, it would be appropriate also to raise some doubts
and questions, so that we might assess correctly the significance of Jawaharlal Nehru's ideas on planned development
and carry them more fully into the future.

It is not always easy to distinguish the premises to which
an individual's thinking may be traced from the concrete
expressions which it may assume. Jawaharlal Nehru's mind
and interests were extraordinarily wide-ranging, and the
line between his premises and his thought is sometimes
difficult to draw. The starting point would appear to be
his concept of India with her history, her geographical
location as the pivot of western, southern and south-eastern
Asia, with her national struggle under the spell of Gandhiji's
teachings and the manner of the final settlement with Britain.

With all her limitations, India was yet unique, and it was her duty and her role to find an answer to fundamental problems of economic, social and political well-being which was truly her own. Jawaharlal Nehru had an abiding faith in the people of India and felt that they had it within their power to find this answer. At the heart of this problem lay the issue of ends and means. It was a cardinal belief with him, from which, in the midst of life's pulls and struggles one might fall now and again, that there was always a close and intimate relationship between the end we aim at and the means adopted to attain it. Even if the end was right but the means were wrong, he said, it would vitiate the end or divert us in a wrong direction.

These two premises led to a third. Admittedly, the tasks to be accomplished were fundamental and involved deep conflicts within society. But they should be approached in a constructive and peaceful way and by methods of persuasion and consent. Sensitive people, Jawaharlal Nehru observed, cannot easily put up with the vast gap between human beings, the difference between them, the lack of opportunities on the one side and the waste on the other. Therefore, the objective must be to put an end to all differences between class and class, to develop ultimately into a classless society. The tendency towards acquisitiveness had to be replaced by the spirit of co-operation. As he put it in 1952,

> Our economy and social structure have outlived their day and it has become a matter of urgent necessity for us to refashion them so that they may promote the happiness of all our people in things material and spiritual. We have to aim deliberately at a social philosophy which seeks a fundamental transformation of this structure, at a society which is not dominated by the urge for private profit and by individual greed and in which there is fair distribution of political and economic power. We must aim at a classless society, based on co-operative effort, with opportunities for all.

These goals could be sought through violence and revolution or by peaceful and evolutionary methods. Jawaharlal Nehru chose the latter and adhered to them through life.

This was one of his basic premises. He came to it by instinct and training as well as with deliberation. Faced by the upheavals of the first few months after Partition, he saw that stability and continuity and, above all, production, were essential. If in our attempt to get something that we like and, to go forward a step in one direction we lose a few steps in another then, he remarked, on balance we have lost, not gained. It took a long time to build, but not very long to destroy. There was more than the circumstances of the moment to support his confidence in the constructive approach. There was, first, the belief in democracy and the democratic process. These were vital to the growth of individual freedom and of the creative and the adventurous spirit of man. It was Jawaharlal Nehru's hope that political democracy would lead to economic and social democracy. He did not have to face the question, which we must now face : what if, in the conditions of India, economic and social disparities continue to grow rather than diminish because democracy does not have the courage and the vigour to achieve institutional changes, and vital economic and social goals continue to elude us ?

The main grounds for Jawaharlal Nehru's optimism appear to be, first, the belief that democracy would bring its own pressures; secondly, a view of the industrial process; and, thirdly, the far-reaching significance of science and technology and of new sources of power. But with all these, in his mind there was hope rather than certainty that democracy would succeed in its social objectives. He did not fail to warn that political democracy would only justify itself if it attained its human and social goals. If it did not, he said in Parliament when presenting the First Five Year Plan, it would have to yield to some other kind of economic or social structure which we might or might not like. Ultimately, he added, it is the results that decide the structure a country will adopt. If, therefore, Jawaharlal Nehru was somewhat pragmatic, attached less value to ideology and doctrine than he might have, and sought the middle way, equally he insisted that the country and its institutions and methods were on test, and there was room neither for complacency nor for long delay. He was eager to set India on the right road but was willing, if one thing failed, to try another. His emphasis on the dynamics of growth included not only big changes in science and technology but also in the minds of men and by way of social forces.

III

The appeal of planning for Jawaharlal Nehru was both emotional and intellectual. The patriot and the historian in him conjured up, to use his own words, the vision of something vast—the mighty theme of a nation building and re-making itself. For him planning embodied the processes by which cumulative forces which made the rich richer could be stopped and those which enabled the poor to get over the barrier of poverty pushed forward. He had asked himself how this barrier could be crossed without human suffering and without infringing human freedom. Planning was at least a major part of the answer, for it helped integrate the social, economic, agricultural, industrial and other aspects of the country into a single framework of thinking.

The significance of planning was even greater. It was a means to sustain and develop national unity and to create a democracy of the masses. In India, the first essential was to maintain the unity of the country, to achieve not merely a political unity but a unity of the mind and the heart, which precludes the narrow urges that make for disunity and which breaks down barriers raised in the name of religion or State or any other barrier. Planning would help us in achieving an emotional awareness of our problems as a whole. It would help us to see the isolated problems in villages or

23

districts or States in their wider context. In this sense,
national plans represent goals for which the people of
India work together as a body transcending every difference
and diversity. These are goals to be achieved within the
framework of democracy. In a democracy, Jawaharlal
Nehru said, even though it may take a little longer, things
are built on a firm foundation and with due consideration
for the individual. He felt that the limitations set by the
democratic method were not final and it should be possible
for a democratic set up, if properly worked, to make provision
for everything we want done, and this would be its real
justification.

Planning was to be undertaken in accordance with the
Constitution, from which it derived its objectives. This is a
thought to which Jawaharlal Nehru attached great importance and he himself worked it into the Resolution in 1950
constituting the Planning Commission and six years later
into the Resolution on Industrial Policy. But the Constitution
was not so sacrosanct that it could not be changed even if
the needs of the country or the nation so demand. To
make change impossible would be to kill the Constitution.
Life is a curve, Jawaharlal Nehru said, not a straight line,
and the life of a nation is even more of a curve in these
changing times. So, he remarked, if you are flexible in your
action and constitution, then you are nearer the living curve
of a nation's growth.

Jawaharlal Nehru saw successive national plans as a
continuous series, as stages in the nation's journey which
knows no resting place. This was part of his approach to
long-term planning. He looked upon the beginning and
the end of each Plan as vital dates in the country's history.
His mind was ever on the future. Scarcely was work on
one Plan over before he asked for work to begin on the
next. In each Plan he watched for the major emphasis and
considered numbers and quantities to be changeable within

PLANNED DEVELOPMENT AND THE NATIONAL SYNTHESIS 355

large limits. His sense of continuity enabled him to resolve the problems posed by the reappraisal of the Second Plan and the gap between requirements and resources at the formulation of the Third Plan. In November 1962, when new challenges had to be faced and within the administration some thought that much of the Third Plan would have to be scrapped, Jawaharlal Nehru left no one in doubt. Our Plan, he said, is not something apart from our national life; it is of the warp and woof of it. In words, which have equal significance in the economic and social situation which we confront today, he said:

For people to say that the Plan must be largely scrapped because we have trouble and invasion to face has no meaning to me. It shows an utter misunderstanding of the situation. It is war effort that requires the Plan.

IV

Jawaharlal Nehru's social approach largely determined his outlook on economic policy and structure. For him an individual's life and philosophy were not made up of compartments but constituted a composite whole. His views on the economic and social system flowed directly from his value premises and his concept of planning. A few days after assuming office as Vice-President of the Interim Government in September, 1946, he declared that we aimed at a co-operative commonwealth in which all would be equal sharers in opportunity and in all things that give meaning and value to life. He went on to say:

The service of India means the service of the millions who suffer. It means the ending of poverty and ignorance and inequality of opportunity.

In later years, specially during the period from 1954 to 1957, in Parliament, in the Indian National Congress, and in relation to the Second Plan, Jawaharlal Nehru developed this theme more fully and gave it the name of socialist pattern of society and socialist society, but the fundamentals remained unchanged. What was put forward at the Karachi

Congress in 1931 and came to be embodied in the Directive Principles of the Constitution was now elaborated and became almost a political ideology.

Basically, Jawaharlal Nehru's socialism consisted of human and social values. In terms of institutions and structures it left too large an area fluid and flexible. He did not wish to be bound by any dogma or rigid frame. His view of land policy and the agrarian system, his support of the co-operative movement, his faith in the approach of community development and in voluntary effort go back to his human and social values. On the other hand, his views on industrial policy and the industrial structure belonged more specifically to his economic thinking and were part of his outlook on science and technology. In this sense, it can be said that his ideas on economic and social development did not amount to a complete and fully worked out system and, given the correct direction, he was willing to leave a great deal to evolve out of future experience.

Yet, what he had to urge on land policy, on co-operation and on community projects was fundamental to the future of the country and could be lost sight of only at the cost of that future. In the crucial discussions which took place on the land policy presented in the Second Plan, he threw his weight wholly on the side of proposals for social change. He was fully convinced of the necessity of ceilings on land holdings. At an earlier stage, he had thought mainly of the abolition of zamindari and of the protection of tenants, but he now saw that these were not sufficient and it was necessary to ensure both limitation of holdings and widespread ownership in land, with tenancy serving essentially as a phase of transition.

However, in piece with his general outlook, Jawaharlal Nehru thought of land reform perhaps less as a programme for redistribution and far more as a necessary condition for the growth of agricultural production and the rural economy. Therefore, during the Second Plan period and more specially between 1957 and 1959, he gave close attention to the problems of co-operative development. As he put it to the National Development Council in November 1958, ceilings on land holdings were essential, but they would not be useful without co-operatives. Both must go together, otherwise something would go wrong. Through the whole of that year, influenced by Vinoba Bhave's *gramdan* movement, by V. T. Krishnamachari's thinking on co-operation, and by reports of co-operative development in China, Jawaharlal Nehru gave much thought to the subject of co-operation. He saw that, despite its merits, in one aspect the Rural Credit Survey had given a questionable lead, namely, in its emphasis on large-sized co-operatives which in practice led to distortions and errors which the Committee had not itself anticipated. The Resolution on Co-operative Policy of the National Development Council in November 1958 and the Nagpur Congress Resolution of January 1959 are important landmarks in agrarian policy. They fall into a consistent pattern and owe everything to Jawaharlal Nehru's insight and ability to discern the implications for the future of policies which, under the inducement of possible short-term benefits, were being pursued at the time at various levels of administration. His address to the Indian Co-operative Congress in April 1958 constitutes perhaps the most complete exposition of his views on co-operation and co-operative farming as voluntary movements based on consent and persuasion, and we can go back to it today with profit.

There has been recently some lack of understanding of the significance of community development and the conditions necessary for its growth. For Jawaharlal Nehru the issue was quite simple. As he put it at the very start, community projects were of vital importance because they seek to build up the community and the individual and to make the latter the builder of his own village centre and of India in the larger sense. To the end Jawaharlal Nehru gave unwavering support to community development and to Panchayati Raj which largely grew out of it, and let pass no occasion for stressing its significance in the structure of India and in securing a certain balance within a growing industrial economy.

V

As we move from Jawaharlal Nehru's outlook on social and rural policy to his approach to economic and industrial policy, we are struck by his three overriding concerns. The first was to ensure continuity of production lest, in the anxiety to pursue the aims of redistribution, production should suffer and the prize itself be lost. The second was to advance the development of science and technology and thereby to build up a strong industrial base. This was the essential appeal to him of the ideas presented by Professor P. C. Mahalanobis towards the end of 1954 and of the experience of the Soviet Union. He saw the growth of basic industries and of heavy industries, specially of steel, machine-building, power and oil, in no exclusive sense, but certainly as a central theme in the economic and technical transformation of India. In this transformation, agriculture provided the foundation and there had to be a large and increasing component of small industries and village industries, including khadi, which would provide a balance to big industry and great machines. Jawaharlal Nehru's third concern was to find a way to counter trends inherent in an acquisitive society.

Emphasis on production led inevitably to a mixed economy in which nationalisation of existing industry had only a nominal role. Jawaharlal Nehru explained his opposition to nationalisation as a policy, as distinct from action on the merits of a case, on the ground of conserving public resources and using them most effectively on the side of new technology rather than old. But the instinctive caution concerning maintenance of existing production also argued in favour of the same conclusion.

Through the support he gave to the Second and the Third Plan and more specially to steel, oil and power, to the training of scientific and technical manpower, and to scientific and technological research, Jawaharlal Nehru helped to lay the foundations of comprehensive industrial development and of self-sustained growth largely in terms of the country's own resources and capacities. For a variety of reasons, balances conceived of in theory did not work out equally well in practice and certainly not in time, and some of the assumptions in the Plans were not borne out by events. Yet, Jawaharlal Nehru's main underlying concepts should stand scrutiny both in principle and in the longer perspective of events.

Jawaharlal Nehru had a natural aversion to capitalism and the capitalist way. In areas assigned to the private sector he was opposed to interference and restriction, because these came in the way of production and initiative. He would have been glad to see industries in the private sector adopt progressive policies following the welfare capitalism of western countries and greater scope given to small and medium-sized entrepreneurs and to new entrants, but he did not himself press hard for changes along these lines. He relied instead on the countervailing role of an efficient public sector in control of basic industries which would grow absolutely and relatively faster than the private sector. He thought somewhat hopefully that the mixed economy would be no more than a transitional stage in the movement towards a socialist economy and a socialist society.

Agricultural setbacks in recent years have induced some critics to question his priorities and to ask whether in fact

Jawaharlal Nehru failed to lay sufficient stress on agriculture. Undoubtedly, there were shortcomings in this as in other fields, and the response from Chief Ministers of States to his suggestion that they should themselves take over the agricultural portfolio was less than adequate. Yet, his own approach, which he maintained at every step, was that agriculture must have an absolute priority over everything else. He explained to Parliament in December 1952:

> If our agricultural foundation is not strong, then the industry we seek to build will not have a strong basis either. Apart from that, if our food front cracks up, everything else will crack up too. Therefore, we dare not weaken our food front. If our agriculture becomes strongly entrenched, as we hope it will, then it will be relatively easy for us to progress more rapidly on the industrial front.

The explanation for slow agricultural progress must be sought, not in the degree of importance which Jawaharlal Nehru gave to agriculture, but on the more practical plane of resources and inputs, efficiency in implementation, the quality of political leadership and administrative and technical organisation, and action to bring about institutional changes. It should be added also that food imports worried Jawaharlal Nehru at many stages. His promise in 1949 to end imports within a year had not come through, nor the promise in the First and the Second Plan, and more than once he expressed his sorrow at the failure which had occurred.

VI

No man's work is ever fully accomplished in his own time. The statesman with power unquestioned is at best an influence, albeit a dominant influence, while he stays at the helm. His insights and values light the path, but alone he can go only a few steps ahead of the system in which he works and the devotion and sincerity with which his colleagues and associates do their part. Ideas can point the way, but how far they will be sustained depends on practical results and achievements. In these, many elements of success and failure, of strength and weakness, play their part. Some are within the control and influence of the statesman. To that extent his responsibility is direct. Some belong to the larger social climate and environment in which he functions and on these his influence may be relatively small and lightly felt. Therefore, an appreciation of the singular achievements and contribution of Jawaharlal Nehru at the present juncture would not be complete without a few observations on how the foundations he laid could be made stronger and used to build a mansion for India such as he had wished to build. As it happens, this is a task which events since his passing have made much more difficult.

Jawaharlal Nehru's ideas could have achieved more for India than they did if the follow-up had been more complete and implementation more efficient. His own wide range of interests and the many goals he cherished together may account for this in part, but by far the greater responsibility rests with those who shared the burdens of office with him, the administrations which were at their disposal, the diffusion of power which characterises a parliamentary and federal system, and the distractions and weaknesses of political parties, more specially those engendered through years of office within the Indian National Congress itself. Secondly, as an economy begins to grow and development brings new stresses, problems of economic management are inextricably linked with and become as important as those of planning. Economic management in all its aspects has been and continues to be one of the main sources of weakness both in India's administrative system and in the scheme of planning. This weakness has a direct bearing on the extent to which many of the assumptions in Jawaharlal Nehru's thinking could be fulfilled in practice.

In considering Jawaharlal Nehru's approach to planned development, it is essential to distinguish his basic values and concepts from more specific priorities. The latter are related to time and circumstance, to concrete experience and assessment of the national situation from time to time. Therefore if, after fifteen years of planned development, with all its gains and shortcomings, there is need now to concentrate overwhelmingly on agriculture, or to stress the urgency of orienting development towards the expansion of employment opportunities and acceleration of education, or to bring dependence on external aid to an end as early as possible, such action would not involve departures from Jawaharlal Nehru's teaching and beliefs.

Jawaharlal Nehru did not either claim or seek to provide a complete system. While he was right regarding the contribution of science and technology to human welfare and economic development, he was too optimistic about the pace at which technical advances can occur without the support of large social and structural changes. Consequently, he did not place as much emphasis as he might have on speeding up these changes and on building up adequate social instruments. In a country so full of divisive forces, Jawaharlal Nehru might have done more to strengthen such organised, secular and national forces, as the trade union movement, the co-operative movement, organisations of landless labourers and poorer peasants and elements which will have both the determination and the resources to fight disintegration tooth and nail. He might have done more to bring all the progressive forces together into a creative working partnership. He knew that in achieving peaceful change and in working the levers of democracy, directions of policy and goodwill, and strong pressures from below from groups and classes whose interests the present economic system fails to safeguard, had to operate together and all the time. His very ideals and the confidence he aroused held back these pressures and to that extent the goals he desired but could not reach have now become harder to achieve at the same time as they have gained in their urgency. He knew that market forces had to be controlled and channelled but, having opted for state trading in foodgrains, he yet permitted them and other like forces to gain sway over the policies of his own Government. Soon after taking office in 1946, he had described the existing administrative structure as a ship of state, old, battered, slow moving and unsuited to this age of swift change, which would have to be scrapped and to give place to another. But he himself initiated no fundamental change and, in his usual generous manner, even permitted willingness to conform to the prevailing fashion of thought to pass off as commitment and sense of purpose. Having made large numbers of people aware of the need for joint co-operative farming undertaken willingly and by consent, later his own silence tended to encourage retreat from this objective. He was always concerned over the growth of economic and social disparities and the spread of slums, but could not move much beyond educating public opinion to the seriousness of these problems.

These and other examples of what might have been are easy to cite. In their essence they are in the nature of tasks which Jawaharlal Nehru could not finish, as much because of his own multifarious roles as the political and administrative limitations under which he worked. To point to them is not criticism, but recognition of our present responsibilities and admission of the fact that India's freedom has yet to be consolidated, that her economic and social system has still to be built up into something just and efficient and capable of resolving the problems of the people, and that her political system must be strengthened and administrative structure recast if we are not to be overwhelmed by current drifts and challenges. These are among the elements in seeking a new national synthesis without which India will remain far short of being a nation with a sense of direction, at peace with herself and able to meet internal and external strains which press upon her. Such a synthesis has to evolve largely around Jawaharlal Nehru's vision of India and his thoughts for her future and go forward from where he left off.

21

PLANNING AND PLAN IMPLEMENTATION: LESSONS FROM THE FIVE YEAR PLANS*

THE PREPARATION of every Five Year Plan involves, in some degree, an appraisal of past experience. Planned development has taken the country forward in many directions and, on the whole, the record will bear scrutiny. Along with a great deal of continuity, there has been considerable variation from one period to another in the problems which have claimed special attention and in the emphasis given to different aims and policies. Changes in methods and machinery have also occurred. While there has been at no time a sense of complacency, there has also not been that sense of conviction widely shared and that degree of concern with speed and attainment of results which are essential to the accomplishment of great tasks. An attempt is made in this paper to list a few of the lessons which could be learnt from our experience in development over the past thirteen or fourteen years.

---

* Based on a paper circulated to the National Development Council at its meeting on October 27 and 28, 1964, when it considered the draft of the *Memorandum on the Fourth Five Year Plan* and published in the *Yojana*, Vol. IX No. 1, January 26, 1965.

INSTRUMENTS OF POLICY

Our plans have presented the social objectives of development in broad terms and without setting time limits, without specifying in detail the means to be employed and without establishing sufficiently effective machinery and instruments for achieving or moving rapidly enough towards the declared objectives. Thus, between the statement of social objectives and the practical ability to achieve them, there has been a gap, whose persistence now throws increasing doubt on the very process of planned development. This statement is true, for instance, of such objectives as establishment of greater equality of opportunity, bringing about reduction in disparities in income and wealth and a more even distribution of economic power, ensuring adequate expansion of employment opportunities, utilising the country's manpower resources and meeting the minimum needs of the bulk of the population. During any given period, frequently there may be a conflict between measures and policies for attaining economic growth and for enlarging social justice. We have been keen that the promise of freedom should take a concrete form as soon as possible. Since this will take a great deal of effort on the part of the country, we have been anxious that the goal should be constantly kept in view. In our thinking, therefore, there has been a certain amount of vagueness at this point and we have not been able to place the problem before the country in bold relief, pointing out clearly what might or might not be possible and the implications for the nation of going forward or turning back on the basic objective.

We should try now to state the essential problem in a precise and realistic manner in relation to the Fourth and Fifth Plans. It will not be enough merely to state the problem. The measures and policies to be implemented will also have to be stated and accepted. Here there are two difficulties. The first is that the savings of the community and the external resources that may be available will not be sufficient to achieve all the objectives we have. Even with correct social and economic policies, the period needed will be somewhat longer than the next two Plans. How much longer, it is at present difficult to say. There are heavy odds to be met, not the least being the rate of growth of population and the demands of current consumption against accumulation of capital. Ultimately, this is a point where there has to be political judgement and political choice. This is true not merely of India but of every society that functions within the framework of democracy.

The second difficulty is that, within the limits of political judgement and deliberate choice, in our setting, the spectrum of political views described under a common label has been rather wide. This has made for unity in approach in a general sense, but not in terms of specific action. Much that is agreed to by way of principle and approach loses in effect in the course of action and implementation. The degree of discipline in policy, so essential for effective and continuous administrative action, has not been available in many key areas. This has been the position over the years, both at the national and State levels and, despite the existence of the National Development Council and several favourable political factors, as between the Centre and the States.

These problems influence the formulation of the Plans to a limited extent, but the shadow they cast over their implementation is larger and more serious. There is no easy way out. At the same time, if we formulate our Plans with greater care and thoroughness and give much more attention to means and instruments through which the objectives are to be attained, the gaps may be progressively reduced.

CURRENT ECONOMIC MANAGEMENT

At best a plan of development is an outline, a framework of policy and action. It cannot be too rigid, for new situations and new facts have to be reckoned with from time to time. In retrospect, a plan, even if correctly conceived, can only be as good as the implementation in detail of the policies and measures embodied in it. Even if there were no contradictions between plan objectives and policies and those adopted currently, success would be far from assured. In many directions administrations have to make their own mistakes and learn from experience. It is true that, with the experience that has been gained since Independence, there are many errors which we can avoid—errors of optimism and pessimism, errors of policy as well as errors of execution. Nevertheless, there has been hitherto a wide gap between plan objectives and policies and current policies. This has reduced the effectiveness of our plans without giving corresponding advantage in managing the current problems of the economy. This observation is true, for instance, of the manner in which we have dealt for several years with such problems as food distribution, fixation of relative prices of agricultural commodities and industrial commodities, control of inflationary pressures, implementation of land reform and growth of corporate enterprise in the private sector. In fairness, it should be said that these are problems which have been found difficult in other countries as well. Yet, the more closely current policies and plan objectives are integrated with one another, the greater will be the measure of success in fulfilling the plans. The implication is not merely that current policies have to conform to the plan but also that in formulating plan objectives and policies, short term requirements and problems should be anticipated and provided for.

THE FEDERAL STRUCTURE

The distribution of subjects under our Constitution between the Union and the States does not give to the Central Government sufficient power to ensure economic and social development for the country as a whole either on an adequate scale or on uniform lines. Our Plans have sought to overcome this limitation to some extent. Through various forums the Central Government is able to initiate consulations over a wide field and thus exert a distinct advisory influence with the States. Through the resources for development which the Centre makes available, a measure of direction can be given to the scheme of development in the States. Rigid procedures for the administration of Central assistance inhibit action in the States. On the other hand, if agreed priorities are not observed and Central assistance meant for given purposes is not well applied or is diverted to other purposes, planning breaks down. There have been indications of this during the Third Plan. In particular, in States whose financial situation was not satisfactory, in several aspects planning has suffered and priorities have been affected. An important lesson for the Fourth Plan, therefore, is that procedures relating to Central assistance, while permitting a reasonable measure of change and flexibility, should have built into them certain sanctions which will ensure that Plan programmes and priorities are not disregarded in any State simply because, for the moment, this seems to be the easier way. This is a matter which merits consideration as much from the point of view of individual Ministries and State Governments as in the larger national perspective.

While financial and regulatory procedures, if well administered, can secure implementation of Plan programmes and projects along approved lines, unless State Governments and those who hold responsible political office are so motivated and determined, the social objectives and the policy

24

approaches implicit in the Plans may not be fulfilled. Several examples could be cited. For instance, failures in implementing programmes of land reform in an efficient and timely manner, which react equally on social stability and on agricultural progress, need not have occurred. Progress in building up co-operatives could be greater in several parts of the country. There could be more integrated development between rural and urban areas and between the more developed and the less developed parts of each State. Much more could have been done by State Governments to strengthen their administrative machinery.

The question of raising standards of administration in the States is of extreme importance. States administer not only for themselves but also on behalf of the Central Government. Theirs is the only administration at levels closest to the people. The Centre depends on them and has few agencies of its own which operate over the country as a whole. The problem of administrative efficiency and of integrity in administration at the Centre and in the States is, in the final analysis, an indivisible one. In the past, weaknesses in State administration were less apparent and mattered less, because of the limited scale of the effort envisaged in the plans. Now the dimensions of the effort to be undertaken are so vast that, unless the administrative assumptions of planning are fulfilled, it is not possible to succeed. In the field of administration, a common approach to the problems of reform, not only in a general way but in considerable detail, should be regarded as an essential national interest.

THE MANAGEMENT FUNCTION

Management lies at the core of the planning process. Earlier, the critical importance of management in relation to projects and in relation to various development programmes was not fully realised and was not stressed enough. It was assumed that the authorities concerned would do whatever was necessary and there was no need to pursue this aspect otherwise than in a broad way. This assumption has proved false. During the past three or four years, the nature of the problem has been seen more clearly, but the administrative Ministries and Departments and technical and other organisations working under them, have on the whole been inadequate in relation to the tasks to be undertaken. The problem, therefore, is one of strengthening these organisations, proposing to them improved methods of management and planning and endeavouring to secure their implementation in detail. The frequency with which projects exceed their cost and time estimates and fail on their targets reflects both on the quality of planning and the quality of implementation. In many large enterprises, inadequacies at the stage of project preparation have led to great difficulties, first in completing the construction phase, and later in operating the new plants economically. Similarly, failure to provide the necessary material, technical and personnel support to many developing projects has been both a fault in planning and in implementation. Deficiencies in management, taking the expression in its wider meaning, are capable of being largely removed. From now on, the utmost concentration should be on the proper working out of projects and ensuring that each enterprise has an adequate organisation and follows sound methods of work.

Inappropriate Targets

In several fields of development, targets have not been proposed after sufficiently critical and detailed study. This is a fault in their technical preparation which tends to be slurred over at the stage of planning, but becomes only too obvious later on.

The failure on targets in many projects often comes to light after the event. With better project preparation, even if certain factors should turn adverse, some measure of re-planning would be possible, not arbitrarily, but as part of an integrated scheme of development. Frequently, this aspect of integration is lost sight of. The adjustments are merely forced upon the project authorities, as if they did not have much control on their own.

Failure on targets may occur for reasons other than those connected with the given project. For instance, adequate resources may not be made available because of other claims. Such failures have to be distinguished from those inherent in the preparation and implementation of the project itself.

One error which has often occurred is to propose targets and judge achievements in terms of expenditure incurred. Wherever they are fixed, the targets should be related to physical tasks and achievements. Against these, certain financial estimates have to be set. Any expenditure is intended to represent a certain performance in the physical sense. Therefore, it is of the utmost importance that performance budgeting should be developed as a tool of planning and plan implementation.

There has also been excessive fixing of targets in fields in which they may not be wholly appropriate. Where large numbers of persons are involved, for instance, in agriculture, co-operation, or small industries or in social services, it is important that only a limited number of targets, each justifiable in itself, should be proposed. For the rest, the main attention should be given to ensuring that the processes of development are thought of along the right lines, the necessary institutions and incentives are being built up, and a process of growth from within is being stimulated.

GESTATION PERIODS

If the gestation period of a project turns out to be longer than has been planned, ordinarily this should be regarded as a failure in the management function. As suggested earlier, the failure constitutes a blot both on planning and on implementation. In the past, frequently, the lengthening out of gestation periods has been ascribed to foreign exchange difficulties. That there have been foreign exchange problems is not denied. However, it is also true that in many instances, there have been other and more serious factors. Delays, for example, in making steel or cement available during the construction phase or in organising procurement of raw materials and components, both from within the country and from abroad, indicate that materials planning and management have not been given that central place in planning and plan implementation which is due to them. This has been realised for the past two years, but the steps taken to correct this known deficiency have been utterly inadequate. As an important preparatory step for the Fourth Plan, a programme of action designed to secure the regular flow of key materials to projects under construction and procurement of raw materials and components for projects in operation should be taken in hand from now on.

Even if gestation periods were not to lengthen out beyond the planned schedules, a central problem in planning is the extent to which projects and schemes requiring long periods of gestation are balanced with those requiring shorter periods of gestation. The problem arises in all sectors. It has drawn repeated attention in the fields of irrigation and industry. It exists also to an extent in agriculture and social services. In their policy formulations, our Plans have emphasised the need for continuous flow of benefits, for phasing, for securing at each stage a composite programme in which results will be forthcoming over the short period without, at the same time, neglecting such basic development as may require longer periods of gestation. Unfortunately, in the actual choice of projects, these suggestions are often ignored, both at the Centre and in the States.

The main reason why it is possible to neglect what is accepted in theory as the correct approach, is that in our planning so far there has been very little insistence on the appraisal of costs and benefits and on comparisons between returns on alternative investments. This is a key area for action in the Fourth plan. Working practices for the preparation of plans in different sectors have to be considerably improved. If project appraisal and evaluation and assessment of returns were to become a normal ingredient of all planning decisions, as they should, the element of political preference and judgment, in itself understandable, can be a positive aid in planning. If the Central Ministries set the right example, the States could be induced to follow. Action in this direction is urgent because, unless the new practices come into sufficient vogue in the next few months, selection of projects for the Fourth Plan will be marked by the same kind of deficiency as in the Third Plan.

It is true that, at the stage of formulating a Five Year Plan, all the projects may not be fully worked out. Yet some decisions have to be taken. The answer lies in introducing greater continuity in the process of considering and approving projects. Every project to be considered for a Five Year Plan should be presented by the appropriate agency with a careful 'project definition', supported by sufficient data for this stage of the project. Projects, which have been fully worked out or for which feasibility studies have been prepared, could be approved specifically for implementation. The allocation of resources in the Five Year Plan should take into account the estimates of requirements for these projects as well as for projects for which only preliminary statements are available. But specific approval leading to action should be given only after the feasibility study for a project has been considered. Within the scheme of resource allocations, approvals to projects should be given as each project is presented in sufficient detail.

Continuity in planning on the lines suggested above, specially for projects, has to be built into the practice of planning and plan implementation right through each plan period. This has two important implications. First, the sharpness with which plan periods have tended to be divided from one another marking, as it were, quite distinctive phases of development, is now unnecessary. There should be greater emphasis on sound technical and economic investigation, on taking correct decisions on the basis of requisite information and data, and on implementation and smooth flow of benefits. Secondly, each year every large enterprise should undertake forward planning, both in physical and in financial terms, for a further period of four or five years. This would ensure that their estimates of cost and time and of physical benefits were reviewed systematically and, whatever changes or re-planning were needed, could be undertaken as a matter of normal practice and incorporated into the plan. Current economic policies could then be more closely related to Plan objectives and targets. This does not mean that for many vital reasons Five Year Plans as such will not be required. These must continue but, at every stage, a Five Year Plan should be up-to-date in its estimates of costs, time schedules and physical targets and further, at each point, at least in respect of major projects and the aggregate projections for the economy, those concerned with planning and financial and economic policies should have a fairly clear view of the future.

DISPERSAL OF RESOURCES

The comments offered above have a bearing on investment policy and on allocation of resources. Another aspect of the same subject is the extent to which in our plans resources should be spread out or deployed in a concentrated manner. Twelve years ago, when the approach of community development and national extension was being worked out, it seemed hard to contemplate that, for years on end, only a proportion of the villages of India should receive the benefits of the proposed development. It was then thought that there would be no contradiction between extension of community development so as to cover the entire country-side and the growth of agricultural production, provided (*a*) the necessary priority which the plans contemplated was always given to agriculture, and (*b*) extension services were established by each State government first in areas which already had irrigation or assured rainfall or which were likely to come under irrigation in accordance with plan programmes. Neither of the two assumptions was fulfilled to the extent our plans and policies had postulated. Be that as it may, the fact that growth in agricultural production, after attaining a certain level, seems to have come to a halt, has led us to stress the strategy of intensive area development. This has special application for agricultural and rural development. In other fields, areas selected for intensive development have a more limited purpose, such as testing of improved methods or the training of pesonnel. A common danger in planning is that certain descriptions may be used, but the content may be quite different. This aspect has to be watched in applying the idea of intensive development in every field and specially in agriculture.

The choice between dispersed and concentrated develop-ment of resources arises in other fields as well, for instance, in determining locations for industrial development, in considering how speedily the less developed areas are to be brought to a level with the more advanced areas, or in considering how the rural industrialisation programme should be implemented. In practice, it is not possible to pursue either course completely at the cost of the other. Where the Fourth Five Year Plan should differ from earlier Plans is in posing the issues in each case, working out the implications with the available tools of economic and statistical analysis, and in formulating precise programmes in which there would be proper time-phasing and assessment of costs and benefits. Admittedly, economic criteria alone will not be decisive, but they should be applied, and political and administrative decisions should be taken after considering the results of the economic appraisal. This is another direction in which, unless the lessons of earlier Plans are applied in the course of the next few months, it will be too late to take advantage of them at least in the formulation of the Fourth Five Year Plan.

Area Development

In any area, the main investments envisaged in a plan, whether public or private, help establish certain potentials for development. These potentials can be realised and progressively enlarged in practice if the human resources and the leadership and administrative set up in an area can be harnessed for achieving integrated development. This would mean that various development programmes and activities are seen as an interdependent system in which each part stimulates and supports the others. These concepts lie behind our planning, but they have not been so far realised in any adequate measure. They do not become wrong for this reason. They need more studied application. The notion of integrated area development may apply to a resource region, to a district, and, within a district, to individual blocks and villages, or to a city or metropolitan region. The most important application is in terms of districts and blocks and villages for which a new system of institutions is being built up under Panchayati Raj. These institutions are conceived of primarily as means for achieving integrated area development based on the participation of the people and on coordination between various agencies. Working with these institutions, various agencies of Government are expected to coordinate and dovetail their efforts. Failure to achieve effective coordination, for instance, between the Agriculture and Irrigation Departments, has led to shortfalls in irrigation. Similarly, there is interdependence between Agriculture and Co-operation, between these and Education and between Health and Family Planning and other aspects of development. In this sphere, there are a number of detailed lessons to be drawn from past experience.

Costs, Productivity and Returns

Costs, productivity and returns are aspects, firstly, of the criteria of investment which are followed and, secondly, of management at each stage of a project or scheme, but something more is also involved. Technological improvement and raising of levels of productivity are basic to economic progress. They have to be built not only into the general design of a plan but into each of the activities included in it. In other words, productivity has to be a matter of continuing concern. In the search for higher productivity, the entire apparatus of scientific and technological knowledge and research has to be involved fully at every stage. Costs and returns are in themselves both tests of productivity and instruments for achieving higher productivity. In the past these aspects have received only casual consideration. It is necessary that both in the formulation of the Fourth Plan and in its implementation, measurement of productivity and setting of productivity standards and norms should be given a key place.

THE PRIVATE SECTOR

At the beginning of the First Plan, a general view was taken of the place of the private sector in the national economy. This led to the passing of the Industries (Development and Regulation) Act of 1951. The industrial Policy Resolution of 1956 carried the matter a little further, specially by way of demarcating fields of industrial development in which the public sector or the private sector would play a major part. In the light of experience over the past several years, it is necessary to review the 1956 Resolution and bring it in line with present day needs. It is also necessary to review the 1951 legislation because, apart from the provisions made for licensing of industries, provisions concerning the machinery of development in the private sector (Development Councils and the Central Advisory Council of Industries) have not fulfilled their purpose. In an economy which is to develop according to a plan and which, at the same time, assigns a considerable role to the private sector, it has now become necessary to give fresh thought to the structure of industrial organisation, to the role of the newly emerging managerial and technical cadres and to the part which labour should play in responsible decisions affecting industrial development and economic policy. Our recent experience of difficulties in ensuring the development of priority industries in the private sector, in obtaining resources, in promoting the application of scientific and technological research and attaining higher levels of productivity, in negotiating collaboration agreements and, finally, in working with Development Councils and industrial associations, deserves close and critical attention.

REPORTING, EVALUATION AND APPRAISAL

This is a field in which responsibility lies with the Planning Commission and with the Ministries for improving the existing system of reporting on progress and on short-comings in implementation. Three aspects are of special importance. First, in respect of projects, reports should enable the authorities concerned to anticipate problems and to judge progress at each stage in relation to pre-determined programmes and objectives. Secondly, over the past two or three years, reporting from the States to the Centre, which was never quite adequate, has become even weaker and less regular. Thirdly, while a system of reports and evaluation can be developed for plan projects and programmes, it is much more difficult to develop tests and data by which to judge progress in achieving important policy objectives. This aspect has not been considered so far, but has become increasingly important. As the scope of plan programmes and policies grows, systematic reporting, study of reports and action on conclusions drawn from reports become matters of great importance for the success of our plans. In any field, unless the reporting system at the base level is placed on a sound footing, satisfactory reporting and use of reports at higher levels cannot be achieved. Therefore, the question of reports has now become one of fundamental importance. Reference was made earlier to the introduction of performance budgeting and evaluation. This is also closely linked with the manner in which pro-grammes are formulated, financial provisions are made and performance is reported upon.

ORGANISATION AND ANALYSIS

Planning and plan implementation are intimately related to one another. Whether in project management or pro-gramme management or area development administration, unless the quality of planning improves, it is not possible to obtain the results which a plan postulates. Nor is it possible to ensure that investments will be correctly made, targets correctly set, and costs and returns correctly established. Therefore, strengthening organisations concerned with planning and equipping them adequately for obtaining and analysing the necessary technical and economic information are of the utmost importance. There is much to be done in this respect within the Planning Commission at the national level. Some steps were initiated after the Third Plan was formulated, but these have to be pursued much more intensively. The technical quality of work in the Planning Commission can and should be considerably raised.

Several Ministries at the Centre do not have adequate planning units of their own, so that their grip on their own plans and projects is much weaker than it should be.

Most of the larger industrial projects and construction projects do not have units assisting the general manager or the managing director in overall coordinated planning and watching of performance.

In the States, although some steps have been taken from the technical aspect, the level of planning cannot be said to be anywhere near that required by the difficult tasks they have to accomplish. There is need for much more overall study and integration. The planning machinery in most States does not function sufficiently above the ordinary departmental level to make the impact needed in terms of policy and approach. This was an important consideration behind the suggestion to the States in April, 1962, to set up State Planning Boards.

In relation to the private sector, planning tends to reduce itself largely to licensing and allocations. The extent to which the leaders of an industry (from amongst employers, managers and technicians and workers) are in fact able to take an active share in planning for the development of the industry as a whole is much less than was hoped for many years ago.

Experience of earlier Plans and, more especially recent experience, has emphasised the need for early action in each of the directions outlined above. Basically, the issue is one of taking positive steps urgently to strengthen planning organisations at various levels, so that they may develop the necessary competence to assemble the essential information required for sound planning, present their analysis and organise up-to-date intelligence and studies in the future.

22

MANAGEMENT AND PLAN FULFILMENT*

DURING THE past few years, the coming up of a number
of new institutions, expansion of facilities for management
development, increase in our knowledge of the operational
problems of the Indian economy, and the varying quality
of success achieved in the public sector as well as in many
parts of the economy where private enterprise has had the
fullest opportunity to develop, have served to draw attention
to the critical role of management in the progress of the
economy and in the execution of our plans of development.
The main propositions can be stated briefly.

I

An achieving society is distinguished from one that fails
to achieve by its capacity to manage and organise, to
motivate and inspire, and to implement and produce results
swiftly. To modernise our economy, as a nation, we are
under deep compulsion also to modernise our methods of
work, to get the utmost out of our resources, whether these
be time, money, machines, materials or, more important

* Adapted from an address at the Twentieth All India Commerce Conference
held at Jiwaji University, Gwalior, on December 29, 1966.

than all else, men, talent and creative ability. There is already consciousness of the size and range of the enormous tasks which must be accomplished. If we had done better in the Third Plan, some of these tasks would have been a little easier. Now they call for additional and more concentrated effort. There are many facets to this problem. A systematic and co-operative approach to problems of management constitutes one of the most promising areas in which to concentrate. Efforts to raise the standards of management in all our enterprises, whether public, private and co-operative, or large and small, in our development and extension activities, in the management of materials and supplies, in the administration of public services and utilities, and in agriculture, industry, transport and other sectors, can yield quick and substantial results. In doing so, they will also generate larger resources for speeding up national development.

In the past decade, in the more advanced countries, there has occurred a near revolution in the concepts of management, in management techniques, in the support which advances in economics and other disciplines and in computational methods can provide to management and, above all, in the extent to which all groups and levels of workers are beginning to participate in the responsibilities of management. In India, too, there have been important developments, but what has been accomplished is still by far the smaller part.

The contribution of management to the speeding up of economic development and to the fulfilment of the Five Year Plans may be considered under several heads, for instance, (i) in relation to different sectors within the economy, (ii) in terms of public enterprises and project preparation and implementation, (iii) in relation to supplies and materials, (iv) in terms of growth of productivity, fairer sharing of the gains and development of human relations conducive to good management, and (v) in building up personnel for achieving efficient planning and management. The scope of management, conceived thus, embraces the entire economy. Hitherto, institutions engaged in the study of Commerce, Business or Management have tended largely to limit their interest to the organised sectors of the economy. However, viewed in the wider perspective of national growth, the tasks falling to them are far more comprehensive and exacting.

II

The size and complexity of problems of management have increased greatly with the growth of population, the expansion of the economy and greater integration between its different parts. What happens in different branches of the economy turns to a large extent on the foresight and wisdom with which the economy is managed in its broader and overall aspects, such as supply of essential components and raw materials and effective use of existing productive capacities, achievement of a continuing balance between investment, savings and consumption, assuring food and other essential supplies to the mass of the people, maintenance of reasonable levels of prices, and maintenance of an outlook of confidence in sustained growth. In recent years, for a variety of reasons, specially the unexpected setbacks in agriculture, large expenditures on defence and development and increases in internal prices accentuated by speculative and anti-social elements, these problems of current management of the economy have been extremely difficult in nature. Perhaps, with greater understanding and better preparation and implementation on the part of the Central and State Governments, and greater concern over the public interest on the part of the business community, this task could have been handled more effectively. It has to

25

be admitted that every one concerned has had to work on
small margins and one difficult situation has succeeded
another. While no completely satisfactory solutions were in
fact available, there have also been many avoidable weaknesses. Thus, problems of management in different sectors
of the economy, whether these are operated by the public
sector or by private enterprise or by small peasants and
small entrepreneurs, have tended to get out of hand. Small
imbalances became larger and cumulative in their impact.
Failures and shortfalls at one point have caused failures and
shortfalls at others in an unbroken vicious circle. Therefore, if the effort to lift the national economy is to bear
fruit, special attention must be given to each critical point
in the overall current management of the economy. If the
economy in the short term is managed in a hand-to-mouth
style and without sufficient insight and knowledge concerning the causal factors at work, not only do many things
tend to go wrong currently, but the longer term prospects
of continuous growth and of plan fulfilment can also be
jeopardised.

In every sector of the economy, we have an area of
organised activity, which is represented by major enterprises,
and an area of dispersed activity, which is represented
by large numbers of small, individual operators. This is
true of industry which comprises, on the one hand, a growing corporate sector and, on the other, a wide range of small
and unorganised activities, including village and household
industries. The bulk of road transport is in the hands of
small operators. In trade, notwithstanding a few outstanding organisations in the public and private sectors and a
widespread chain of wholesalers and retailers, the greater
part of activity is of an unorganised character. In power,
while generation presents one set of problems, rural electrification has the aspect of extension activity. Agriculture,
in itself by far the largest sector of the economy, offers

also in some ways the most difficult problems of management. Broadly, it may be said that the problems of management in these different sectors fall into four distinct groups, namely, (a) management at the enterprise level, (b) public regulation of private activity, (c) management in relation to extension, including organisation of small, dispersed units into co-operative or other associations, and (d) management of supplies and materials.

III

Of these aspects, one which has been studied perhaps more fully than others pertains to large enterprises. As is well known, major projects in sectors such as industry, irrigation, power and transport account for a high proportion of new investment during any plan period. They make demands on resources in men, money, materials and organisation which are frequently under-estimated. They call, on the one hand, for decisions and procedures at the level of policy which would facilitate their preparation and execution and, on the other, they cannot be successfully undertaken without a high degree of efficiency, initiative and compactness in the organisations responsible for them. Thus, in the scheme of development, large projects constitute a major challenge to administrative and technical capacity which has to be met more adequately than in the past. Projects in different sectors of the economy present special problems, but many essential features are common.

Project management embraces the life cycle of a project from inception to operation. The main propositions which are thrown up by the experience of recent years and by the special studies which have been undertaken fall under four broad heads. These are project definition and pre-construction phase, construction management, operations management, and management issues concerning organisation, planning and policy.

A major project comes to be defined with increasing precision in three distinct stages, namely preliminary project formulation, feasibility study and the detailed project report. The first two steps are indispensable to sound decision-making, while the third is essentially a tool of implementation. The preparation of the feasibility study is the critical stage for reaching correct economic and technical decisions and one which is still not being handled as well as it should be. Judgments concerning size, location, product patterns and technical processes depend upon the quality of work undertaken for the feasibility study. On the basis of the feasibility study, it should be possible to mark out all the steps to be taken prior to the commencement of construction and, in particular, to draw up the necessary technical and managerial plans for handling the subsequent construction phase and synchronizing the work of different agencies. Secondly, it should be possible to provide for each of the specific points of integration with other interdependent projects, whether these are in the public or the private sector. From the start, it is imperative that there should be a total systems approach to the conception, planning and management of each project, so that the total systems cost of operation is reduced to the minimum.

Construction of a major project is a large and complex management task. A complete master plan, which includes all important allocations of the work to be undertaken, is essential to a management control system. More than in any other sphere, network planning techniques, which are now obtaining increasing recognition in the country and which the Planning Commission is at present engaged in developing, can facilitate better management of the construction stage of major projects.

In the course of implementation, major projects are faced with two different sets of operational problems, those which require action at the level of Government or other higher authority and those which lie within their own sphere of action. A project authority, acting within its own limits, can do much to achieve better management through the introduction of modern production schedules and cost control systems, scientific materials management and inventory practices, improvement of existing budget and accounts procedures, and forward planning. There are, however, other problems affecting management at the enterprise level which can be resolved satisfactorily only if project managements have adequate authority and personnel, if overall materials planning for scarce materials is undertaken in a satisfactory manner, if capital resources and foreign exchange are correctly allocated and, finally, if industrial relations are so managed as to provide a climate for co-operative working between labour and management.

IV

A few words should be said on the critical place of the planning of supplies and materials for the smooth functioning of the economy and for the efficient use of available capacities in all sectors, including industry, transport, power and agriculture. It is not yet sufficiently recognised that there is an intimate two-way connection between materials planning at the national level in respect of key items and economic management of materials at the project or area level. Both are essential for obtaining physical outputs at minimum cost and within prescribed time-schedules. At the national level, it is essential to undertake systematic planning, keeping in view both internal demands and available capacities as well as indigenous outputs and supplies which have to be secured from abroad. In particular, materials planning is an imperative need in respect of certain imported materials such as sulphur, rock phosphate, copper, lead, zinc, tin, mercury, tool and alloy steel and rubber. Within each sector of development, it is necessary to undertake an assessment of materials requirements and their phasing along with supplies likely to be available. There is a constant tendency to accept larger commitments than can be sustained with the resources which may be foreseen at any given time, so that what is available is spread too thin, and few projects or units are able to work to capacity or in accordance with the schedules which are prescribed. Yet, with better management and a clearer direction of priorities, this failure need not occur. Careful assessment of financial and material resources and adequate programming to achieve given outputs should be built into the scheme of planning in each sector far more precisely than has been done so far.

V

Standards of management in different parts of the economy cannot be raised continuously and in significant measure, unless, from now on, we adopt a thorough and comprehensive approach to the preparation and orientation of key personnel, more specially at the middle and higher levels. In planning courses of training at the graduate and postgraduate level in institutions concerned with the teaching of Commerce, Business or Management, there should be the fullest awareness of priorities in the larger national context and of the areas in which new skills will be most needed. Two conditions have to be secured. Firstly, there should be much closer association between these institutions and agencies of Government, enterprises and associations which represent organised industry and trade as well as co-operative and other organisations concerned with operations in the decentralised sectors of the economy. Such association would be of mutual benefit. Secondly, it is highly desirable that institutions engaged in the teaching of Commerce, Business and Management, specially those equipped with postgraduate departments and adequate faculties for research, should participate actively in training programmes which have been visualised in the Fourth Plan. These concern enterprise management, programme planning and management, methods and techniques for economic planning, specially in relation to private and dispersed activities, and the training and orientation, not only of managers, but also of supervisors and workers in such important areas as reduction in costs and increase in productivity.

By themselves, government agencies are seldom equipped to provide for training. Of course, their personnel should be enabled freely to participate in training programmes. The role of training belongs properly to institutions engaged in teaching and research. In a co-operative national programme, each selected institution could develop plans for training, appropriate to its field of interest, which it could implement continuously over several years. From the side of the users also, whether government agencies, private industry, trade unions or local authorities, there should be corresponding plans for preparing personnel for receiving the necessary training over a period of years and treating trained persons as a scarce resource to be used effectively. Work along these lines would open up new opportunities for the development of institutions and strengthening of training facilities and would even begin to transform the methods and substance of teaching. At the same time, it would have far-reaching and cumulative effects on the quality of management and on the growth of efficiency as a habit of mind and as a style of work which we bring to bear on every task we may attempt.

23

ADMINISTRATION FOR DEVELOPMENT*

THE THEME of administration for development covers such wide ground that one can at best pinpoint certain aspects which should receive special attention in an overall review.

The political and administrative framework within which development is undertaken sets the conditions which determine largely what can be accomplished and how it is to be accomplished. Within the framework, it is possible to suggest how better results may be obtained, and how any limitations inherent in it may be overcome. We do not get far if, in answer to many important problems, we can only propose that the Constitution should be changed or that relations between the Centre and the States should be redefined, or that certain basic value commitments should be given up. If the main institutional premises which have hitherto formed part of the scheme of national development are challenged, the discussion moves on to another plane altogether.

* The substance of this paper was presented in March, 1965, to an orientation course on development administration at the Indian Institute of Public Administration, New Delhi.

POLITICAL AND ADMINISTRATIVE ASSUMPTIONS

There are three major political assumptions underlying development administration.

Plans of development are being undertaken within a federal system which gives much responsibility to the States. In many vital areas, planning is based on a scheme of partnership between the Centre and the States, in which the role of execution, accompanied by considerable initiative and the right to change, rests with the States. The best that the Centre can do, in co-operation with the States, is to aim at a national approach, at a broad consensus, and then to devise means for following up the agreed decisions as systematically as possible. This situation is not without its problems. Quite often what is agreed between the Centre and the States is not sufficiently precise and may not be a sufficient guide for obtaining results. The consequence is that in taking follow-up action, agencies at the Centre become less effective than they need be even within a federal structure. The problem, therefore, is to identify the weak points within the existing framework and to examine how they could be eliminated without either departing from the principle of joint planning between the Centre and the States or creating a situation in which States do not have sufficient flexibility and opportunity to adapt and innovate.

The second assumption for development administration arises from the parliamentary system, from the responsibility, both at the Centre and in the States, of the executive to the legislature. In a parliamentary system of democracy, authority tends to be more diffused than under a presidential system. Therefore, the techniques and instruments through which coordinaton is achieved between different agencies become matters of close study. Coordination has to be achieved between agencies functioning at a given level as well as with agencies above and below it. A number of lines criss cross and connect different levels. Looking at the problem from the angle of a State, various departments have to provide technical and administrative leadership to their own regional, district and block organisations, and have also to coordinate in some manner with Ministries at the Centre. Moreover, agencies at each of the lower levels must coordinate with one another. A thread of common purpose running through the administration, therefore, becomes essential. This explains the coordinating role of the Planning Commission at the Centre and of Planning Departments in the States, which may have been far from neat, but fulfilled an essential function.

In a parliamentary system it is difficult to establish completely the principle of command and responsibility; yet effective administration depends on carrying the principle of responsibility to the farthest extent possible. Moreover in a parliamentary system, with Ministers having to answer questions and meet criticism from day to day and Parliamentary Committees carrying out their wide-ranging investigations, the Minister and his Secretary and other senior officials tend to draw a considerable amount of decision-making authority towards themselves. This raises the issue of how there could be much greater delegation of authority than there has been so far. Part of the answer may lie in the Minister and the Department doing a great deal of concentrated thinking in advance and obtaining the approval of Parliament to a framework of action in broad terms, within which they can delegate further responsibility. If they choose to proceed in piece-meal fashion, without a plan worked out to cover all essential aspects, they will be less effective and will frequently be compelled to seek cover.

The third political assumption, which has to be reckoned with, is the acceptance of the institutions of local democracy and the desire to enhance their effectiveness in meeting the needs of the people. There are good reasons why so much emphasis should be placed on Panchayati Raj institutions in rural areas and on municipal bodies in towns and cities. It is simply beyond the capacity of the public services functioning alone to achieve development seen as a process of growth on the part of the people. The general body of citizens have to come into the scheme of development, not merely as beneficiaries, not merely as individuals reacting to events, decisions and possibilities, but as partners, as active groups equipped increasingly to do much of their own planning and to undertake a great deal together. One could say with truth that by far the most creative principle of India's development planning is the opportunity sought to be given to every community and every area, with some measure of technical help and resources from outside, to plan for itself, to solve its own problems, and to grow according to the capacity of the people and of the leadership they throw up as they move forward.

Though participation of the people in the process of development is a potentially creative factor, on a short view, it could easily become a source of difficulties and of much diffusion of authority and responsibility. It should not be beyond our capacity to analyse this problem and to suggest the pattern of relationships between democratic institutions and the public services which could yield more satisfactory results. Such thinking has to be evolved urgently and tested and communicated widely. In the absence of such an effort, the essential meaning and role of Panchayati Raj are often misunderstood. Panchayati Raj comprises three sets of institutions working together which are intended to enable the people of each area to develop largely on their own initiative. These are, firstly, the elected representative bodies; secondly, popular movements like co-operative organisations and voluntary agencies; and, thirdly, the administrative and technical services which function at each level as part of the administrative and technical structure of the State. Difficulties arise when Panchayati Raj is taken to refer only to the elected bodies, with their accent more sharply on power and support than on trust and responsibility, and there is failure to distinguish the function of deliberation from that of execution. The law gives to public servants the power to enforce and execute within the framework of broad decisions and rules emanating from representative bodies. At each point in the structure, the respective functions must be clearly defined and insisted upon. In given situations, or from time to time, public servants may not act with sufficient courage or elected representatives with sufficient widsom, but this should not affect our view of the nature of relationships which make local democracy a working proposition.

Beyond the three political conditions discussed above—the federal structure, the parliamentary system and local democracy—we have to reckon with the machinery of administration inherited at Independence. It has two features which are a source of some difficulty. Firstly, for any branch of activity, there is a secretariat department which has functioned in the past with a small number of highly trained officers and a large body of subordinate staff. Secondly, for executive functions, the department is aided by an executive agency or, in the case of enterprises, by a corporation or company with its own board of management. In the States where the regional level is important, there may be authorities such as Commissioners of Divisions. Under this dual system, the essential decision-making authority rests with the secretariat department, which functions directly under the Minister, who owes responsibility to the legislature. A notable development since Independence has been the steady weakening of executive agencies and regional authorities. Because of constraints arising from allocations of resources, foreign exchange or scarce materials, even corporations and companies have found themselves in a situation not far removed from that of attached and subordinate departments. Unless the process of reorganisation and of delegation of authority is pushed through in a radical sense, concentration of decision-making power within secretariat departments, both at the Centre and in the States, is a burden on development and clogs the entire structure from within.

There is much to be said on these aspects. Perhaps it will be sufficient to emphasise here the need to move speedily towards a system in which the framework of policy and action within which an executive agency is expected to act on its own is clearly defined in advance and the necessary means are at its disposal. Within such a framework, both in the secretariat departments and in the executive agencies, there has to be much clearer assignment of responsibility and marking out of tasks and much greater accountability for results. The entire administrative structure has to be reconstructed on the basis, not merely of how authority will flow, but of what results are to be secured and what conditions of delegation and responsibility and of assignment of personnel and other resources will assure the results demanded of the administration.

In brief, both in dealing with the wider political assumptions and in bringing about large changes within the machinery of government, the key is to be found in advance planning of policy and action, defining of tasks and responsibilities, determining the results to be obtained, ensuring the necessary resources, personnel and inputs and, finally, in judging men and institutions by the test of results. A system in which promotions may come, even though the results may not, is not a system built to last.

DEVELOPMENT ADMINISTRATION AND GENERAL ADMINISTRATION

The administrative system has to be seen as a whole, including both its developmental and its general aspects. A discussion on the distinction between development and general administration may begin with consideration of the relative place of planning and of implementation. Some care is needed in defining the limits of planning because planning can and does easily flow into implementation. In fact, a considerable part of planning consists in evolving the means by which those responsible for implementation may organise their action more precisely and effectively. In other words, both at the Centre and in the States, a great deal of planning should be devoted to working out how to plan, how to prepare projects, what kind of details these projects should embody, the controls which should be built into each project and each programme, and their practical use in watching progress, in anticipating problems and in taking such remedial action as may be necessary. The greater the skill with which these aspects of planning are undertaken, the larger will be the results which implementing agencies can achieve.

A warning is, however, necessary. Experience in the socialist countries over many years taught planners, as our own experience in India also teaches, that progressively planning ought to move to a somewhat higher level and to become broader, making use of more refined tools, and that many activities which pass for planning really fall within the sphere of execution or of planning such as should be undertaken by the executive agency itself. Therefore, a test for good planning will be whether, from phase to phase, it is gaining an overall or comprehensive character in the best sense of the term and whether it is helping to establish conditions in which implementation becomes more precise, more specific and more certain. This means that, progressively, the authority to decide and to change should be pushed forward, not through weakening of vigilance, but as an act of deliberate policy.

Here also, as we saw earlier, what is involved is the extension of the principle of delegation of authority, of defining tasks, determining what has to be done, fixing responsibility and giving at each point the tools and resources needed to complete the tasks. In this context, meaningful reporting can be looked upon as a link, on the one hand, between different levels of implementation and, on the other, between planning and implementation. Such reporting implies a clear view of what is significant at each level in planning and in implementation and calls for much advance sifting and analysis and separation of one operation from another.

While administration pertaining to development programmes and projects offers a great deal of scope for the use of advanced techniques of analysis, it is important to see this entire area in its relationship to general administration. The character of the prevailing structure of general administration has a decisive influence on the strength and weakness of development administration. Both general and development administration have a common source of authority within the structure of government, for instance, a cabinet responsible to a legislature. Secondly, a number of key functionaries combine both general and development functions, such as the Chief Minister of a State, the Commissioner of a Division or the Collector of a district. Thirdly, the citizen sees and judges the acts of administration as a whole, drawing no fine distinctions between general and development administration.

In emphasising these links between general and developmental administration, it is important also to underline the distinctive features of development administration. There is the preliminary point that, because of resources which are specially made available for development by way of Central loans and grants, the Centre has a certain role in the administration of development which is more continuing and more detailed than its interest in problems of general administration in the States. Far more important than this is the consideration that the Centre is under obligation to view the nation as a whole. Aside from these issues, three special features of development administration may be mentioned. In all branches of administration there is an element of hierarchy and of levels of responsibility. But, if the lines of authority, as they operate in revenue administration or police administration, were to prevail in the field of development, it would be extremely difficult to draw the potential knowledge and creative capacities of individuals working at different levels into the general scheme of development. In other words, the very process of development demands a system of open exchange and communication between various levels, so that in a real sense the gaps caused by hierarchy may be overcome. This is not easy to achieve because many public servants are not too well trained in taking along those functioning at lower levels of responsibility as colleagues and partners in a common enterprise.

The second distinction between general and development administration is that when there is so much to accomplish and development embraces a very wide range of activities, the only way work can get done is to divide it between a number of agencies. Therefore, ways have to be found for achieving coordination between many agencies engaged in allied and complementary tasks. This is the reason why it becomes both more difficult to escape from boards and committees and more essential to undertake pre-planning, to have in view a clear scheme for enmeshing diverse activities into a common design and to define responsibilities with great care. Thus, we are brought back once again to the basic approach of a plan of action and of eliminating at the stage of planning as much of guess-work as may be possible.

The third special feature of development administration is that in development many agencies and institutions which do not belong to the main structure of the administration have a vital role to fill. Examples of this are the co-operative movement, voluntary organisations, institutions for research and teaching, and trade unions. These represent an aspect of administration where only the first steps have yet been taken, but there is little doubt that the entire scheme of development in India would fan out and strike deeper roots if we could ensure in real life an organic and continuous role at key points for institutions and groups outside the government. To say this is in fact to emphasise that, far more than physical targets or the investments undertaken, development implies a process of change at the level of the community in skills and practices and in ways of thinking and behaviour.

AREAS OF DEVELOPMENT ADMINISTRATION

The field of study and action represented by development administration may be conveniently divided into the following areas, though other classifications could also be thought of:

(i)   Extension and community services.
(ii)   Programme management.
(iii)   Project management.
(iv)   Area development.
(v)   Urban administration.
(vi)   Personnel development and administration.

This is by no means a complete list and leaves out, for instance, areas like the role of administration in guiding and regulating private activity, labour administration, financial administration and others. A few words may be said here to draw attention to some significant features in each of the areas mentioned above, although frequently many different elements have to be seen together.

Extension and community services are best seen as a form of partnership between the government agencies which pro-

26

vide technical, institutional or financial services and the people. Their significance derives from the fact that they are in part substitutes for a system based on governmental action alone and are rooted in the belief that it is the community at the local level which receives the services, responds to them and, in the process, itself grows in initiative and responsibility. They imply community organisations of one kind or another at the base. The most difficult problem met with in extension is that, within the limits of the resources available, benefits do not easily reach the sections of the population who are in a situation of weakness, and are unable to contribute their own share or to claim what is due to them. Therefore, there is need both for first hand investigation of social situations, for better devices and instruments for dealing with social disabilities, psychological handicaps and other 'lacks', and for more comprehensive social and economic policies.

Problems of programme managment run right through the entire range of development in various sectors of the economy. They include questions of organisation, personnel, delegation and attitudes in administration, but if one issue should be identified more sharply than any other, it is the critical role in programme management of planning for supplies and inputs. Invariably, though facts will assert themselves soon enough, plans err in accepting commitments and targets in excess of supplies and inputs and other material resources which are in fact likely to be available. This failure in planning, itself a cause of much failure in implementation, may occur partly for lack of measurement and systematic estimation, partly because pressures have a way of persuading, and planners are sometimes tempted to leave difficult choices to others.

Project management, more specially the management of public enterprises, has become an altogether crucial area, because major projects account for a high proportion of new investment and make demands on resources in men,

materials and organisation which are frequently under-
estimated. They call for decisions and procedures at the level
of policy which would facilitate their preparation and
execution and, at the same time, there must be efficiency,
initiative and compactness in the organisations responsible
for them. They are undoubtedly a major challenge to administrative and technical capacity for achieving results.
From the various management studies which have been
undertaken, it can be said that, whatever may have been the
difficulties in the early stages, success and failure in the
management of enterprises are not matters of chance or only
of favourable circumstance. It is proper to ask for complete
accountability at every point and to judge by results. It is
essential also to be ruthless in the event of failure. The life
cycle of a project from inception to operation contains well
marked stages such as project definition and pre-construction
phase, construction management and operations management, and the techniques and methods required in each
phase as a matter of sound planning and execution have now
been sufficiently established in terms of India's own experience
and the analysis to which this has been subjected. In presenting this view, it is also important to recognise that project
authorities face several problems beyond their power, which
can only be resolved by agencies concerned at the level of
government. The responsibility of these agencies should,
therefore, be equally stressed. For instance, it is for them
to ensure that each enterprise has the requisite organisation,
competent top level personnel and boards of directors with
the necessary authority. They have to secure effective communication with the project and a system of management information and control which will help anticipate problems
and provide for them in advance.

Area development is an extremely difficult field of administration and one of which we do not yet have sufficient
successful experience. It was perhaps too readily assumed

in the past that the problems which arise at the area level would be adequately dealt with by men and institutions on the spot. It was not realised that area development requires a clear frame of delegations and procedures within which, both at the state level and in districts and blocks, each agency could act on its own, as well as careful identification of the points at which the activities of different agencies should become mutually complementary to one another. Again, at the district level there are three sets of institutions which have to work together—Panchayati Raj institutions in the rural areas, district officials functioning with the Collector outside the scheme of Panchayati Raj, and local self-governing institutions in towns and cities. The role of co-operative organisations and voluntary agencies at the area level should also be noted. Before we can make a success of area development, far more knowledge and understanding will have to be brought to bear on problems at the local level. Local problems are best regarded as facets of difficult national problems, looked at in terms of given areas and communities. They demand no less expertise and knowledge from the higher levels of administration and from universities and research institutions than problems at the state or national level.

Municipal institutions in the urban areas first came into existence in the eighties of the last century, but they have yet to become the primary means for involving urban communities in the solution of their own problems or for the efficient administration of social services. To secure their effective working in relation to civic life and development, there is need as much for a changed outlook towards urban problems and allocations of larger resources as for more intensive and systematic training and for appropriate public policies.

Over the past decade, training facilities have expanded at a rapid pace. To a large extent the problem of numbers has been taken care of, but not that of quality and motivation. There are still important areas requiring attention, specially where links between different sectors of activity and systems planning are involved. The organisation of training programmes, availability of personnel at each level for receiving training, intelligent use of trained personnel, and adoption of improved methods of planning and management should form a composite scheme of development. In such a scheme, equally with technical skills, it would be necessary to impart to each individual wider understanding of the objectives for which he is working, greater commitment towards them, capacity to co-operate and to lead, and the courage to work for what may be right and to dissociate from what may be wrong. In other words, in all personnel development, what has to be achieved is a combination of skills, character and motivation.

When we pass from individual aspects of development administration to the theme as a whole, three other issues call for brief comment—the place of appraisal and evaluation, the contribution of pilot projects and action research, and relations between citizens and the administration.

We may think of appraisal and reporting as being undertaken within the system of administration and of evaluation as being carried out by an agency which is not itself responsible for implementing a programme or a project. Evaluation has to be selective and can only be done at intervals. On the other hand, appraisal has to be built into the very mode of operation and therefore links up with the complete scheme of planning and action against which progress has to be continuously reported.

One of the main features of development administration is that there must be a great deal of experimentation, of testing, of exploration. Often big ideas are launched without working out their implications on the ground and ascertaining the difficulties to be watched and overcome. Therefore, as an attitude of mind, everyone engaged in development should be encouraged to experiment. There is need also for institutions which are specially equipped to undertake and guide field studies, pilot projects and action research. To feel our way with a new idea on a small scale can save enormous sums of money, bring more assured results and avoid frustration later.

Our plans envisage citizens participating in development as individuals, in groups, and through a network of institutions. At each level they assign to citizen leaders a role which is responsible and purposeful, to which prestige should be attached, and which assumes a degree of wisdom, good judgment and sense of public interest in the use of power and resources. Therefore, as an important element in accomplishing any significant development task, thought must be given from the beginning to ways of involving citizens, to their training, and to growth in their capacity to assume larger functions in the future.

As we delve more deeply into our own experience in India over the past fifteen years, study the efforts made, and reflect upon where they succeeded and where they failed and the elements which were found wanting, we gain useful insights into the problems of development administration. If we can go back and forth from the general to the particular and from the particular to the general, seeing where specific events suggest conclusions of wider significance and where general propositions may be relevant to specific situations, in time it may become possible to present the subject of development administration as a fairly well-defined system of institutions, methods and principles relevant to the conditions of economic and social development in India and in other countries similarly placed.

24

ADMINISTRATIVE LEADERSHIP AND LOCAL DEMOCRACY*

ON THE eve of Independence, the country passed through a testing period when much that was familiar was being dismantled and the shape of the new structure was uncertain. This was a moment when, side by side with political vision and judgment, there was need for administrative leadership of the highest calibre—for clarity of mind, speed in the making of decisions, vigilance for national interest, team work and dedication, and cordial relations with those with whom one negotiated and would differ almost at every turn. In recalling this phase of the national struggle, one thought which comes to mind is the role of leadership in administration, more specially when, as at present, difficulties, hitherto latent, have come to the surface.

Since Independence, the country's administrative machinery has a record which is marked both by achievements which are impressive by any standard and by weaknesses which have persisted beyond their time. If we were to single out one direction in which the administration needs to be strengthened above all, we might point to the need for

---

* Adapted from a countribution to Shri H. M. Patel 60th Birthday Commemoration Volume (1964), Charutar Vidya Mandal, pages 34-37.

training and practice of leadership within the administrative machinery, irrespective of the level of functioning or the scope of the tasks undertaken. In administration, as in other spheres, competence, discipline, comradeship, unselfishness, firmness, and a sense of loyalty to common purpose constitute the essential ingredients of leadership. On a superficial view, it may be thought that these qualities come more naturally to public servants when they function in a close and protected hierachy whose even tenor remains immune to external influence. For the larger number engaged in the administration of the country to be so sealed off from forces and pressures operating from without is an unnatural condition which could not in any circumstance last long. Already, with the establishment of responsible parliamentary government at the national and state level, the picture was transformed. With the introduction of democratic institutions, the Zilla Parishad and the Panchayat Samiti at the district and block level, the process of democracy has been taken to points at which the ground is not yet well prepared, but where success or failure might make all the difference to the future. In brief, these democratic institutions at the local level imply a challenge to the capacity and wisdom of those engaged in administration which is in every sense more critical than any presented by developments over the past decade and more. Will this challenge be met and in what manner?

Local democratic institutions, which are now being established in most States, are as much a product of faith as they are of the logic of a scheme of national development with and through the people. It must be admitted that they are an exceedingly difficult set of institutions to operate. The relationships between institutions at different levels and between public servants and non-official representatives who participate in their functioning are still far from clearly defined. There are areas of overlap and conflict in jurisdic-

tion and functions. There is considerable scope for quarrel-
ing over shadows. The nature of authority and of obligations
may not always be clear and both may be misunderstood or
distorted. Under certain conditions, independence of judgment and concern for the public interest may bring difficulties and trials rather than appreciation and co-operation.
In any event, initiative may be cramped. These are problems
one should be aware of and should make special efforts
to resolve, for the successful working of democracy at
the local level is a fundamental national goal which cannot
be permitted to fail or to succeed merely to an indifferent
degree. There are many conditions to be met before this
goal can be reached. Of these, in the immediate future,
one of the most important is the acceptance by the
public services as a whole of an obligation to assist,
advise and guide the new institutions in carrying out the
wide range of tasks given to them. It has to be remembered
that in undertaking legislation for Panchayati Raj and in
establishing the new institutions many of the administrative
problems, which were no doubt implicit, have still to be
worked out and practical solutions evolved for them. There
are real problems in the actual functioning of the institutions. At the same time, the tasks placed upon them are complex enough to tax the ingenuity of even mature democracies.

There are signs at present in some States of initial optimism about the possibilities of the new democratic institutions giving place to greater caution and scepticism.
At the same time, States also provide examples of well-
considered efforts to redesign administrative arrangements
and procedures to meet the requirements of the new institutions. In both groups of States, there appears to be a
tendency for the technical and administrative services of the
State Government, both at the State and district level, to
pull back from too active a role in the working and development of Panchayati Raj bodies. Perhaps they feel that this is

the better and the safer course and prefer not to tread on sensitive corns. In some degree this is an understandable approach, but it may easily become a source of weakness in the growth of effective democracy and competent public administration at the local level.

There are three great assets which the public service of an open democratic society must necessarily come to have. These should go a long way to give it confidence in its own values and purposes, a feeling for public interest, and freedom from all fear of unjust action. The first asset is the existence of complete identification between the duties one undertakes and the welfare and interests of the community as a whole. The true public servant seeks neither power nor wealth; he finds satisfaction in the unique opportunities that come to him to serve the entire community unfettered by fear or favour. The second asset lies in the fact that public servants are in a position to gain experience and competence such as enable them to make a distinctive contribution and, at the same time, make them indispensable to the smooth functioning of representative democracy. The third asset arises from the sense of continuity and stability which belongs to the permanent cadres in the public service. This must give them independence from the ups and downs to which those participating in the electoral process are necessarily subject, and, therefore, a capacity to take a detached and dispassionate view unaffected by personal or political anxiety. If these assets are harnessed to the full in the coming years, persons with strength of character and a sense of duty, who choose public service as their vocation, will not only contribute greatly to the building up of the country, but will also receive genuine respect from all shades of opinion.

Given the approach implicit in these observations, it is apparent that, acting in harmony with those who have political responsibility and leadership in the States and at the

Centre, public servants have much to give to democracy at all levels, and more specially to the strengthening of democratic institutions in districts and blocks. No one can doubt that only an upsurge of popular effort, massive local initiative, and movements deriving energy from the soil, can hope to fulfil the far-reaching social and economic objectives set in our Five Year Plans. Active involvement of citizens and citizen leaders at every point holds the key to progress, but the same institutions which can mould and strengthen a nation, if torn by faction and misused, can damage public welfare beyond repair. Therefore, while assuring the widest measure of initiative in advancing the interest of the community, citizen leaders who serve in representative and popular institutions have to be trained and oriented to carry the burdens placed on them. In the right setting they will welcome a great deal of help and guidance from those with greater technical and administrative knowledge and experience. Such help is due to them and the necessary climate for a genuinely co-operative approach can surely be created.

At all levels, democratic institutions demand integrity and a high quality of leadership and dedication, equally from the representatives of the people and from the public services. This has to be specially stressed at the local level, in districts and blocks and close to the people in the villages where, in the nature of things, it will take time for a sufficient number of citizen leaders to equip themselves adequately for the onerous tasks which our national plans place upon them. These citizen leaders have great advantages on their side, such as local knowledge, intimate understanding of the people, and a sense of belonging to the area and the community. But they also work under certain limitations inherent in the traditional situation, such as those deriving from ties of caste, tribe and economic interest and even local conflict. As they gain experience and come into a wide world, more and more of the citizen leaders of each area will overcome these limitations and grow into sentinels of the interest of the community as a whole and a force for radical social and economic reform and the building up of a co-operative rural economy. In this process they should receive all the practical and constructive help which it is within the power of leaders at higher levels and of experienced public servants to render. It is in the early years of a national movement that the gains are consolidated and new paths laid. The next few years are, therefore, a crucial period for the fulfilment of democracy at the grass-roots, through which alone can our vision of India become one with the mind and life of the millions in our villages.

25

ADMINISTRATIVE RELATIONS
IN PLANNING*

PLANNING belongs to that small group of social concepts which are difficult to define and yet become a medium of common thinking and expression, whose impact on institutions and human relations has a pervasive quality, although their meaning depends altogether on the situations and the objectives they are intended to serve. Reduced to essentials, to plan is to determine the use of resources available to a community. Planning, thus, is an aspect of decision-making. It is concerned with resources in the widest sense —material, manpower and capital resources, no less than resources of a non-material character such as the values, ideals and urges of a community and of its individual members. Since resources can only be used and developed over time, planning involves always an attempt to balance short term and long term aims. Determining what the resources are and how they can and should be employed and augmented and assessing and preparing the conditions for

* Adapted from an article published in the Indian Journal of Public Administration, April-June 1955. Vol. I No. 2, pages 137-151 which was based on a talk given at the Delhi School of Economics, University of Delhi, on March 30, 1955.

economic and social action are processes which fall within the scope of planning.

Planning would be an infructuous exercise unless important decisions flowed from it. The agencies and methods employed in planning are closely allied to those involved in taking and implementing decisions. In other words, planning is an aspect of government. Its range is nearly as large as that of governmental activity, its association with the people as great as the extent to which the people have a share in the activities of government at different levels. All phases of governmental activity are influenced by planning, though economic and social development is, naturally, its special field.

Administrative relations implicit in the process of planning do not stand by themselves. They are part of a wider context, influencing and in turn being influenced by other prevailing relationships. Moreover, the context itself changes from time to time; with it, there may be changes in administrative, economic and political relations large enough to require fresh evaluation at frequent intervals. The main determining factors at any time or in any situation are:

(1) the major aims and objectives which are sought to be achieved,

(2) the political assumptions,

(3) the administrative assumptions, and

(4) the nature of the planning machinery.

These different factors interact all the time and it is seldom easy to separate individual elements in them as cause or effect. Beyond them, there is the human factor, the personality and attitudes of individuals, specially those in positions of key responsibility on whom, in the final analysis, the smooth functioning of any set of institutions largely turns.

Choice of Objectives

The principal objectives in planning at any given moment are determined mainly by two sets of conditions, namely, (a) the needs, short term and long term, of the economic and social situation as judged at the time, and (b) the relative pressure of defence and of welfare and development.

How far the objectives can be attained will depend on the behaviour of the other assumptions in planning and on whether the initial judgment from which planning starts proves correct or adequate. Historically, there are important examples of considerable economic progress without deliberate planning. Planning, however, is the strategy of forcing the pace of development. For those who have a long distance to cover, there is no choice. Much, therefore, depends on how accurately the economic situation is assessed by those responsible for planning and on the manner in which their judgment is modified on grounds of national security.

The economic assessment is invariably subordinate to the demands of national security as judged by those who are in control of the apparatus of the State. If defence is given the first place—there may sometimes be no option but to do so—the emphasis in planning will be on:

(i) planning to achieve the maximum results during relatively short periods,

(ii) the highest possible rate of capital formation involving reduction of consumption through high prices, reduced supplies, and measures for withdrawing as much of the purchasing power of the community as may be feasible, and

(iii) maximum attainable control over economic operations in different fields, including internal trade and distribution and measures to secure food surpluses through obligatory deliveries and procurement systems.

It is possible to visualise such an approach in planning for its own sake, even if defence considerations were not paramount. There is no instance of this, however, in actual practice, and on the whole it seems correct to associate the acceptance of the rigours involved with objectives more compelling than the desire to build up a fully developed socialist economy.

On the other hand, if the assumption is that conditions of peace will prevail and that there is no urgent threat to national security, planning is likely to be marked by the following features:

(i) defining short term goals in terms of more long term aims for increasing national income and national well-being and acceptance of a somewhat gradual approach;

(ii) balancing consumption and investment so as to avoid excessive strain on the economy and hardship to the poorer sections of the community;

(iii) insistence on certain human values and on changes in institutions taking place in large part pari passu with changes in the attitudes and outlook of men, with equal emphasis given to the moulding of the human material and to the correction of economic and social disparities and reorganisation of institutions;

(iv) balanced development in different sectors with emphasis on those activities which will contribute to the welfare of the largest numbers;

(v) expansion of the public sector and of the co-operative sector, accompanied by a certain amount of general regulation by the State but without detailed control in relation to the private sector; and

(vi) maintenance of the framework of a market economy.

Planning with defence requirements as the focal point involves widespread conscription of human and material resources; it carries the techniques of management commonly employed in war into the realm of economic development. Necessarily, such planning is not possible without considerable concentration of authority. Planning with the welfare of the largest number and continuing peace as the basic assumptions also calls for certain common ideas and a degree of discipline in fulfilling them. There is, however, a wider distribution of authority and conclusions emerge as a rule from the process of consultation and consensus. It is obvious that administrative and other relations have a share in determining the kind of planning that may be practicable, but to a large extent they are a product of the approach adopted in planning.

All planning places a certain amount of power in the hands of those with whom decisions lie and gives influence to those whose knowledge or assessment shapes the decisions. Whichever pattern of planning comes to be adopted in the circumstances of a country and within its given assumptions, there is need for balance, restraint, flexibility and delegation of authority if large mistakes in planning are to be avoided. Many failures of policy in planning occur when those responsible for making decisions do not give sufficient weight to elements from which is woven the texture of human relations in the day to day life of the community. Under any system there can be an easy transition from intelligent and well-informed management of the economic machine to wasteful exercise of authority and direction. For its own sake, therefore, planning, like government, needs a number of internal checks and balances. The use of a tool of such far-reaching value for social and economic progress has to be watched jealously lest through its own excesses it should destroy with one hand what it creates with the other.

POLITICAL PRE-CONDITIONS

The political assumptions on which planning is based are closely allied to the basic conditions which determine its objectives. The elements to be considered are:

(i) the size and population of a country,

(ii) whether the political structure is based on the existence or possibility of one or of more than one political party,

(iii) in the case of a large country, the pattern of constitutional relations between the Central Government and the governments of States, and regions, and

(iv) the resources available to the Centre and the States.

27

The size and population of India with her vast problems, the existence of a federal system in which the States are important units in their own right, with resources accounting for half the national budget, and adherence to the democratic method in political organisation are factors which give to India's planning unique historical and practical importance.

The adoption of the Indian Constitution in January, 1950, was followed within a few weeks by the setting up of the Planning Commission. The preamble to the Government of India's Resolution of March 15, 1950, announcing the terms of reference of the Planning Commission drew inspiration from the Directive Principles of State Policy in the Constitution, so that these principles became the frame of reference for all future planning.

The ideas embodied in the Constitution correspond to the principles of a welfare state. Now, through further elaboration and interpretation, they can be said to provide for the basic objectives of a welfare state as well as of a socialist pattern of society. This widening of the concept has a moral. It illustrates how democratic growth makes for continuity, how, within the framework of democratic values, major advances in policy may take place through the process of political interpretation and adjustment to new economic situations, how the very words one uses change and grow in meaning. The influence of such a method of development on administrative and human relations in the process of planning can be highly significant.

In a large country there are very definite limits to central planning. These limits are sharper where the Constitution vests in the States vital powers and functions and accords to them considerable independence in the manner in which the resources available to them may be developed and utilised. National planning, while proceeding to a large extent on the basis of consultation and consent, yet widens the role of the Central Government and tends to reduce the distinction between Central and State responsibilities. This occurs for a number of reasons, notably the following:

(i) Planning determines, both for the Centre and the States, the directions in which the available resources may be used both over short and long periods.

(ii) In joining with all the States to formulate a national plan, the Centre underwrites its implementation in a large measure. In other words, on the one hand, it has a concern and must develop an apparatus for seeing that States fulfil their part of the obligations; on the other hand, it undertakes to use its own resources and its powers of management over the economic and financial system in the service of the whole plan, including the obligations assumed by the States.

(iii) Important new impulses and drives emanate from the Centre and develop into nation-wide programmes.

In some cases, part of the direction and finance may come from the Centre, but the execution may be wholly with the States, for instance, the Grow More Food campaign, the national malaria control programme, the welfare of backward classes, or the conversion of primary schools to the basic and of secondary schools to the multi-purpose pattern. The power of the purse is the main instrument in such cases.

Distinct in quality from these activities are the Community Projects and the National Extension Service. These do call for finance and direction from the Centre, but their real meaning lies in the new approach they embody towards community responsibility and welfare and the conception that every agency in the administration should work with and not merely for the people. Community Projects and the National Extension Service began with emphasis on agriculture and rural development as these are the first needs. Their scope and range of interests will steadily extend to other fields and, in the long run, it is as a method of development inherent in and growing out of the democratic approach which encompasses every vital need of local communities that they will be best integrated into the scheme of national planning. The approach which they imply, provided only that excessive centralisation is vigilantly guarded against, should survive long after particular forms of assistance which they take from the national or the state capital to village homes have changed.

(iv) Large scale industrial development places a major responsibility on the Central Government both for the public sector and for the regulation of the private sector.

It would be wise to find ways of associating the States to the utmost extent possible in the development of new industries for, as economic development proceeds, industry will dominate the national scene.

The ultimate problems which the growth of industry is intended to solve—diversification of employment, work for all, and raising of standards of living through the maximum development of the local resources of each region—are of deep concern to the States. It would be unfortunate if, in the system of planning that comes to be evolved, the plans of States are without a significant industrial component of their own and a degree of participation in the growth of the national public sector.

Thus, in Indian conditions, as formal lines of demarcation between the Centre and the States inevitably weaken through national planning, new ways need to be devised to enable the States to work as partners, responsible and sufficiently self-determining, yet subserving the common goals and conforming broadly to the national pattern of economic and social development. As the initial political assumptions of planning become less important, new assumptions have to be built in their place to effect the transition from formal distribution of powers and responsibilities to fruitful partnership in action.

ADMINISTRATIVE ASSUMPTIONS

The administrative assumptions of planning flow in large part from the political assumptions. In so far as they are distinct they are specially related to questions of personnel. The first aspect to consider is the extent to which administrative and technical personnel concerned with planning are drawn from the same sources as those which provide the personnel for execution. At the level of the region or the State, planning is not yet specialised enough for any differentiation to have taken place between these two categories of personnel. At the national level, although planning is by no means such a specialised field, the personnel drawn into planning come from a number of different sources. On the whole, however, there has been so far a large degree of common experience and tradition between the principal officials concerned with planning and with execution.

This has made for a co-operative approach. In the future, it is to be expected that greater specialisation will develop in planning. It is in the interest of sound planning and fulfilment of the plans which are formulated that the planning organisation should not attempt to become altogether self-contained and all-knowing and that there should continue to be a steady exchange of personnel and ideas between it and the Ministries and the States and institutions and agencies outside the government. Ideas and attitudes which are reared through similar work and experience are not by themselves sufficient and need to be supplemented; they do, however, lead to easier human relations. Both aspects have to be borne in mind in organising the administration for a planned economy. Good human relations are as important for planning as they are for implementation and for working with and through the people.

In the first phase of India's planning—this will be true largely also of the second phase—both at the Centre and as between the Centre and the States, a considerable proportion of the administrative and technical personnel concerned with planning belonged to the former all-India services. It would help national planning if in the future there were all-India or joint service cadres in the principal fields of technical development. Such service cadres are a means for carrying a wider stock of talent to the States, some of which may otherwise accept the second or the third best, that is, in effect, a lower rate of development. These cadres will also prevent isolation between the thinking and experience of those who serve at the Centre and those who serve in the States. This is of the highest importance for national progress along democratic lines. Equally, it can help avoid differences in outlook between those who plan and those who execute, for such differences reduce greatly the contribution which planning can make to national well-being.

As a result of the growth of planning in India, the Centre

is assuming increasing responsibilities in providing facilities
for training and research. Earlier, the Centre's interest was
confined to the higher levels of scientific and technical
education. Now, it views the problems of personnel more
comprehensively. For the first time, perhaps, the role of
trained personnel in the execution of major programmes
was fully recognised in the field of community development.
While several valuable steps have been taken, there are many
directions in which rapid progress will become possible only
when resources and techniques are carried to the people
by men and women who have first acquired the skills needed.
As a result of the experience gained in planning during
recent years, the Centre and the States now approach training
programmes with equal concern and as partners in a common task. This augurs well for the success of future plans.

MACHINERY FOR PLANNING

Thus, in terms both of political and administrative assumptions, in the developments that have taken place so far,
planning has been pre-eminently a method for achieving
co-operation and evolving a body of common aims to be
pursued on a national scale. This is one of the most important
tests of the quality of planning and one on which much
else turns. In this respect, during recent years, the role of
the Planning Commission as the national planning body
has been clearly helpful and influential. In its work the
Planning Commission was favoured by several circumstances, such as the position of the Prime Minister, who is
chairman of the Commission, the support given to the
Commission's work on the political plane, the eminence
and the place in public life of its individual members, the
close links between the Planning Commission and the
Finance Ministry at the Centre, the co-operation freely
given and received at all levels both at the Centre and in the

States, specially on the part of the Chief Ministers, the objectivity and judgment which the Planning Commission has shown in pressing its own ideas and in entertaining those of others and, finally, the favourable results flowing from much of the effort in the First Five Year Plan. The setting up of the National Development Council, in which all the States are represented through their Chief Ministers and of a Standing Committee of that Council, to consider matters of common interest from a national point of view, are important new developments whose significance may well grow in the future.

If, however, we consider the character of the machinery of planning over a longer span of time, there are a number of questions bearing on administrative relations in planning which deserve to be considered:

(1) *Should the national planning organisation be an advisory or an executive body* ?

The Planning Commission has stood out generally for the principle that it will not accept responsibility for implementation of the plan. In practice, however, it has had to assume for a period duties wider than those represented by planning. It has a range of other duties which have grown up in recent years, such as watching the implementation of plans specially in the States through its team of Programme Administration Advisers, assisting and guiding economic and social research programmes in the universities through the Research Programmes Committee, considering land reform programmes all over the country through a high level Central Committee for Land Reforms, and from time to time pursuing various questions of long term policy with the Central Ministries and the States. For the strength of personnel at its command, the functions of the Planning Commission have become more extensive than could be foreseen in the beginning.

Public opinion in India expects much from the Planning Commission, regarding it as a group engaged in the search for disinterested solutions, reaching into the depths in its appreciation of the needs and hopes of the people, moulding public thinking on the basic problems of planning, stimulating right action within and outside the government, and at all times watching for what is true and lasting in the interest of the community as a whole. This is no small task to been-trusted to any body of men and, let it be added, one to which there is no parallel elsewhere.

(2) *What is the level at which, within the Government, members of the planning organisation are expected to function ?*

In several countries with planned economies, planning bodies have chairmen who have a high place in the Council of Ministers, but their other members are only high level executives or experts. There is, however, no country other than India in which the Prime Minister is himself the chairman of the planning body and where its members not only function at the level of ministers but also include in their ranks ministers with key responsibilities in the national government. This latter development has come from historical circumstance rather than deliberate purpose.

For the planning body to have the requisite amount of independence in judgment and time for thought, it is essential that the original intention should be fulfilled to the extent of a sufficient number of members being available who do not carry departmental and political responsibilities and who, by devoting their entire attention to planning, seek to develop and maintain under all circumstances a balanced and integrated approach towards major national problems. If some of the factors which have so far specially favoured the fortunes of planning in India are viewed in this perspective, it is apparent that in the last analysis the authority of the planning body in a democratic system derives mainly from the comprehensive character of its social approach, the quality of the experience and judgment expressed in its work, the sources of knowledge and information which it commands, and its ability to adapt its thinking to the changing needs of the economic and social structure, and, what is not less important, to changes that take place at an increasingly rapid pace in the minds of ordinary citizens. One aspect needs specially to be stressed. The national planning body should be in a position to draw upon sources of statistical and technical information, which place it in a position to consider important issues from a wider standpoint and without any time lag in comparison with those concerned with execution.

(3) *What should be the character of planning organisations in the States ?*

In India, partly for lack of personnel, planning at the State level has the aspect largely of inter-departmental coordination. This is not now adequate because in the next phase in national planning two new features have to be reckoned with. In the first place, State plans will be based to a substantial extent on local plans, that is, the plans of villages, towns, districts, and blocks. The programmes which they embody will bear closely on the work and welfare of the people and will need for their fulfilment a large and expanding social and institutional base through village panchayats, local bodies and the co-operative movement. Within a State, therefore, the body co-ordinating plans has to be able to function above the level and outlook of administrative departments. Secondly, the employment goals of the national plan require that the plans of States should be similarly motivated. Considerable technical study is, therefore, needed to ensure that the plans of all regions are sufficiently integrated within themselves and with the overall national plan.

(4) *What kind of connection exists between planning in the public sector and planning in the private sector ?*

This is one of the weak points revealed by the experience of recent years. The approach envisaged in setting up

Development Councils for individual industries, composed of persons representing the interests of industry, labour and others, discharging a continuing public responsibility in the planning and development of each industry and in close touch with the programmes of individual units, has not taken the shape which the First Plan had contemplated. An important task remains for the future. Perhaps so far the Government's role in relation to the private sector is seen mainly as being one of regulation and to some extent of assistance. The Plan envisaged a private sector functioning in harmony with the rest of national planning, based on different labour-management relations from those now existing, each industry providing largely its own leadership, technical personnel and machinery for planning and also the impulse to development in terms of the essential interests of the community as a whole. In the coming years, these will be some of the conditions of stability and acceptance for the private sector in large scale, organised industry. Steps to establish the necessary institutions and methods for planning in the private sector have an importance which has not yet been fully recognised.

(5) *What is the nature of the links which connect the work of the planning body with the political organisation or organisations supporting the government at the Centre and in the States ?*

A planning organisation is not and, in a democratic system, should never be a political body. Existence of political confidence is, however, a material condition for success in planning. Therefore, for planning under democratic conditions to have sufficient integrity and continuity and to provide a basis for co-operation over a wide field, the work of the planning organisation should be regarded scrupulously as falling outside the strictly political field, even as the national planning body must function somewhat apart from the normal structure of government.

In this paper an attempt has been made to touch briefly

upon some salient aspects of planning so as to explain the relationships, specially in administration, which planning may throw up. The analysis is based upon the experience of India and a few other countries.

To obtain a fuller picture, it would be necessary to elaborate in detail upon the whole structure of relationships in several fields of economic and social development under varying degrees of planning. In real life, the various relationships are so intertwined that, wherever we may begin, we are led by small steps to an enquiry into the ends of planning and the means to be employed in attaining them.

Planning is perhaps best viewed as a body of techniques of social management, still imperfectly developed, which can be employed, under given conditions, to accelerate the rate of economic and social progress. In applying these techniques, it is well to remember that they are but the instruments and that the central problems of planning concern the aims we set for ourselves and the scheme of political, economic and human relationships generally which we seek to build.

26

RE-ORIENTING TASKS AND
ORGANISATION IN PLANNING*

THE PLANNING Commission is one of the major administrative innovations India has made since Independence. In the light of experience and in view of the stage reached in planning and economic development and the country's evolving political structure, there is need for some re-orientation in the tasks and organisation for planning. This paper examines the problem and offers suggestions. The discussion is divided into five parts: (a) general considerations, (b) changes in emphasis in planning, (c) Centre-State relations in planning, (d) role of the Planning Commission within the Central Government, and (e) changes in organisation.

GENERAL CONSIDERATIONS

Compared to many other countries, planning and the structure of the national planning agency in India have enjoyed greater continuity, both in aims and direction and in

*Except for a few minor changes, this paper was completed and circulated to the responsible authorities early in March, 1967, following the results of the fourth General Elections, and before the formation of the new Government at the Centre.

terms of organisation and relationships with other agencies. Seventeen years ago, when planning was introduced and the Planning Commission was set up, there was little by way of examples to draw upon. To a large extent, therefore, the shape which planning and institutions connected with it have taken has been a response to the special conditions prevailing in India, its constitutional and administrative structure, appreciation of the country's basic economic and social needs and the outlook on national problems developed in the course of India's struggle for freedom, more specially in the two closing decades.

Since the Constitution had been already promulgated and planning came as a relatively new factor into a structure of administration which already existed, while acting in conformity with the system as a whole, the Planning Commission had a measure of freedom in evolving its machinery, its methods of work and its relationships with Ministries, States and other agencies. Now that the institutional set up in the country in its economic and political aspects has become much more complete, it is possible to take a fresh look at assumptions and relationships, to replace informal by formal arrangements, to distinguish the intangible from the tangible, and to subject practices and procedures which may have grown up over the years to critical and objective tests.

In reviewing the place of planning and the national planning agency in the structure, there are certain important considerations which should be kept in view. First, planning is, on the one hand, a process of assisting and integrating the making of policy and, on the other, of translating policy into concrete programmes of action and of ensuring their systematic implementation. The object of planning is to study and analyse the structure of the economy and its functioning, to bring out the main interconnections both at the level of policy and of implementation, and to relate policy and implementation to wider objectives such as economic growth, development of resources, utilisation of manpower, social justice and equitable distribution, regional development and others. Since all the objectives cannot be achieved simultaneously during any given period and there are inherent conflicts among them, priorities have to be determined both inter se and over time, resources allocated in relation to them, programmes formulated for realising the chosen objectives, and the quality of implementation continuously raised. This is the main work of the Planning Commission and involves technical and analytical as well as policy and programme-oriented formulations.

Secondly, by its nature, the scope of planning cannot be too rigidly confined. In fact, as an economy develops and new problems emerge, the planning operation increases in range and depth. The study of problems of implementation, evaluation and appraisal, and development of new methods and techniques are aspects of planning which have become more important with each Five Year Plan. However, every process and operation which is seen to be a part of planning does not have to be undertaken by the planning agency. In some instances, for a period, the planning agency may undertake a pioneering piece of work or may give a push to an idea or a programme. As soon as circumstances may permit or another organisation is able to take over, many functions initially performed by the planning agency can and should be passed on with such changes as may be necessary. In other words, while the major continuing tasks of the planning agency are fixed and must be undertaken with the maximum thoroughness, there should be sufficient flexibility to enable a planning agency to take up new tasks for a period if there are good reasons to do so. A degree of flexibility and capacity to experiment with new ideas should be regarded as useful attributes in a national planning agency.

In the third place, while planning is undertaken with reference to a framework of social, economic and political objectives, there is increasingly close interaction between the longer term needs of the economy and its current management. The formulation of plans is only the first step in planning. Plans cannot be implemented unless current economic policies are in accord with them or, in turn, lead to changes in the plans themselves. As an economy becomes more complex, its current management assumes a still larger role. Therefore, planning and the planning agency have to be closely and continuously concerned with the working of the economy in all its aspects. Whatever influences the future and the present is of concern to planning. In this sense, the economic implications of defence and of current monetary, fiscal and other policies have a significant bearing on the shape of plans proposed by the planning agency, the means through which they are to be fulfilled, the rate at which the economy grows, and the extent to which the social objectives of development are realised. While planning should aim always at a longer time span than the day to day operation of the economy and the horizon set by agencies directly concerned with implementation, the planning agency has to be sufficiently in touch with the events to appreciate their significance and, at the same time, to be sufficiently removed from them to be able to look beyond the immediate cares, to point to future implications for policy and action, and to prepare for later developments.

Finally, neither planning nor the national planning agency should be looked at in isolation. Whatever may be the measure of success or failure at any given time, these have to be shared between policy, planning and implementation. Similarly, the national planning agency has to be seen as one important element in a network of national agencies, including the key ministries concerned with economic policy and administration and economic and social development and the Reserve Bank and others. In a parliamentary democracy, in the working of different institutions, there is a high degree of interdependence. Under certain conditions, most of the institutions of government will be seen to be working well and giving mutual support to one another; at other times, contrary impressions may prevail. Also, when economic conditions are favourable, and the going seems good, weaknesses in the working of institutions are obscured; at other times, they are highlighted. Much recent thinking on planning and the national planning agency and the questions raised have been influenced by the severe strains under which the economy has functioned over the past three or four years as well as the series of political events which have affected the course of events since the Chinese aggression in 1962. Objectively, it is necessary to distinguish the economic from other elements and the problems of current management of the economy from the longer term plans of development. It is all too easy to quarrel with one's tools. Therefore, wisdom lies in identifying weaknesses and suggesting how they could be best removed. In this way, whatever is of value in India's own experience of planning and in the working of the national planning agency could be seen more clearly and improved upon to meet the economic and political needs which have emerged and are likely to become even more pressing in the future.

CHANGES IN EMPHASIS IN PLANNING

The Resolution of March 15, 1950, setting up the Planning Commission throws light on how the Commission was expected to function. Four main propositions are implicit in the thinking at the time:

(1) The need for comprehensive planning based on careful appraisal of resources and on objective analysis of all the relevant economic factors had become imperative. The Planning Commission was to be the main instrument of such planning;

(2) The Planning Commission was to be an organisation free from the burden of day to day administration, but in constant touch with the Government at the highest policy level;

(3) Responsibility for taking and implementing decisions would rest with the Central and State Governments. In framing its recommendations, the Planning Commission would act in close understanding and consultation with the Ministers of the Central Government and the Governments of States; and

(4) The work of the Planning Commission would affect decisively the future welfare of the people in every sphere of national life. Its success would depend on the extent to which it enlisted the association and co-operation of the people at all levels. Therefore, the Resolution of the Government of India expressed the hope that in carrying out its tasks, the Planning Commission would receive the maximum support and goodwill from all interests and, in particular, from industry and labour.

Thus, in its basic conception, the Planning Commission was seen as a body rendering advice and assistance both to the Central and the State Governments. It was an agency created by the Government of India, but not forming part of its normal administration. It was intended to function above the level of Departments and, more specifically, in relation to matters of policy. Finally, it was seen as an organisation with a certain public image, stimulating public response and co-operation, and deriving support from the larger community.

The basic conditions for the existence and functioning of a planning agency at the national level have not altered materially from those postulated in 1950. However, over this period certain lessons have been learnt, and the tasks to be accomplished have assumed new dimensions. Economic and social development has been found to be a much more uphill and complex task than it seemed some years ago. The growth of population places the economy under extremely heavy burdens. Stagnation in agriculture, which has occurred in recent years, has placed the agricultural problem at the centre of institutional and organisational planning as well as of investment planning and industrial policy. Under the pressure of economic facts bearing on the supply of

28

foreign exchange, policies and programmes for industrialisation are already undergoing significant change. The impact on development and on current economic trends of the larger expenditures on defence undertaken after 1962 has to be reckoned with. Food and prices have become the critical issues both for short term economic management and for longer term planning. Current fiscal and monetary policies and plan policies and programmes cannot be considered separately from one another. The very progress which has been achieved, added to other factors which have now emerged, compels a period of activity devoted to the stabilisation of the economy and to the consolidation of past gains at the same time as ground is prepared for more rapid development in the future. On the one side, there is the federal structure, with its distribution of subjects; on the other, there are the facts of a growing and increasingly integrated economy in which action must be taken simultaneously at a number of points, so that the urgent economic problems of the people can be solved and their expectations met. In such a situation, planning, economic policies and the instruments and programmes through which they are to be fulfilled have to be based altogether on careful and objective analysis of facts. Greater attention has to be focussed on results in the short term and conditions have to be created in which, while keeping the larger design of development in view, efforts are made to resolve the main outstanding problems one by one.

The statement of functions of the Planning Commission, as conceived in 1950, was directed towards the longer term development of the economy. In the sixties the more dominant elements bearing on development have been of a shorter term character. The Planning Commission has to equip itself more adequately for economic and statistical analysis of the working of the economy. The Commission has to be involved more intimately in the consideration of current economic measures and policies, so that the course of development over a longer period may be guided more smoothly and with greater knowledge. Hence the far greater importance now of annual planning and of short term balance between different sectors of the economy. For the same reason, the statistical information on which current policies are based needs to be greatly enlarged and refined and its processing for use made more swift and accurate. The working of the private sector of the economy, both organised and unorganised, needs to be followed through much more closely than before. As with more developed economies, the stage has now reached when the emphasis in planning and in the working of institutions associated with it has to go much more definitely beyond policies to precise programmes of action, beyond formulation to implementation, beyond institutions to personnel and skills and to techniques and methods. In other words, the major contribution of planning to the making of policy and to the implementation of development programmes has to be in terms of objective understanding of the elements at work, analysis and appraisal, application of new methods and techniques, and ability to take an informed view of shorter term developments, both in relation to one another and in relation to longer term objectives and plans.

In the initial phase of planned development, which covers broadly the period of the first three Five Year Plans, much new ground had to be broken in terms of economic and social policy and the spelling out of a general design of development. By the nature of its composition and the manner of its functioning, the Planning Commission helped define many of the basic aims of development and the institutional changes required for their realisation. With the economic and other developments which have occurred, in future major structural changes are likely to emerge more and more from new and often unexpected situations or from prolonged study by specially constituted commissions, committees and expert groups. The national planning agency will probably be concerned to a somewhat smaller extent than in the past with the formulation of fundamental social and economic policies. These are likely to ensue in greater degree from public debate in Parliament and State Legislatures and from the play of new social and political forces which take shape within the community and press their claims on society and the kind of national consensus that may be achieved on changes in the economic and social fabric. The work of the Planning Commission at the Centre and of planning bodies in the States is, therefore, likely to be related more to the secondary levels of policy, to analysis of experience, evaluation and appraisal, considered comments and forecasts based on current developments, and the formulation of long and medium term investment and consumption goals and of annual plans. The process of planning and development will inevitably be marked by greater flexibility and adaptation to changing conditions. The work of planning agencies will call for greater use of advanced statistical and other computational techniques and for profounder understanding of the economy and of changes occurring in the social structure, including motivations and tensions. The tasks will not be less important than before, but the changes in them are indication of the transformation which has taken place over the past decade. In turn, this transformation calls for a certain re-orientation of planning, for closer links between planning for development and the current management of economy and for greater contact between the work of the planing agency and the universities and other centres of research.

CENTRE-STATE RELATIONS IN PLANNING

When the Planning Commission was constituted, it was assumed that it would assist and advise both the Central and the State Governments. At that time it was far from clear how the Planning Commission would in fact function in relation to the States. Over the years, in the context of planning, a pattern of Centre-State relationships has taken shape. The main elements in this pattern can be briefly described.

The Five Year Plans embrace the entire range of developmental activities. Responsibility for legislation and execution derive from the Constitution, but consideration of policies bearing on development and the setting of development goals and the preparation of plans to fulfil them have been regarded as tasks to be undertaken by the country as a whole, jointly by the Centre and the States in co-operation with one another. At the first meeting of the National Development Council, in November, 1952, and at many subsequent meetings of the Council, Jawaharlal Nehru stressed that the Chief Ministers of the States bore intimate responsibility for the Plan in all its phases. As Chief Ministers, they shouldered heavy responsibility for the whole of India and had to look upon every question from a national point of view. Both in their preparation and in their implementation, therefore, the Five Year Plans have developed as a continuing partnership between the Centre and the States.

For many years, the more important policies and directions on priorities have either emerged from or have been considered and approved in meetings of the National Development Council or in conferences of Chief Ministers or in inter-State conferences and other similar forums. In future, the National Development Council could play an even larger role both as a body and through its committees.

Since assessment of resources and their mobilisation are a necessary basis for the formulation of five year and annual plans, review of the financial position of States and of measures to mobilise resources for the future has been undertaken systematically by the Planning Commission in co-operation with each State. For the Third Five Year Plan, the major directions on resource mobilisation came from a committee of the National Development Council, including Chief Ministers and others, which was specially constituted for the purpose.

The five year plans of States, which form an integral part of the national plan and of plans for different sectors, entail a flow of resources from the Centre to the States by way of loans and grants, in addition to transfers of revenues effected periodically on the recommendation of the Finance Commission. Procedures pertaining to Central assistance have come under systematic revision on three occasions— in 1958, 1962 and 1966. The broad aim, specially during the past year, has been to pass on as much responsibility as possible to the States, to enable them to utilise resources made available by the Centre with greater flexibility, but in accordance with the general scheme of the Plan. With due attention to overall national concerns, an effort is also being made to limit strictly the areas in which development schemes should continue to be 'sponsored' by the Central Ministries.

An important point to stress is that the procedures followed in respect of all States are identical although, in the nature of things, some States are in a position to contribute larger resources for their own development than others. The Planning Commission has been concerned to enable each State to develop its own resource potential and its agriculture and social and economic overheads to the utmost extent. It has, therefore, considered the problems of each State both in relation to wider national priorities and in relation to its own needs and capabilities. The close contacts which, at the level of the Commission, have been maintained with the States, the assistance afforded through the Planning Commission's Programme Administration Advisers, and the opportunities provided by working groups including representatives of States, Ministries and the Commission, have made it possible, on the one hand, to bring to the attention of the Central Government the special needs of different States and, on the other, to bring to the attention of the States wider national priorities and national policies and the results of evaluation and experience in other States. At any rate, the effort has been consistently along these lines.

The general scheme of Centre-State relationships in planning outlined above has functioned satisfactorily on the whole. No difficulties were experienced during periods when, in as many as three States, governments were formed by political parties other than those responsible for administration elsewhere. Within a framework of certain common premises, Centre-State relationships in planning, as they have evolved thus far, have been a product of mutual interest between the Centre and the States. The Centre accepted its special responsibility for supporting development in the States by way of resources and technical and other assistance. The States appreciated the close interdependence which exists between the economic advance of different parts of the country and of the nation as a whole. This scheme of Centre-State co-operation in planning can be reckoned to be an important asset for the nation. But it is necessary to emphasise that it hinges heavily on the existence of a national planning agency which stands outside the normal apparatus of the Central Government, yet enjoys its confidence as well as the confidence of the State Governments, and a certain intangible quality marked by prestige in the community and genuine acceptance and support within the apparatus of the State. The tasks undertaken by the Planning Commission have involved not only careful study of facts but also appreciation of the compulsions under which the Centre and the States have to operate. To the extent to which the Planning Commission is intimately concerned with the consideration of policies and of current economic develop-

ments at the Centre and is aware of the implications, acting
in co-operation with other agencies, it is able to communicate
to the States the national interest and the limitations under
which the Centre has to function. Correspondingly, to the
extent State Governments share their experience and difficulties with the Planning Commission and readily make all
facts and data available to it, the Planning Commission
is able to bring their needs and problems more effectively
to the attention of the Prime Minister, the Finance Minister
and others at the Centre. But it should be added that while
the scheme of Centre-State relations in planning is good as
far as broad decisions are concerned, it has not been found
sufficient for securing concerted action in detail between the
Centre and the States, for instance, in limiting expenditures,
in mobilising resources, in food distribution and in implementing agricultural programmes. This aspect requires
serious consideration afresh and jointly with the States.

Role Within the Central Government

Within the Central Government, the Planning Commission
is called upon to advise in two main areas—questions of policy and allocations of resources. From the beginning, the
practice has developed that, in common with the other
agencies concerned, the Planning Commission is given the
opportunity of commenting on policy proposals evloved by
Ministries and of making its own recommendations to Ministries and the Cabinet for action at the level of policy. Similarly, from the inception of planning, the Ministry of Finance
have sought the views of the Planning Commission before
accepting new financial proposals from the Ministries.
Specific expenditure sanctions have been always related to
Plan allocations.

On the whole, these relationships between the Planning
Commission, the Ministry of Finance and other Ministries

have worked smoothly. For many years, the Deputy Chairman and Members of the Planning Commission have participated in meetings of the Cabinet and of Cabinet Committees on subjects pertaining to development and economic policy. A practice followed for several years, though recently somewhat less frequently, was that important matters of policy were discussed in the Planning Commission with the officials concerned and, when necessary, with the Ministers concerned, before any view was expressed on behalf of the Commission. Instances in which the Planning Commission felt it necessary to set out formally views different from those presented by a Ministry to the Cabinet or a Committee of the Cabinet were comparatively infrequent, although some notable examples to the contrary could also be cited.

Within the Government, different points of view are often expressed and resolved at the official level. By convention, the Planning Commission's representatives have participated for many years in inter-departmental committees of Secretaries and other senior officials. If issues involving policy in which the Planning Commission had a special interest remained unresolved at official level, steps were taken to discuss them in meetings in the Planning Commission to which the respresentatives of the Ministries concerned were invited. In this way, to the maximum extent possible, agreed views could be submitted to the Government. Where there might have been difficulties in reaching a common view between the Minister and the Member concerned, in the Planning Commission, further discussions were arranged at the level of the Commission and, more often than not, agreed views emerged.

Three institutional devices have greatly helped in the past in the smooth and effective functioning of the Planning Commission in relation to the Ministry of Finance and other Central Ministries.

The personal interest of Jawaharlal Nehru as Prime
Minister in planning as an administrative practice and in the
success of the Five Year Plans and his readiness to participate personally in meetings of the Planning Commission were
known to all concerned. Sometimes, the Prime Minister's
attention was drawn to specific issues by a Minister, sometimes on behalf of the Planning Commission.

As a Member of the Planning Commission, the Finance
Minister is concerned with financial matters as well as with
broader economic and social policies. The frequent participation of the Finance Minister in meetings of the Planning
Commission was an important factor in producing a common
outlook as between the officials of the Planning Commission
and the Finance Ministry and in enabling both to give a
measure of constructive help to Ministries in the formulation of their proposals. On matters bearing on resources
and allied policies, the fact that the Economic Adviser was
common to the Planning Commission and the Finance
Ministry and enjoyed the support of both proved to be of
great value.

When the Planning Commission was set up, the Cabinet
Secretary was also appointed as Secretary to the Planning
Commission. The Cabinet Secretary, as chairman of the
Committee of Secretaries and by virtue of his standing
among Secretaries to the Government, was able frequently
to place before the Secretaries of Ministries considerations
of a wider nature. He was also able to apprise the Planning
Commission of any aspects which it would need to take into
account. As the Cabinet Secretary had an office in the Planning Commission, he himself became aware of many aspects
of Government's activities and of the problems of States
to an extent which would otherwise have been difficult.
The loss of the link with the Cabinet Secretary since early
1964 has been a handicap in the work of the Planning
Commission.

Experience over several years would, therefore, support the conclusion that for an agency like the Planning Commission to be able to function at the level of policy and to give effective assistance to the Ministries and the Cabinet, the continuing interest of the Prime Minister, the active participation in the work of the Commission by the Finance Minister and an institutional link with the Cabinet Secretary are elements of great value. The relationship of the Planning Commission and its Members with Union Ministers and their senior officials has to be based on mutual respect for the integrity of views which may be urged on either side. The Ministries have the advantage of knowledge of detail. The Planning Commission has the advantage of a larger and a more long range view. The facts available to both in relation to any decision that may be required are or should be the same, so that consideration of important issues jointly and objectively, far from leading to differences, should make for right decisions and for effective implementation on the part of the system as a whole. In any structure, it may sometimes happen that the dialogue stops short and differences are allowed to persist or grow, but this is not inherent in the institutions of planning which have been built up or in the relationships with Ministries which came to be established. In the measure in which the Planning Commission's advice is based on objective study of data and the facts of experience and on a wider understanding of basic problems, it can provide assistance of real value to the Cabinet.

CHANGES IN ORGANISATION

The tasks now envisaged are in harmony with the original stipulation that the national planning agency should be a body of individuals thinking and working jointly and concerning itself with the problems of economic and social development for the economy as a whole. This conception is best fulfilled through a body constituted as a Commission and charged with functions broadly indicated in the Resolution of 1950. It would be an error to suggest that a body functioning on the lines of a Ministry or in subordination to a Minister could fill this role, whether at the Centre or in relation to the States. Therefore, in the light of experience the sound course would be to continue the form and structure of the Planning Commission broadly as at present.

Over the past year and more, the strength of the Planning Commission has diminished seriously. If thought is given to the range of subjects which planning embraces and the responsibilities which, as a body, the Planning Commission is required to fulfil in relation to the Centre and the State and the national economy, six full-time Members seem to be the minimum required to do justice to the technical work of the Commission. Planning calls for much intensive study and thought on the part of Members and for collective consideration of different aspects of development. For the Planning Commission to be able to function as a body of competent individuals who have a distinct contribution to make and endeavour to reach conclusions and recommendations of real value to the Centre and the States implies an enormous amount of application, teamwork and cohesion. These latter elements have to be provided largely by the Deputy Chairman who would need to give all his time to the work of the Commission. It is physically impossible for even a gifted individual to fulfil his political responsibilities as a Minister, including responsibilities in Parliament and, at the same time, to devote the attention needed to the study of problems in depth, both individually and jointly with his colleagues. The Deputy Chairman of the Planning Commission would have to give the greater part of his time to coordination of work on the Plan as a whole, coordination with States, review of current economic trends, and the preparation of perspective plans for the economy.

The question is sometimes raised whether the full-time Members of the Planning Commission should be responsible for any specific subjects or should function only as a collective body, considering matters placed before them and generally keeping in touch with developments. This concept is more appropriate to the judicial than to the executive branch of Government. Every aspect of development involves extensive study and, therefore, calls for a degree of specialisation.

Within the scheme of planning, certain fields mark themselves out as being of central interest, for instance, Agriculture; Industries; Transport; Engineering and Technology, including Irrigation, Power, Construction and Housing; and Education and Manpower. These five areas constitute the core. Besides these, there are several other aspects of development which could be added on to the responsibilities of different Members, depending upon their interests and background. To cover the entire range of interests which fall within the scope of planning, therefore, as suggested earlier, six full-time Members, including the Deputy Chairman, are by no means too many. Among the essential skills which should be found within the membership of the Planning Commission are those of the economist, the student of agriculture and the rural economy, the engineer and the technologist, the educationist, the administrator, and firsthand experience of industrial enterprise. These qualities will need to be supplemented to a great extent by knowledge available among specialists in the Ministries and outside the Government as well as by competent supporting staff units within the Planning Commission.

For some years it has been recognised that Central Ministries which are concerned with industrial and economic development need to be more adequately equipped for planning.

In a number of Ministries dealing with the social aspects of development also, there is scope for more systematic work on planning. To the extent to which planning units in the Ministries are better organised, it should be possible for the Planning Commission to draw upon them and, correspondingly, to limit its own work to the broader questions of policy and planning and the appraisal of progress.

In the States, each Department does its own planning, coordination being provided by the Planning Department and overall direction by the Chief Minister and a committee of the State Cabinet. In a few States useful work on evaluation has also been done, but by and large planning at the State level has tended to concentrate on the preparation of projects and schemes and their consolidation into plans to be presented to the Planning Commission. There is need for continuous study of the resource potential of each State and its different regions, of the patterns of development which would best meet their needs and of the extent to which different regions and areas could mobilise their own resources and efforts for development. With the completion of ten years or more of community development and the establishment of Panchayati Raj institutions, area development planning represents an important line of advance. Several States have special problems such as those of unemployment, under-employment, hilly areas, tribal areas, growth of industrial towns and others. While it is difficult to suggest a general pattern of organisation applicable to all States, the stage has come when it is essential for State Governments to set up their own expert and high level bodies for planning. These could take the form of State Planning Boards or State Planning Commissions, each including three or four full-time members and headed by the Chief Minister as chairman. These Boards or Commissions could take a perspective view of the developmental needs and prospects of their States and of the measures required to enable them to develop their own resources, to extend employment and other opportunities for the landless, and to diversify the rural economy.* The existence of such State Planning Boards or Commissions would ensure greater continuity in planning at the State level, provide informed guidance to urban local authorities and to Panchayati Raj institutions and strengthen the technical apparatus of State planning.

Apart from annual plan discussions, each year the Planning Commission and the Planning Board of a State could jointly review progress and consider problems requiring special attention. If States have adequate planning machinery, a great deal of consideration of detail which now enters into discussions on planning could be undertaken by them. The work of the Planning Commission would be facilitated and all unnecessary references to the Centre avoided. Technical and analytical work required in planning has to be undertaken on scientific lines equally for individual States as for the country as a whole. Systematic training programmes should be developed both for planning in general and for planning in specific fields and at the area level. Implementation by local authorities has to be observed more closely and

---

* The functions of the State Planning Boards or Commissions may be defined, broadly, as follows:

  (i) to formulate long term, medium term and short term plans of economic and social development;

  (ii) to advise on the evaluation and selection of projects and programmes;

  (iii) to undertake continuous appraisal of the progress of the State economy, and make proposals for effective utilisation and development of the State's natural, material and human resources;

  (iv) to assist the State Government and its Departments in planning for the integrated development of different regions within the State;

  (v) to assist and advise Panchayati Raj institutions and municipal bodies in formulating development plans, in mobilising resources at the district and local level, and in improving implementation; and

  (vi) to undertake and arrange for the study of the special problems of the State.

reported upon authoritatively. All these steps will become easier if the planning apparatus in the States is strengthened.

Parliament has a vital and continuing interest in the success of planning and in keeping itself informed about policies proposed and problems encountered in giving effect to the plans. Therefore, it is necessary to designate a senior member of the Council of Ministers as the Minister of Planning. Since it is envisaged that the Planning Commission should have a full-time Deputy Chairman, the national interest may be best served if the Minister of Finance, who is in a position to take a view of the national economy as a whole, also functions as the Minister of Planning and provides the essential link with Parliament.

Every effort will have to be made to secure a broadly agreed approach with representatives of various groups in Parliament over as large an area of planning as possible. A forum such as the Prime Minister's Committee on Planning, on which leaders of the main groups in Parliament are invited to serve, and which functioned effectively when Jawaharlal Nehru guided work on the Third Five Year Plan, should prove to be of special value in imparting a broad national sanction to major policies and programmes undertaken for the economic and social development of the country and for meeting the basic needs of the people.

PART THREE

SOCIAL POLICY

27

THE PROCESS OF SOCIAL PLANNING*

IN INDIA and other countries similarly placed, the aims of planning are necessarily comprehensive. The community has to advance as a whole and simultaneously in a number of directions. In each direction its progress suffers from limitations. Many of these are interacting and cumulative in effect and are inherent in the social structure inherited from the past. In dealing with the social aspects of planning, priorities are essential, but difficult to determine and apply. In smaller or larger degree, there are numerous participants in the process of planning and implementation, but scarcely any of them can see the entire design and the links by which its different parts are held. In fact, it would be too much to claim that a design of social change and development, fully worked out and expressed in terms of institutions, men, motivations and resources, has come into being even after more than a decade of planning in India.

The objectives of planning are both economic and social and are interrelated. In its economic aspect, planning seeks

---

* Adapted from a paper which formed part of the contribution from India for the Twelfth International Conference of Social Work held at Athens in September, 1964. See *Indian Journal of Social Work*, Vol. XXV, No. 3. October, 1964, pages 207-212.

a higher rate of growth, greater balance between industry and agriculture, better harnessing of natural and human resources and employment opportunities at a reasonable level of income for the entire labour force. These are but different aspects of the long-drawn war against mass poverty, a war that has to be waged for decades, inevitably under the pressure of increasing numbers, despite severe limitations by way of resources, skills and leadership, and in the background of persistent strains and conflicts of interest between different groups of which society is composed. The human and social factor has to be reckoned at every turn. Its response is both a result of various forces and developments and a positive element in the continuing process of change.

In comparison with social planning, the aims and methods of economic planning are more narrowly defined and easier to measure. Poverty has deep social roots, but its various concrete expressions—low levels of productivity and skill, lack of tools and machinery, unemployment and others—are matters which demand and can be given specific attention as well as an immediate claim on the available resources. On the other hand, social planning has broader goals, notably, creation of conditions of equal opportunity for different sections of the population and a fuller life for every citizen, and these can become precise only over a period of effort and struggle. Conditions differ from one country to another to such a degree that in the main, at the present age of interchange of experience, problems of social planning have to be resolved by each culture in its own indigenous setting.

On a broad view, social planning may be said to comprise four main areas of effort:

(a) development of basic social services such as education, health and housing,
(b) social welfare, including provision of minimum amenities and rural and urban welfare,
(c) welfare of the weaker and more vulnerable sections of the community, and
(d) social security.

In their preparation and execution, social plans call for a combined approach between governmental agencies at the national, regional and local levels, voluntary organisations and individual communities. At the inception of planning, the agencies needed, both governmental and others, are either not available or are without common objectives. The first task, therefore, is to visualise the character of the requisite agencies and to initiate steps for building them up over a period of years. Secondly, the resources available are meagre and claims to economic development and productive investment so pressing that social plans tend to be starved for finance. Lack of adequate agencies and trained personnel comes in the way of even such resources as are available being put to the most effective use. In turn, the scanty resources available for social plans fail to give to existing agencies the necessary vitality or to create conditions under which there may be vigorous social action at the level of the community. In the third place, social development is seldom envisaged in an integral manner, and in practice each aspect and each activity tends to be pursued in isolation, as if it stood alone. Consequently, the various agencies engaged in planning and implementing schemes of social development at different levels do not have a well-organised system of communication between them, in which the functions and responsibilities of each would be known to and accepted by the others. Finally, there is the question of methods and techniques of social work, of informing and educating the people and of seeking from them a sustained response to the challenge of the many problems they confront, thus enabling each local community to become its own primary agent of change. These different problems arise in each of the four areas of social planning mentioned above, and it may be useful to set out briefly the approach which has been developed thus far in the context of India's development and the directions in which it has still to be strengthened and extended.

Rapid economic development is contingent upon the expansion of basic social services. The connection is apparent in plans for the training of skilled manpower, provision of adequate health and medical facilities in growing urban centres and housing of industrial workers. It is no less important in relation to the development of facilities for mass education, expansion of health and medical facilities for the general population, provision of water supply and drainage and improved housing conditions for the entire community. It would be correct to say that greater emphasis is now being placed on these social services than in the initial stage of planning, more specially, on the development of education and elementary medical facilities. However, in the intervening years, the gap in housing has become larger and it has not been possible to secure any significant improvement in living conditions for a large proportion of the population, particularly in cities and towns. In other words, in terms of resources and in the institutional apparatus for making the essential social services available, important lags persist. In this field, while methods and techniques of development are being continually improved, local communities, municipal councils and democratic bodies functioning at the district, block and village levels have not yet assumed a sufficient measure of responsibility in social planning which they could be depended upon to discharge effectively to the satisfaction of the people. It is true that in a number of directions advances have occurred. The process of social planning has, nevertheless, to be greatly strengthened in terms of the contribution of different agencies and the resources on which they are in a position to operate.

The concept of social welfare is essentially supplementary to the provision of elementary social services for the population as a whole. In extending social services, the major role is that of governmental agencies at different levels along with greater participation and interest on the part of local communities. In social welfare, however, the contribution of voluntary organisations working with local communities and providing a bridge, as it were, between them and the various governmental agencies is much greater and can be progressively enlarged. In the early fifties, with the setting up of the Central and State Social Welfare Boards, which sought to assist and mobilise voluntary workers and organisations, social welfare became an element of promise in India's development plans. Considerable numbers of welfare extension projects were initiated in the rural areas, specially for promoting the welfare of women and children. It was soon apparent that in the rural areas such projects could not be undertaken as a distinct and separate programme and must eventually merge into the main stream of effort under community development programmes. From the beginning, community development envisaged an increasing share of responsibility for planning and implementation being assumed by local communities and local leadership. This notion has now been institutionalised through the setting up of democratic bodies at the village level as well as for development blocks and districts.

The scope for social welfare will be even greater when it comes to be assimilated into the wider ideal of community development, provided democratically constituted bodies evolve ways of promoting and utilising voluntary organisations. To an extent this object is being sought to be achieved through voluntary organisations being enabled to set up voluntary rural welfare projects in rural areas. These are intended to harness local resources and manpower for building up community assets, meeting such felt needs of local communities as do not fall easily within the normal pattern of development, and involving to a larger degree the spirit of mutual self-help and co-operation and sense of obligation within each community. An important step in the process of social planning would be to enhance the feeling of mutual responsibility within each community and establish favourable conditions for local effort and initiative. In a few cities, beginnings have been made with experimental urban community development projects but, on the whole, in the urban areas social planning is still limited to the extension of elementary social services supplemented to a small extent by voluntary welfare work.

A decade and more of planned development, which has been marked by rapid urban growth, increase in agricultural and industrial production and improvements in the conditions of living of only a small fraction of the population, has highlighted the problem of the weaker and vulnerable sections of the community. In the past, to an extent, the joint family and the prevailing sense of cohesion and obligation which distinguished castes and sub-castes and many small social groups, as well as the unsophisticated living conditions which generally prevailed, made the problem of the weaker and vulnerable sections much less conspicuous and demanding of special attention. In recent years, though the scale of the effort remains very short of the minimum needed, this problem has been approached by way of planning from three different directions. Firstly, the five year plans have embodied supplementary development programmes for such groups in the population as the tribal people, scheduled castes and other sections of the population who are adjudged to be backward on various economic and social criteria. The plans have provided for these groups limited resources in addition to their share in development as members of the general community. Secondly, areas which are predominantly inhabited by the tribal people are organised as tribal development blocks with schemes of development which are intended to be better adjusted to their needs and conditions. Similarly, in areas with considerable pressure of population and a high proportion of agricultural labour, rural works programmes are being undertaken with a view to supplementing employment opportunities available under the normal scheme of development. The need is being felt also for taking up intensive development in a number of areas in which there is a high degree of poverty and pressure on land and resources. The third approach to the problem of the weaker and vulnerable sections may be described as organisational. Thus, forest labourers are being organised into forest co-operatives, and industries subsidiary to agriculture are being established in rural areas. In each of the directions mentioned above, only the merest beginnings are to be observed and there is need for doing a great deal more by bringing local democratic bodies and local communities into the scheme of planning and placing greater responsibility on them.

Finally, different aspects of the programme for social services, for social welfare and for making a greater impact on the conditions of life and opportunity for the weaker sections of the population merge into the broader idea of social security. In this direction, a small start has been made, first, through schemes for health insurance, provident funds and retrenchment benefits for industrial workers; secondly, through social assistance funds for aiding those handicapped by age and infirmity, widows and orphans; and, thirdly, through the introduction in a few States of old age pensions. In extending social security, there is a wealth of experience in other countries to be drawn upon. It is obvious that State agencies will have a dominant role in this field. However, in a country in the early phase of development and facing acute shortage in resources, unless local communities, organs of local self-government and voluntary welfare organisations participate together in the planning and administration of social security measures, inadequacy of resources in men and money which the State alone can make available will be a serious limiting factor. There is already some readiness now to accept new social burdens as an organic element in plans for development. In the course of the next two or three plans a fairly well-knit scheme of social security should take shape. Social security itself becomes a vital link between economic and social planning since the most important single condition for assuring social security is the provision of adequate and stable employment opportunities.

To sum up, the processes of social planning are much more complex than those of economic planning. Neither can go far without the support of the other. In the first decade or more of planned development, certain lags in social development have become more marked. This would indicate greater priority for social plans in the next phase, specially for ensuring the essential services and a minimum for all citizens. Social development implies a considerably larger transfer of resources from those at higher levels of income, whether these be groups or regions, to others at lower levels of income. Until the idea of the Welfare State came to be widely accepted, such transfers of resources were frequently preceded by prolonged social conflict. In India, the Directive Principles of State Policy embodied the ethos of democracy, and planning has to be based on the assumption that the community as a whole is under obligation to secure welfare and equal opportunity to all its members and more specially to those who have been denied or left behind in the past Planning, thus, becomes a means to social change in the widest sense. In achieving a better balance between social and economic planning, at the stage now reached, there has to be much greater stress on allocation of resources distinctly in favour of social services and the development of human resources. Equally, in strengthening the institutional apparatus for social planning, particular attention has to be given to the role of local communities, of local self-governing bodies and of voluntary organisations. These have to function in the closest association with governmental agencies and, at each step, they must endeavour to involve the people as a whole in the common effort.

28

SOCIAL POLICY PERSPECTIVES*

WITHIN LESS than two years since the departure of Jawaharlal Nehru from the horizon of India, a large number of baffling problems already confront us. Much negative and non-rational thinking and action have come to the surface. There have been moments when it has seemed that India may be overtaken by her problems, passing in uncertain manner from one crisis to another. The comparatively even course of progress, which marked the first fifteen years of our Independence, was disturbed in the latter part of 1962. More recently, there has been a feeling of inadequacy over the ideas and institutions which have long provided the formal basis for public policy. At such a juncture, more than ever before, we need to draw fresh strength from the ideals which Jawaharlal Nehru pursued through life. Jawaharlal Nehru saw society as a whole. To him its many components were interdependent parts of an organic structure, which

---

* Adapted from the Jawaharlal Nehru Memorial Lectures, 1966, delivered on March 30 and 31, 1966, at the Tata Institute of Social Sciences, Bombay. The first lecture was devoted to a broad statement of social tasks and problems and the second to an outline of how they might be approached, the objectives and instruments of social policy and some of the limitations to be overcome. See *Indian Journal of Social Work*, Vol. XXVII, No. 2, July 1966, pages 107-118.

became stronger as each separate part gained in vitality and self-expression. Jawaharlal Nehru's vision of India was itself a force for building the future. With this vision as our guide, it is possible to face up to weaknesses inherent in our economic, social and political life and to accept harsh truths and, at the same time, to enrich our faith and confidence in the destiny of India.

I

A discussion of social policy should begin perhaps by identifying the social tasks and problems to which it relates, the factors whose interplay throws up these tasks and problems, and the changes which may be expected to occur, say, over the next decade. The subject has wide ramifications and does not lend itself readily to precise analysis, nor is it easy to mark off social aspects of development from the economic, political and institutional. A useful starting point may, therefore, be to emphasise the links which exist between social, economic and political problems and how they have shaped and influenced one another and, even more, the directions in which they are likely to interact upon one another in the future. For, in the main, it is to these inter-relationships that we may trace many of the most urgent and pressing social problems of our day.

Over the past fifteen years and more, we have placed our main reliance on the approach of planned development. It was thought that poverty and lack of development lay at the root of most social problems. With more rapid economic growth and more equitable distribution, social problems would become easier to solve and new and dynamic social and economic relationships would replace those derived from the rigid social structures and institutions inherited from our past. On the political aspect, there was confidence that the institutions of democracy and freedom, which the Constitution embodied, were capable not only of giving to the people at each level a sense of participation and fulfilment, but also of solving economic and social problems and taking the country forward steadily towards a classless, progressive and essentially co-operative social order.

We have gained sufficient experience to know that while the major decisions have been right and the national goals have been correctly set, there is a wide gulf between them and the reality. For the assumptions underlying our philosophy of economic, social and political advance to be fulfilled, it is necessary to probe more fully into our failures and weaknesses, to evolve a series of supporting strategies for effective implementation and to secure a range and scale of national effort sufficient to bring within its fold every urban and rural community and all institutions and individuals who can contribute to the welfare of the people. Both democracy and planning must be so worked from day to day as to enlarge the common effort and serve the interest of the people as a whole.

Before Independence, the principal social problems which attracted the interest of social workers were those in the nature of social evils. Some of these were attributed to the working of caste institutions, and their elimination was considered a necessary step in strengthening the social fabric. To a large extent, where their work did not become part of some wider religious movement, social reformers limited their activities to urban areas and to certain selected problems. The search for the welfare of the entire community, emphasis on the obligations of each community towards its weaker and more vulnerable sections, and the acceptance of equal worth for every individual without consideration of accidents of birth or fortune are comparatively recent developments. Until a few years ago, the problems which exercised social workers were, therefore, primarily social in their origin and context.

An important consequence of planned economic evelopment has been to give to most social problems an economic

dimension and to bring about a closer link between the
economic and the social. Thus, if in practice the rights established for scheduled castes under the Constitution have not
brought equal dignity and equal opportunity to them, a large
part of the explanation is to be found in the economic factors
at work. If scheduled tribes in different States have remained
apart from the main Indian community, the explanation
may lie in the manner in which the processes of economic
development have operated close to the tribal people. Or,
again, if the growth of towns has led to a variety of new
social problems, the reasons are to be sought mainly in
the economic factors. As we shall see, both the older social
problems which have continued to grow and new social
problems which now claim special attention are linked with
the manner in which the economic process has proceeded.
More generally, even as rapid expansion of the economy
makes possible solutions to social problems which would
otherwise be greatly prolonged, the pace and pattern of
economic advance may accentuate old problems and create
new ones. Thus, in each phase, it becomes necessary to view
together the social aspects of economic development and
the economic implications of social facts and policies and to
seek a correct balance between them.

An important link between economic and social development is provided by the institutions which subserve both
needs. In the last analysis, these institutions are political
in nature, for they form part of the political and administrative structure envisaged in the constitution. This institutions at the national and State levels, and their counterparts
in the form of municipal institutions for urban areas and
Panchayati Raj institutions for rural areas, have both economic and social responsibilities. They can discharge these
responsibilities in the measure in which they are able efficiently to carry out the political and administrative processes
and function so as to create public satisfaction, evoke res-

ponse and meet rising expectations. The working of political, civic and administrative institutions has, therefore, critical significance equally for the success of economic as well as social programmes and policies. Conflicts of social and economic interest, growth of consciousness of their needs on the part of various sections of the people in different parts of the country, and the emergence of new leaders lead to the formulation of new aspirations and demands. More frequently than not, these must take political form if they do not receive timely attention.

Following this analysis, from the events of the past three or four years, it is possible to draw certain inferences relevant to future social policy. First, economic planning is but a partial approach to the problems of society unless the political, administrative and civic institutions on which it depends can in practice work with integrity, efficiency and goodwill and secure a large measure of popular support. Secondly, economic growth in overall statistical terms will yet leave large regions and numerous groups out of its pale. To that extent, it will provide fertile soil for discontent. Every important act of economic and social policy should, therefore, be seen and understood widely as part of a larger design of social change and development, a scheme for bringing greater opportunity to all parts of the country and to all sections of the population. During any given period, these latter cannot all advance equally or to the same level, but there has to be a basic harmony and interdependence between the advance of society as a whole and of its different constituent units. Political education and training, effective communication between different sections of the community, and clear grasp of their concerns and aspirations and of the tensions and discontents to which they might give rise, are essential elements in the success and stability of a system based on the values of freedom and democracy. If during recent years, divisive forces have sometimes appeared stronger and cementing forces weaker, if discontents have found at times unexpectedly brazen and anti-social expression, could this be because our view of social and economic problems and their inter-relationships has not been complete enough, because the factors which make for successful political development have not received adequate thought, and because some crucial social and economic problems have been allowed to grow unresolved ?

II

Our ability to solve social problems and pursue long range continuing social policies is largely conditioned by the rate of economic progress. The tasks of economic development have proved less amenable than was assumed at the beginning of planning. In each phase of development, a series of limitations have to be overcome. These include limitations of resources, including foreign exchange, difficulties in finding acceptable ways for the accumulation of developmental capital, diversity of claims on the available resources, including defence and non-plan commitments, and the choice which has to be frequently made between concentration and dispersal, between quality and quantity, between different agencies and between different technologies. As the economy develops, its problems of implementation become more complex, so that it has constantly to balance shorter term with longer term objectives. These various elements in the economic situation tend to take away from planning some of the emphasis on more fundamental social tasks and problems at the very moment when these begin to assume greater importance and when stability and growth depend increasingly on our success in turning the energies and aspirations of the people into constructive and positive activity.

Against this background, the tasks which social policy should accomplish have to be defined more specifically, and
30

indeed more modestly than one may wish to. These tasks
may be looked at in three different ways. First, social policy
may comprise programmes and measures directed towards
such objectives as :

(a) expansion of social services and their qualitative improvement, for
    instance, in education, health, family planning, nutrition and housing;
(b) welfare and development of the weaker and more vulnerable sections
    of the population and, more specially, of non-integrated groups, such
    as scheduled castes and the tribal people;
(c) development of supplementary welfare services at the level of the local
    area and the local community;
(d) social reform;
(e) provision of social security; and
(f) social change, including reduction in disparities of income and wealth,
    prevention of concentration of economic power and steps to equalise
    opportunities within the community.

Whatever the present limitations in terms of resources and
the freedom with which they may be allocated, social
problems have accumulated to such an extent that they
cannot now be regarded lightly. Therefore, even as action
proceeds, ways to overcome the existing limitations will
need to be found. Wherever there are openings and opportunities for reducing the social lag, these must be pressed.
In the social field, even more than the economic, relatively
small resources can go a long way and, in turn, generate
more resources from within the community and through
voluntary effort.

Whatever their scope, social policies cannot succeed
without ensuring the necessary economic conditions. Of
these, the most important are a significant and steady rate
of growth for the economy as a whole, employment policies
which will absorb into productive work at least the addition
to the labour force during each plan period, maintenance
of reasonable price levels and efforts to assure a national
minimum. The provision of minimum needs is sometimes
thought of as being an attempt to share poverty. The truth

is that for all its limitaions in resources and organisation,
given the necessary will and direction, even over the short
period, the Indian economy could become capable of providing the minimum work opportunities and meeting the
minium needs of all citizens. It should certainly be within
the capacity of the nation to eliminate the more serious
forms of poverty and unemployment. This is by far the
most important condition for uninterrupted economic and
social development in the coming years and for resolving
present and future social imbalances.

A second way of looking at problems of social policy could
be in terms of different sections of the population. A developing economy, specially one in which the`process of modernisa-
tion and industrialisation is actively under way, consists
of groups at varying stages of development and integration
into the wider movement for change and growth. Thus,
at one end there are progressive and dynamic groups who
are able to take advantage of new opportunities and are
in the vanguard of economic progress. Examples of these
are a considerble body of new industrial and commercial
entrepreneurs, both large and small, technicians, managers
and salaried employees, and a growing number of large and
middle farmers. At the other end, we have groups, still largely
outside the main current, for whose problems our present
development plans have failed so far to provide an adequate
or effective approach. Examples of these groups are the landless agricultural workers, tribal communities and an increasing urban proletariat comprising groups of industrial, manual
and other workers engaged in unorganised industries and,
to an extent, even in organised industries. The great body
of small peasants and cultivators also represent a wide range
of conditions and levels of development, a small but increasing number being drawn into the scheme of agricultural
and economic expansion, while large numbers remain close
to the condition of landless agricultural workers.

In the first approach to social policy, we had in view types of activity to be undertaken within the scheme of social development. In the second approach, we see social problems in terms of certain economic and functional groups and enquire how social development may be planned and social policy pursued, so that the groups which have lagged behind or remained out of the main stream of economic development and expansion can be best enabled to advance more rapidly and overcome the social and economic handicaps from which they have suffered. There is a third way also of looking at problems of social policy and social development. Within any community, in addition to general schemes for the expansion of social services, there are sections of the population whose developmental needs must become a matter of special concern to the community as a whole. These are, for instance, women, pre-school children, children out of school and school drop-outs, and youth. The welfare of these sections of the community has to be achieved largely through the efforts of the community itself. Development plans can provide resources and support in some measure to enable local communities to assume responsibility for their own total welfare.

III

The three ways of looking at social tasks and problems described above are complementary to one another. Each of them throws up certain questions of approach and planning and suggests elements which should enter into the general design of social policy and the instruments through which its implementation is to be secured. In this light, the social tasks and problems with which we are concerned at present are different in nature and range from those which we faced ten or fifteen years ago. Similarly, if we look ahead over the next decade, the social tasks and problems will have changed a great deal and will in fact become much more complex. An understanding of the main economic factors likely to give rise to social tasks and problems over the next decade will also suggest certain essential priorities.

The social situation will change appreciably during the next decade on account of growth of population. India's population now stands at 494 million, 55 million more than at the 1961 census. In another decade, on present expectations, the population will rise by 135 million to 629 million. Over the next decade, the addition to the labour force will be of the order of 53 million. The urban population rose from 62 to 79 million between 1951 and 1961 and is expected to increase by about 4 per cent per annum, rising to 134 million in 1976. Development plans for the next decade proceed on the basis of growth rates varying from 6 to 7 per cent per annum. These are the minimum rates of development needed to sustain India's economy and take it out of the ruts of poverty.

The precise social tasks and problems which will have to be faced over the next ten years will depend greatly on the pace at which the economy develops and solves its problems of agricultural production and employment. These are the crucial objectives. There will be large increases in the rural population, including landless agricultural and manual workers. Diversification of the occupational structure of rural areas, productive use of their manpower resources, and planned growth of towns and cities, are essential premises for successful social planning and for systematic pursuit of social policies. At the same time since, in the ordinary course, economic development during the next decade is likely to strengthen the more dynamic groups, measures for enabling those groups which have fallen behind in the past to catch up with the rest will have to be intensified.

As the economy and the social configuration change, during each period, we shall need to redefine our problems, modify approaches followed in the past and seek fresh solutions. An increasing number of social and economic groups, will assert their aspirations for a better living and for sharing in new opportunities. Their problems will have to be studied objectively and with sympathy and their urges and desires anticipated. Social research in all its aspects will have a vital contribution to offer. Disparities in economic opportunity and conflicts of social interest will be continually with us. They will put our political, administrative and civic institutions to severe test. Much will depend on the quality of planning and implementation at the national, state and local levels and on the adequacy of political response. Universities, research institutions and scientific and academic forums can do a great deal to present a long range view of national, regional and sectional problems and needs. Standing aside from the day to day strife and clash of interest, scholars and research workers have the opportunity, as they have the obligation, to present the problems of different groups in the larger setting of economic, social and political development of the country as a whole, viewing these different facets as parts of a single composite scheme for achieving growth and stability.

In the last analysis, through many separate movements for enlarging community welfare and assuring a fuller life to all groups, big and small, throughout the country, our plans and the social policies associated with them do seek to build up a nation working for a social order which would give to millions of people a sense of satisfaction and opportunity in their daily lives and a feeling of identification with a larger cause. Even under favourable conditions, this would be a difficult objective to realise. Yet, nothing short of this will bring home to every citizen that larger purpose without which both planning and social policy may well leave behind trails of frustration and missed opportunities.

IV

We have so far viewed problems of social policy, firstly, in terms of programmes and measures directed towards broad social objectives; secondly, in terms of the problems which confront specially those groups which have either lagged behind or face peculiar difficulties in their development; and thirdly, in relation to sections of the population such as women, children and youth, for which communities may assume special responsibility within the framework of general public policy. These three different ways of looking at social policy are not exclusive of one another. Though they overlap at certain points, they are intended to supplement one another and could together constitute a fairly comprehensive approach to the subject.

In current planning an attempt is being made to allocate comparatively larger resources, specially for the expansion of education and health services. This may help correct, to some extent, inadequacies in earlier plans. There are, however, other essential social services such as housing and urban development and general welfare services where the resource allocations at present envisaged will not be sufficient to make the impact needed.

In the development of basic health and education services, there are still large disparities between States and regions. Over the next decade, these disparities have to be eliminated if different parts of the country are to provide some measure of equality of opportunity for the local population. In this sense, the Central Government will be called upon to give additional help in certain areas.

The problem of reducing disparities goes beyond the expansion of basic services in the case of the rural areas, scheduled castes and other backward classes and tribal communities. Here, in addition to limitations of resources, which can perhaps be overcome at least in part, there are serious limitations in organisation and personnel and in the ability of the groups concerned to profit fully from the available facilities. Supporting programmes for training, for scholarships, for assuring the supply of teachers, doctors and other personnel must be an essential component of development. Moreover, this component should be provided precisely in the form called for by local needs and conditions, that is, in a flexible manner and not in terms of set prescriptions and formulae without consideration of whether or not they meet the needs as identified in each area or within each group.

There are certain weaknesses in general programmes for the expansion of social services which need to be combated as matters of broad social policy. First, there should be a proper balance between quantitative expansion and consolidation and improvement of quality. Critical appraisal from time to time of the status of education and health services from this angle in each area could provide a corrective. Secondly, general schemes of expansion of social services leave little room for experiment and innovation and even discourage efforts at adaptation to local needs and conditions. Thirdly, too often, schools and institutions such as health centres, far from becoming nerve centres in the life of the communities they are intended to serve, remain merely isolated structures, contributing little to creative activity.

Whatever aspect of social development we touch, the central purpose of social policy should be to create conditions in which each area, urban or rural, and each group with distinctive and identifiable problems, is able to lift itself, overcome its limitations, and improve its living conditions and economic opportunities, thus becoming part of the larger integrated Indian community. This has two implications for the development of the basic social services. First, these services have to be developed according to the needs and conditions of each area and community so that, together with other developmental activities, they will produce the maximum impact. Secondly, while every effort should be made to provide adequate resources under the plans for the expansion of social services, the general direction should be to encourage increasing self-reliance at the level of the area and the community. The long-term goal of policy should be that the provision of *elementary* social srvices is ultimately a responsibility that any sizeable community should bear for itself. This will leave the resources of the Centre and the States more free for the development of the higher stages of social services and for more generous support to the weaker groups as well as for new experimental initiatives. For social services such as housing, urban development and slum clearance, if the pace of development were determined altogether by allocations directly feasible under the plans, the progress likely to be registered will be altogether too small and the problems will get out of hand. Therefore, the aim should be to develop a strong network of institutions which can draw resources from several different directions and function in an autonomous manner. In turn, these institutions can aid and stimulate planned effort on the part of local areas and local communities.

In dealing with the weaker and more vulnerable groups, and, more specially, with non-integrated groups, we are face to face with perhaps the most fundamental area of social policy. The groups we might identify for this purpose are (a) the scheduled castes and other backward classes living mainly in the villages as part of larger communities, (b) the tribal communities, and (c) industrial, manual and other workers in the towns who form a kind of urban proletariat steadily increasing in numbers and frequently living under slum conditions. Each group presents special problems which call both for broader public policy and for specific local action. Moreover, the problems are both economic and social and have to be dealt with together.

The scheduled castes and other backward classes in the villages are in the main an economically dependent group. They suffer from chronic shortage of employment opportunities. The growth of population has borne on them with particular harshness and will do so to an even greater degree in the future. To a large extent, they remain socially a non-integrated group in the rural community and from the economic aspect our present development plans are not oriented to provide sufficient relief and support to them. We are yet far from having an effective social policy to deal with the problems of this group. Only the elements of such a social policy can be indicated at this stage. These are:

(1) bold educational programmes, including imparting of skills and support by way of scholarships and special coaching sufficient to ensure that the benefits of reservation of posts and seats accrue in full;

(2) rural works programmes for the slack agricultural season so as to assure a minimum family income, accompanied by a movement for labour co-operatives on a national scale;

(3) to the extent feasible, allotment of land to co-operative groups;

(4) a common housing programme in the villages which will progressively integrate the scheduled castes with other sections of the rural community; and

(5) migration to urban and industrial centres accompanied by appropriate welfare and resettlement policies.

Concerted efforts along these lines in different States may point the way, but they will also bring out the extraordinarily difficult tasks which remain to be undertaken and the extensive, nation-wide nature of the problem of bringing scheduled castes and other backward classes in the villages on par with the rest of the community. It is unfortunately true that in terms of policy and action we are still at the outskirts of a major national responsibility.

The problems of tribal communities have been studied by several expert bodies and efforts have been made to bring larger communication, education and other facilities to them. The requirements of social planning are not the same in areas in which tribals are in comparatively small numbers in the midst of non-tribal communities as in areas in which they themselves constitute the main population. In the former, a considerable amount of contact and integration has already come about. The main concern is to ensure that the tribal groups are able to obtain a fair share of developmental support and their educational and economic programmes are implemented with vigour in keeping with their needs and cultural background. The more difficult task is to carry out the development of predominantly tribal areas with the full support and participation of the tribal communities and through their own leadership and institutions. The problems of each such area need to be investigated carefully and adequate resources and facilities brought to bear on them. General programmes and schematic patterns of development, which are not closely adapted to the actual conditions and needs of each area, will be of little avail. The impact hitherto has been superficial, often leaving unattended the basic problems of transformation of the forest-based agricultural economy, development of trained personnel from within the tribal groups, and active involvement of tribal village communities in their own future development. In each tribal area, the burden of development must eventually be borne largely by the tribal people themselves. For this they have to be prepared and equipped. In the transitional period, which will be a long one, it is essential to organise special cadres of technical and administrative personnel who will be trained for service among the tribal people, will identify themselves with their welfare and, by their work and association, evoke genuine confidence and initiative from within the tribal communities themselves.

The third non-integrated group mentioned earlier, the growing and amorphous mass of urban workers, are less easy to identify than scheduled castes and other backward classes in the villages or the tribal communities. Not enough is known about their precise numbers and the economic and social conditions in which they live and work. Moreover, the composition of such groups, at any rate, in the larger cities goes on changing along with changes in the urban economy and the increasing influx from the smaller towns and the villages. City development plans, including control over use of land, development of civic amenities and planned expansion, and urban community development, may together provide an approach to the problems of this and other groups in the urban area. These problems are likely to grow to unmanageable dimensions over the next decade. Therefore, a substantial beginning must now be made. To this end, the strengthening of municipal institutions in personnel and resources and insistence on their functioning as key organs for planning and implementation of plans in the urban areas have become essential steps. Universities and educational institutions and schools of social work are in a position to render valuable assistance to municipal institutions by identifying the problems of different groups, collecting accurate social and economic data, and pointing to practical solutions. In the nature of things, large heterogenous populations are characteristic of growing cities. Communication and mutual knowledge within such populations present peculiar problems. For a long time the consequences of social and civic neglect may not come to the surface, but discontent and tension go on simmering. Under these conditions, healthy urban development becomes extraordinarily difficult. The approach and methods being currently developed for work among the poorer sections in the towns under the anti-poverty programme in the United States deserve to be followed closely. The social, psychological and economic problems of the urban poor have yet to receive systematic attention from those concerned with policy, administration, social work and research.

Over the past decade, through the work of the Central Social Welfare Board and State Social Welfare Boards and voluntary organisations, an attempt has been made to provide supplementary social services, specially for women and children in the rural areas. Midday meals in schools and the applied nutrition programme supported by UNICEF are other examples of such supplementary welfare services. In the more advanced countries, the scope of the main social services has gradually expanded to include some of the supplementary services. Thus, provision of facilities for pre-school children and for children out-of-school and school drop-outs and midday meals in schools has become a part of the general scheme of education. Measures for improving nutrition and promoting health education are an integral part of the development of health services. The general trend, therefore, is to limit the scope of supplementary welfare services to activities which the local community is best placed to undertake. In the transition, the range of supplementary welfare services will be somewhat larger and action in relation to them correspondingly less intensive. In the Indian context, even allowing for enlargement in the scope of the main social services, specially health and education, the role of the community in providing supplementary welfare services will be of the greatest importance. For this, neither urban nor rural communities are at present equipped and organised. Experience over the past decade has brought out a series of difficult problems for which satisfactory solutions have yet to be found. Welfare extension projects, which were coordinated with the community development programme, do not appear, on the whole, to have stimulated much community action, and their impact appears to have been small. Their future as an integral part of services provided through community development has also been uncertain. Similarly, welfare extension projects and centres entrusted to voluntary organisations have come up against difficulties arising from the provision of recurring and committed expenditures. It is now apparent that the solution will lie perhaps along the lines of an institutional set up at the block level which can provide for sustained development with the support of the Panchayat Samiti and the State Social Welfare Board as well as voluntary workers and village organisations. Such an institutional set up might take the form of a family and child welfare centre located within each development block, from which activities could be carried into villages in co-operation with local village organisations, and through which adequate financial, administrative and technical help could be given by higher organisations and by extension agencies. Side by side with such an institutional set up, it will also be essential to formulate appropriate national policies and programmes for making available special training facilities for women in rural areas, affording employment opportunities to them, assuring training and orientation for children out-of-school and school drop-outs, and providing openings for youth, both in the towns and in rural areas, to play a constructive and dynamic role in the life and development of the community.*

VI

Some of the other aspects of social policy, which have been mentioned already, may be touched upon more briefly. Numerous social evils have persisted through the years and legislation by itself, even where adequately conceived, has

* These suggestions are developed further in Chapter 31 on Family and Child Welfare in the Rural Community.

proved ineffective. Examples of social action needed urgently are the uprooting of beggary, including juvenile and professional beggary, attack on moral vice in urban areas, removal of slums and shanties which disfigure our towns, provision of night shelters in towns, and a rural housing programme based on composite villages in which scheduled castes and others live together as members of the same community rather than on the basis of segregation. In view of the size of the problems involved, in each case local effort will need to be stimulated and the necessary public support given to it. Such action has to be organised on a sufficient scale to become the nucleus of more widespread movements for dealing with the basic causes.

The beginnings of social security for workers in organised industries have been made already through the provision of health insurance and provident fund schemes. For these workers unemployment insurance schemes can also be progressively introduced. However, for the bulk of the people, at the present stage of development, social assistance programmes will be more feasible and of greater practical value. The Central and State Governments will have to provide nucleus resources to enable municipal bodies, Panchayat Samitis, village panchayats and voluntary organisations to participate in schemes for providing timely assistance to at least three groups of persons who may be altogether lacking in the means of livelihood and support, namely, physically handicapped persons, old persons unable to work, and women and children. Some State Governments have made a limited beginning with old age pensions. There is scope for extending schemes for old age pensions, but it has to be recognised that at present it would be difficult to provide resources on any scale for this purpose. While, as a longer term objective to be achieved in stages through the joint efforts of the Centre and the States, the importance of old age pensions should be stressed, the major accent during the next few years should be on social assistance programmes at the local level in which civic bodies, voluntary organisations and urban and rural communities can co-operate closely.

VII

Social problems touch groups and individuals at many points. They do not lend themselves readily to specific forms of public action since the sequence of cause and effect runs through innumerable human, social and economic relationships. Conditions vary to an extraordinary extent in different areas and within different communities. Formal development programmes drawn up at the national and state levels often lead to the application of pre-conceived patterns of social action in varying situations. In consequence, they may prove to be barren of results and fail to secure the best use of resources. Sometimes, they benefit only small numbers of favoured individuals and leave the problems of the mass untouched. Social policy and social planning should aim, above all, at providing a favourable environment for continuing action at the community and area level. This will no doubt involve provision of resources, but even more important than these is the building up of an integrated view of community welfare, each community accepting the obligation of looking after the interests of all its members and specially of those who need help most.

Significant leadership resources are latent in most communities. Potential leaders are held back frequently from lack of knowledge and lack of resources. These are the two elements which plans at the national and state levels should seek specially to provide. Few investments will yield larger results than the training of leaders and workers at the community level. Experience in the working of voluntary organisations suggests that priority should be given to building up their capability for continuous work. For special types of projects, support should no doubt be given by way of grants for equipment and other facilities, but the greater emphasis should be on the strengthening of these organisations through nucleus staffs of trained workers who can be maintained on a permanent basis and can serve as catalysts for getting the best out of the available human resources. With greater freedom and flexibility in using the resources made available to it, each community and the voluntary organisations which serve it will be able to develop greater capacity to solve their social problems and enlarge the area of welfare activity.

Owing to their complexities, social problems do not admit of simple solutions. In a changing and developing society, as old problems diminish or become less urgent, new ones arise. Social policy is composed of many different strands and calls for sustained action at every point in the national structure. Its ultimate purpose is to achieve integration between diverse elements and a sense of common citizenship and common values. Development plans, national policies and public resources are but means to one end. This is to enable each area and each community to find answers to its own basic problems and to seek the welfare of all its members.

29

ECONOMIC ASPECTS AND ORGANISATION OF WELFARE SERVICES*

THERE is much general agreement on the directions in which welfare services, for instance, for children and youth should be developed. The difficult problem is to set priorities within a given time span and to assign resources from within what is invariably a strictly limited total after balancing various conflicting economic and social claims. Anything like a uniform approach between different countries is not to be expected. The best that can be hoped for is to arrive at some broad guide lines which may assist a country, according to its needs and conditions, to pick upon certain central tasks and activities and turn them into points of advance and attack upon what is everywhere a major area of national concern.

I

Welfare problems of children and youth, in themselves illustrative of a wider range of social needs, may be regarded as a special case of two more general problems. The first concerns the manner in which the claims of economic and social

* Based on two contributions at the Asian Conference on Children and Youth in National Planning and Development convened by the UNICEF at Bangkok in March, 1966.

development are to be assessed and balanced and how investment in human resources is to be assured in the midst of a multiplicity of claims. The second bears on the extent to which the needs of the less developed areas, of which the rural areas are typical, and of the under-privileged and needy sections of the community are to be met. Since the great majority of children and youth in the countries of Asia live in rural areas, their welfare forms part of the larger rural problem. At the same time, of course, there are critical emerging problems in the growing urban areas as well.

At any given time, the room for manoeuvre, for freedom in the disposition of resources is extremely limited. Therefore the aim of policy is to discover new openings and possibilities and to enlarge the area of advance during any given period. In doing so, it is important that long term development should be so planned for and organised that, to an extent, short term and immediate problems are also resolved at the same time. Too frequently, in the name of long term planning, present problems are allowed to grow and become less manageable.

II

In the economic and social sphere, public policy has a wider role than the actual size of public expenditures may suggest. This is specially true of welfare policies, for instance, for children and youth. While all advanced societies, whether socialist or non-socialist, have similar welfare objectives, there is a basic difference between the more developed and the less developed countries. This arises from the inescapable limitations under which the latter have to function. In the under-developed countries it is specially important that, both in their objectives and in the means adopted, economic policies should be such as to influence the welfare of the mass of the people, not merely the welfare of comparatively small numbers.

The main advance in mass welfare has to come from rapid economic growth accompanied by expansion in the elementary social services, specially education, health, family planning, water supply and sanitation and housing. But these will not be enough and must be supplemented by more specific action. In this area of supplementary social services, it is possible to evolve an approach which will meet even strict tests for planning and allocation of resources. Such an approach might underline the need for action in five important directions.

Firstly, priority should be given to policies designed to mobilise local resources and strengthen community effort. To a large extent, much larger in fact than is generally recognised, welfare objectives have to be realised at the level of the local community. National policy can at best provide a favourable framework and an environment which will stimulate local effort. Central plans and policies frequently also centralise resources; to this extent they may even reduce the scope for local action. Therefore, in the poorer countries, national planning and economic policy should seek to create a sound economic and social base for self-reliance within local communities and at each level below the nation as a whole. To this end, national fiscal policy should be designed to leave a large enough field for taxation by local and regional authorities and for voluntary local effort.

Secondly, there should be emphasis on policies for promoting activities which will combine production and increase in productive capacity with improvements in consumption and increase in welfare. The applied nutrition programme in India, undertaken with support from UNICEF, is a good example of such activities, which can be augmented continuously.

In the third place, since fuller and more continuous employment is the key to minimum income and, therefore, to minimum levels of welfare in the rural areas, high priority attaches to policies for expanding employment opportunities and reducing disguised unemployment. Such additional opportunities must be found both for men and for women.

In the fourth place, there should be marked stress on policies for promoting social assistance, at any rate, until general systems of social insurance and security can be established. There is little doubt that it is the younger people from families who are in a condition of dependence and comparative helplessness whose welfare needs tend to be conspicuously neglected.

Finally, an approach to welfare consistent with economic criteria should embody a complex of policies for training personnel and making trained personnel available for welfare and other services, not only at higher levels, but within each community.

Two further aspects deserve to be brought out. In choosing priorities for the use of resources allocated to any supplementary social plan, as far as possible, the objectives should be such as will help unify the social effort and induce other resources to come into the field of welfare, for instance, of children and youth. In other words, to the extent resources provided by the State can serve as magnets and catalysts, community welfare and the welfare of particular sections can be greatly enlarged. Secondly, welfare problems should be seen in relation to the total social structure. Thus, the problem of welfare for children and youth is by no means identical for such different sections of the community as peasants, agricultural labourers, industrial workers, slum dwellers, low income groups in urban areas and middle class families. While promoting social mobility between lower and higher income groups, concentrated attention should be given to the specific handicaps under which each group labours, and all the available institutions and services should be harnessed together in the service of tasks which have been identified in advance with the help of social workers and on the basis of careful study.

The approaches and the criteria of public policy outlined above should go some distance in obtaining the maximum benefits from such resources as are allocated for welfare. This aspect is as important as the total volume of resources provided for welfare in any given period. For resources which are used effectively and produce an impact, in turn, create more resources from within and also attract additional resources from other sectors of activity.

III

We may turn next to the manner in which welfare services in any sphere are to be organised and responsibilities for execution shared. These responsibilities have to be assigned in three different ways: first, between different agencies at the national level; second, between various governmental agencies operating at different levels within the national structure; and thirdly, between public agencies on the one hand and voluntary and community agencies on the other. Questions of organisation in any field cannot be dealt with in isolation from the administrative and political framework in which policies are translated into action and welfare services are made available. It is all too easy to carry the institutional assumptions of one structure into another and to suggest as principles and general propositions what may in fact be only significant but special illustrations. Therefore, conclusions on organisation must be formulated and expressed with some degree of caution, recognising at every step that there are difficult practical problems to resolve, that there must be much continuing trial and error, and that in the main each country has to find the appropriate solutions from within its own experience and its own struggles with the realities of economic, social and political development.

Before the problem of organisation and implementation can be discussed in a meaningful way, it is necessary to assume that the welfare services to be provided over a given period have been broadly determined and the resources needed allocated within the national plan. In practice, there is much groping for precise objectives and this stage is not easily reached, for means and ends continuously influence each other. Nor is it sufficient, in devising administrative arrangements and taking steps to build up appropriate agencies for execution, to establish priorities and resources merely in terms of the time span common to most plans of development. For this, there are at least three practical reasons. First, during any specific period, only a small part of the journey can be covered. Almost always, the larger part of the task lies ahead. To provide fully and effectively for any system of welfare services is a task which may take a period of fifteen years or more to accomplish. Secondly, trained personnel are needed and must be thought of in terms of comparatively long periods, and training of personnel has to be followed by adequate opportunities for using the trained manpower in a continuing manner. Thirdly, services established during any plan period have to be maintained in later periods, at the same time as new and extended services are introduced. In other words, along with developmental outlays, the community has to bear a growing burden of recurring and maintenance outlays. This is a rock on which much expansion in social services tends to flounder in underdeveloped economies, because it is not easy for governmental budgets to expand sufficiently rapidly to meet the liability for maintaining existing social services without slowing down new development and expansion.

IV

We have referred earlier to the broad distinction between the main social services and services which enter into the supplementary social plan. Organisational arrangements for the former will be embodied in the appropriate sectoral plans; here we are concerned with the organisation and execution of the second group of welfare services. It is in the nature of these latter services that frequently they call for complementary action from more than one sector. Thus, for nutritional and school health services, for care of pre-school children or for education and work for those who have never gone to school or have dropped out of school before their time, a co-operative approach has to be evolved between two or more sectors of social activity before the services can be effectively organised and developed.

It is characteristic of an economically developed society, as distinguished from a less developed one, that the principal social services steadily expand in scope, so that the supplementary social plan becomes smaller in range at the same time as it is pursued more intensively. For instance, in several advanced countries, as a process of evolution, the education of the pre-school child in the age group 3-5, through the kindergarten, has now come to be included within the ordinary school system. The same development has occurred in respect of full-time and part-time schools, correspondence schools, midday meals in schools, special courses for youth and the welfare of children in need of protection. Therefore, from the aspect of welfare services, the primary emphasis has to be on rapid expansion and increase in the scope of the principal social services, such as education, health and employment. The educational system should come to comprehend the needs of pre-school children and of drop-outs and of children who have not gone to school. Health services should come to include not only family planning, but also nutrition and school health. Employment programmes should be expanded to provide for the imparting of new skills for rural youth and for additional work opportunities, both for men and for women, so that family incomes may be materially increased, and thereby family welfare may be strengthened.

The significance of this proposition for policy and administration is that, progressively, the supplementary social plan will include chiefly those welfare services which have to be organised at the level of the local area and the local community and at the level of the local city or town or neighbourhood. During the period of transition, until the principal social services develop adequately, the supplementary social plan will be somewhat wider in scope. But, to that extent, the impact on the community will be less intensive and penetrating. The local community, the local area and the city have, of course, to co-operate in implementing the whole range of social services, but the services for which they are primarily responsible and have to take greater initiative should be sufficiently limited for this specific obligation to be fulfilled effectively.

V

We may now consider some specific problems of organisation. Much time need not be spent on the question of responsibility as between different ministries at the national level. Within any system of government, two aims are being constantly pursued. On the one hand, in setting up agencies and arranging for their work, there is the search for greater specialisation and differentiation in functions; on the other, there is the pressure for greater coordination and integration and avoidance of overlapping responsibilities. This is the very process by which agencies first multiply and then seek ways of coming together, within every government, there are always internal pressures for change in structure and functions at the national as well as regional levels and, between one administrative compromise and another the end is never reached. What is of real importance in developing and carrying out the supplementary social services is that

the higher level agencies should content themselves with
setting the broad goals, providing the resources needed on a
stable and assured basis, and creating a favourable environment for co-operative working between various agencies, governmental and non-governmental, which operate
at the local level. These agencies and the communities they
serve directly should have freedom to administer, to change
and adapt, and to find solutions for the many problems
which must arise from day to day in the course of implementation. The higher agencies have to persuade themselves
not to plan and direct in detail. Their primary task is to
create conditions in which others may succeed.

From this reasoning follows another proposition. If
welfare services, specially those which form part of the
supplementary social plan, are to be carried out with the
full involvement and participation of the people, and if each
community is to seek the welfare of all as a common and
fundamental obligation, everything possible must be done
to strengthen local self-governing institutions and voluntary
organisations. Within the framework of national policy
and national planning, these are our major instruments.
Even with the help of these institutions, the task of reaching
every section of the community is an extraordinarily difficult one; without them, it cannot be accomplished in any
serious measure.

The structure of self-governing institutions varies in
different countries. In India, within the scheme of democracy
and human freedom, with many imperfections yet, we are
seeking to build up a system of rural democracy at various
levels. To enable these and other grass-root institutions to
work for the welfare of the community, with the support
of the people, and without being too greatly distracted by
political or factional considerations, is not an easy task.
But, to the extent they can succeed, the capacity of each
community to prepare for its own advance and harness the

energies of the people also grows, and the future is secured. Therefore, local self-governing institutions should be given the necessary resources and should have the opportunity of augmenting them by their own efforts. They should also have adequately trained personnel at their disposal and should be in a position to provide them with fair careers in social service. On their part, local self-governing institutions have to recognize that they can achieve the aims of welfare for the community only on the basis of complete partnership with voluntary organisations.

In their turn, as much is expected of them, voluntary organisations have to be supported and nurtured with care. There is a vast amount of energy to be mobilised at every level. Voluntary work has to be valued and given social prestige, so that public spirited workers may be drawn to it. Voluntary organisations should receive adequate maintenance grants from the government, so that they can attract and retain competent trained workers and be in a position to provide them with satisfying opportunities for work and service.

In devising arrangements for organising welfare services, one further proposition may be advanced. In the villages, in the main such arrangements will fall within the framework of rural community development. In the towns, they will come within the scope of municipal services and urban community development. In both cases, the aim is to build up institutions which will grow from within, which will have the capacity to operate social services with competence and to develop them in depth, and which will attract active and constructive support from the local communities which they serve.

VI

In extending and implementing welfare services, inevitably, we encounter many difficult and unsolved problems.

We must be prepared to experiment, to evaluate closely and to learn constantly from our own experience and the experience of others. There are of course some tried and tested answers we can turn to. But we need many more if we are to reach the weakest in our midst. Therefore, the search for practical devices and institutions suited to the conditions of non-affluent societies will have to be a prolonged one and each step, in whichever country it may be taken, has to be followed with sympathy and understanding and readiness to profit from the success and failure of others no less than from our own.

30

FAMILY AND CHILD WELFARE IN THE RURAL COMMUNITY*

IN COMMON with many other countries, India owes a debt of gratitude to the UNICEF for bringing to bear concentrated thought and experience on the problem of planning for the needs of children. With the co-operation of international agencies and individual countries and through conferences, much that is of value in the efforts of pioneers of national organisations has been brought together. In this way clearer concepts of development are emerging, and there is greater opportunity for translating general aspirations into specific objectives and measures as an integral part of the scheme of national development suited to the conditions of each country.

---

* This paper was prepared for the Indian Council of Child Welfare for publication in their Children's Annual on November 14, 1965, and was later circulated for the Asian Conference on Children and Youth in National Planning and Development convened by the UNICEF at Bangkok in March, 1966. The analysis and suggestions set out in the paper were considered at length between various agencies of the Government of India during 1965 and 1966 and assisted in the evolution of the programme of Family and Child Welfare embodied in *The Fourth Five Year Plan—A Draft Outline* (August, 1966), pages 365-69.

The requirements to be met are now much better appreciated than a few years ago. Yet, there are many baffling and unsolved problems for which, in the main, each country must evolve its own appropriate solutions. There is little doubt that much more would be done for children if larger resources became available. An even more fundamental problem, however, may lie in the fact that satisfactory institutional and organisational means have still to be established for harnessing to common purpose the continuing concern and efforts of the local community and the contribution which various other agencies can make. The problem may be illustrated in relation to family and child welfare in rural communities in India. Similar questions arise for family and child welfare in urban communities, but obviously the rural problem is both larger and more basic.

Social workers have agreed that the welfare of the child and of the family to which it belongs are closely linked. Whatever will promote and assure the welfare of the family will also secure that of the child. Much thought has been devoted in recent years to defining the needs of children, in health, nutrition, education, welfare services, vocational preparation and conditions of work. The gaps which exist btween the desirable standards and those which prevail are indeed large. They can be reduced only through a long period of steady work. Only as the essential needs are met will it become possible to approach anything like an environment which will make for growth of personality, ensure a sense of equal opportunity to one and all and nurture true citizens of the future.

Even under conditions of rapid economic development, rural areas tend to lag behind the urban in income, in work opportunities and in social services. Rural children as a body remain under some degree of comparative handicap. Again, while many of their problems are common, a considerable proportion among the rural children, specially those belonging to the families of smaller cultivators, agricultural labourers and others suffering from acute poverty, are under still greater handicap than others. Difficult as it is to reach out to the rural children as a whole, it is even more difficult to come close enough to the core of the problem where economic and social factors merge and present a formidable obstacle to achievement of family and child welfare. A few can be touched under almost any scheme of work, but if we are to reach the many and deal with the heart of the problem of welfare of the family and the child in the villages, the rural community and its sense of social obligation and responsibility have to be fully roused. Within its means and capacity, each community has to be enabled to develop and implement its own plan of social action.

Our rural communities are face to face with many difficult problems. The most fundamental of these are problems which arise from the prevalence of poverty and lack of work opportunities, that is to say, from pressure of population, dependence on agriculture and inadequate diversification in the occupational structure. Side by side with these are problems which arise from ignorance and ill-health, from lack of the necessary social services, from conditions of living which are not only bare and harsh but also prevent social integration and the development of a sense of community. There is yet another set of problems which can be traced to lack of adequate civic organs and agencies and leadership within the community and failure to identify the nature and extent of the social responsibility which each community must bear for the well-being of all its members.

It follows, thus, that family and child welfare in rural areas should be set in the larger context of the way the rural community is helped to develop and function and solve its own problems. Economic policies and programmes which lift the rural population as a whole, solve its problems of employment, diversify opportunities for work and reduce

the gap between rural and urban incomes and living conditions have a vital bearing on family and child welfare. They
will provide the conditions under which families, specially
those from groups nearest to the poverty line, can do well
by their children and give them education and training and
better levels of living. As the village economy is diversified,
its nutritional base will improve, both through greater
production of milk, vegetables, eggs and other essential
foods and through such supplementary foods as may be
needed from outside the village for the very young. In other
words, family and child welfare should be thought of not
only as services by way of relief and amelioration reaching
progressively larger numbers, but as an essential and integral
part of the scheme of rural community development.

How the integration between family and child welfare and
development at the community level is achieved in any
country will depend upon its economic and social background, administrative and political structure, resources
and stage of development. Case studies for different countries assembled for the round table conference at Bellagio
in April, 1964 and, more recently, for the Asian Conference
at Bangkok provide valuable material deserving careful
study. There is much to be learnt, for instance, from the
experience of countries like Poland, the Soviet Union and
the United States and others which have done so much to
assure that as 'the riches, the power and the future of the
country' children will receive all that is due to them. India
cannot yet count among such countries, for public consciousness and plans of action which have been adopted are still
far removed from the stage when children become in fact a
national interest above class and status and above the limitations under which different sections within the community
live and labour. By whatever means it may be attained, only
a classless society or a society which is rapidly on the way to
becoming classless can break the barriers to the welfare of

those who are weak and vulnerable. Again, whatever the structure of the state or the social configuration, only when the community at the local level makes itself responsible for the welfare of all children without distinction as to the circumstances of their parents, does it become truly possible to provide for children as a concern ranking above all others.

In this background, it is useful to review briefly the experience gained in India over the past ten or twelve years, to define the nature of the institutional and organisational problem which still remains to be solved, and to indicate some of the more specific questions to which appropriate answers should be found in the near future, so that a large and continuous advance towards family and child welfare can be secured throughout the country.

In India, the credit for pioneering work on any scale in the field of family and child welfare belongs to the Central Social Welfare Board. When the Board was constituted in 1952, its primary aim was to harness the efforts of social workers and voluntary agencies for enlarging welfare, specially for women and children. It soon emerged that women and children in the rural areas could not be reached without programmes which specially catered for them. This took the form of a series of welfare extension projects. Under these projects, centres were established in rural areas where activities of interest to women and children could be undertaken. Resources in personnel, finance, materials and equipment were carried to these centres and attempts were made to secure local interest and co-operation in their working. At first, these welfare extension projects remained independent of efforts under way through the community development programme for rural areas. Each development block under the community development programme also provided for some funds and personnel for work among women and children. A scheme of coordination was then

32

introduced. 'Coordinated' welfare extension projects, in which both community development agencies and the Central and State Social Welfare Boards contribute resources, are now being carried out in 267 development blocks at 2390 centres. These arrangements are at present intended for the period of the Third Plan and arrangements for the future have still to be worked out. Side by side with these, there are other welfare extension projects and centres which were entrusted to the care and management of selected voluntary organisations on the understanding that three-fourths of the cost would be met from the resources of the Central Social Welfare Board and the balance would be found by them. A proportion of these projects and centres have closed down for want of resources and organisation and, in relation to many which still function, there is some uncertainty about the financial and other arrangements for the future.

In addition to welfare extension projects for work among women and children, 19 pilot projects in child welfare were also initiated in different parts of the country during the Third Five Year Plan. In sponsoring this programme, the Indian Council for Child Welfare stressed the need for services bearing upon the welfare and development of the child, such as health, nutrition, recreation, education and training, being provided together in a coordinated manner with attention to the specific requirements of different age groups. In some measure a number of these services already exist, but they tend to function independently of one another. In these 'integrated' child welfare projects it was also intended to give special emphasis to pre-school education and to the provision of child welfare workers (*bal sevikas*).

As a result of experience gained, both in welfare extension projects and in child welfare projects, there is general agreement among experienced social workers in favour of presenting the task of the future as being one of securing the welfare of the family and the child together rather than that of women and children or of children reckoned as a group apart. This re-orientation of objectives should make it possible to secure the necessary integration between the welfare of the family and the child and community welfare and should also help evolve the necessary organisation for the future.

A study of past experience suggests some important conclusions:

(1) A plan of action such as welfare extension projects, undertaken independently of the general programme of rural community development, is apt to suffer from want of resources and continuity and does not benefit sufficiently from the total scheme of development under way in any area;

(2) Civic organisations serving an area, specially the Panchayat Samiti at the block level and the panchayats at the village level, should be given full responsibility for organising family and child welfare work;

(3) In the nature of things, personnel serving under Government or civic agencies find it difficult to reach women and children and to work intensively among them. For many years, under the community development programme, there have been three women workers in each block, a *mukhya sevika* at the block level and two *gram sevikas* at the village level. The number of women workers at the block and village level has remained static for more than a decade. Their impact in the villages has been necessarily small. Therefore, some means other than the normal extension machinery provided in each area have to be found for making effective use of women workers in rural community development and for reaching women and children in the villages. This is yet an

unsolved problem in India's rural development
plans;

(4)   In devising an organisational set up from the
point of view of family and child welfare and for
work among women and children, two conditions
have to be fulfilled:

(a) The set up should be such that, while functioning under the aegis of the civic body and
within its overall responsibility, it can yet be
a distinct entity, able to work directly with
village panchayats, women's organisations in
the villages (*mahila mandals*) and voluntary
workers and agencies;

(b) It should be possible in this set up to use
resources provided by the civic body, resources provided by agencies outside the
area (such as a State Social Welfare Board
or voluntary organisations at the district and
higher levels) and also such resources as
may become locally available.

These conditions are likely to be best fulfilled if in a development block in which work among women and children is
to be organised, in its role as the civic body at the block
level, the Panchayat Samiti were to establish a separate institution which might function as a family and child welfare
centre. Such an institution could be a registered body promoted by the Panchayat Samiti. The Panchyat Samiti might
constitute its managing committee and appoint the chairman.
The managing committee should include persons drawn
from within the membership of the Panchyat Samiti as well
as other workers. In the scheme of organisation, women
workers attached to the block extension staff should be
deputed to work with the family and child welfare centre.
In addition, there would be additional personnel employed
directly by the centre, such as *bal sevikas* or women workers

trained to work with children. Thus, the centre would have a larger complement of staff than are available either under the existing welfare extension projects or under the community development programme. The family and child welfare centre would be expected to develop as an institution working directly with village communities for family and child welfare. The centre would serve as an institutional base for focussing the contribution of different agencies within the block on problems affecting women and children. Thus, such centres could promote and stimulate those activities in which women in the villages might participate more and more by organising themselves in associations. Work at the village level could then be undertaken to an increasing extent by women's own organisations functioning with the general support and assistance of village panchayats. Progressively, as economic conditions improve, village panchayats would accept greater responsibility for financing the activities of associations which they have helped bring into existence, including provision of staff and services. The family and child welfare centre in the block could not only pay special attention to such problems as health needs, girls' education, better nutrition, care of the pre-school child and welfare of working women, but could also promote and support activities for providing supplementary work opportunities for women in the villages. The latter is at present a large and relatively unexplored aspect of rural welfare. There is little doubt that much more has to be done to support family income in this manner and to bring considerable numbers of women into gainful and productive work. Once a family and child welfare centre is established along these lines at the block level, given the necessary support and continuity, its programme of work should expand both in the range of activities undertaken and in depth. In this way, its activities could reach increasing numbers of women and children in the villages, including sections of the community such as the smaller cultivators, agricultural labourers and artisans whose needs are specially acute.

Naturally, in a scheme of organisation such as this, there would be many practical problems to solve and much need for experimentation. There would be problems such as the structure at the block level, relations between different constituent elements like the Panchayat Samiti, voluntary organisations within the block and promotional organisations at the district and State level, patterns of staff and their training, securing an adequate share of benefits from various development programmes for women and children, developing subsidiary employment schemes for women, finding out the best techniques for encouraging and helping women in the villages to organise their efforts through associations and run their activities themselves with the maximum support from the village community as a whole. It is important that voluntary organisations working for women and children —and indeed all voluntary organisations—should be rooted more and more in the soil, drawing the best leadership which the local community can offer and being sustained by local efforts. The role of promotional agencies at the district and higher levels should be one of helping, guiding and advising, and making new experience and knowledge available, but always avoiding control or excessive influence.

If the approach outlined above is correct, and if it is recognised that a somewhat crucial stage has been reached in programmes for the welfare of women and children, it will be seen readily that a period for consolidating the work already done is now essential. In each of the areas in which welfare extension projects are being implemented, either through voluntary organisations or in integration with the community development agency, a fresh scheme of work for the future has to be drawn up broadly along the principles explained above. Many adjustments peculiar to each area will be necessary. The objectives and the methods of development in family and child welfare as an organic element in community welfare will have to be much more widely explained and understood. In a difficult area of social work such as this, each group or agency is apt to see less than the whole picture, and there is always scope for misunderstanding and waste of effort. Yet the tasks to be accomplished are vital and of great significance, as much for the welfare of the family and the child, as for the balanced economic and social development of the community as a whole.

31

RURAL-URBAN IMBALANCE*

THE RAPID growth of urban population in India over the past two decades has recently drawn greater attention on account of its bearing on the food situation, the problem of urban housing and slums and the preparation of master plans. During the ten years, 1941 to 1951, the population of cities, that is, towns with population exceeding 100,000, rose by 36.2 per cent as against the general population increase of 13.3 per cent. In 1951, urban population accounted for about 62 million or a little over 17 per cent of the total population of India; of this, 38 per cent lived in cities with a population of 100,000 or more, 30 per cent in towns with a population of 20,000 to 100,000, and about 32 per cent in towns with population below 20,000.**

* A draft of this paper was contributed in 1958 to a discussion on urban problems arranged at Ankara by the Rural-Urban Sociology Committee of the International Sociological Association.
** The corresponding data for the period 1951-61 are as follows. Against the increase of about 27 per cent in the total urban population, the population of cities, that is, towns with more than 100,000 inhabitants, rose by 39 per cent. In 1961, urban population accounted for about 79 million or about 18 per cent of the total population. Of this, 44·5 per cent lived in cities with a population of 100,000 or more, 32 per cent in towns with a population of 20,000 to 100,000, and about 23·5 per cent in towns with a population below 20,000.

With the object of obtaining a precise picture of the processes of urbanisation, a series of studies were initiated several years ago by the Planning Commission through the research staffs of various universities. These studies comprised a programme of socio-economic surveys of 21 cities.* The surveys were based on a common scheme of concepts and classification. The main object was to ascertain facts which would throw light on the dynamics of city growth and, in particular, on such aspects as changes in occupational patterns, distribution of incomes, migration, housing and the development of community facilities.

Once an economy begins to develop and in place of stagnation there is purposeful effort to push forward in various directions, it becomes ever more necessary to relate its different facets to one another. Urban studies cannot, therefore, reveal fully all the major factors which influence the character and prospects of urban growth. The results of these studies have to be considered side by side with studies of rural areas. The observations offered in this paper and the conclusions suggested are, therefore, necessarily incomplete and provisional. It should be stated, nevertheless, that as the economy becomes more complex and its problems come to be more closely interrelated to one another, scientific socio-economic studies provide an essential basis for objective assessment without which it would be difficult to plan on sound lines. Many assumptions need to be re-examined from time to time and goals set afresh.

FEATURES OF URBAN GROWTH

The growth of population and the movement of indi-

---

* The cities selected for study were: Agra, Allahabad, Aligarh, Amritsar, Baroda, Bhopal, Bombay, Calcutta, Cuttack, Delhi, Gorakhpur, Madras, Hyderabad, Hubli, Jaipur, Jamshedpur, Kanpur, Lucknow, Poona, Surat and Vishakhapatnam.

viduals and groups are in themselves familiar age-old pheno-
mena. The distinguishing marks of recent urban growth are
its continuity and the steadily increasing rate at which it
occurs. Concern with the implications of urban growth is a
necessary part of the effort to analyse the processes of social
development, to guide them as far as may be possible, and
to assimilate their consequences into the scheme of national
planning.

When we speak of urbanisation, it is essential to recognise
that there are wide variations between the process as it
occurs in different situations. One could distinguish, for
instance, the various forms of urbanisation associated with
(a) local trading and marketing centres, (b) places of administrative and cultural importance, (c) commercial centres,
especially those connected with foreign trade, and (d) industrial towns. Until the latter part of the nineteenth century,
most towns in India belonged to the first two categories.
Commercial centres, some of which grew later into metropolitan towns of immense size, developed in the wake of
increasing trade with western countries. Industrial towns
are a relatively recent development. Thus in India, in the
development of cities like Agra, Allahabad, Amritsar,
Baroda, Bhopal, Lucknow or Poona, administrative and
cultural factors were the first dominant factor. In cities like
Bombay, Calcutta and Madras, the growth of commerce
was the major initial influence although, after a time, the
industrial possibilities of these towns came also to be recognised and exploited. Towns like Jamshedpur or Vishakhapatnam grew up over short periods as a result of massive
investment on new development. Their experience will now
be repeated more intensively and over an even shorter period
in the new steel towns which are under construction at
Bhilai in Madhya Pradesh, Rourkela in Orissa and Durgapur
in West Bengal. Elsewhere, except in relation to new industries, the new population infiltrates somewhat slowly and the

growth of the town is not accompanied by large or immediate accretion to the total investment.

In future, by far the greater part of urban growth may be
expected to occur as a consequence of the industrialisation
and modernisation of the economy. The rate at which it
occurs will, therefore, be governed almost wholly by the
volume of investment and the pace at which the economy
as a whole develops. The large increase in the population
of many towns in India which occurred on account of the
movement of displaced persons following the partition of
the sub-continent in 1947 is to be regarded as an illustration of 'development through crisis' rather than as a feature
of economic progress. In turn, however, it has important
economic and other implications for the areas in which the
new population came to concentrate.

Although it is customary to speak of migration from rural
to urban areas, it is useful to distinguish between migration
from one type of urban area to another (as from a small
to a large town) and from rural to urban areas. The latter
could be further analysed in terms of distance from the receiving centre. The situation is different, for instance, where an
individual moves into a town from a surrounding rural area
or from a more distant rural area within the same cultural
region or from a rural area situated in another cultural
region. As a rule, the rural influx comes largely from those
areas which are either situated within the direct influence
of a town or, at any rate, lie within the same cultural region.
On the other hand, those migrating from towns come from
considerably longer distances. Frequently, therefore, the
movement from a village to an urban centre is but the
first stage of a subsequent movement from a smaller to a
larger town. Where towns grow rapidly because of large
investment undertaken over a short period, the movement
of population between towns is perhaps a more marked
feature, the gaps left being filled in turn by fresh movement

from rural areas. In other words, while there is a continuous trend towards movement from rural to urban areas, the movement itself is frequently marked by distinctive stages.

Where the movement of population occurs as a result of large scale industrial investment undertaken over a short period, the first impact is necessarily on the population of the area where the new industry is being set up and its immediate neighbourhood. Thus, at Bhilai in Madhya Pradesh while the steel plant was being established, a bench mark survey divided the region into five different strata. The first of these included 19 villages which came within the site of the plant and were to be acquired. The second included 40 villages which might also be acquired in due course. The third included 102 villages, situated within a ten-mile-belt. The fourth included two towns which represented an urban block under the immediate influence of the steel town. Finally, there were 59 villages which were marked out for the mining of iron, coal, manganese, etc. which would gradually become important centres for quarrying and for transport of material to plant site. This example illustrates the process by which, for instance, a town like Jamshedpur, now widely known for its steel and engineering industries, has grown from a mere village at the beginning of the century to a town with a population of about 328,044 in 1961. The industrial and commercial activities of every urban centre and the needs of the growing population exert a powerful influence on the surrounding rural areas and help to create new enterprises within its boundaries.

It is usual to study the new population coming into a town from the point of view of age composition, education and occupational pattern before and after migration. The kind of population a town will attract depends necessarily on the character of the activities developed there and the further prospects of development. As the market economy began to grow, the development of local trading centres enhanced the influence on rural life of those sections of the population who were engaged in trade and moneylending. The world of the village merchant was inevitably wider than that of the cultivators. It was, therefore, natural that, with the development of new commercial centres, some among those who were engaged in rural trade should move into the new towns. This was one of the main factors in the peculiar pattern of growth of nineteenth century Indian capitalism. As educational facilities increased, the movement of professional classes and middle classes into towns was a necessary consequence. In recent years, however, apart from the process of growth inherent in any urban centre, the pace and pattern of development and the types of individuals likely to be attracted into towns are influenced to an increasing extent by the development of new industries. There is relatively less scope for the illiterate village worker who has only his labour to sell. On the other hand, there is greater scope for the skilled craftsman, the literate apprentice and the young student from the secondary school whom it is easy to turn to a new vocation.

In every town which has been studied recently, a degree of unemployment and under-employment has been observed. Thus, in Poona whose population more than doubled over the twenty years between 1931 and 1951, a survey showed that 9 per cent of the total earners were unemployed. In a number of other towns also unemployment of this order is by no means exceptional. There is, besides, in every town a great deal of under-employment. This is not always easy to measure but is reflected clearly enough in the high percentage of the population engaged in occupations other than production and transport and, more especially, in various miscellaneous services. The existence of unemployment and under-employment in various towns points to the fact that, even apart from the serious lack of housing and other social services, scarcely any town is able to offer work to the bulk of the people who come into it. From several aspects, the social economy of urban areas shows an imbalance which is in part a reflection of the imbalance which exists within the rural economy and in part an aspect of that total imbalance which exists within the national economy of an under-developed country.

IMBALANCE IN RURAL COMMUNITIES

Young people tend to move out of a village when they have acquired a little education or a measure of skill. This often evokes the comment that the countryside is being denuded of some of its best potential leaders—a fact which in the long run may weaken the rural areas in relation to urban areas. The exodus from villages is both a response to wider opportunities emerging in other sectors of the economy and an expression of the growing inadequacy of the rural economy in meeting the challenge of modern economic development. For several decades past, the village economy, which was once largely self-contained and functioned within its own scheme of rights and obligations, has been exposed to a variety of new influences. Its cohesive elements have weakened and in a sense a process of disintegration has been under way. The increase in population has borne harshly on the greater part of the village community and more especially on the landless sections. Their employment opportunities are smaller relatively to their numbers, and more of them have been driven to casual and intermittent labour. Legislation of the past twenty years and more relating to moneylenders has gradually sent an increasing number among them into towns. Recent legislation giving security to the tiller of the soil makes it more difficult for the non-cultivating landholder to retain a place within the fabric of village society. For those who own land but work outside the village, it is now much less easy to continue to maintain a close enough link with the village community. At the same time, the continuing dependence on agriculture, the failure so far to diversify rural economic life in any substantial measure and the slow expansion of agricultural production (except in irrigated areas) are reflected in the low levels of income and low levels of productivity which characterise much of rural economic life. The spread of educational facilities and of social services generally should help strengthen rural life and provide progressive leadership. However, since economic opportunities have not developed at the same rate, there is disparity between economic development and the development of social services which, in turn, strengthens the trend in favour of a continuing exodus from rural areas.

As at present organised, rural society fails to offer anything like a reasonable measure of opportunity for those who have education, skill and ambition. It is in the nature of the process of economic development and of industrialisation that there should be powerful factors tending to widen the disparities between urban levels of income, employment and living and those prevalent in rural areas. Within the existing agrarian structure, which is based on small and frequently uneconomic holdings and excessive dependence on agriculture, there are scarcely any counteracting factors. In recent years, as part of India's development plans, there is some emphasis on rural development and on the reconstruction of village life. This has to be strengthened further through basic changes in the pattern of agricultural production and through the introduction on a much larger scale of non-agricultural activities. An efficient and diversified rural economic structure organised along co-operative lines offers the main solution. It is now clear that, as at present situated, despite the efforts which are being made, rural communities cannot develop at a rate at all commensurate with the rate of growth of the urban economy. They are not only unable to provide the minimum employment opportunities and livelihood for the bulk of the rural population but are also unable to keep within their fold those sections of the population which are progressive and are able to take advantage of opportunities for better education and training. Without reorganisation in a basic sense and the creation of a socially just and economically viable structure, in the midst of poverty, the tensions and conflicts of rural life tend to be accentuated and become a further factor in driving forward-looking elements away from the village. The problems of reconstruction of rural life cannot, however, be solved in an isolated manner, and it becomes essential not only to link the reconstruction of each village with that of the area of which it forms part but also to visualise in an integrated manner the problems of balanced growth for each area or region, including both its rural and urban components.

URBAN IMBALANCE

To become a reality for the average citizen, the 'welfare state' has to find an effective counterpart in the 'welfare village' and the 'welfare city'. The population of a city is drawn from a variety of sources and lacks homogeneity and the capacity for community action. A large proportion, often as much as three-fourths of the population of a city, are wage-earners and salaried employees. They are, therefore, dependent in a high degree on the services provided by the city administration, whether these concern education or health facilities or housing or water supply. In varying degrees, all towns and cities find themselves unable to provide the minimum services needed to more than a proportion of their population. Even in a city like Jamshedpur, which is noted for its stability of employment, 67 per cent of the population live in rented houses. Few employers can provide housing for more than a fraction of their workers. Gradually, the movement of individuals into a town turns into a movement of families. An increasing proportion of the population of the towns become wholly urbanised and links with the village break off completely.

Unless urban development can keep pace in respect of employment opportunities, education, housing, health facilities and water supply, growing numbers in each town tend to fall into deeper poverty. In Poona, a survey in 1937 showed that 65 per cent of the families studied were below the 'poverty line'. In 1954, this proportion stood around 70 per cent of the families studied. Numbers below the destitution line increased from about 15 per cent in 1937 to 25 per cent of the families studied in 1954. Thus, there is a widening gap on all sides—between rural and urban areas, within each rural area, and within each urban area. Migration into towns is an important aspect of social mobility which makes it possible for individuals to move from one place to another, from one occupation to another, and indeed from one class to another. While they limited progress, old bonds often made for greater security. They are inevitably loosened as a result of rural-urban migration. If society does not replace them by a new scheme of opportunities and obligations, to a larger or smaller extent, the creative value of social mobility remains unrealised and, as psychological and other tensions grow, further imbalances develop. Yet, while it is neither possible nor desirable to intervene in the processes of social mobility in a negative sense, there is everything to be said for creating conditions in which social mobility could make its maximum contribution towards the growth of a social order which offers adequate economic opportunity to all sections of the community.

Recent studies in India have shown perhaps more clearly than had been realised in the past how close a connection exists between rural and urban poverty. Both are facets of the larger problem of economic development and neither

33

can be resolved alone. The problems of the village and the town interpenetrate in the economic, the social and the political fields. Within each urban area, there is a process of centralisation at work. The individual becomes less and less part of an identifiable community and is scarcely associated with the governance of the city to which he belongs. As the process of urbanisation develops, new elements come into the town, and on the whole the break with the surrounding rural area tends to become more complete. This has important implications for countries in which even fifty years hence the majority of the population will be living in rural areas. In the absence of special measures, the chasm between urban and rural areas is likely to grow. In the measure in which this occurs, there is risk of conflict of interests between urban and rural areas which will, in turn, affect adversely the tempo of development within the economy as a whole. Such conflicts may express themselves in various forms, not the least of these being disparities in levels of income, employment and educational and other opportunities, and in the price policies adopted for manufactured products and agricultural commodities.

DIRECTIONS OF CHANGE

This statement of the problem carries us to a theme beyond the scope of the present paper. Certain directions of change can, however, be briefly indicated.

Each city or town requires a scheme of development which embraces not merely the establishment and maintenance of the minimum services but also a plan of economic development for the future. A master plan for an urban area necessarily embodies also a view of population growth, industrial development and location, provision of housing facilities, extension of education and other services.

Unemployment is most visible in urban areas but, even in this form, it is a reflection of the malaise common both to the urban and to the rural economy, namely, the inability to provide for the potential labour force. This and other problems can only be solved if for each composite urban and rural area there is a well-knit economic and social plan of development, based on the maximum utilisation of local resources and a complete identity of interests. Hitherto, even in the manner in which urban and rural administrations are conceived, there is a great deal of rigidity, and little consideration is given to the essential unity of their problems. The concentration of population in large towns occurs mainly because the smaller towns fail to offer adequate opportunities. If the development of smaller towns is planned along with that of the rural areas which they serve and which, in turn, largely supply their needs, the local economy of each area would offer much greater opportunity than it does at present.

To achieve the balanced development of rural and urban areas in themselves and as between one another, it is essential that the general pattern of industrialisation should be devised so as to provide for a large and growing sector of small industry which is closely linked with basic and large scale industries and is organised to the extent possible on co-operative lines. Only within the framework of such a pattern will it become possible to disperse industry and carry employment opportunities in adequate measure to the smaller centres. Under-developed countries with large populations have enormous employment problems to which basic and heavy industries can make their main contribution if they are, at the same time, supported by a well-developed structure of industrial production reaching out to the small town and the village.

A combined plan of economic and social development for an urban-rural region assumes that the movement of skilled and educated persons from rural areas into the towns to seek new livelihood would be matched by corresponding movement of trained workers from urban areas going into the villages to help in improving techniques, raising levels of living, extending educational facilities and providing relief where needed.

Both rural and urban development should be informed by the same essential principles of the development of local resources by each community, largely through its own efforts, but accompanied by special concern for assisting vulnerable sections of the population in overcoming their limitations and attaining, in fact no less than in name, the status of equal citizens. This approach applies in several fields and most notably in the extension of minimum opportunities by way of education and housing and the provision of employment.

To sum up, it is only in the context of overall economic development and a studied effort at social and economic integration within individual rural and urban communities and within each composite rural-urban area that we can hope to resolve some of the urgent problems thrown up by the migration trends which have been in evidence in India over the past two decades and more and which are likely in the future to become an increasingly significant factor in all under-developed economies.

32

INTEGRATION OF RURAL, URBAN AND INDUSTRIAL DEVELOPMENT*

LARGE changes are in progress both in rural life and in urban life. While studies to assess the impact of rural-urban migration and the employment situation in urban areas have been undertaken, there have been few investigations into the other changes which are currently taking place in urban areas. In some ways more has been done in the evaluation and study of rural change. Work in this field has, however, not extended far enough to permit a comparative analysis of the factors which are bringing about changes in rural and urban life, the pace at which these changes are taking place, and the effects of these changes on different sections of the rural and the urban community.

Urbanisation is both a consequence and a causal factor in economic development. The rate of urban growth is an important index of progress in the economy. Some allowance should be made for the fact that many of the problems of urbanisation are relatively new and social policies for dealing with the emerging symptoms are being but slowly evolved.

* Slightly adapted from a paper presented at the Seminar on Urbanisation in India held at the University of California, Berkeley, in June 1960, and included in *India's Urban Future*, edited by Roy Turner, University of California Press, 1962, pages 327-334.

Nevertheless, there are some aspects of the present urban situation which point to larger problems. For instance, the recent city surveys almost uniformly report a high degree of unemployment and under-employment. In one city, 40 per cent of all the earners interviewed felt a sense of insecurity in the jobs they held. Planned townships set up for new industries often seem to begin their course like walled cities of old isolated from and not too greatly concerned with what develops beyond. The inevitable expansion of these towns and the need to mark out for future acquisition successive rings of villages introduce in the latter a feeling of decay to which current policies do not give enough thought. The tendency to grab land and push up land prices introduces around every large town undeniable elements of exploitation and conflict. Further away from urban areas, there is the discontent on the part of the more conscious opinion in the rural areas of a growing disparity between urban and rural conditions, opportunities and levels of income. A more imaginative solution of the problems of urbanisation and better urban planning and administration are essential and will doubtless help, but the issues go deeper. In what manner are rural and urban development, both essential parts of the scheme of economic and social development, to be related to or 'integrated' with one another?

'Integration' is never an easy expression to define. In the context of rural and urban development, to 'integrate' means to ensure coordinated development such as will secure even progress between rural and urban areas and minimise social and economic conflict between them and within the urban communities themselves. In advanced countries, the distinction between urban and rural life has become less significant. In countries like India too, this phenomenon may take place after some 40 or 50 years of growth. The manner in which the distance between rural and urban life diminishes differs according to such factors as the intensity of industrialisation, density of population, the role assigned to individual intitiative and to co-operative and collective organisation, the system of local administration and other factors. In the Indian situation, therefore, there is room for departing in some measure from experience, for instance, of USA or USSR and considering afresh how, over the coming decades, the rural and urban economies might be developed so that they merge into one another and become, as it were, parts of a composite structure. Here it is perhaps pertinent to suggest that, at the present stage of development in India, the contrast between the rural and the urban way of life cannot yet be said to have been fully established, for it is confined to those sections in the urban community who have become wholly identified with industrial and commercial activity, skilled workers and others with incomes high enough and stable enough to sustain the main urban amenities. Large sections of the population may not be able easily to retreat from the town, but the situation is sufficiently fluid for them to move from a large city to a small or middle-sized town. There are also others for whom the time for a final choice between village and town has not yet come.

The problem of integrated development of rural and urban areas is posed in relation to industry because of the leading role of industrialisation in changing the pattern of resource allocation within the community and in bringing new productive forces into play. It would be more correct to speak of industry, along with agriculture, as providing the spearhead of the attack upon problems of mass poverty, an attack which can only succeed if, at the same time, a corresponding measure of development is assured in education, in the building up of skills, improvement in the conditions of health and housing, development of power and transport and, more generally, in scientific and social research and in efforts to raise the productivity of large numbers of persons.

If some urban areas generally present greater attraction to new industries than others, perhaps the main explanation is to be sought in the differences in the level of development in economic and social overheads. To a large extent, therefore, the problem of spreading the benefits of industrialisation and of realising them sooner rather than later, is one of deciding upon the lines along which economic and social overheads should be developed in the future. In this, both long range and short range considerations have to be taken into account, the question being one of assessment of economic and social costs in the wider perspective of national development.

In considering the broad approach to this problem, the first observation to be made is that the choices are by no means clear cut. In any scheme of development, large cities, medium-sized and small towns and rural areas have to receive, according to the urgent problems to be met, a fair share of the total resources that can be assigned for economic and social overheads. Within these limits, however, there is room for relative emphasis and for a degree of orientation in terms of future development which, over a period, may exert a significant influence. There is a large measure of agreement that concentration of urbanisation in metropolitan cities, unavoidable as it may have seemed, entails high social and economic costs, and serious efforts should be made to promote other patterns of urbanisation, economic and social overheads being used as an important lever of development. For this four main suggestions have been advanced. The first is that middle-sized towns offer an environment in which, having regard to various economic considerations, industry can find roots strong enough to compare with the attractions of large metropolitan cities. Definitions in terms of the population of towns fulfilling this condition differ, some favouring towns with a population of 250,000 to a million, others 50,000 to 100,000 or even 20,000 to 50,000.

The location of industry involves a variety of factors. A rigid view as to size is, therefore, difficult to support and is indeed unnecessary. The second broad approach, closely related to the first, is that middle-sized and small towns should be developed as 'counter-magnets' to the large cities. The third approach which has been put forward is that in each area small towns and large villages should be selected for the development specially of medium-sized and small scale industries which may have the capacity to grow. In the second proposal, the emphasis was on finding an efficient alternative to the large cities. Here the stress is on bringing into the rural areas in a more direct way than may be otherwise possible a further dimension in development, namely, the introduction of industry on a scale sufficient to change their occupational structure. Finally, there is an allied proposal summed up in the expression 'village clusters', which involves the development of a local industry with its ancillary facilities in a village selected as being 'central' out of a small group of adjacent villages.

The important consideration is not so much to choose between these various proposals as if they excluded one another, but to recognise them as gradations in a general scheme of development aiming at a wider dispersal of industry away from the large cities. The different proposals mentioned above are, in reality, parallel patterns of growth, each being adopted in the measure in which it is appropriate to the prevailing conditions. The problem has to be approached from both ends—outwards from the village, seeking a varied system of work opportunities and, secondly, away from the large cities, seeking a wider distribution of industrial and economic activity so as to avoid the admittedly undesirable effects of over-concentration. Expressions in common use, such as 'decentralisation of industry', do not succeed in conveying the more positive idea of balanced development between rural and urban areas, between large, medium-sized and small

towns, between economic and social objectives conceived
in terms of long term development. Viewed thus, there is
little need to pose the issue, as some have done, of the individual village being an insufficient basis for rural
industrialisation. In this form, the proposition has never
really been advanced, and those who have appeared to
suggest this course have in fact done no more than point
to one aspect of the balanced development which has to be
achieved.

Although urbanisation is more frequently associated with
industrial development, which is doubtless a major influence
now and in the future, one could distinguish between the
processes associated with the initial stimulus to urbanisation
in at least four different types of urban situations, namely,
(a) local trading and marketing centres, (b) places of administrative and cultural importance, (c) commercial centres,
specially those connected with foreign trade, and (d) industrial towns. After a period of growth, these aspects are to be
found together in most towns, the proportion varying from
one to another. This is illustrated, for instance, in the table
below in the distribution of population on the basis of

Percentage distribution of population according to means of livelihood.

City	Production other than cultivation	Commerce	Transport	Other services and miscellaneous means of livelihood
Allahabad	22	20	10	48
Baroda	27	22	5	44
Bhopal	21	18	7	52
Gorakhpur	25	19	13	37
Hyderabad	19	20	8	51
Hubli	39	22	8	24
Jamshedpur	70	11	3	15
Kanpur	42	24	4	28
Lucknow	24	21	7	45
Madras	25	22	9	42
Poona	27	18	7	27
Surat	44	25	3	27

livelihood in twelve of the cities studied under the auspices of the Research Programmes Committee of the Planning Commission.*

The existing towns will witness considerable growth in the next 15 or 20 years. Many new towns will also come into existence. The average rate of growth in urban population is estimated at about 4 per cent per annum although, according to the studies which have been made, in the metropolitan cities, it might be even higher. Against this background, the idea of balanced development mentioned above might be interpreted as comprising the following main objectives:

(1) As far as possible, new industries should be established away from the large and congested cities. The new centres might be middle-sized towns, small towns or new locations selected on account of the accessibility of raw materials or other considerations;

(2) In the planning of large industries, the concept of region should be adopted. Thus, where a steel plant or a heavy machinery project is established, the area of planning should extend beyond the immediate environs to a larger area for whose development the new industry could serve as a major focal point;

(3) Generally, in community development projects or other areas within districts, the rural and the urban components of development should be knit into a composite plan. This will involve an attempt to work out carefully the interdependence between each town and the surrounding rural area emphasising, for instance, the supplies to be drawn from the villages, the market in the rural area to be served from the town, communications, expansion of power facilities and the provision of facilities for training and education;

(4) Within each area, apart from the medium-sized or other industries located on the basis of economic and other criteria in the selected towns, the effort should be to secure a diversified occupational pattern in place of the present extreme dependence on agriculture. In the main, this will involve the building up of processing industries, meeting local needs to the extent feasible through local production, and improvement of tools and equipment in the traditional village industries and their gradual transformation into small scale industries through the introduction of power and machinery.

* *See Chapter 31, Rural-Urban Imbalance,* pp. 505-507. *op cit.*

These objectives are consistent with one another and may be said to be facets of the same basic approach. The next question to be considered concerns the conditions necessary for realising these objectives. The most important of these is the concept of the pattern of industrialisation on which the plans are based. In the Indian situation, it is assumed that, apart from fields in which large capital intensive industries are unavoidable for technological reasons, the bulk of industry will take the form of medium and small industries, making use of the available human resources and, at the same time, applying a forward-looking technology. It is also assumed that as between large or medium-sized and small scale industries, the object will be to widen the field for small scale operations by way of manufacture of parts and components and arrangements for the production of ancillaries. These general propositions have long been accepted, but their concrete applications have to be worked out systematically industry by industry. Conditions have to be created in which large numbers of small entrepreneurs and artisans' co-operatives can take up new activities with a measure of assistance in finance, techniques and designs from the appropriate institutions. Therefore, apart from big industries, many of which might fall appropriately in India within the sphere of the public sector, these are the essentials of an industrial policy designed to facilitate balanced industrial development and seeking to fulfil the four objectives outlined above. Decisions as to location of industries and the related development of economic and social overheads follow from these broad principles.

In giving effect to these concepts, the next question to examine is whether the machinery of planning below the national and State level is adequate for sustaining development on the lines envisaged. This is a theme by itself, but a few suggestions could perhaps be offered.

In the first place, it is clear that plans for developing

economic and social overheads in the larger cities, in the new industrial townships and in the more important middle-sized towns, in which industries are located, should become integral parts of national and State plans, in each case along with plans for the associated regions. Thus, it is no longer adequate to consider the building up of a township for a steel plant as a project by itself without at the same time coordinating the development of a larger area which, along with the township, should be appropriately viewed as a planning region for a great deal of development in the future.

Secondly, the concept of local administration will need to be strengthened in two ways—in terms of area falling within the jurisdiction of a municipal body and in terms of the functions to be undertaken by it. In the past, the municipal limits of towns have been expanded under the pressure of circumstances, because industrial, commercial and building activities overstepped these limits or speculation in land disorganised the life of the neighbouring villages or ribbon development began to disfigure the countryside. It would, therefore, appear desirable from the beginning to provide for larger rather than smaller limits for every growing town. This would bring a city and its hinterland within the same scheme of planning and administration. Extending the idea further, such an approach would also facilitate the economic and social integration of a large surrounding rural area with the town on rational lines, thus enabling the town and the village to influence each other directly to mutual advantage.

The third aspect which may be considered is the role of the village community and its likely future. It is sometimes thought that the stress on the village community is an attempt to cling to the past, a failure to see the forces of change. This is a misapprehension in relation to the underlying concepts of co-operative development and the community approach in India's plans. It is clearly envisaged that as technological changes take place in agriculture and as transport facilities improve, the unit of effective community organisation will become larger. Gradually, the operational area of local planning and decision will be a group of villages rather than the individual village. This trend is stimulated both by the growing requirements of the village which have to be met from without and the institutional arrangements needed for meeting those requirements. The process, however, is seen as being one of evolution largely from below in response to developing needs, rather than as an imposition from above justified by convenience of administration alone.

A more fundamental aspect is the need to assure integrated development of all sections of the village community and through it of rural society as a whole. In urban populations the composition is heterogenous, the bonds of community life are few, and the cohesive forces are weak. On the other hand, within the rural community there are still vital elements of common obligation and common interest which can be turned to account in the development of a co-operative and diversified rural economy. To the extent this is achieved, it will be easier to secure a larger measure of integration between the rural, urban and industrial economy for the country as a whole.

33

PLANNING FOR
A SELF-RELIANT DEMOCRACY*

THE PRESENT emergency takes us back to some of the fundamental premises of economic and social development and gives to them a new sharpness and urgency. In a matter of weeks, the wider context in which a country lives and works can change radically. A national crisis throws up new problems; it also brings forth new possibilities and new opportunities which can do much to increase the capacity of the people to bear greater responsibilities and labour together for larger goals.

Self-reliance has been a basic objective of India's planning for about a decade. Progress in this direction, though steady and well-marked, has not been conclusive enough. Rising demand for imports of components and raw materials, pressure on the part of much Indian enterprise for collaboration with foreign parties, frequent resort to foreign consultants for designs and other know-how and the inadequate measure in which India's own scientists and technologists

---

* Adapted from a contribution to *Yojana*, Vol. IX, No. 20, dated October 10, 1965, following the conflict between India and Pakistan when supplies and economic aid in relation to both were suspended by a number of Western countries.

have been pressed to find immediate and practical answers to unresolved problems, are illustrations of a gap which has been allowed to persist. Yet, through the very processes of development which have been under way, facilities and talents are at hand for reducing this gap and even eliminating it through intensive and purposeful effort over a short period of years.

CHANGED ROLE OF PLANNING

The emergency now upon us, while changing the character and purpose of planning, also enlarges its scope and role in national life. Hitherto, we have tended to think of plans as being spread in terms of a year or five years or longer periods. Plans covered wide ground, their special feature being increasing comprehensiveness in the economic and social fields. The objectives were defined broadly rather than pointedly. Time dimensions were not precise enough and, if those concerned took longer to execute the tasks entrusted to them, explanations were given and accepted readily. Planning has now to become wholly problem and task-oriented. The emergency marks out the more from the less essential. It demands concentration of effort and resources. Failures cannot be excused. Explanations cease to be relevant. Performance becomes the single test to be applied. Resources strictly follow priorities. Planning assumes all the characteristics of a military operation designed to succeed—precision in objectives and targets, well thought-out strategy and tactics, an assured line of supply, coordination in action, command responsibility, and bold initiative in the field.

In any modern country, there is close interdependence between the quality and range of the defence effort and the strength of the economic and industrial base. The economy supports defence; defence guides and stimulates the economy. This interdependence is as good as the planning that lies behind it. There has to be coordination between defence and economic planning in considerable depth, continuous and sustained, followed through every branch of activity in all its intricate detail. A major lesson of the national emergency of 1962 has been impressed upon us once again and with even greater force. Economic planning must comprehend the entire national effort, including defence and the needs of defence, both immediate and long-term, in all their varied aspects. Short of this, defence receives much less support from the economy than it has a right to, planning contributes much less to national security than it can. Fortunately, India's economy has now reached the stage when such coordination can bring the maximum benefit both to defence and to economic development.

The Larger Objective

Self-reliance for defence and development is not to be confused with autarky or with the approach of isolation. Its essential purpose is to put indigenous resources, capacities, expertise and institutions to the maximum advantage and to achieve a high degree of initiative and autonomy of action in vital sectors of national life. In pursuing a policy of self-reliance in her development, it would be necessary for India to work for wider and more intimate relations with a large number of countries and, as far as possible, to strive for continuing multiple partnerships. Along with economic bonds, cultural and other links will have to be equally fostered. To the extent to which, for a period, the flow of capital resources and know-how has to be in larger measure from the more to the less developed nations, international and multilateral arrangements should receive precedence. Such re-orientation would lead eventually to greater balance and diversification in relation to other countries as well as to a more purposeful advance within the economy.

34

A self-reliant economy has to be viewed as a major aspect of a larger objective—the building up of a self-reliant, technologically progressive, socialist democracy. In recent years the concern for economic advance and the role assigned in it to economic aid and private foreign investment have tended to push back some of the broader social and economic aims and institutional changes which are an essential ingredient of India's scheme of development. The technological aspects of a policy of self-reliance are undoubtedly of great importance, but such a policy has to be pursued continuously over years and must involve some degree of hardship and deprivation and deferment of benefits for *all* sections of the community. Therefore, its real strength will lie in the degree of mass support and mass satisfaction which can be generated while specific economic objectives are being pursued. The struggle for self-reliance will be a long-drawn one, involving years of effort and acceptance of stern ways of living. It has, therefore, to assume the shape of a national movement from which no one can stand aside and which encompasses every facet of life and activity. The springs of action and the ultimate sanctions of such an all-embracing effort must lie deep within the soul of the people, giving to each individual and each group the sense of sharing in a common endeavour and a common sacrifice.

ADMINISTRATION AND LEADERSHIP

Of the several lines along which action should proceed, changes in administration and in the style of work come first. These become a pre-condition for securing greater participation and response from the people. Each point in the administration has to be enabled to carry a greater load of decision-making and responsibility for action. The main task of the higher levels of policy and administration is to provide clear direction, ensure the essential resources needed, fix responsibility, and insist upon results. In time, wider

changes of a structural nature will also be required but, as a
first step, there has to be concentration on increasing the capability of each organisation and, within it, of each individual, to act to the maximum extent on its own initiative. No
unit within the administration can do much without co-operation and team work from other units. These processes must
be so organised that behind each specific task it is possible
to identify an individual who has the necessary authority
and can be held accountable. One of the first tests of the
approach of self-reliance should, therefore, be the conferment of larger responsibilities within the structure, increase
in trust, reduction of references and consultations, and
greater emphasis on action and decision. For large numbers
of individuals engaged in implementing the present plans,
the re-orientation demanded by the new circumstances
of the country involves intensification, speeding up and
improved communication rather than a basic change in the
tasks to be accomplished.

Closely connected with administration is the larger role of
non-official leaders at every level. In recent years, although
new institutions for providing opportunities to non-official
workers have grown through Panchayati Raj, co-operatives
and other agencies, dependence on local and other officials
has also increased. In consequence, contacts between
non-official workers in different walks of life and the mass of
the people have tended to become more formal and functional and, therefore, less intimate. This has reduced the
ability of non-official workers genuinely to influence and
motivate the mass of the people. Though declining, the
potential of leadership available at the local level, both in
urban and in rural areas, and through institutions such as
trade unions and co-operatives, is still considerable. The
policy of self-reliance has to be fully understood by non-
official workers closest to the people. Only then will they
be able to help translate it into practical action and assist

groups of citizens such as peasants, workers and others to assume greater responsibility.

The concept of self-reliance implies that the greatest possible effort that can be physically made at each level will be forthcoming, the next level above being asked to provide only the minimum assistance and support needed. This notion has to be applied within every village and neighbourhood and, progressively thereafter, to the larger entities of which they form part, such as block, district, city or State. It is through such self-reliance, organised by local leaders working in partnership with the administration, that it will become possible to ensure that every citizen has a task cut out for him, a duty to render, a defined role in the larger national effort. Once the scope of the idea of self-reliance is understood, the media of mass communication assume critical importance. In this respect, the traditional thinking and practice will not be equal to the challenge without a great deal of new effort. Resources on a large scale will have to be made available for reaching the people in every possible way.

Re-defining Economic Tasks

The considerations stressed above are in a sense preliminary in nature, and set certain essential conditions for achieving self-reliance. The crux of the economic problem turns on availability of foreign exchange, of scarce materials, of needed capacities and of food and other consumer goods. At the very least, whatever turn events may take, the foreign exchange assumptions on which planning has been based in recent years will change in a fundamental sense. The objectives of industrial production must be defined afresh as clearly as possible, so that the available capacities can be put to the best use. Given these objectives and the selective approach implicit in them, the key to action is given by these four words: Improvise, Adapt, Substitute, Conserve.

It is in this context that scientists and technologists engaged in industry, in research institutions and in universities have to be drawn in a meaningful and rewarding way into the national effort. Ways have to be found for giving to many thousands of them working in teams specific problems to solve. Tasks facing each industry and each branch of the economy have to be broken down, the existing knowledge and resources assessed and, in accordance with clear schemes of priorities, all the available talent put to work. The truth is that there is even now an extraordinarily large unused or partially used reservoir of ability and knowledge in the country. To the extent this reservoir is drawn upon effectively, it will grow and add to national wealth. This is also a time to consider calling back to India many of the scientists, technologists and other specialists who are still serving abroad. They should be offered worthwhile opportunities to work in vital tasks at home. This thought has come up from time to time, but there is need for a new approach and one supported by the necessary organisation, flexibility in administrative and financial procedures, and conditions of work in which there is a sense of equal worth.

Along with measures to reduce dependence on foreign exchange resources, we have to face up to the most urgent task of all—increasing food and agricultural production and so managing the country's food economy that imports play no more than a marginal and occasional role. Whether or not continued dependence on food imports has come in the way of the maximum effort being made to increase agricultural production, the opposite may still be true, namely, that to know that we cannot count on food imports to a significant extent should induce the greatest effort physically possible being made in every nook and corner of the land to achieve food self-sufficiency. There may still be a food gap, but through rationing and other means the shortage can be so shared as to enable the country to go through the difficult period unscathed. The successful management of the food economy becomes something more than a matter of marketing, prices, regulation and control. Producers, traders, consumers and the various administrative agencies become jointly accountable for fulfilling their social and economic obligations with complete responsibility to the community. This is itself a good instance of the kind of combination of administrative and popular leadership, mass communication, mass organisation and harnessing of local resources which is essential for achieving self-reliance in different sectors of the economy and at different levels of national life.

The same combination is called for in dealing with the problem of civil supplies and essential consumer goods. Here, it is equally important that consumption patterns should be re-oriented so as to secure to the mass of the people their most essential needs, cutting out demands on scarce materials and on vital fabricating capacities for which there are more urgent uses. Restraint in consumption is no less necessary for mobilising resources to sustain the burdens of defence and development.

These burdens are likely to be far bigger than we know or can readily envisage. The management of a mixed economy under the double strain of defence and development is an extremely complex undertaking and one entailing many risks. Here, it may be enough to refer to only one of its important components, the mobilisation of savings. The intensification of the savings movement in all its aspects is a task that cannot wait.

Solving Urgent Social Problems

Planning for a self-reliant democracy is a total effort. Economic problems are undoubtedly the most important, but they will prove overwhelming unless urgent social problems also receive equal attention at the same time. In

working for self-reliance, a nation such as ours seeks to libe-
rate itself both from external limitations and from weaknesses and failures that lie within. For millions the content
of freedom is still meagre. To create enough work, to use
our manpower resources in a gainful and productive manner,
to extend the principle of social responsibility to the relief
of distress and suffering within the community, to implement completely and swiftly our programmes of land reform
and social justice, are tasks wholly within the capacity of a
nation such as ours.

34

CHALLENGE AND OPPORTUNITY*

As A NATION, we are now at the beginning of a difficult period and a time of trial and danger and, one hopes, of renewed endeavour and faith. Since Independence, India has many achievements to her credit. The rehabilitation of millions of displaced persons was accomplished with considerable success. Democracy has been consolidated. The economic stagnation of the preceding half century has been broken. There have been impressive advances in agriculture, industry, transport, science, education, and other services. The institutions of democracy have reached down to the people in the villages. India has made a notable contribution to the preservation of world peace and of sane values in the midst of hatred and conflict. Everywhere she has held aloft the torch of freedom and justice. Yet, on account of changes and developments within and without, today India finds that she is under compulsion to come to terms with herself and, at the same time, to establish a new equation with the

* Adapted from an address at the Second Annual Convocation of the Panjabi University at Patiala on January 16, 1965.

Unfortunately, the grounds for confidence expressed early in 1965 have since visibly weakened. The doubts then felt give cause for greater anxiety. Altogether, the theme has gained in urgency.

rest of the world. At such a juncture, our foremost duty as a nation is to hasten to solve our urgent domestic problems and eliminate such weaknesses as there may be, so as to be better able to enter upon the new and difficult tasks that lie ahead.

There were many factors to encourage us in the belief that in her political institutions, her economic and social planning and her policy of peace and goodwill, India was pursuing paths which were just and certain to succeed. However, the burdens which have had to be borne over the past two years, the imbalances in the economy which have been recently accentuated, the slow rate of economic growth during the Third Plan and developments abroad have combined to cause a measure of doubt and confusion. The prevailing mood in the country is not marked by that intense attitude of positive response to challenge, however great, which is a necessary condition of success. There are symptoms that make one feel uneasy. Slow economic growth has tended to diminish the tempo of social change. Sections of the community which have in fact benefited from economic development seem more eager to consolidate and add to their gains than to lift the levels of living of the community as a whole. Misguided aspirations hold sway among many groups. The more common desire is to receive, giving little in return. The social conscience is not as fiercely roused by wrongs done to the community as a whole as one might expect. One witnesses a certain hardening of privilege and of vested interest. Freedom brought to the mass of the people hope of eliminating poverty and social injustice from our midst. This promise is being delayed. In current thinking and action less weight seems to be given to self-reliance as a social value.

These are disturbing trends; yet, they are relatively recent. They are in fact alien to the traditions of India's national movement. They are opposed to the very goals and strategy of economic and social planning to which we are committed through our Five Year Plans. Nor are they justified in terms of the objecive facts of the economic, social or political situation. Even harsh critics will grant that in size and range of activity, India's economy is now considerably larger and more developed than a decade or more ago. Thanks to her advances in education and in science and technology, India's resources in trained manpower and in skill and knowledge are richer than those of any country in comparable situation. Her democratic institutions are intended to provide to the bulk of the people opportunities for self-expression and growth which remain unique among the poorer countries. Her public services and the apparatus of administration are capable, under proper guidance and leadership, of carrying out the most exacting tasks. In village and town alike, the people are ready to respond to new initiatives, to take upon themselves larger responsibilities in the process of transforming a static and fragmented economy into a dynamic and co-operative structure. There is a wealth of new leadership which can be trained and harnessed through political and social institutions. In the universities and in educational institutions, in the professions and in other walks of life, there are men of talent and courage who can do much to speed processes of economic and social change. The growth of the public and the co-operative sectors has greatly enhanced the capacity of the State and of the community as a whole to achieve rapid economic advance and a just social order.

Among those engaged in private business and industry, there is a growing proportion of individuals who recognise the precedence of social interest above private interest. These are some of the assets which form part of our legacy from Jawaharlal Nehru. No other nation similarly placed has these assets in equal measure.

Does this mean, then, that the phase of doubt and pessimism which we sense around us is a passing one? Will such clouds as there may be disappear with greater advance in agriculture and industry and a favourable turn in the international climate ? This counter question is not without substance, but such optimism could prove a false guide. Even more than an individual, a nation must test its performance by the strictest standards. We must admit that while there has been marked and widespread progress, in this very process, economic and social problems have grown in size and complexity and, in turn, make larger demands on leadership at all levels. Between 1961 and 1966, India's population will have grown by some 60 million and will rise by about 130 million in the next decade. Without assuring appreciable relief to the vast amount of disguised unemployment which exists in the villages, the backlog of unemployment will have grown significantly. In other words, despite growth in production, sizeable numbers among the rural population, specially the landless, continue to live under the stress of deep poverty. They are still nearly as far from being integrated as equal members of the rural community as they were before the commencement of planned development. At the eve of Independence, there was general agreement that without the reconstruction of the rural economy in fundamental terms, including development of a system of co-operative farming suited to Indian conditions, the problem of agricultural productivity and rapid technological change would not be solved. Through the years the social perception of this basic fact has become much dimmer. Some of the central problems of rural reconstruction have tended to be put off to a large extent, perhaps unconsciously, perhaps through pressure of other concerns and interests. Thus, without creating the necessary social and economic conditions for rapid application of science and technology among the vast majority of the people, the apparatus of research and higher education developed over the years frequently functions remotely from those very problems which bear most closely upon the welfare of the people. The ranks of the middle

classes have been steadily expanding, but they form a small
proportion in the total mass and do not yet fully comprehend
their function in the social structure. Progress in bringing the
unorganised sectors of the economy such as trade, small
industry and agriculture within the scope of organised effort
has been slow. Equally, sections of the population in a position to exploit the pressing needs of industrial and urban
centres have not felt the impact either of social obligation or
of social sanction. Wherever the causes of failure or of slow
progress might lie, the small advance made in co-operative
marketing and in state trading leave the community as a
whole insufficiently equipped to deal with anti-social action
affecting its vital needs. The lesson is being but slowly learnt
that a growing economy must place itself in a position to
obtain the entire marketable surplus of food and raw
materials or else it will constantly remain at the mercy of one
section of interest or another.

The tasks of management, organisation and administration in the context of development have been under-estimated. Sufficient value has not been placed on performance,
action and results. The consequence is that failure in accomplishing tasks assigned to individuals and organisations,
instead of being regarded as an offence against society, has
been too often condoned. Similarly, injury done to the
community has frequently remained unnoticed and un-
punished. Where democracy should have placed far greater
stress on duty and obligations, the accent has tended to shift
to rights and safeguards. One of the main lessons to be drawn
from the past years is that a society without a stern cons-
science against evil and disregard of public interest and a
democracy which develops soft habits of mind cannot secure
the full fruits of freedom or fulfil the essential needs of the
mass of the people.

It is out duty at this time to face up to weaknesses such
as these with frankness and courage. For, they are not

inherent in the scheme of democracy envisaged in our Constitution, or in the system of social, economic and political objectives to which Parliament and the nation have pledged themselves. On the contrary, within the limits of our resources and capacity, our institutions and our ideals are designed to produce the largest measure of well-being possible, to assist the mass of our people to grow in stature and dignity and find a larger fulfilment, to counter injustice and privilege in all its forms, to achieve an integrated society and an integrated economy. Although the economic base is yet weak, our concepts of socialism are far-reaching in their implications. They envisage that over a period of years, we shall achieve a society without caste, without class and without privilege, a society which guarantees equality of opportunity to all and assures his minimum needs to every citizen, a society based on a sense of sharing and co-operation in which the greater burdens will fall on those who are in a position to bear them. Such a social order cannot be established without rapid economic growth and widespread diffusion of industry and application of science and technology. Socialism is not merely a set of economic institutions. Even more, it is a system of human and social relationships. It is a way of life marked, above all, by respect for the citizen and a sense of equal consideration and opportunity for every individual. Within the framework of democracy, a socialist society has to be based on fulfilment of duties and obligations and, as Gandhiji would have said, in such a society, real rights are a result of performance of duty.

In our scheme of development, we have visualised a private sector, widely dispersed and functioning in harmony with public interest and with an attitude of responsibility towards the well-being of the community. More and more, the private sector should serve the community on the basis of mutual co-operation and accepted standards of performance. On any other assumption, planned development within the framework of democratic socialism would come into sharp conflict with a growing private corporate sector. Over large parts of the economy, both economic progress and social integration demand the organisation of economic activity through co-operative institutions. Without rapid transformation of the rural economy along co-operative lines, the gap in productivity, incomes and opportunities between rural and urban areas will inevitably grow. A co-operative rural economy, including co-operative farming and land management, is, therefore, for India a social and economic necessity. It is no longer a matter of choice or volition, nor is it a phase of development that can be pursued in future at leisure when other problems have been solved. It is so much in the interest of the vast majority of the rural population that, given the necessary conviction and determination, the transition to a co-operative rural economy can be achieved as a national movement among the people largely through adequate leadership and organisation and appropriate support and incentives. The growth of the public sector has been rightly regarded as being a necessary condition for advance along socialist lines. But the notion of monopoly is not a part of this concept. On the other hand, it is fully realised that efficiency of management, initiative and innovation are of the utmost importance in the success of the public sector. In all its economic activities, Government itself must be at pains to fight the elements of inertia, hierarchical authority and failure in human relationships.

Underlying those different aspects of economic and social development is the basic thought that, at each level, the community should organise itself for the maximum effort of which it is capable. It must draw upon its untapped reserves of energy, manpower and leadership and its potential for savings. While functioning in the larger context of the national and the regional economy, each community should work hard to reduce its dependence on assistance from with-

in community life—these must become over the next decade the common possession of every citizen in the land. This would be our best assurance for realising these values speedily and translating them into social and human relationships of every day life and into action programmes implemented through our economic and social institutions with the support and participation of the people.

Through many faltering steps, since we gained our freedom, we have now the knowledge, the resources and the social institutions by which it is within the bounds of practical action to achieve a rapidly advancing economy and a society integrated from within. In the 'Hind Swaraj', written as far back as 1908, Gandhiji declared that by patriotism he meant the welfare of the whole people. Later he called it Sarvodaya, the welfare of all. A few days before the end came, he referred to Sarvodaya as true democracy in which we would regard the humblest and lowest Indian as being equally the ruler of India with the tallest in the land. This comes close to defining the mission and the faith which we of this generation and students and youth, who are the harbingers and leaders of the next phase in our national life, are together called upon to work for, to live for. The challenge and the opportunity are great and rewarding. The battle will not be easily won. Our own failings will often pull us back and undo some of our own work from time to time. But if we labour on, we shall win through. In his poem, 'Boundless Sky', Poet Tagore spoke of—

a call to some desperate task,

in the pride of poignant suffering.

Suffering there is all around us, the tasks are urgent and critical and the time in which to accomplish them is now desperately short.

GLOSSARY OF INDIAN TERMS

ANNA

Coin equivalent to one-sixteenth of a rupee, frequently used as a measure in land revenue operations

BAJRA

Bulrush or spiked millet

BAL SEVIKA

A woman worker trained in child welfare work

BENAMI

A fictitious transfer of land or other immovable property

BHOODAN

Donation of land for the landless

CRORE

10 million; 100 lakhs

GAUSHALA

An institution for the care and protection of cows

GHEE

Butter processed to serve as cooking material

GRAM

Village

GRAMDAN

Voluntary surrender by the landholders of a village of their individual proprietary rights, wholly or substantially, in favour of the entire village community

HARIJAN

Expression for members of scheduled castes, first used by Mahatma Gandhi

JOWAR

Sorghum

KHADI

Hand-spun and hand-woven cloth

KHARIF

Crop season corresponding to the summer months

LAKH

100,000; 0.1 million

MAHILA MANDAL

An association of women

MUKHIYA SEVIKA — A woman social worker at the Block level

PANCHAYAT — A representative local council at the village level for one or more villages

PANCHAYAT SAMITI — A representative local council at the level of the Block, a unit in the scheme of rural community development comprising generally about 100 villages and a population of 60,000 to 70,000

PANCHAYATI RAJ — An integrated system or network of rural democratic institutions at the Village, Block and District levels, set up under State legislation, and entrusted with responsibility for local development. Expression also stands for local democracy in rural areas.

RABI — Crop season corresponding to the winter months

RAIYAT — An occupancy tenant in areas under zamindari tenures

TAHSIL, TEHSIL — Subdivision of a district

TALUK — Subdivision of a district

TINKAL — Fodder famine or scarcity

TRIKAL — The three facets of a famine, namely, food, water and fodder

ZAMINDARI — A system of land tenure involving possession of intermediary rights

ZILLA PARISHAD, ZILA PARISHAD — A representative local council at the District level

MAHILA SEVIKA	A woman social worker at the Block level
PANCHAYAT	A representative local council at the village level for one or more villages
PANCHAYAT SAMITI	A representative local council at the level of the Block, a unit in the scheme of rural community development comprising generally about 100 villages and a population of 60,000 to 70,000
PANCHAYATI RAJ	An integrated system or network of rural democratic institutions at the Village, Block and District levels, set up under State legislation, and entrusted with responsibility for local development. Expression also stands for local democracy in rural areas.
RABI	Crop season corresponding to the winter months
RAIYAT	An occupancy tenant in areas under zamindari tenures
TAHSIL, TEHSIL	Subdivision of a district
TALUKA	Subdivision of a district
TAKAVI	Fodder famine or scarcity
TRIKAL	The three facets of a famine, namely, food, water and fodder
ZAMINDARI	A system of land tenure involving possession of intermediary rights
ZILLA PARISHAD, ZILA PARISHAD	A representative local council at the District level

INDEX